WITTGENSTEIN'S THOUGHT IN TRANSITION

**Purdue University Press Series
in the History of Philosophy**

General Editors
Adriaan Peperzak, Editor-in-chief
Arion Kelkel
Joseph J. Kockelmans
Calvin O. Schrag
Thomas Seebohm

WITTGENSTEIN'S THOUGHT IN TRANSITION

Dale Jacquette

Purdue University Press
West Lafayette, Indiana

02   01   00   99   98   5   4   3   2   1

∞ The paper used in this book meets the minimum requirements of
American National Standard for Information Sciences—Permanence
of Paper Printed Library Materials, ANSI Z39.48-1992.

Printed in the United States of America

Interior design by Anita Noble

Library of Congress Cataloging-in-Publication Data

Jacquette, Dale.
    Wittgenstein's thought in transition / Dale Jacquette.
        p.   cm. — (Purdue University Press series in the history of
    philosophy)
        Includes bibliographical references and index.
        ISBN 1-55753-103-X (alk. paper). — ISBN 1-55753-104-8
    (pbk. : alk. paper)
        1. Wittgenstein, Ludwig, 1889–1951. I. Title. II. Series.
    B3376.W564J33 1997   97-9813
    192—dc21   CIP

For Tina, with love

This is how philosophers should
salute each other:
'Take your time!'

—WITTGENSTEIN, *CULTURE AND VALUE*

C O N T E N T S

In 1922, Wittgenstein believed he had eliminated all philosophical problems. The explanation of meaning advanced in his *Tractatus Logico-Philosophicus* excludes traditional philosophical questions and answers as nonsensical. There was nothing more to do but withdraw in silence from meaningless philosophical speculation, as the final sentence of his treatise recommends.

By 1929, after a period of philosophical inactivity, Wittgenstein began to doubt the adequacy of his early semantic philosophy, and tried to repair the analysis in response to a particular logical difficulty. When the theory proved unable to deliver a satisfactory solution within the general framework of the *Tractatus,* Wittgenstein concluded that his early account of meaning was deeply flawed. By 1933, he had gone back to the drawing board to rethink the semantics of language and its implications for the right method of philosophy. The misgivings he had at this time can conjecturally be inferred from the argument of his 1929 essay, "Some Remarks on Logical Form," and from the historical circumstances surrounding his rejection and disowning of the work, including his decision not to read the paper at the philosophical meeting for which it was intended.

Wittgenstein thereafter until the time of his death in 1951 develops a radically new philosophy. He criticizes his early work, and offers a different approach to the same cluster of questions that had motivated his first reflections on language, the self, moral and aesthetic value, and the proper aim and practice of philosophy. Wittgenstein's reconsideration of these problems in light of the failure of the *Tractatus* first appears in the *Blue and Brown Books,* as lecture notes from his seminars at Cambridge University in 1933 and 1934, and culminates in the posthumous

Philosophical Investigations, most of which was completed by 1945, with additions written between 1946 and 1949. These essential works are but the tip of an iceberg of unpublished manuscripts on a wide range of topics. As in his early philosophy, Wittgenstein in the later period seeks to eliminate philosophical problems from the standpoint of a correct understanding of the meaning of language. The puzzles and paradoxes of philosophy are no longer dismissed as meaningless in one fell swoop, because Wittgenstein now sees the legitimate use of language as more complicated and multidimensional than the *Tractatus* had allowed. Wittgenstein maintains that the proper practice of philosophy amounts to a therapy from the intellectual anxiety produced by improper philosophical questioning. Philosophical problems melt away in the course of arriving at a correct understanding of the meanings of innocent-appearing terms like 'know', 'pain', 'believe', 'free', that give rise to conceptual confusions. The meanings of these terms are determined by the rules of a philosophical grammar, discovered in the therapeutic exercise of specifying what Wittgenstein calls a perspicuous representation of their nonphilosophical pragmatic uses as ordinary language tools in the diverse linguistic transactions of everyday human activity.

Considered by many today as among the greatest twentieth-century philosophers, Wittgenstein is so admired even by those who vehemently disagree with both his early and later thought as to rank him in company with Plato, Aristotle, and Kant. Yet Wittgenstein's achievement is of quite a different kind than any of these historical comparisons would suggest. Had the project of the *Tractatus* succeeded, Wittgenstein would have overturned all of past traditionally conceived philosophy as literal nonsense. Even in the later period of the *Philosophical Investigations,* when he has rejected nearly all of the content of his early philosophy, Wittgenstein finds himself thoroughly opposed to philosophy as a system of propositions modeled on mathematics or the sciences to be accepted as doctrine about a special subject matter. The difficulty in understanding Wittgenstein's thought in the early, transition, or later periods is not merely one of grasping its imposing technicalities, but its revolutionary purpose and direction, as an anti-philosophical philosophy. It is the challenge of coming to terms with a philosophy in which there are finally no real philosophical problems, no substantive philosophical theses, and no philosophical work to be done beyond the clarification of meaning in language, by which the need for philosophy evaporates.

This is a book about Wittgenstein's (anti-) philosophy in all three major periods, with an emphasis on the transition between his early and later work. The main purpose is to situate Wittgenstein's ideas in the broader context of the evolution of his thought in its two major phases, represented by the *Tractatus* and *Philosophical Investigations,* and divided in the transition period by the essay "Some Remarks on Logical Form." The exposition includes a detailed critical interpretation of the 1929 essay, explaining its historical and philosophical importance. In the space of a few pages in this remarkable document, Wittgenstein offers his first and only attempt to apply the abstract principles of logical analysis posited by the *Tractatus* to experiential phenomena. Yet, because Wittgenstein disowned the essay, its merits have been overlooked and underappreciated by many commentators. Despite the extensive literature surrounding Wittgenstein's other major texts, very little of a systematic nature has been written about the essay. The fact that Wittgenstein in "Some Remarks on Logical Form" tries but fails to carry forward the *Tractatus* analysis of complex to simpler facts, the precise way in which the effort fails, and the fact that Wittgenstein recognized the essay's defects and refused to read it to a philosophical audience, far from being an excuse to ignore the work, suggests that it deserves the most careful attention as an episode of major significance in the transition from Wittgenstein's early to later philosophy. The irony is that those who downplay "Some Remarks on Logical Form" as unworthy of serious study on the grounds that Wittgenstein rejected it do not by the same reasoning conclude that the *Tractatus* itself, which Wittgenstein also later condemns, can safely be discounted in trying to understand his thought—yet it is only when he renounces "Some Remarks on Logical Form" that Wittgenstein finally abandons the program of the *Tractatus.*

Wittgenstein in his early, transitional, and later thought is continuously engaged in a struggle to uncover the principles of the meaningfulness of language and the implications of philosophical semantics for the proper conduct of philosophy. He thinks he has the right answer in the early period. Then, in the transitional period, he doubts the adequacy of his first solution, and begins to move toward a different approach. This is developed at length, though not completed, in the later philosophy. The following account defends an interpretation of the philosophical reasons for the transition in Wittgenstein's thought from the early to the later periods, tracing the sources of Wittgenstein's dissatisfaction with his early theory of the nature of language in the *Tractatus* to the problems he addresses in the 1929 essay. Why did Wittgenstein after 1929 renounce his earlier solution to the problem of language, when in the preface to the *Tractatus* (29) he so confidently asserts that "the *truth* of the thoughts communicated here seems to me unassailable and definitive. I am therefore of the opinion that the problems have in essentials been finally solved"? It is this question about the shift in Wittgenstein's philosophy from the early to the later period in all its implications for understanding his thought as a whole that the book attempts to answer. I shall try to show that Wittgenstein's 1929 essay "Some Remarks on Logical Form" provides the key to this historical puzzle.

ACKNOWLEDGMENTS

I am grateful to many persons who have influenced my thinking about Wittgenstein's philosophy. My first studies of Wittgenstein began in seminars with P. T. Geach, Peter Long, and Roger White, and continued later with Roderick M. Chisholm and Ernest Sosa. The authors from whom I have benefited most in arriving at my own view of Wittgenstein's ideas include G. E. M. Anscombe, G. P. Baker, Max Black, Rudolf Carnap, K. T. Fann, Robert J. Fogelin, Newton Garver, James Griffin, P. M. S. Hacker, Rudolf Haller, Garth Hallett, Jaakko Hintikka, Anthony Kenny, Colin McGinn, Brian McGuinness, Norman Malcolm, Ray Monk, David Pears, F. P. Ramsey, Rush Rhees, Joachim Schulte, Erik Stenius, Friedrich Waismann, and G. H. von Wright. My debt to these scholars is profound; some have directly shaped and informed my attitudes, while others have helped me more clearly to define my own dissenting ideas. I was delighted by the invitation of my friend and colleague Joseph Kockelmans to contribute this monograph on Wittgenstein to the Purdue University Press Series in the History of Philosophy. The study was supported by a Melvin and Rosalind Jacobs University Endowed Faculty Research Fellowship in the Humanities at The Pennsylvania State University, and by the J. William Fulbright Commission for Cultural, Scientific, and Educational Exchange Between Italy and the United States, during my tenure as Distinguished Lecture Chair in Contemporary Philosophy of Language at the University of Venice in spring 1996. The editors of *Australasian Journal of Philosophy, Brentano Studien, History of Philosophy Quarterly, International Studies in Philosophy, Philosophy and Cognitive Science (Proceedings of the 16th International Wittgenstein Symposium),* and *Wittgenstein Studien* kindly gave permission to incorporate rewritten passages from previously published essays. Finally, I offer special thanks to Margaret Hunt, editor at Purdue University Press, for patient and expert editorial supervision in guiding the work to publication, and to Anita Noble for her superb graphic design.

A NOTE ON READING WITTGENSTEIN

Wittgenstein's writings consist primarily of philosophical aphorisms, remarks, and epigrams. It is often difficult to understand these individually, and even more challenging to follow the thoughts that link successive items. Accordingly, I have introduced large selections with detailed connecting commentary from what for my purposes are three of Wittgenstein's most important works. These are the *Tractatus Logico-Philosophicus,* the essay "Some Remarks on Logical Form," reprinted here in its entirety, and *Philosophical Investigations,* in the editions and translations indicated in the bibliography.

All references to the *Tractatus* are numbered by Wittgenstein's decimal system. The method he devised to rank his remarks according to relative importance is explained in a note to the first page: "The decimal figures as numbers of the separate propositions indicate the logical importance of the propositions, the emphasis laid on them in my exposition. The propositions $n.1$, $n.2$, $n.3$, etc., are comments on proposition No. n; the propositions $n.m1$, $n.m2$, etc., are comments on the proposition No. $n.m$; and so on" (31). References to the 1929 essay "Some Remarks on Logical Form" are given in parentheses as page numbers from its first publication in *Knowledge, Experience and Realism (Aristotelian Society Supplementary Volume 9),* reproduced below with original pagination indicated in brackets as the text of part 2. The *Philosophical Investigations* is divided into two parts. I follow the standard convention of designating Wittgenstein's numbered paragraph sections in part 1 as §n, §§m-n, or §§m, n, and in part 2 by page number. All references to Wittgenstein's other writings are given by date and page or section number, according to the usual practice, with full documentation in the notes and bibliography.

The numbering of *Tractatus* entries from propositions 1 through 7 with subsidiary development of main ideas added to all but the last suggests a variety of different reading itineraries. It is possible simply to read through the text sequentially from beginning to end, which is advisable in a first encounter with Wittgenstein's treatise. It is also instructive to read the text backwards from end to beginning, to read and consider just the whole-numbered propositions 1,2,3,4,5,6,7 (although these do not necessarily represent Wittgenstein's most important ideas), and then the supplementary decimal-numbered comments to each main whole-numbered proposition as 1.1, 2.01, 3.001, 4.001, 5.01, 6.001, and then 1.11, 2.011, 3.01, etc. (although there is not an equal number of these for each main whole-numbered proposition), or to seek out corresponding decimal groupings for each whole-numbered proposition, as in 1.1, 2.1, 3.1, 4.1, 5.1, 6.1, and then 1.11, 2.11, 3.11, etc., and to reflect on why in some cases there are and in others there are no parallel elaborations of main propositions in different combinations.

Wittgenstein clearly intended the numbering of propositions in the book to invite such alternative readings, with the idea that approaching the subject from many alternative perspectives would throw light on different aspects of his thought. He experimented with several different orderings of the propositions, as his surviving *Notebooks 1914–1916* and *Prototractatus* indicate. He adopted the decimal-numbering system almost from the start as a way of managing a complexly interrelated subject matter that did not lend itself to any single linear ordering. To a lesser degree, similar considerations apply to the whole-numbered paragraphs of *Philosophical Investigations,* which Wittgenstein describes in the preface to that work as "a number of sketches of landscapes which were made in the course of these long journeyings . . . really only an album," adding, "The best that I could write would never be more than philosophical remarks; my thoughts were soon crippled if I tried to force them on in any single direction against their natural inclination.—And this was, of course, connected with the very nature of the investigation. For this compels us to travel over a wide field of thought crisscross in every direction" (v). We are thus encouraged to approach Wittgenstein's philosophy as a collection of postcards, to be considered in different chronological or thematically intertwined arrangements and rearrangements, to which we must supply the interconnecting narrative by which the pictures tell a story.

There are currently two published translations of Wittgenstein's *Tractatus.* The first appeared in 1922, dictated by Frank

P. Ramsey and edited by C. K. Ogden. A more recent and in some ways improved translation was published in 1961 by David F. Pears and Brian F. McGuinness. I prefer the Ogden translation to the Pears-McGuinness partly because I am less satisfied with the Pears-McGuinness handling of Wittgenstein's technical term 'Sachverhalt' as 'state of affairs' than with the Ogden edition's 'atomic fact'. Pears and McGuinness probably regard this substitution as one of the major improvements in their translation, because Wittgenstein in the *Tractatus* does not use the words 'atomar' or 'atomisch'. But where both versions correctly render 'Tatsache' simply as 'fact', the Pears-McGuinness translation of 'Sachverhalt' as 'state of affairs' obscures the logical, metaphysical, and etymological connection between *Tatsache* and *Sachverhalt*. Wittgenstein frequently uses the term 'Sachlage', which is standardly translated as 'state of affairs'. But because the Pears-McGuinness translation is committed to using 'state of affairs' for 'Sachverhalt', they have opted infelicitously to translate 'Sachlage' as 'situation'. Wittgenstein collaborated on and personally approved the Ogden translation (but not the Pears-McGuinness, which appeared only after his death), working sentence-by-sentence on the manuscript with Ramsey, Ogden, and G. E. Moore (as we know from his correspondence with Ogden, edited by G. H. von Wright). In "Some Remarks on Logical Form," written only in English, Wittgenstein explicitly uses the phrase 'atomic proposition', citing Russell's "Lectures on Logical Atomism" for its derivation, a work in which Russell credits Wittgenstein with having influenced his thinking on the topic beginning in 1914. Since the 1929 essay is the centerpiece of my commentary, I have chosen the Ogden edition as more directly relevant to Wittgenstein's terminology in the 1929 essay.

I hope that the present book will help readers unfamiliar with Wittgenstein's enigmatic philosophical style to an improved understanding and appreciation of his ideas. As a guide to Wittgenstein's thought, it will serve its purpose if it inspires readers to return again and again to Wittgenstein's original writings. It is Wittgenstein's own way of expressing himself, even where his thoughts are most difficult to grasp, and what they mean to individual readers as philosophy and as poetry, to which critical commentary in my view should at most contribute as the means to a higher philosophical and aesthetic end.

| Wittgenstein's Life and Times

Ludwig Josef Johann Wittgenstein was born in Vienna, Austria, 26 April 1889, and died in Cambridge, England, where he had spent the greatest part of his philosophical career, on 29 April 1951.[1]

Wittgenstein was the son of Karl and Leopoldine ("Poldy") (née Kalmus). His father's family was of Jewish descent, but Wittgenstein's grandfather had converted to Protestantism.[2] Wittgenstein's mother was Jewish only on her father's side, and a Roman Catholic, in which church Wittgenstein was baptized. Wittgenstein was the youngest of eight children, five brothers and three sisters.

Karl was an engineer and entrepreneur who accumulated a fortune in the iron and steel industry. The Palais Wittgenstein in the Alleegasse in Vienna (no longer standing, in what has since been renamed the Argentinergasse), was one of the wealthiest and most important cultural centers of late-nineteenth- and early-twentieth-century Vienna. The palace was decorated with fine artworks, including the new Austrian *Jugenstil* painting and sculpture by Egon Schiele, Gustav Klimt, and Kolo Moser, then becoming fashionable among the avant-garde, but considered too outré by the conservative Vienna Akadamie.

Music was especially important in Wittgenstein's upbringing. All the children were musically gifted. Wittgenstein's brother Hans was a composer and virtuoso performer, until his presumed suicide during a visit to the United States, probably as the result of psychological conflict over his father's insistence that he give up music to enter a career in industry. Their brother Paul was a famous concert pianist, both before and after losing his right arm in World War I, and had piano works for one hand written for him by some of the most famous composers of the day. Wittgenstein, who did not learn an instrument until required to do so for a school-teaching position later in life, and was considered by his mother to lack a sense of rhythm, also had unusual musical abilities, a detailed knowledge of classical music, and at one time considered becoming a conductor. The Wittgenstein home, primarily through the efforts of Leopoldine, herself a talented pianist, hosted premier salon performances of works by Johannes Brahms, Gustav Mahler, Bruno Malter, and Joseph Labor.[3]

Wittgenstein thus entered the world as a modern-day industrial prince in a house of tremendous wealth and high culture. Yet it was also an environment of social democratic ideals outside the mainstream of traditional Austrian aristocracy dominated by the established royal houses. It was, for those in the upper ranks of society, the last golden days of the Biedermeier era under Emperor Franz Josef, before the breakup of the Austro-Hungarian empire at the conclusion of World War I.[4] More immediately in the Austrian chain of command, Ludwig and his siblings, some fifteen years apart, were under the control of Karl Wittgenstein, a self-made baron of nineteenth-century European industrialism, and, as his biographers unanimously suggest, a man with definite if not always welcome ideas about what was best for everyone around him.[5] The first six children in the family were most forcefully molded, while, chastened especially by Hans's suicide, Ludwig and his brother Paul were given more free rein to develop individually according to their personal inclinations. The Wittgensteins were all intellectually and artistically talented, but of such a temperament that they naturally resisted at the same time that they felt an overwhelming need to obey Karl's patriarchal efforts to prepare them as his successors in the family business. It may be in part as a result of such pressure that two other brothers, Kurt and Rudolf, also later committed suicide under quite different circumstances.[6]

Wittgenstein was educated at home until the age of fourteen. He was then sent to the Realschule in Linz for a broad pretechnical training, where he passed his Matura degree examination in 1906. He had hoped to study physics with Ludwig Boltzmann in Vienna, but was prevented by Boltzmann's suicide. Instead, Wittgenstein enrolled at the Technische Hochschule in Berlin-Charlottenburg, where he earned his certificate in engineering after two years in 1908. Wittgenstein's first professional work was in designing and building large experimental kites at The Kite Flying Open Atmosphere Station in Derbyshire, England. In the fall of 1908, Wittgenstein registered as an engineering research student at Manchester University. It was at this time that Wittgenstein's philosophical interests in mathematics began to emerge. Wittgenstein's discussions of mathematics with Horace Lamb, and his attendance at lectures by J. E. Littlewood at Manchester, inspired him to a consideration of the logical foundations of mathematics, an inquiry in which he found a stimulating source of ideas in Bertrand Russell's recently published (1903) *The Principles of Mathematics.*

After this, Wittgenstein became absorbed in problems of mathematical logic and the philosophy of mathematics. He abandoned his ambitious initial research project to design, build, and fly the first jet engine aircraft, and concentrated instead on designing a more efficient nautical turbo-propeller, which he patented. On leaving Manchester, Wittgenstein turned his attention from engineering to problems of the foundations of mathematics. He visited Gottlob Frege, author of the *Grundlagen der Arithmetik, Grundgesetze der Arithmetik,* and numerous influential essays in the philosophy of language and mathematics that had also been seminal in Russell's thinking after 1904. Wittgenstein followed Frege's advice to study logic with Russell at Cambridge University. There he quickly impressed Russell with his intelligence and culture, was invited to join the elite discussion group of Cambridge Apostles, including Russell, G. E. Moore, John Maynard Keynes, Lytton Strachey, and others, and became Russell's protégé. Before long, Wittgenstein, through brilliant devastating criticisms, began to overpower Russell in their philosophical interactions, and their master-disciple relationship was in some ways reversed.[7]

When World War I broke out, Wittgenstein, who was twenty-five, volunteered for active service. He had already left Cambridge and was working on problems of logic and philosophy in a secluded hut he had rebuilt on a fjord in the fishing village of Skjolden, Norway. Upon enlisting, he was first stationed on the patrol boat *Goplana* on the river Vistula in Cracow, and later put his engineering skills to use in the artillery at the Polish front, where he was decorated for bravery with the Silver Medal of Valor. Late in the war he was captured by the Italian army and imprisoned with other officers in the castle at Monte Cassino near Como. In prison he discussed logic with interested inmates, and meticulously studied Immanuel Kant's *Critique of Pure Reason (Kritik der reinen Vernunft)* with one of his compatriots, Ludwig Hänsel. Wittgenstein carried a few well-thumbed books through the war. By reputation, he had in his possession Dostoyevsky's *The Brothers Karamazov,* and a collection of Tolstoy's ethical and religious writings on the Gospels, which he repeatedly reread. He also kept notebooks in which he recorded philosophical aphorisms, somewhat in the style of Georg Christoph Lichtenberg and Arthur Schopenhauer, concerning problems of logic, the philosophical semantics of everyday language, the nature of the world, the limits of language, solipsism, mysticism, the transcendence of the self as metaphysical ego, and the unity of ethics and aesthetics. These are the central ideas of Wittgenstein's so-called early philosophy. His reflections began in Cambridge before the war, were partly worked out during his stay in Norway, written down in penultimate form mostly while on leave during the war in the late summer of 1918, and carried through the trenches into the castle prison, where with the help of Keynes his manuscript finally reached the world through copies sent to Russell and Frege. This was a short treatise Wittgenstein titled the *Logisch-Philosophische Abhandlung,* published in German in the last issue of the philosophical journal *Annalen der Naturphilosophie* in 1921, and in a German-English bilingual edition in 1922, as the *Tractatus Logico-Philosophicus.*[8]

Wittgenstein's father, Karl, died in 1912, about the time Wittgenstein went to Cambridge. Wittgenstein inherited a share of the family fortune, which after the war he promptly gave away. He secretly aided philosophers, poets, and artists, some of whose work, such as that of Rainer Maria Rilke, he did not particularly esteem. The *Tractatus* had supposedly eliminated all philosophical problems, and Wittgenstein, after its publication, accordingly stopped doing philosophy. With wealth, the war, and philosophy for the time being behind him, Wittgenstein turned to something practical that he must have thought could benefit the world in a small way by becoming an elementary school teacher. He was trained as schoolmaster at the Lehrerbildungsanstalt in Vienna from 1919 to 1920, and from 1920 to 1926 he taught at several elementary schools and in local continuing adult education programs in a few remote villages in Trattenbach and Otterthal in the lower Austrian Alps. The experience was in many ways frustrating for Wittgenstein, as he complains in much of his personal correspondence during this period.[9] Wittgenstein tried to introduce innovative teaching methods based on hands-on constructive activity. He emphasized the teaching of mathematics including algebra for students, many of whose parents regarded such a level of education for their rustic way of life as a senseless extravagance, if not an inroad of moral corruption.[10]

Wittgenstein resigned his teaching position, and became a gardener's assistant at the monastery Klosterneuberg at Hütteldorf outside Vienna, where for three months he lived in the tool shed. At this time, Wittgenstein considered entering a cloister, which it would have been possible to do as a lay person without taking holy orders. The religious dimensions of Wittgenstein's life, the appeal of mysticism even as it relates to the study of mathematical logic in his early philosophy, the denial of the will and renunciation of the world imbibed from his early reading of Schopenhauer and wartime contemplation of Tolstoy, manifested themselves in his immersion in the Bible, his recurring need to make confession of sins to certain of his friends, and his occasional desire to join a monastery, and later in his idealistic plan to immigrate to the young Soviet republic in Russia.[11] This spiritual aspect of Wittgenstein's personality might usefully be compared with that of Vincent van Gogh. Although the two did not know each other, they were each distinctively modern personalities who shared immense intellectual and artistic talents and a passionate devotion to the most uncompromising idiosyncratic standards of moral conduct and aesthetic value, as judged by the social conventions of their time. They also shared a compulsion toward religious self-denial and service to humankind, a desperate search for love and the understanding of another like soul that was inevitably disappointed by the persons they first chose as friends and then severely repulsed as unworthy, and a fierce untiring energy and manic need to pour forth visionary new ideas on canvas or in notebooks and typescripts, much of which the world is only now beginning to appreciate. In remarkably similar ways, Wittgenstein and van Gogh experienced the frustrations and torments on the emotional roller coaster of aesthetic and philosophical genius.[12]

The facts about Wittgenstein's early biography must be seen against the backdrop of Vienna as one of the major centers of European fin-de-siècle culture in the last days of the Austro-Hungarian empire. The sudden dismantling of this major political power sphere in the aftermath of World War I, the disillusionment with modern society in the wake of the unprecedented mechanized horrors of the war, was widely perceived by an entire generation of young European intellectuals as a failure of reason and betrayal of idealism. Wittgenstein had been a soldier for five years in a war that defied rational justification. The crisis contradicted what was supposed to have been the enlightened spirit of the era, that to no purpose resulted in terrible destruction, and had as its traumatic conclusion the dissolution of a great empire that for two hundred years had defined the political and cultural identity of much of Europe. The fall of the Habsburg dynasty had been foretold by the pessimist novelists and sociologists of the time, such as Robert Musil, Otto Weininger, and Karl Kraus. These writers propagated an Austrian cult of social despair and suicide, and popularized the notion of the empire and the modern world generally as having fallen into an irreversible state of decay and moral lassitude.[13] Wittgenstein's struggles to find new meaning in life after the war were shared by many young veterans and survivors of the conflict. The postwar malaise was even more complicated for Wittgenstein because of his exceptional intellect, intense and finely-tuned moral and aesthetic sensibilities, and the fact that he had convinced himself that there was no possible future for philosophy. The symbol of Wittgenstein's religious-ascetic renunciation of the world during the rest of his life can be seen in the modest furnishings of his school teacher's room outside Trattenbach, across the road from the inn *Zum braunen Hirsch,* and the similar humble university digs in which he later lived in Cambridge. The rooms can still be seen, austerely furnished like a monk's cell, with a cot, washstand, writing table, folding chairs, and in Cambridge a fireproof safe for protecting his manuscripts, about which he suffered fears bordering on paranoia.

After resigning his teaching position, Wittgenstein tried his hand at a number of artistic projects. Back in Vienna, he undertook partly to redesign and supervise the construction of a modernist city mansion for his sister Gretl (Margarete, married to Jerome Stonborough) in the Kundmanngasse.[14] The building was first drafted by architect Paul Englemann and later annotated in the final plans as a collaborative effort between Englemann and Wittgenstein. It can be visited today, and has recently been restored, having been used for many years as the Bulgarian cultural embassy. Wittgenstein conceived the townhouse as an embodiment of the minimalist spirit of the architectural critic Adolf Loos, whom he had met in 1914, and whose writings on architectural aesthetics he greatly admired.[15] Wittgenstein worked at the construction site for two years. During this time, sculpting the head of a woman with modernist neoclassical lines in the studio of Michael Drobil, whom he had met when they were both prisoners of war, he demonstrated further untapped artistic abilities. Here Wittgenstein frequented the café Museum, near the Vienna Secession—the celebrated temple to modern art, constructed as a gleaming white box surmounted by a golden lattice leaf-and-tendril dome—where artists who had broken away from the rigid standards of the Austrian art academy staged their own independent exhibits, and whose work the Wittgenstein family and Wittgenstein later anonymously supported.

A single anecdote from this time reveals much about Wittgenstein's unyielding aesthetic standards of exactness. The attitude no doubt derived from his training in engineering and lifelong fascination with the problems of logic and mathematics, but is more a reflection of something deeply characteristic about his personality. The story is told by Wittgenstein's sister Hermine, in connection with his 1926–28 architectural venture:

> A second great problem that Ludwig told me about concerned the doors and windows. They were all made of iron, and the construction of the unusually high glass doors with their narrow iron mullions was exceedingly difficult, for there were no supporting horizontal rails, and a precision was demanded which seemed impossible to attain. Of eight firms with which long, detailed negotiations were held only one thought it could undertake the work, but the finished door, which had taken months to construct, had to be rejected as unusable. During the discussions with the firm which eventually built the doors, the engineer handling the negotiations broke down in a fit of sobbing. He did not want to give up the commission but despaired of ever being able to complete it in accordance with Ludwig's wishes. . . . Perhaps the most telling proof of Ludwig's relentlessness when it came to getting proportions exactly right is the fact that he had the ceiling of one of the rooms, which was almost big enough to be a hall, raised by three centimetres, just when it was almost time to start cleaning the completed house.[16]

Then, in 1929, after a seven-year moratorium, Wittgenstein attended a lecture given in Vienna by the Dutch intuitionist mathematician and philosopher of mathematics, L. E. J. Brouwer. After this, Wittgenstein is reported to have believed himself able again to make worthwhile contributions to philosophical work, and his return to philosophy is usually dated from the time of the Brouwer lecture.[17]

Wittgenstein returned to Cambridge, where he first enrolled as a postgraduate research student, was made lecturer in 1930, and finally ascended to Moore's chair, near the beginning of World War II. What became the *Blue and Brown Books,* issued in dictation to his lecture seminars in 1933 and 1934, were privately circulated, but not published until several years after his death. Concerned because of his family's Jewish origins about the safety of his sisters who remained in Vienna after the Nazi Anschluss, Wittgenstein wanted a useful part to play in the wartime mobilization. Unable to reconcile himself to what he always regarded as the detestable duties of an academic philosopher while the world again waged war, Wittgenstein took temporary leave of his chair in philosophy to serve as an orderly at Guy's Hospital in London, attending to the wounded, and later worked as a technician in a medical laboratory in Newcastle. The *Philosophical Investigations,* Wittgenstein's second great work, was mostly complete by the war's end in 1945, with additions and corrections drafted between 1946 and 1949. Wittgenstein never intercollated these as he intended into the first part of the text, but they have been collected in the posthumous edition as part 2, more or less in the order in which he left them in manuscript.

The other typescripts, folios of remarks about specialized subjects, student lecture notes, diaries, journals, and shoe boxes filled with strips of paper snipped from typed pages for rearrangement, were written during this time. There is a monumental body of work, only about a third of which has been published to date. The manuscripts consist largely of philosophical reflections on a large number of subjects of such profound originality and depth of penetration as to constitute one of the most remarkable philosophical achievements. During his brief tenure as lecturer at Cambridge, Wittgenstein, by virtue of the *Tractatus's* reputation and reports of his new teaching, attracted some of the brightest philosophy students from all over the world, especially from England, the United States, and Scandinavia. The list of those who attended his lectures and whose intellectual and personal lives he touched, even while dissuading many of them from philosophy to more practical pursuits, reads like a who's who of some of the most prominent thinkers of the last half-century. Of equal importance is the impact Wittgenstein's ideas have had since the time of his death especially on recent analytic thought, through the early and later writings that have contributed to the influence of his attitude toward and distinctive way of doing philosophy.

In 1948, Wittgenstein resigned his chair at Cambridge and moved to Ireland, where he lived on a farm in the countryside to resume full-time philosophical writing. Later, he again occupied a simple hut among fishermen in Galway, on the western Irish coast, where he impressed local residents with his ability to tame sea birds. In 1949, during a brief visit to the United States with his former student, the philosopher Norman Malcolm, Wittgenstein was diagnosed with prostate cancer. In 1950, he returned again to Norway. Here he intermittently continued work in philosophy, to the extent his failing health permitted, writing with characteristic clarity despite his advancing illness, as he did upon his final return to Cambridge in the following year, until two days before his death. Wittgenstein's last days are described in these closing words of Malcolm's personal *Memoir:*

On Friday, April 27th, he took a walk in the afternoon. That night he fell violently ill. He remained conscious and when informed by the doctor that he could live only a few days, he exclaimed 'Good!' Before losing consciousness he said to Mrs. Bevan (who was with him throughout the night) 'Tell them I've had a wonderful life!' By 'them' he undoubtedly meant his close friends. When I think of his profound pessimism, the intensity of his mental and moral suffering, the relentless way in which he drove his intellect, his need for love together with the harshness that repelled love, I am inclined to believe that his life was fiercely unhappy. Yet at the end he himself exclaimed that it had been 'wonderful'! To me this seems a mysterious and strangely moving utterance.[18]

At a glance, this is the life of the thinker whose extraordinary contributions to contemporary philosophy we are about to consider. In what follows, I offer a detailed interpretation and commentary on the development of Wittgenstein's philosophy. The story inevitably is simplified, but I hope not oversimplified. I begin with what others have referred to as the early philosophy, dating approximately from the years 1914 to 1929, to the later philosophy, from about 1934 to his death in 1951, with special emphasis on the historical-philosophical events of the transition period, which I designate from 1929 to 1933.[19]

The dates are significant and by no means arbitrary. Wittgenstein's early surviving *Notebooks 1914–1916*, which were preparatory to the *Tractatus*, begin in 1914. Wittgenstein's much-neglected but extraordinarily important essay, "Some Remarks on Logical Form," was written in 1929. It is the only substantive philosophical work other than the *Tractatus* to be published in Wittgenstein's lifetime, but he rejected it before it appeared and refused to read it at the philosophical meeting for which it was written.[20] In 1930, Wittgenstein began lecturing at Cambridge University. The end of the transition period can be dated approximately to 1933, because Wittgenstein's lectures from this term recorded in the *Blue Book,* together with the *Brown Book* of 1934, already contain his new methodology and nearly all of the central ideas of his later philosophy as they were to appear in the *Philosophical Investigations*. The *Philosophical Remarks* and *Philosophical Grammar,* lifted from the so-called *Big Typescript,* the *Remarks on the Foundations of Mathematics, On Certainty, Remarks on Colour, Remarks on Frazer's Golden Bough, Lectures on Philosophical Psychology, Culture and Value, Zettel, Diaries,* and other posthumously collected writings of the *Nachlaß,* student lecture notes on ethics, aesthetics, and religion, are worlds unto themselves, of which I can take only passing notice.

My main topic is Wittgenstein's philosophy of language from the early through the transitional to the later period, and to a lesser extent its implications for Wittgenstein's philosophical psychology and philosophy of logic and mathematics. The scope and limits of languages in which traditional philosophical puzzles and paradoxes about the nature of substance, causation, the self, free will, beauty and the good purport to be thought about and expressed have a direct bearing on the scope and limits of philosophy. I am interested in clarifying Wittgenstein's ideas about the relevance of language and the conditions of the meaningfulness of language for philosophy in each of the three major periods of his thought. Wittgenstein radically changed his opinions about some aspects of the relation between language and philosophy, but held steadfast throughout his philosophical career to others. The transition in Wittgenstein's thought from the early to the later philosophy is an important chapter in the history of philosophy. It reveals the complex workings of one of the greatest philosophical minds, struggling through self-criticism of an original wide-ranging and highly integrated set of solutions to reach new insights about the most difficult problems of meaning and the conduct of philosophy. The concepts I shall explore as central to Wittgenstein's work offer a brief glimpse into just a few related dimensions of a vastly more multifaceted philosophical intelligence and cultural presence. Yet the conclusions of Wittgenstein's reflections about language and proper philosophical method are fundamental to his philosophy in the early, transitional, and later periods.

In this commentary, I shall concentrate almost exclusively on the *Tractatus Logico-Philosophicus,* "Some Remarks on Logical Form," and *Philosophical Investigations,* with secondary emphasis on the *Notebooks 1914–1916* and the *Blue and Brown Books,* while making only incidental references to the other writings. There is a wealth of philosophical material collateral to my interpretation of Wittgenstein's philosophy which for reasons of space I cannot fully take into account. Nor, for the same reason, can I enter deeply into detailed consideration or critical evaluation of previous analyses of Wittgenstein's thought by other commentators, with almost all of which I partly agree and, sometimes in the most important points, also partly disagree. From the fact that I do not always individually acknowledge received views about Wittgenstein that I accept or with which I implicitly take issue, it should not be inferred that I am unmindful that what I say about Wittgenstein has been said before, or, alternatively, that on other matters of interpretation that have become established as standard in the field, my remarks may seem controversial, even heretical. In the notes to each chapter and in the bibliography I include additional sources from an extensive secondary literature that offer complementary perspectives on Wittgenstein's philosophy.

I do not claim to convey any startlingly new discoveries about Wittgenstein's life or thought. I have merely tried to put together what is already mostly common coin in Wittgenstein studies in what I hope to be a provocative way. There is a danger in this method of imposing a different order on the subject than it naturally admits. I can only say that I am aware of the risks, and that I believe I am explaining an existent order rather than foisting an imaginary structure onto Wittgenstein's thought. I have avoided explicit criticism of received interpretations wherever possible, even when I sharply dissent, because I have no wish to detract from other attempts to shed light on Wittgenstein's thought from different points of view. Wittgenstein, who frequently describes the practice of philosophy as rightly organizing what we are given to see clearly before us if we will only try to look without philosophical prejudice, might have approved of this method of understanding his work. In his writings, Wittgenstein presents his ideas as so many colorful tesserae to be arranged and rearranged in different mosaics to be seen experimentally in different ways from different angles in a many-sided philosophical portrait of the relations that must hold between thought, language, and world.

To anticipate and give the most succinct précis of my overview of Wittgenstein's philosophy, I maintain that Wittgenstein in the early period is an idealist semantic transcendentalist of a roughly Schopenhauerian kind; the later Wittgenstein is a staunchly antitranscendentalist empirical realist and semantic pragmatist or instrumentalist (of his own stripe, despite points of similarity and some bibliographic connections, independent of the American pragmatist tradition); while the transition between these changes of philosophical approach between the early and later periods is brought about by Wittgenstein's rejection of the *Tractatus* theory of meaning due to the color incompatibility problem, and his subsequent need to rethink the foundations of philosophical semantics and its implications for philosophical psychology, the philosophy of mathematics, religion, ethics and aesthetics, and the practice of philosophy.

There are, as might be expected and as I shall point out along the way, continuities that extend throughout all of Wittgenstein's thought from the early to the later philosophy through the transitional period. Yet there are also dramatic discontinuities, abrupt rejections of previous positions, experiments with solutions under different formulations, new insights and an ongoing development of concepts and methods to replace others that Wittgenstein discards. In this book I try to chart the main features of this difficult terrain, offering a unified historical-critical interpretation of Wittgenstein's lifework. My interests are philosophical rather than purely historical. While I do not profess to being a Wittgensteinian, I find Wittgenstein's involvement with the problems of meaning, mind, and philosophical method more stimulating and rewarding even in matters about which I disagree than those of almost any other philosopher. It is in the effort to understand Wittgenstein's thought on its own terms that I am motivated to offer this historical reconstruction, a project in which my own thinking for twenty-odd years remains in transition.

I NOTES

1. I am indebted to the memoirs and biographies of Wittgenstein by Malcolm (with von Wright) 1958, McGuinness 1988, and Monk 1991.

2. Monk, 5: "By the time they moved to Vienna in the 1850s the Wittgensteins probably no longer regarded themselves as Jewish. Hermann Christian [Ludwig's paternal grandfather], indeed, acquired something of a reputation as an anti-Semite, and firmly forbade his offspring to marry Jews. . . . The Wittgensteins (unlike, say, the Freuds) were in no way part of a Jewish community—except in the elusive sense in which the whole of Vienna could be so described; nor did Judaism play any part in their upbringing. Their culture was entirely Germanic."

3. See Janik and Toulmin 1973, 102–12, 244–61.

4. Johnston 1972, 19–23 and passim.

5. Monk, 11–15.

6. Monk, 11: "The régime within which Karl's eldest sons were raised was shaped by Karl's determination to see them continue his business. They were not to be sent to schools (where they would acquire the bad habits of mind of the Austrian establishment), but were to be educated privately in a way designed to train their minds for the intellectual rigours of commerce. They were then to be sent to some part of the Wittgenstein business empire, where they would acquire the technical and commercial expertise necessary for success in industry."

7. The shift is apparent in Wittgenstein 1974b, 7–104. See also Monk, 36–90.

8. Russell regarded the *Tractatus* as brilliant, but Wittgenstein thought he did not fully understand it; Frege claimed not to understand it. Russell's introduction is in many ways useful, but in other respects, such as its description of Wittgenstein's purpose as the construction of an ideal language and complaint about the theory's lack of provision for transfinite numbers, it is neither an accurate exposition nor a sensitive criticism of Wittgenstein's early philosophy. Wittgenstein met with Russell in The Hague in 1919 to discuss certain details of the introduction and publishing arrangements, and came away feeling that Russell had largely misunderstood the work. He contemplated refusing permission to have the book published with Russell's introductory essay. The manuscript Wittgenstein had in his possession at the time of his imprisonment was the so-called *Prototractatus*. See von Wright 1982, 68–74. Wittgenstein 1973, editor's Introduction, 1–13.

9. See Wittgenstein's letters to Engelmann dated 2.1.21 and 24.2.25, in Wittgenstein 1967b; also his letter to Russell dated 28.11.21, in Wittgenstein 1974b.

10. The most detailed account appears in Monk, 192–233. See also Wünsche 1985. Wittgenstein during this period also wrote a useful inexpensive student dictionary, the *Wörterbuch für Volksschulen*, edited and reprinted by Leinfellner, Leinfellner, and Hübner 1977.

11. It was Schopenhauer's *The World as Will and Representation* and other writings that Wittgenstein claims provided the foundation of his first idealist-transcendentalist philosophy in a broadly Kantian vein. See Janik 1966; Engel 1969. Von Wright 1982, 18: "If I remember rightly, Wittgenstein told me that he had read Schopenhauer's *Die Welt als Wille und Vorstellung* in his youth and that his first philosophy was a Schopenhauerian epistemological idealism." Ayer 1985, 13: "Wittgenstein was not entirely dismissive of the philosophers of the past, but his reading of them was markedly eclectic. As a boy he was strongly influenced by Schopenhauer's principal work *The World as Will and Representation*, and we shall see that this influence persists in the *Tractatus*, though the only philosophers to whom he acknowledges a debt in the *Tractatus* are Frege and Russell. The book contains a passing reference to Kant and has been thought by some critics to display a Kantian approach, but there is no evidence that Wittgenstein made any serious study of Kant's writings and his knowledge of Kant was most probably filtered through Schopenhauer." Haller 1988, 74: "Wittgenstein's preoccupation with Schopenhauer—whose work visibly displays the principal themes of Kant's philosophy—is apparent from his earliest notes onwards." Jacquette 1996b. Yet von Wright in Malcolm 1958, 21–22, writes: "It may appear strange that Schopenhauer, one of the masters of philosophic prose, did not influence Wittgenstein's style. An author, however, who reminds one, often astonishingly, of Wittgenstein is [Georg Christoph] Lichtenberg. Wittgenstein esteemed him highly. To what extent, if any, he can be said to have learned from him I do not know. It is deserving of mention that some of Lichtenberg's thoughts on philosophic questions show a striking resemblance to Wittgenstein's." Compare von Wright 1942, 201–17. See also Drury, in Rhees 1984, 158: "WITTGENSTEIN: My fundamental ideas came to me very early in life. DRURY: Schopenhauer? WITTGENSTEIN: No; I think I see quite clearly what Schopenhauer got out of his philosophy—but when I read Schopenhauer I seem to see to the bottom very easily. He is not deep in the sense that Kant and Berkeley are deep." Wittgenstein's consideration and eventual rejection of the plan to move to the USSR is described by his Russian language tutor, Fania Pascal, in Rhees 1984, 12–49.

12. As a basis for comparison with van Gogh's life, see Edwards 1989. The connections between Wittgenstein's work in philosophical logic and his religious struggles are examined in Shields 1993. See Malcolm 1994.

13. Musil 1953–60; 1964. Weininger 1906. See Dallago 1912; Engelmann 1967; Iggers 1967; Janik 1985; Kraft 1961.

14. Kapfinger 1984; Leitner 1970, 1973; Wijdeveld 1994.

15. Loos 1962; Munz and Kunstler 1966; Gravagnuolo 1982; Kubinszky 1970.

16. Hermine Wittgenstein, in Rhees 1984, 8. Wittgenstein's hypergraphia, excessive attention to detail, need to redo flawed work from the beginning in order to satisfy an elevated ideal of perfection, and obsession with the problem of solipsism have led some to speculate that Wittgenstein may have been partially autistic. Sachs 1995, 295: "Christopher Gillberg, one of the finest clinical observers of autism, feels that autistic people of the Asperger type . . . may be capable of major creativity and wonders whether indeed Bartók and Wittgenstein may have been autistic."

17. Von Wright, in Malcolm 1958, 12–13; Monk, 248–51. See also Redpath 1990. Findlay 1973, 167–85.

18. Malcolm 1958, 100. I am inspired to close my biographical remarks on this note by Herbert's essay, "Spinoza's Bed," in his 1991, 144: "It is an amazing thing that our memory best retains images of great philosophers when their lives were coming to an end. Socrates raising the chalice with hemlock to his mouth, Seneca whose veins were opened by a slave (there is a painting of this by Rubens), Descartes roaming cold palace rooms with a foreboding that his role of teacher of the Swedish queen would be his last, old Kant smelling a grated horseradish before his daily walk (the cane preceding him, sinking deeper and deeper into the sand), Spinoza consumed by tuberculosis and patiently polishing lenses, so weak he is unable to finish his *Treatise on the Rainbow.* . . . A gallery of noble moribunds, pale masks, plaster casts."

19. It is on this basis that I disagree with and wish to refine the chronology offered by Pitcher in the preface to his 1966 collection, v: "If I were forced to distinguish the aspects or phases of Wittgenstein's work for the purpose, say, of writing a chapter in a history-of-philosophy text, I might make the following broad divisions: 1. *Tractatus* period, from just before 1913 to about 1929, when 'Some Remarks on Logical Form' was published. 2. Transitional period, from 1929 through 1935. Here, the ideas of the *Tractatus* were being criticized and largely rejected, and the leading themes of his later work were being developed. 3. *Investigations* period, from about 1936 until his death."

20. The only other philosophical publications to appear in Wittgenstein's lifetime are his scathing 1913 review of Peter Coffey, *The Science of Logic,* and his 1933 letter to the editor of the journal *Mind.*

The Early Philosophy

Logic must take care of itself.
— WITTGENSTEIN, *NOTEBOOKS 1914–1916*
(22.8.14)

CHAPTER
O   N   E | **Logical Atomism**

To understand Wittgenstein's early philosophy, we must begin with the problem of language. Wittgenstein's *Tractatus* seeks to explicate the conditions by which it is possible for language to have meaning. When language expresses an idea, typically in formulating a proposition to convey a thought, it can be used to say something that is definitely true or definitely false. The *Tractatus* offers a philosophical semantics to explain how this can be so, taking as its general topic the question of how meaning is achieved in any logically possible language under any logically possible circumstances.

The account Wittgenstein presents has three main parts. It combines a metaphysics of logical atomism with a picture theory of meaning and a definition of the general form of proposition. The idea of logical atomism can best be understood in terms of an analogy with physical atomism. Physical atomism is the building up of material objects by combinations of atoms into molecules, and molecules into macrophysical things like tables and chairs and solar systems, the sum total of which constitute the furniture of the universe. Wittgenstein's semantics is committed to a logical rather than physical atomism, and we must see in what respects logical atomism is like and in what respects it is unlike physical atomism.

Any particular use of language, such as the disturbance of air produced when someone speaks or the marks made on paper in writing and printing, is a concrete expression of thought. Regarding its concrete expressions only as such, language is not only analogous to but is itself a material entity consisting of physical molecules of graphite, ink, or air in motion, which in turn are composed of physical atoms. Logical atomism as distinct from purely physical atomism in Wittgenstein's sense requires that we think of language in more abstract terms. Language on this conception is like any material object, in that it involves simple units of meaning put together in complex ways. The book you are now reading is a meaningful expression of thoughts that can be understood and communicated in language from mind to mind. A book consists of individual chapters in a certain order; the chapters consist of individual sections and paragraphs, again in a certain order; the paragraphs consist of individual sentences; the sentences consist of individual words; and the words consist of individual letters of the alphabet.

The idea of interpreting the meaning of complex linguistic expressions as a semantic function of the meaning of simpler meaningful units was already known in ancient Greek philosophy.[1] Among more recent thinkers the concept is perhaps most often associated with Frege's theory of language. Frege is understood by Wittgenstein to accept such a principle, for example, when he writes in the *Tractatus* 3.318: "I conceive the proposition—like Frege and Russell—as a function of the expressions contained in it."[2] It was Russell who coined the term 'logical atomism', and Wittgenstein later reports that he adopted the term 'atomic proposition' from Russell's 1917–18 "Lectures on Logical Atomism."[3] Yet the doctrine of logical atomism in Russell's or Wittgenstein's philosophy requires more than the thesis that larger meaningful expressions in a language can be built up out of smaller meaningful expressions. What is needed for logical *atomism* is the further thesis that there are ultimately simple or irreducible semantic units of meaning. These will be genuine logical atoms that, like genuine physical atoms, cannot be subdivided into more basic constituents. Otherwise, there is no reason to suppose that the decomposition of meaning could not continue indefinitely. Logical atoms, if there are any, must provide the absolutely fundamental starting place for the constructive elaboration of meaning, the semantic building blocks of all language.

Wittgenstein proposes to explain language in its most abstract general terms. He must therefore identify the logically most basic elements in the analysis of meaning for any logically possible language, including natural languages like English, French, German, Russian, Japanese, and special mathematical and scientific languages. Since Wittgenstein's goal is to find whatever it is that makes any language work—that by virtue of which any conceivable language is capable of expressing determinate meaning—it will not do for him to settle on the words or sentences of any particular language as its logical atoms. That there must be logical atoms is in one sense necessitated for Wittgenstein by this fact alone. If we accept the reductive model by which the meaning of more complex constructions is a function of the meaning of the simpler meaningful units they contain and out of which they are built, then, if we suppose that language has determinate meaning, we cannot imagine that the reduction of meaning from larger to smaller units continues indefinitely, but that it comes to an end in some ultimate semantic foundation. The reason is obvious when we reflect that actual uses of language have determinate meaning in speaking and writing, that two persons can understand one another's thoughts when formulated in language, but that meaning is expressed and communicated in a finite amount of time. If there are logical atoms, if they explain the conditions that make possible the determinate meaningfulness of any logically possible language, and if logical atoms cannot merely be the paragraphs, sentences, words, or letters of the alphabet of any particular language, but must be more abstract units, what kinds of things are they, and how exactly are they combined into more complicated constructions?

Wittgenstein begins to answer this question by explaining how the world must be constituted in order to be represented in language. The first propositions of Wittgenstein's treatise introduce the metaphysical presuppositions of any language:

1   The world is everything that is the case.

1.1   The world is the totality of facts, not of things.

1.11   The world is determined by the facts, and by these being *all* the facts.

1.12   For the totality of facts determines both what is the case, and also all that is not the case.

1.13   The facts in logical space are the world.

The opening statements offer a compact expression of some of Wittgenstein's most important ideas. Propositions 1 and 1.1 explain Wittgenstein's first approximation to a world ontology. The world is everything that is the case, a totality of facts rather than of things. Although the translation is excellent, Wittgenstein's German in proposition 1 is worth considering. He asserts that "Die Welt ist alles was der Fall ist." This might be rendered with better emphasis as 'The world is everything that *happens* to be the case', where by punning on the German we might say that the world is everything as it occurs or falls out. The point is that for Wittgenstein the world is a totality specifically of contingent or logically possible but not logically necessary facts. This at once excludes logical, mathematical, and analytic truths, which are also sometimes informally referred to as 'facts', such as the 'fact' that $2 + 2 = 4$, or the 'fact' that all bachelors are unmarried male adults, that are excluded by Wittgenstein's technical sense of the term *Tatsache,* translated here as 'fact'.

Things can be differently configured. But the totality of facts or states of affairs is inflexible. A group of planets can be placed in indeterminately many different relations to one another. Venus could be between Earth and Mars, or Mars between Earth and Venus, or Earth between Venus and Mars. We get distinct logically possible worlds, different from the actual world, if we consider the same things reordered in different ways, as if Mercury and Mars were to change places in our solar system. The fact that Earth is between Venus and Mars fixes their relation and allows for no indeterminacy with respect to their relative locations. If the totality of facts is considered for each and every thing in the universe, then there is no room for indeterminateness, but the world as a whole is fixed and determined, as 1.11 and 1.12 state. We are not to think of facts as occurrent events in physical space, but rather as obtaining in what Wittgenstein calls logical space. Logical space is more abstract than physical space. Logical space is a logical 'enclosure' or ideal range of logical possibilities that could be occupied by different logically possible worlds, each with its own physical space. It is the abstract space in which any logically possible world can be constructed as a distinct totality of facts, and, more particularly, as Wittgenstein is about to say, as a totality of logically possible atomic facts. When Wittgenstein speaks of 'the world' (*die Welt*) in these passages, it is evident, therefore, that he means any world, including but not necessarily limited to the actual world, as when we speak generically of 'the law' to denote any legislation in force, rather than a particular set of statutes.

Wittgenstein next maintains the logical independence of the facts that in their totality constitute a world:

> 1.2   The world divides into facts.
>
> 1.21   Any one can either be the case or not be the case,
> and everything else remain the same.

These remarks do not make the matter sufficiently apparent, but 1.2 and 1.21 already contain within their implications Wittgenstein's commitment to the reduction of any logically possible world to a totality of atomic facts. As we shall see, it is only the logically most elementary or atomic facts that can be logically independent of one another, or such that any can either be the case or not be the case, without affecting the existence or nonexistence of any other. Ordinary complex facts, such as those we have so far considered, are not mutually logically independent. If the ordinary fact that Earth is between Venus and Mars should fail to obtain, then many other ordinary facts about the universe cannot simply 'remain the same' but are accordingly altered. This includes the appearance of the night sky from the Earth, gravitational equilibria throughout and distances between centers of gravity within the solar system, and many other things.

If the world is the totality of facts, and if the world is determined by and divides into facts, the facts in question cannot be ordinary facts or states of affairs as we typically think of them. The concept of an atomic fact now appropriately makes its debut:

> 2   What is the case, the fact, is the existence of atomic facts.
>
> 2.01   An atomic fact is a combination of objects (entities, things).

Wittgenstein draws an important distinction between ordinary complex facts and atomic facts. He writes in 2: "Was der Fall ist, die Tatsache, ist das Bestehen von Sachverhalten." The terms made to serve the purposes of his technical contrast are 'Tatsache' for ordinary fact, and 'Sachverhalt' for atomic fact. The world is everything that is or happens to be the case, and what is or happens to be the case is the existence of atomic facts. From this it seems to follow that the world (generically) is just the existence of atomic facts. The sequel in 2.01 explains that an atomic fact or Sachverhalt is a combination of objects (von Gegenständen). That the objects combined into atomic facts are not ordinary objects is required by the argument that atomic facts are not ordinary facts. The objects in atomic facts are said in the parenthetical remark of 2.01 to be entities (Sachen) or things (Dinge). Yet again and for the same reasons these cannot be ordinary entities or ordinary things. If the Gegenstände of which Sachverhalte are composed were ordinary objects like tables and chairs, Earth, Venus, and Mars, or even the material atomic and subatomic particles of microphysics, then we should have already run into contradiction with the ontic independence of the facts into which the world divides in 1.21.

We learn next what Wittgenstein intends by the objects that in combination constitute atomic facts. Wittgenstein invokes the Aristotelian distinction between a thing's essential and accidental properties. He explains:

> 2.011   It is essential to a thing that it can be a constituent part of an atomic fact.

2.012   In logic nothing is accidental: if a thing *can* occur in
an atomic fact the possibility of that atomic fact
must already be prejudged in the thing.

2.0121   It would, so to speak, appear as an accident, when
to a thing that could exist alone on its own account,
subsequently a state of affairs could be made to fit.

If things can occur in atomic facts, this possibility
must already lie in them.

(A logical entity cannot be merely possible. Logic
treats of every possibility, and all possibilities are
its facts.)

Wittgenstein claims that the objects that make up ontically
independent atomic facts are essentially potential constituents of
atomic facts. We are presumably to think of the objects that are
combined into atomic facts as being essentially such that they
can be so combined. An object might belong to many different
atomic facts. Then the possibility of its entering into these facts
will define the object's nature or essence, in the sense that it
could not exist as just that object if it failed to have the property
of possibly belonging to any of these facts.

Atomic facts cannot exist without their objects because particular atomic facts are particular combinations of objects. Yet
the objects of atomic facts cannot exist (*bestehen*) independently
of the possibility of entering into particular atomic facts. We are
not to imagine a pool of objects that in some sense have their
identity and individuality preestablished as discrete autonomous
entities that might then be combined to constitute different
atomic facts. Wittgenstein states that this would make the combination of any selection of ontically independent objects an accidental property of the objects. The objects are the ultimate
constituents of atomic facts in logical space, and are in that sense
logical objects, where in logic nothing is accidental. The possibility of an object's occurrence in an atomic fact must therefore be,
as Wittgenstein puts it in 2.012, 'prejudged' in the thing. Wittgenstein's metaphysics of atomic facts entails the possibility of
the occurrence of an object in any of the atomic facts into which it
may be combined as logically necessary or essential (*wesentlich*)
to it, and as such cannot merely be one among the contingent or
accidental facts that collectively constitute the world.

We must think of the objects that in combination comprise
all atomic facts as already containing within themselves, among
their internal or constitutive properties, the possibility of entering into all the atomic facts to which logically they can belong.
This not only offers insight into the essential as opposed to accidental properties of objects in Wittgenstein's technical sense, but

more importantly, Wittgenstein in this way stipulates what he means by the concept of an object. The objects that combine to comprise atomic facts are in essence whatever things have the logical possibility of entering into such combinations so as to constitute atomic facts. Wittgenstein elaborates on this definition of object in the ensuing passages, where he speaks of the essence or nature of objects as belonging to certain atomic facts as among its internal as opposed to external qualities. He draws the distinction epistemically, in terms of what can be known about the properties of an object:

> 2.0123 If I know an object, then I also know all the possibilities of its occurrence in atomic facts.
>
> (Every such possibility must lie in the nature of the object.)
>
> A new possibility cannot subsequently be found.
>
> 2.01231 In order to know an object, I must know not its external but all its internal qualities.

An internal quality is one that uniquely identifies and individuates a thing; an external quality is a quality a thing has only in its outward relations to other things. We might regard an apple in its internal qualities as being the fruit of a certain kind of tree, the ripened ovary of a blossom with a certain texture and shape and color and so on, while the external qualities of the apple would include its spatial relation to other apples, the gravitational force exerted on it by the planet Neptune, and the fact that a passerby admires and desires it. This gives us a working idea of the distinction between internal and external qualities. Wittgenstein says more particularly, in the case of the objects of which atomic facts are composed, that, whatever external qualities they may have, their internal qualities are specifically the possibility of entering into the logically possible facts that they may be put together to constitute. To know an object is thus to know the atomic facts into which it can be combined. Since this is a matter of logical necessity, logic exhausts the possibility for the combination of objects into atomic facts, and new possibilities cannot be empirically discovered, but are, so to speak, already known to logic.

The complete set of logically possible atomic facts constituted by combinations of the objects is determined by the complete set of objects. This is implied by the requirement that the nature or essence of each object is defined by its internal properties of possibly belonging to a given set of atomic facts. Wittgenstein only states the inevitable in the following passages when he concludes:

2.0124   If all objects are given, then thereby are all *possible* atomic facts also given.

2.013   Every thing is, as it were, in a space of possible atomic facts. I can think of this space as empty, but not of the thing without the space.

2.014   Objects contain the possibility of all states of affairs.

The observation in 2.013 looks back to the concept of logical space introduced in 1.13. Wittgenstein now adds the condition that the objects occupy an abstract space of logical possibilities. This, as 2.011–2.0123 imply, is not something an object does entirely on its own, but only in the context of its combination with other objects in an atomic fact. We learn in 2.013 that logical space is a space of possible atomic facts. The contextualism of objects in atomic facts within logical space parallels Wittgenstein's commitment to Frege's semantic contextualism, whereby words do not have meaning considered entirely on their own, but only holistically in the context of a sentence or larger unit of meaning.[4]

Wittgenstein adds that an object's form is its essential internal qualities of possibly belonging to atomic facts in combination with other objects, and that the object is simple. He thereby finally touches the ontic bedrock of logical atomism. Simple objects are the metaphysical foundation of the world, the true logical atoms out of which atomic facts are constituted, and as such enter into ordinary facts composed of atomic facts at the logically and ontically deepest level of analysis.

2.0141   The possibility of its occurrence in atomic facts is the form of the object.

2.02   The object is simple.

Wittgenstein has already explained that the internal qualities of objects are logical properties. So it is not surprising that he should now equate their internal qualities, the possibilities of their occurrences in atomic facts, as their essential logical forms. The ontic simplicity of objects follows as a consequence of the claim in 1.21 that the facts into which the world divides, the nonordinary atomic facts, must be composed of nonordinary objects. If the objects were themselves complex, then atomic facts would be endlessly further reducible to facts involving complex relations of their constitutive complex components. If there are atomic facts constituted by combinations of objects, then the objects of which atomic facts are constituted must themselves be simple rather than complex.

Wittgenstein for the first time now interjects an application of logical atomism to the problem of understanding the meaning of language. Language is ordinarily about complexes, as when we say that the Earth orbits the Sun between Venus and Mars. Wittgenstein asserts that such a description of an ordinary complex can be analyzed as a statement about the complex's constitutive parts, and that such a statement can further be reduced to propositions that completely describe complex facts and objects:

> 2.0201 Every statement about complexes can be analysed into a statement about their constituent parts, and into those propositions which completely describe the complexes.

This is the first installment in a continuing theme. Wittgenstein establishes an exact parallelism between logical atomism as the metaphysics of any logically possible world, and the picture theory of meaning he has yet to develop as the semantics of any logically possible language. Wittgenstein posits a mirroring of parallel logical atomic structures of facts and the propositions of languages that describe the world. The connection between the structures of facts and the structures of propositions is even more intimate than this parallelism suggests, as Wittgenstein implies in 2.141 when he says that propositions as pictures of facts are themselves facts. We get a first glance in 2.0201 of how Wittgenstein's metaphysics of logical atomism is eventually related to his picture theory semantics.

Taking up the thread of his conclusion in 2.02 that the object is simple, Wittgenstein, having offered this gesture toward the picture theory parallelism between the atomic structures of world and language, turns instead to a knotty argument in support of the simplicity of objects that comprise atomic facts. He declares:

> 2.021 Objects form the substance of the world. Therefore they cannot be compound.
> 2.0211 If the world had no substance, then whether a proposition had sense would depend on whether another proposition was true.
> 2.0212 It would then be impossible to form a picture of the world (true or false).

Wittgenstein's concept of the substance of the world, like the distinction between essential and accidental properties, is adapted from Aristotle's metaphysics. What does Wittgenstein mean by 'substance', and how does he arrive at the view that objects form the substance of the world? If objects form the substance of the world, how is it supposed to follow that therefore the objects must be simple rather than compound?

Atomic facts can differ from logically possible world to logically possible world. That indeed is what distinguishes one logically possible world from another. But all logically possible atomic facts are given as 2.0124 asserts by a single set of atomic-fact-constituting objects. It follows that any logically possible world, no matter how different its complexes and its ordinary and even atomic facts might be from any other logically possible world, must contain as its logically ultimate atoms precisely the same set of objects. This is what Wittgenstein means when he states in the first sentence of 2.021 that objects form the substance of the world. They are what is common to and fixed or unchanging in every logically possible world. Such a concept answers nicely to the traditional doctrine of substance, beginning with Aristotle's metaphysics and proceeding through the Scholastic era to the rationalist metaphysics of the seventeenth century and beyond. Substance is what underlies the changes that take place in the world, that which remains the same while different configurations and arrangements of the substance of the world are played out in time in different ways from world to world. Wittgenstein continues immediately thereafter in this vein:

> 2.022 It is clear that however different from the real one an imagined world may be, it must have something—a form—in common with the real world.
>
> 2.023 This fixed form consists of the objects.
>
> 2.0231 The substance of the world *can* only determine a form and not any material properties. For these are first presented by the propositions—first formed by the configuration of the objects.

In this way, Wittgenstein answers the first question posed by 2.021. The objects are the substance of the world, in that they combine to constitute the atomic facts that in their totality constitute the world. We are now prepared for the next problem, of understanding Wittgenstein's inference that therefore the objects must be simple rather than compound.

This is a more difficult topic. Wittgenstein holds that if the world had no substance, then the meaningfulness of a proposition would depend on whether another proposition was true, and that it would then be impossible to form a true or false picture of the world. This argument compresses a chain of reasoning that must be more carefully explicated if it is to shed light on Wittgenstein's conclusion about the objects' simplicity or atomicity. Wittgenstein appeals to the unargued claim in 1.21 that the facts that in totality constitute the world and into which the world divides are logically independent of one another, in the sense that any one can either be the case or not be the case, while nothing else is changed. There is more to be said about this, and it is time to consider this previous assertion more critically with an eye to unpacking its implications and assessing its validity.

Wittgenstein's argument in 2.021–2.0212 has the form of a dilemma. If the objects required by the analysis of a proposition's meaning concerning a complex state of affairs are themselves complex, then no proposition can have determinate meaning. In that case, semantic reduction results in an infinite regress of descriptions of endlessly further reducible complexes. The regress can only be avoided by appealing in a circular way to the preestablished truth and hence the preestablished determinate meaning of another proposition. Thus, the dilemma shows that if the objects that constitute facts are irreducibly complex, then there can be no fully general philosophical semantics. The only alternative is to conclude as Wittgenstein does that the objects that in combination constitute atomic facts are simple rather than complex. In concluding that there must be simple objects in order to avoid a semantic circle or regress, Wittgenstein's argument is structurally much the same as Aristotle's classic proof of the existence of an unmoved mover as the only alternative to an infinite regress in time or circularity of cosmic causation.[5]

This interpretation also explains why Wittgenstein in 1.21 maintains without further ado that any fact into which the world divides can either be the case or not be the case, and everything else remain the same. The ontic independence of the atomic facts that in their totality constitute a logically possible world is thus a requirement of the determinate meaningfulness of propositions about complex facts. Were it otherwise, there could be no fully general philosophical semantics, but at best a semantics that presupposes the determinate meaningfulness of at least one definitely true proposition. A general philosophical semantics thereby fails to achieve its purpose of explaining the meaning of all propositions on pain of vicious circularity. Wittgenstein reaffirms the ontic independence of atomic facts:

2.061 Atomic facts are independent of one another.

2.062 From the existence or non-existence of an atomic fact we cannot infer the existence or non-existence of another.

Wittgenstein's argument for simple objects and the logical independence of atomic facts relies on considerations about the requirements of language and of the determinate meaningfulness of language. The strategy is appropriate on the assumption that Wittgenstein's inquiry takes as its point of departure the fact that language is determinate in meaning, and asks in Kantian transcendental fashion after the conditions that must obtain in order for the determinate meaning of language to be possible. Although the text opens with a series of metaphysical assertions, it is the problem of language that motivates Wittgenstein's treatment of the fundamental formal ontology of the world as a structure of atomic facts in logical space.[6]

Wittgenstein proceeds next to expand on the thesis that simple objects are the fixed unchanging substance of the world. The world is whatever happens to be the case. Simple objects as the substance of the world exist independently of their contingent configurations that constitute the world as a particular totality of atomic facts:

2.024   Substance is what exists independently of what is the case.

2.025   It is form and content.

2.0251   Space, time and colour (colouredness) are forms of objects.

2.026   Only if there are objects can there be a fixed form of the world.

2.027   The fixed, the existent and the object are one.

2.0271   The object is the fixed, the existent; the configuration is the changing, the variable.

Importantly, at this stage of exposition, Wittgenstein now reveals something more informative about the forms of simple objects that constitute the world's substance. The model is virtually complete. We see that for Wittgenstein the world generically speaking in the sense of any logically possible world is a totality of logically independent atomic facts. This must be so if there is to be a fully general philosophical semantics, or, that is, if any logically possible language is to be determinately meaningful. Atomic facts are constituted by combinations of simple objects. Simple objects are the substance of the world in that they exist in any logical possible world, and remain the same in any logically possible world, and at any time within any logically possible world. They are what is essential to the world because they underlie the differences between logically possible worlds and persist through the changes that take place within a world. It is only the accidental configuration or particular combination and arrangement of objects that changes from world to world and over time within a world.

Wittgenstein's concept of substance, again like Aristotle's, is an amalgam of form and content. Propositions 2.025 and 2.0251 offer the only glimpse in the *Tractatus* of how Wittgenstein thinks of the simple objects. He says in 2.0251 that space, time, and color or coloredness are the objects' forms. As befits a treatise on the logical form of language and the world, Wittgenstein says next to nothing about the content of simple objects. The study of the content of objects is presumably a problem for natural science rather than logic or philosophy. This is probably why Wittgenstein in 2.0231 maintains that simple objects as the substance of the world, despite having content, as 2.025 now declares, determine only the world's form and not its material properties, which are constituted by the combining of objects into atomic facts. Wittgenstein describes the forms of simple objects as space, time, and color or coloredness. We may assume that by 'color' and 'coloredness' Wittgenstein does not merely mean the visual tonalities of illuminated surfaces of physical entities, but any phenomenal or experienceable property of any material complex. This follows the convention of physical theorists and mathematicians, who, after the geometer Bernard Riemann, speak of color generally as including color in the ordinary sense along with other sense data. The term 'color' in this technical generic sense does duty for the content of phenomena.[7]

If we accept Wittgenstein's statement that the forms of the simple objects as the substance of the world are space, time, and (generic) color, then we can think of the objects as falling literally into three different categories, each for a different form of simple object. There are objects that have a spatial form (the content of each of which will then be particular spaces, places, or locations in space), temporal form (the content of each of which will then be particular times, instants or extents of time), and (generic) color or chromatic form (the content of each of which will then be particular conceptually primitive generic phenomenal colors, red, loud, rough, salty, etc.).

With an account of the form and reference to the content of simple objects in hand, Wittgenstein next explains how the simple objects are combined with one another to constitute atomic facts:

2.0272 The configuration of the objects forms the atomic fact.

2.03 In the atomic fact objects hang one in another, like the links of a chain.

2.031 In the atomic fact the objects are combined in a definite way.

2.032   The way in which objects hang together in the
         atomic fact is the structure of the atomic fact.

2.033   The form is the possibility of the structure.

2.034   The structure of the fact consists of the structures
         of the atomic facts.

The simple objects are supposed to hook up to each other, as
Wittgenstein remarks, "like the links of a chain" and "in a definite way." The definite way in which the simple objects are linked
together in an atomic fact Wittgenstein calls the atomic fact's
structure. The possibility of such a structure he regards as the
atomic fact's logical form. This complements Wittgenstein's prior
use of the term 'form' of a simple object as the possibility of its
combinations in all logically possible atomic facts. Finally, working from bottom to top, in the reverse direction as previously,
Wittgenstein describes the structure of an ordinary fact or *Tatsache* as consisting of the structures of its component atomic facts
or *Sachverhalte*.

We can imagine a bin of object forms consisting of three com-
partments, where each compartment contains simple objects,
each of which has one of three forms, and each of which accordingly has a special spatial, temporal, or chromatic content. The
objects are said by Wittgenstein to have different forms, so that
we might represent them as differently shaped, depending on
which of the three interlocking forms each has. Then they can be
fit together only in a particular way. A diagram showing Wittgenstein's three categories of the forms of the simple objects might
look like this:

I Forms of Simple Objects

Space   Time   Color

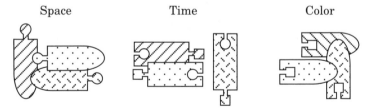

The image this presents is rather like the phosphate and
sugar units assembled into polypeptide chains of DNA and RNA.
Their different shapes limit the ways in which the objects can be
assembled, so that, as 2.031 requires, they must be combined in
an atomic fact in a definite way, according to a definite structure.
Their different markings, dots, stripes, and hatching in the dia-

gram indicate the different content that different simple objects of each form might have. Yet we must not suppose that Wittgenstein would consider that the simple objects themselves could exist independently in bins like interchangeable parts to be fit together into atomic facts like the links in a chain. We recall that Wittgenstein states:

> 2.0122 The thing is independent, in so far as it can occur in all *possible* circumstances, but this form of independence is a form of connexion with the atomic fact, a form of dependence. (It is impossible for words to occur in two different ways, alone and in the proposition).

The diagram represents the three categories of logical forms—spatial, temporal, and (generically) chromatic—not the objects themselves existing independently of one another. Objects occur only dependently in atomic facts. Moreover, as 2.0232 states: "Roughly speaking: objects are colourless." An object with the form 'red' by itself contributes no color to the world, but only in combination with two other objects whose forms are space and time, in the atomic fact 'Red-here-now'. We should not conclude from this way of representing space, time, and color content in the diagram that individual objects considered by themselves are 'colored' with particular spatial, temporal, or chromatic values. Nor, finally, can simple objects be divided into smaller parts, like physical complexes, as the diagram might otherwise be understood to suggest.

If, as in the diagram, there are three simple objects with different content in each of three forms, then the objects can be shown as connected together like the links in a chain in the following atomic facts. There is a total of $3^3 = 27$ possible combinations of such simple objects, which in the above account is highly simplified. Here is a representative selection of three possible atomic facts, each of which is chain-linked in a definite order by virtue of its particular space, time, and generic color form:

▮ Atomic Facts

Space   Time   Color

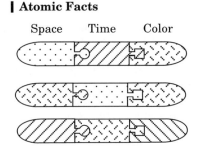

Wittgenstein on philosophical grounds refrains from speculating about the number of objects. But it seems only reasonable that to describe the world in all its rich diversity and complexity would require many more than nine simple objects. We may therefore suppose that the complete set of atomic propositions given by the complete set of objects is astronomical even if finite.

Continuing from bottom to top in the reverse direction of the first characterization of the reductive analysis of the world into facts, atomic facts, and objects, Wittgenstein at last explains how the totality of existent atomic facts logically determines what atomic facts do not exist, so as to constitute a world. The existence and nonexistence of a given set of atomic facts Wittgenstein calls the reality (*die Wirklichkeit*), and the total reality he identifies, as with the totality of existent atomic facts, as the world:

2.04　　The totality of existent atomic facts is the world.

2.05　　The totality of existent atomic facts also determines which atomic facts do not exist.

2.06　　The existence and non-existence of atomic facts is the reality.

　　　　(The existence of atomic facts we also call a positive fact, their non-existence a negative fact.)

2.063　The total reality is the world.

It may at first appear that Wittgenstein contradicts himself. The world is the totality of existent atomic facts. The reality by contrast is the combined existence of some atomic facts and non-existence of others. The total reality, therefore, despite 2.063, would seem to be something more than the world. But since the world as the totality of existent atomic facts also determines the totality of nonexistent atomic facts, the world and the total reality in Wittgenstein's technical sense are identical. The determination of the totality of nonexistent by existent atomic facts (and conversely) reflects the complementarity of these opposite totalities. Wittgenstein's reasoning goes something like this:

1.　　The world = the totality of existent atomic facts.
　　　　　　　　　　　　　　　　　　(Definition)

2.　　The reality = the existence of some atomic facts and nonexistence of others.　　　　(Definition)

3.　　The totality of existent atomic facts determines (and is determined by) the totality of nonexistent facts.
　　　　　　　　　　　　　　　　　　(Complementarity)

4.　　The world = the totality of existent and nonexistent atomic facts.　　　　　　　　(1, 3)

5.   The total reality = the totality of existent and
       nonexistent atomic facts.   (2)
6.   The total reality = the world.   (4, 5)

Wittgenstein's logical atomism explains the world as a structure of facts whose unchanging substance is the simple objects. But an ontology by itself is not yet a semantics. Wittgenstein's metaphysics accounts for the meaningfulness of language only when it joins forces with the picture theory of meaning. Wittgenstein speaks of picturing the world in his 2.0212 argument for the simplicity of objects. The analysis of language now requires Wittgenstein in the next stages of the *Tractatus* to supplement the metaphysics of logical atomism with the semantics of the picture theory.[8]

NOTES

1. Plato, *Theaetetus* 201c–202d. Wittgenstein refers to the passage in 1968b §46.

2. Black 1964, 129–30, disputes Wittgenstein's attribution of the functional compositionality thesis of meaning to Frege. The thesis is rightly attributed to Whitehead and Russell 1910, 1, 14–15.

3. Russell 1985. Wittgenstein acknowledges Russell as the source of his concept of an 'atomic proposition' in 1929, 163 (reprinted below). Wittgenstein does not use the phrase 'logical atomism' in the *Tractatus,* but this seems the most appropriate term for his metaphysics (another term he does not use) of simple objects. Black 1964, 28: "The world is a mosaic of atomic facts, of which any selection might be imagined removed without detriment to the remainder, a view now known as 'logical atomism'." See also 28, 39, 46, 58–61, 206–7.

4. Frege 1950, x, maintains that we are "never to ask for the meaning of a word in isolation, but only in the context of a proposition"; 71: "only in a proposition have words really a meaning." See also *Tractatus* 3.3.

5. Aristotle, *Physics* 256a13–21: "If then everything that is in motion must be moved by something, and the movent must either itself be moved by something else or not, and in the former case there must be some first movent that is not itself moved by anything else, while in the case of the immediate movent being of this kind there is no need of an intermediate movent that is also moved (for it is impossible that there should be an infinite series of movents, each of which is itself moved by something else, since in an infinite series there is no first term)—if then everything that is in motion is moved by something, and the first movent is moved but not by anything else, it must be moved by itself." See also *Metaphysics* 1074a28–29, and *De Caelo* 300a29–b2.

6. The Kantian transcendental argument structure of the *Tractatus* was first remarked by Stenius 1960, especially 214–26. Wittgenstein's references to the transcendence of logic, of logical, pictorial, and representational form, ethics and aesthetics, and the metaphysical self, soul, or subject, are discussed below in chapters 4 and 5. Engel 1970,

483–513; Hintikka 1981, 375–90; Schwyzer 1986, 2, 150–62; Garver 1994, 6, 100–101, 107–10.

7. Riemann's writings on geometry are collected in Weber and Dedekind, eds., 1990. Riemann's account of color space is criticized by Russell in 1897, 66–67. Finch 1971, argues, 258–61: "Wittgenstein's conception of space, time and color as multiply-extended manifolds in all likehood [sic] has its origin in Russell's *Foundation* [sic] *of Geometry* which contains a detailed discussion of Riemann's original formulation of this idea. . . . Wittgenstein's statement that 'In a manner of speaking objects are colorless' (2.0232) indicates his adherence to the Riemann rather than the Russell view." Finch further refers to Wittgenstein's *Notebooks* entry for 11.9.16: "That the colours are not properties is shown by the analysis of physics, by the internal relations in which physics displays the colours. Apply this to sounds too."

8. See also Bradley 1992; Caruthers 1990; Cook 1994; Goddard and Judge 1982; Griffin 1964; Schulte 1992, 46–48; White 1974.

CHAPTER
T   W   O | **The Picture Theory of Meaning**

Logical atomism explains meaning only if language and the world have the same logical structure. Wittgenstein's conviction that there must be an exact parallelism, isomorphism, mirroring, picturing, or representing of the world in language at some level of analysis between any logically possible language and any logically possible world is the central thesis of the picture theory of meaning. Wittgenstein begins his exposition of the picture theory with the down-to-earth observation that

2.1   We make to ourselves pictures of facts.

Why does Wittgenstein find it worthwhile to mention this obvious fact about human picture-making? Facts are pictured in photography and in historical and other kinds of representational painting, and even splatter art is a pictorial record of the artist's activity and aesthetic or random choices in shooting paint from squirt guns against a canvas. What relevance does any of this have for understanding language?

To the claim that we make ordinary pictures and that ordinary pictures are pictures of ordinary facts, Wittgenstein further adds that any descriptive use of language is a true or false picture that truly or falsely pictures the facts of the world. The picturing of facts is not as evident to casual inspection in the case of ordinary language propositions as in artworks. Wittgenstein distinguishes between the perceptible sign and imperceptible symbol that transcends concrete language use at the deepest level of logical analysis. He maintains that the picturing of facts in language takes place where we cannot see it, beyond the logically arbitrary conventionality of ordinary language signs, in the transcendental order of imperceptible symbols.

I 35

The anthropological starting place for Wittgenstein's picture theory of meaning is emphasized in the following passages. Wittgenstein again touches base with language use as a human activity, part of the same world about which language speaks and in which pictures of the world are made. But he admits that ordinary language in the conventionality of its sign systems does not reveal its underlying logical pictorial form:

4.002   Man possesses the capacity of constructing languages, in which every sense can be expressed, without having an idea how and what each word means—just as one speaks without knowing how the single sounds are produced.

Colloquial language is a part of the human organism and is not less complicated than it.

From it it is humanly impossible to gather immediately the logic of language.

Language disguises the thought; so that from the external form of the clothes one cannot infer the form of the thought they clothe, because the external form of the clothes is constructed with quite another object than to let the form of the body be recognized.

The sign-symbol distinction marks a difference between perceptible and imperceptible aspects of symbols. Wittgenstein introduces the distinction in terms of sense experience, defining signs as the perceptible guises of symbols. He first writes:

3.1   In the proposition the thought is expressed perceptibly through the senses.

3.11   We use the sensibly perceptible sign (sound or written sign, etc.) of the proposition as a projection of the possible state of affairs.

The method of projection is the thinking of the sense of the proposition.

3.32   The sign is the part of the symbol perceptible by the senses.

3.34   A proposition possesses essential and accidental features.

Accidental are the features which are due to a particular way of producing the propositional sign. Essential are those which alone enable the proposition to express its sense.

The symbols in any logically possible language have a perceptible and an imperceptible part. The perceptible part Wittgenstein calls the sign. Governed by the logically arbitrary conventions of ordinary language, signs are subject to the vicissitudes of the historical development of natural languages, which conceals their real underlying logical structures. The picturing of the world in language—language as a picture of the world—occurs in the transcendental order of the imperceptible aspect of symbols. The symbol transcends the perceptible sign in ordinary language, where it disguises and conceals a proposition's pictorial form. It is in the transcendental order of symbols, and not necessarily or even typically in the phenomenal empirical order of natural language signs as we perceive them, that we are to think of language as picturing the world. Wittgenstein offers a practical analogy and an application to the interpretation of logical formalisms to explain the linguistic picturing latent even in conventional sign systems:

> 3.1431 The essential nature of the propositional sign becomes very clear when we imagine it made up of spatial objects (such as tables, chairs, books) instead of written signs.
>
> The mutual spatial position of these things then expresses the sense of the proposition.
>
> 3.1432 We must not say, "The complex sign 'aRb' says 'a stands in relation R to b'"; but we must say, "*That* 'a' stands in a certain relation to 'b' says *that aRb*".

The observation in 3.1431, that the pictorial essence of a propositional sign is more transparent when we think of it as made of ordinary objects in spatial relations, recalls a famous anecdote about how the picture theory of meaning is supposed to have first occurred to Wittgenstein. In reading about a Paris court trial involving a car accident, Wittgenstein was reportedly impressed by the use of toy figures to represent the circumstances of the case. The *Notebooks 1914–1916* entry for 29.9.14 states:

> In the proposition a world is as it were put together experimentally. (As when in the law-court in Paris a motor-car accident is represented by means of dolls, etc.)[1]

This modeling apparently suggested to Wittgenstein the idea that all language might function by picturing states of affairs. We can represent the fact that Earth is between Venus and Mars by placing a book to represent the Earth between a chair to represent Venus and a table to represent Mars. This is logically equally as good a way of representing the fact as the written English sentence, 'The Earth is between Venus and Mars'. The table, chair, and book method is much more obviously pictorial or representational, though it is less permanent, reproducible, and transportable than written or spoken language, and in that sense more impractical.

What remains unexplained in Wittgenstein's remark is why the table, chair, and book should be thought to offer better insight into the nature of the propositional sign. The argument in 3.1432 is more complicated, but makes the same point with respect to the picturing of facts by an arrangement of the elements of a propositional sign, as in the relational expression aRb. We should not say that aRb says that a stands in relation R to b; but rather, the fact that the object term 'a' is written to the left of relation term 'R', and that object term 'b' is written to the right, conventionally says that a is R-related to b. It is by virtue of these facts about how propositional signs are constituted that signs picture facts.

Language, any logically possible language, correctly analyzed in its imperceptible transcendental aspect, is a right or wrong picturing of the facts that might belong to any logically possible world. The explanation is meant to apply not only to idealized artificial or formal symbolic languages, but to concrete linguistic expression in natural languages. Wittgenstein in 5.5563 later insists: "All propositions of our colloquial language are actually, just as they are, logically completely in order." Picturing occurs at the deepest level of the analysis of proposition and state of affairs, where the logical form of the proposition in the transcendental order of symbols is reduced to a truth function (conjunction) of elementary propositions, each of which in turn is a concatenation of simple names for simple objects. There is a one-one picturing correlation in Wittgenstein's picture theory between concatenations of simple objects in atomic facts in the world and juxtapositions of simple names for simple objects in atomic propositions. The world reduces logically to a totality of atomic facts. Atomic facts are chain-linkings of simple objects belonging to the three forms of space, time, and (generic phenomenal) color (coloredness), in a definite way and with a definite structure. The elementary propositions express such atomic facts as we might colloquially render in sentences like 'Red-here-now' ('Place-P_1-time-T_1-red') and 'Blue-there-then' ('Place-P_2-time-T_2-blue'). When the places in logical space are filled with logical pictures of the existence or nonexistence of all such possible atomic facts, then a logically possible world is completely metaphysically determined and completely linguistically described.

Wittgenstein's attempt to spell out an adequate general philosophical semantics in the *Tractatus* is commendable for taking the anthropological data of real language use as its starting place. In this, he goes against the grain of some of the philosophers and logicians who were most influential in his early thinking. Frege and Russell find ordinary language so hopelessly vague, ambiguous, and imprecise, that they see no alternative but to replace it with the ideal formal symbolic languages they develop in the logics of the *Begriffsschrift* and *Principia Mathematica*.[2] The fact that ordinary language is enormously complex, vague, and ambiguous, and that it is sometimes simpler and easier to specify a semantics for formal symbolic languages, does not by itself imply that we can understand the semantics of ordinary language in terms of the semantics of artificial languages, nor that we can apply the specialized semantics of formal symbolic languages to everyday discourse. Frege and Russell turn away from ordinary language, but Wittgenstein is undeterred by its superficial defects. By distinguishing between perceptible sign and imperceptible symbol, Wittgenstein finds an ingenious way to explain the meaningfulness of language as determined by its transcendent symbols, without requiring semantic analysis to confront the daunting conventions of natural language signs. Formal languages like symbolic logic, pure and applied mathematical notations, and computer programming protocols, are not essentially different from ordinary languages. As languages, they must answer to the same set of principles. The adequacy test for Wittgenstein's picture theory is whether or not it can satisfactorily explain how ordinary language works to express determinate meaning in everyday applications as we find them in books and newspapers, street corner and breakfast table conversations, scientific reports and political speeches. If a theory does not explain the meaning of expressions in ordinary language, then it cannot provide an adequate fully general philosophical semantics, and methodologically it is likely to be proceeding in the wrong direction. It is a mistake to begin by trying to interpret the meaningfulness of artificial languages designed as formal logical systems, and then applying their semantic principles to ordinary language. The meaning of ordinary language must come first, because historically formal languages develop only later and depend for their meaning ultimately on the meaningfulness of ordinary thought and ordinary language.

What we need to get started in philosophical semantics is the assumption that some language in which determinate meaning is expressed is logically possible. It is enough to know that we think, speak, and write and thereby sometimes express thoughts that might be true or false, and that we sometimes understand one another. The task of an adequate philosophical semantics as Wittgenstein conceives it in the *Tractatus* is to explain the concept or essence of language by explaining the conditions for the possibility of determinate meaning in any logically possible language. Wittgenstein never loses sight of his anthropological starting point, by which he concludes that language is logically possible because experience teaches that we make to ourselves pictures of facts. Whatever else we may need to do in an adequate philosophical semantics, we must be able satisfactorily to explain the determinate meaningfulness of everyday uses of language in their concrete, spoken, written, or otherwise expressed or recorded applications, since these are the facts with which semantic inquiry begins. We cannot achieve this purpose if like Frege and Russell we try to detach semantics from its roots in ordinary thought and language, and construe the task of logic as an effort to design an ideal language to be substituted as a logically more well-behaved replacement for less exact natural languages.

All language pictures facts, and the expressions in a language that picture facts are themselves facts. At the deepest level of formal logical analysis in the transcendental order of symbols, according to Wittgenstein, there is an exact one-one correlation of the logically atomic elements of the world and the logically atomic elements of linguistic descriptions of facts. The correlation constitutes a possible picturing, where thought can intend any fact with what Wittgenstein calls a definite logical form or mathematical multiplicity (*eine bestimmte mathematische Mannigfaltigkeit*) as a picture of another fact with the very same logical form or mathematical multiplicity. This means that, upon a deep and complete reductive analysis into their atomic components, states of affairs in the world and true or false propositions about those states of affairs must have precisely the same number of discernible parts in one-one correlation obtaining in precisely the same formal logical structures.

The transcendent symbolic isomorphism of logical structure between propositions under analysis and the facts they picture is necessary but not sufficient to make one fact a picture of the other. What is additionally required is that thought take one set of facts as its picture, that thought be projected from picturing to pictured facts. Wittgenstein makes the projection requirement clear in *Tractatus* 3.11 quoted above. Picturing occurs when thought takes a fact to represent another fact. The representation of one fact by another in turn presupposes that under analysis in the transcendental order of symbols picturing and pictured facts have precisely the same logical form or identical mathematical multiplicity of correlated simple objects.

Although the concept of a proposition as a picture appears earlier in the text at 2.0122, 2.0201, and 2.0211–2.0212, Wittgenstein explains the picture theory of meaning in a relatively dense cluster of remarks beginning abruptly with 2.1 and extending through 4.1212. It is by far the most extensive development of any line of thought in the *Tractatus,* and in its implications has the most fundamental and wide-reaching importance in Wittgenstein's early philosophy. Wittgenstein first clarifies the nature of picturing in the abstract, and then concludes that propositions in language function pictorially in the same way in representing facts. Wittgenstein states:

2.11   The picture presents the facts in logical space, the existence and non-existence of atomic facts.

2.12   The picture is a model of reality.

2.13   To the objects correspond in the picture the elements of the picture.

2.131   The elements of the picture stand, in the picture, for the objects.

2.14   The picture consists in the fact that its elements are combined with one another in a definite way.

2.141   The picture is a fact.

The picture theory explains the representation of facts. Pictures represent facts by virtue of one-one correspondences between the elements of the pictures and the elements of the facts they picture, combined in each in a certain way with a definite logical structure. The picture moreover is itself a fact, a part of the world some of whose facts it can also depict. This is the sense in which Wittgenstein's philosophical semantics maintains contact with its anthropological starting place in 2.1 in the claim that we make to ourselves pictures of facts. Wittgenstein argues that picturing requires an exact isomorphism of the logical structures of picture and pictured fact. The picture by this account in Wittgenstein's simile is like the lines of a scale or measuring stick held up to reality, matching each and only the elements of its logical structure point for point. The 'points' at the ends of the measuring lines that 'touch' what is to be measured are the simple names that make contact with the atomic facts pictured in elementary propositions only by matching up with the corresponding simple objects they name. It is by virtue of this logical isomorphism that a picture pictures a fact, as a fact that correctly or incorrectly represents another fact:

2.15   That the elements of the picture are combined with one another in a definite way, represents that the things are so combined with one another.

This connexion of the elements of the picture is called its structure, and the possibility of this structure is called the form of representation of the picture.

2.151   The form of representation is the possibility that the things are combined with one another as are the elements of the picture.

2.1511   Thus the picture is linked with reality; it reaches up to it.

2.1512   It is like a scale applied to reality.

2.15121   Only the outermost points of the dividing lines *touch* the object to be measured.

The representing relation in the picture of a fact is itself part of the picture. This is reasonable, because, by limiting consideration to the picture and pictured fact, the representing relation cannot belong to the pictured fact rather than the picture, since it is the picture rather than the pictured fact that represents. The only alternative would be for the representing relation to belong to another entity, presumably a third fact. If the relation resides in the third entity, then, as Wittgenstein proposes, we might as well say that the representing relation belongs to the picture, and eliminate the third fact as an unnecessary semantic middleman. If the relation resides in yet another entity, then we are launched on an indefinite regress that, like the other semantic regresses we have considered, necessarily precludes the determinate meaningfulness of ordinary language. All we need for the representing relation in picturing facts by conventional signs, according to Wittgenstein, is the one-one correspondences that hold between the transcendental symbolic structures of a picture and the facts it pictures. If a picture represents a fact, the picture must share something identical with the fact. Wittgenstein describes this as the form of representation (*Form der Abbildung*):

2.1513   According to this view the representing relation which makes it a picture, also belongs to the picture.

2.1514   The representing relation consists of the co-ordinations of the elements of the picture and the things.

2.1515   These co-ordinations are as it were the feelers of its elements with which the picture touches reality.

2.16   In order to be a picture a fact must have something in common with what it pictures.

2.161   In the picture and the pictured there must be
something identical in order that the one can be a
picture of the other at all.

2.17   What the picture must have in common with reality
in order to be able to represent it after its manner—rightly or falsely—is its form of representation.

Wittgenstein has not yet categorized propositions as linguistic pictures of facts to be explained by the picture theory. He observes an important limitation about what can and what cannot
be pictorially represented. This is the basis for his later efforts to
discount all philosophical problems as pseudoproblems. In particular, a picture cannot represent its own form of representation. To do so, a picture would need to stand outside itself in order
to depict its own form of representation. A picture therefore cannot pictorially describe its own form or anything else about itself.
The facts about a picture can only be pictured by another picture
large enough to contain and depict something true or false about
the first picture. Instead, a picture 'shows forth' its logical form
(*weist sie auf*). In these disclaimers about a picture's form of representation being showable but unsayable, we discover the first
inklings of Wittgenstein's saying-showing distinction:

2.171   The picture can represent every reality whose form
it has.

The spatial picture, everything spatial, the
coloured, everything coloured, etc.

2.172   The picture, however, cannot represent its form of
representation; it shows it forth.

2.173   The picture represents its object from without (its
standpoint is its form of representation), therefore
the picture represents its object rightly or falsely.

2.174   But the picture cannot place itself outside of its
form of representation.

We are reminded that Wittgenstein regards the isomorphism between picture and pictured fact, the sharing of an identical form of representation based on the possibility of structure
in the picture and the fact it pictures, as a necessary but not sufficient condition of picturing. Wittgenstein says that the picture
can represent every reality whose form it has; everything spatial
can be represented by a spatial picture, everything colored can be
represented by a colored picture, and so on. A spatial picture has
the right form of representation to represent something, and
hence anything, spatial; similarly for the colored picture. We can
represent a complex as being located two meters or two hundred

kilometers away from another complex by a picture in which a pictured entity is two centimeters or any other reasonable distance we prefer from any other object. We can represent a blue or yellow complex by a picture of a red complex. To actualize this picturing potential, we must project the sense of the thought from fact to logically isomorphic fact, or, as we might also say, thought must intend one fact or set of facts as a picture of another with which it shares an identical form of representation.

Wittgenstein now presents logical form as the most general and universal type of representational form. Wittgenstein does not wish to hold that there are forms of representation other than logical form for pictures other than logical pictures. On the contrary, he explicitly asserts that every picture, whatever other kind of picture it may be, is at least a logical picture, and he assimilates representational form into the more embracing category of logical form. This brings us one step closer to the picturing of facts by propositions interpreted as pictures of facts:

2.18   What every picture, of whatever form, must have in common with reality in order to be able to represent it at all—rightly or falsely—is the logical form, that is, the form of reality.

2.181 If the form of representation is the logical form, then the picture is called a logical picture.

2.182 Every picture is *also* a logical picture. (On the other hand, for example, not every picture is spatial.)

The contrast between representational and logical form is indicated most clearly in 2.182. There is no picture that is not also a logical picture, because the sharing of logical form as the most fundamental form of representation is a prerequisite of the picturing relation. Yet there are other kinds of pictures that are not spatial pictures, because they do not involve a specifically spatial form of representation.

We can represent the fact that Earth is between Venus and Mars by a picture in which a green circle representing the Earth is shown located between a red circle representing Mars and a yellow circle representing Venus. Here the relative location of the color-identifying circles in the picture (according to a legend or glossary) has a certain spatial form, by virtue of which it pictures the fact that Earth is between Venus and Mars. Not all pictures represent facts by a spatial form of representation, but by other representational forms superimposed on a foundational logical form. An example suggested by Wittgenstein's prior remarks is the colored form of representation for depicting the fact that something is colored, without benefit of any discernible spatial features.

A colored spot on paper can picture the fact that something has any chosen color, but not necessarily by virtue of its size, shape, or location.

When Wittgenstein asserts that every picture is also a logical picture, he implies that a picture, disregarding its perceptible representational form, must minimally possess an identical imperceptible logical form which it shares with whatever it is capable of picturing. The picturing of facts by pictures of identical logical form or possibility of logical structure requires a projection of thought like the projection of geometrical figures from one surface to another, in which logical form is preserved in a logical isomorphism that is not necessarily perceptible. A logical picture, which is to say any picture considered with respect to its sharing the logical form of whatever it is capable of picturing, can represent facts in any logically possible world, including the existent facts of the actual world. Wittgenstein, drawing together several lines of previous argument, now concludes that a logical picture (truly or falsely) depicts reality by representing the existence and nonexistence of atomic facts:

2.19   The logical picture can depict the world.

2.2   The picture has the logical form of representation in common with what it pictures.

2.201 The picture depicts reality by representing a possibility of the existence and non-existence of atomic facts.

2.202 The picture represents a possible state of affairs in logical space.

2.203 The picture contains the possibility of the state of affairs which it represents.

At last Wittgenstein finds himself in a position to explain how a picture can be a true or false, right or wrong, correct or incorrect, representation of reality. The picture represents its sense (Sinn), which either agrees with reality or not. A picture in agreement with reality is true, and a picture lacking such agreement is false. It is only by comparing the picture with reality that it is possible to judge the picture's truth or falsehood. It follows that no picture is a priori true, as Wittgenstein states below in 2.225; equally, as he might also have said but does not venture to say, no picture is a priori false. Wittgenstein's account of truth requires that picturing or representing take place independently of a picture's being true or false. We must first have a picture, correct or incorrect, and only then can the secondary question of its truth or falsehood intelligibly arise. No picture depicts its own truth or falsehood, from which it directly follows that no picture is logically necessary or logically impossible, but is in every case a logically contingent true or false representation of fact. This is well in keeping with the principles of Wittgenstein's logical atomism, by which he declares in the first statement of the text that the world is everything that happens to be the case:

2.21   The picture agrees with reality or not; it is right or wrong, true or false.

2.22   The picture represents what it represents, independently of its truth or falsehood, through the form of representation.

2.221   What the picture represents is its sense.

2.222   In the agreement or disagreement of its sense with reality, its truth or falsity consists.

2.223   In order to discover whether the picture is true or false we must compare it with reality.

2.224   It cannot be discovered from the picture alone whether it is true or false.

2.225   There is no picture which is a priori true.

From this conclusion, Wittgenstein moves in the next passage to what appears to be an extension of the picture theory from semantics to psychology or philosophy of mind. He states that:

3   The logical picture of the facts is the thought.

There is a nuance in this pronouncement that cannot be fully appreciated without background information about Frege's philosophy of logic and language. The original German formulation of Wittgenstein's statement 3 reads: "Das logische Bild der Tatsachen ist der Gedanke." Significantly, Frege also uses the word *'Gedanke'* for the abstract Platonic meaning of a concrete linguistic expression, including written and spoken sentences in various natural languages or formulated in alternative logical notations. This is clearly different from what we might ordinarily think of as a thought in the sense of an occurrent psychological episode.[3] Wittgenstein makes it clear time and again that he is distinctly uninterested in the accidental properties of psychological occurrences. "Psychology," he says in 4.1121, "is no nearer related to philosophy, than is any other natural science. The theory of knowledge is the philosophy of psychology." Nevertheless, in the following passage Wittgenstein writes:

3.001   "An atomic fact is thinkable"—means: we can imagine it.

Wittgenstein's *Gedanke* is the thought or idea expressed by a picture. Yet it is more faithful to the spirit of Frege's conclusions in his essay "Der Gedanke," in a discussion relevant to Wittgenstein's remarks, to think of his reference to *Gedanke* in 3 as a picture's abstract true or false meaning.[4] This is usually understood as equivalent to the concept of a transcendent proposition, related to sentences in different natural languages and alternative formal symbolisms in the same way that abstract numbers are related to numerals in different arithmetical notations. Another precedent for Wittgenstein's introduction of *Gedanken* in 3 is Bernard Bolzano's doctrine of the *Satz an sich* or sentence-in-itself.[5] This is a concept that even in terminology bears an obvious debt to Kant's theory of the noumenal *Ding an sich* or thing-in-itself that transcends experience, the reality that imperceptibly exists independently of how the empirical or phenomenal world is encountered in sensation and conceived by the mind.[6] When Wittgenstein refers to the logical picture of the facts as a thought or *Gedanke,* he brings the semantics of abstract propositions under the principles of the picture theory of meaning.

Wittgenstein now extends his conclusions about the totality of facts into which the world divides to the totality of true thoughts as a picture of the world. Presumably, he means the actual world or total reality, since by his account of the truth conditions for pictures the only true pictures are pictures of 'the reality':

> 3.01   The totality of true thoughts is a picture of the world.

Wittgenstein does not claim that the totality of true thoughts is a complete picture of the entire world, but only that it is *a* picture of the world (*ein Bild der Welt*). The connection between thought and proposition is not made explicit until Wittgenstein adds:

> 4   The thought is the significant proposition.
>
> 4.001   The totality of propositions is the language.

It is in this way that Wittgenstein eventually applies the picture theory to explain the meaning of propositions considered as pictures of facts. The first step is taken when Wittgenstein in 2.18–2.2 speaks of logical form as the most general form of representation, essential to every picture. The second occurs in 3–3.01 when he states that the logical picture of the facts is the 'thought', where by this he seems to mean something like Frege's notion of

Gedanken as abstract propositions or transcendent symbolic *Sätze an sich.*[7] At this juncture, Wittgenstein takes the final step by including the proposition (*der Satz*) as a picture of reality, falling under the picture theory of meaning:

> 4.01 The proposition is a picture of reality.
>
> The proposition is a model of the reality as we think it is.

The second part of this remark recalls Wittgenstein's view in 3.11 that signs express thoughts, and that thinking the sense of the proposition is the method of establishing "lines of projection" from fact to logically isomorphic fact whereby a state of affairs in projected into a perceptible sign. To describe the proposition as a 'model of the reality' (*Modell der Wirklichkeit*) "as we think it is" (*so wie wir sie uns denken*) seems to acknowledge a subjective perspectival element in the (true or false) picturing of reality as a human activity, but more importantly to extend the psychological "method of projection" to propositions as pictures of reality.

A proposition in the transcendental order of imperceptible symbols, according to Wittgenstein's logical atomist picture theory, is a truth function of what he calls elementary propositions, where elementary propositions are concatenations of logically simple names for logically simple objects. Wittgenstein discusses names and elementary propositions in these passages, the interpretation of which is straightforward enough without extensive commentary. Wittgenstein first observes that just as the world is made up of facts rather than a set of things, so only facts and not a mere set of names can be logically meaningful. A jumble of names by itself cannot express a fact, but only a definite structure of names corresponding as linguistic elements to the elements of pictured facts. Wittgenstein explains:

> 3.141 The proposition is not a mixture of words (just as the musical theme is not a mixture of tones).
>
> The proposition is articulate.
>
> 3.142 Only facts can express a sense, a class of names cannot.

The nature of names is then explicated in a series of important remarks. Wittgenstein regards the names for simple objects as themselves absolutely simple, so that in language under analysis they are the logical counterparts of the simple objects in atomic facts. Wittgenstein emphasizes the one-one correspondences required by propositions as pictures of facts at the deepest level of their symbolic logical structures, in the absolutely simple names that name absolutely simple objects. The names of objects are introduced as satisfying the requirements of simple signs in the complete analysis of a proposition entailed by logical atomism and the picture theory, while names in their object designating function are contrasted with propositions as truth-value-vehicles for describing states of affairs:

3.144   States of affairs can be described but not *named*.
(Names resemble points; propositions resemble arrows, they have sense.)

3.2   In propositions thoughts can be so expressed that to the objects of the thoughts correspond the elements of the propositional sign.

3.201   These elements I call "simple signs" and the proposition "completely analysed".

3.202   The simple signs employed in propositions are called names.

3.203   The name means the object. The object is its meaning. ("A" is the same sign as "A".)

3.21   To the configuration of the simple signs in the propositional sign corresponds the configuration of the objects in the state of affairs.

3.22   In the proposition the name represents the object.

3.221   Objects I can only *name*. Signs represent them. I can only speak *of* them. I cannot *assert them*. A proposition can only say *how* a thing is, not *what* it is.

An obvious objection to the picture theory of meaning is that propositions in ordinary language do not look like ordinary pictures. Wittgenstein concedes the nonpictorial appearance of most language, while emphasizing the exceptions in pictographic and hieroglyphic languages and certain logical formalisms, as relics of the cultural genealogy of propositions in logical pictures of facts:

4.011   At the first glance the proposition—say as it stands printed on paper—does not seem to be a picture of the reality of which it treats. But nor does the musical score appear at first sight to be a picture of a musical piece; nor does our phonetic spelling (letters) seem to be a picture of our spoken language. And yet these symbolisms prove to be pictures—even in the ordinary sense of the word—of what they represent.

4.012   It is obvious that we perceive a proposition of the form aRb as a picture. Here the sign is obviously a likeness of the signified.

4.013   And if we penetrate to the essence of this pictorial nature we see that this is not disturbed by *apparent irregularities* (like the use of # and b in the score).

For these irregularities also picture what they are
to express; only in another way.

4.014   The gramophone record, the musical thought, the
score, the waves of sound, all stand to one another
in that pictorial internal relation, which holds
between language and the world.

To all of them the logical structure is common.

(Like the two youths, their two horses and their
lilies in the story. They are all in a certain sense
one.)

To argue by analogy, as Wittgenstein does in 4.011, that we
might discount the nonpictorial appearance of ordinary language on
the grounds that a musical score also does not appear at first sight to
be a picture of a musical piece, seems to beg the question. It might be
objected that the musical score does not appear even at second sight
as a picture of the music that can be performed from it. If we are not
already convinced that the picture theory of meaning is correct, we
are unlikely to excuse the nonpictorial appearance of ordinary language by comparison with what is basically the same nonpictorial
appearance of musical scores. Wittgenstein does little more than
reassert the picture theory when in the final sentence of the passage
he flatly declares: "And yet these symbolisms prove to be pictures—
even in the ordinary sense of the word—of what they represent."
The 'proof' that such symbolisms are pictures, such as it is, comes
only with acceptance of the picture theory as the best explanation of
the meaning of expressions of thoughts in ordinary languages and
musical notations.

Where musical scores might be regarded as pictures of music
or musical ideas, Wittgenstein offers this further consideration:

4.0141 In the fact that there is a general rule by which
the musician is able to read the symphony out of
the score, and that there is a rule by which one
could reconstruct the symphony from the line on a
gramophone record and from this again—by means
of the first rule—construct the score, herein lies
the internal similarity between these things which
at first sight seem to be entirely different. And
the rule is the law of projection which projects the
symphony into the language of the musical score.
It is the rule of translation of this language into
the language of the gramophone record.

The best explanation of the fact that a symphony can be re-
played from a musical score, and recorded physically in and reconstructed from phonograph grooves, may be that they are
projections of facts into logically isomorphic facts, in an essen-

tially pictorial relation. If we find the explanation persuasive, then Wittgenstein has shown despite appearances to the contrary that even the musical score is a picture of a piece of music. If we cannot soundly deduce from this analogy that ordinary languages are also pictorial despite their nonpictorial appearance, we may at least begin to be more receptive to the possibility.

Wittgenstein takes his next example from the pictorial features of formal predicate-quantificational logic. In the relational expression aRb, symbolizing the proposition that b is to the right (R) of a, the proposition pictures its meaning by placing the term 'b' spatially to the right of term 'a', with 'R' between them. The propositions of logic might be thought to embody more of the essential features of propositions as linguistic pictures. Yet the relation is an unusual case, and by the standard conventions for symbolization, to express the converse proposition that a is to the right of b, the picture theory must assume a contrary projection in order to represent the fact pictorially by the construction bRa. As Wittgenstein observes in other cases, this can also be a picture of the fact that a is to the right of b, just as a spot of blue can picture red. The illustration is impressive, but only adds luster to the picture theory for those who have already accepted the thesis that propositions are pictures of facts. Wittgenstein nevertheless shows that not all language is nonpictorial even in superficial appearance.

Wittgenstein describes the origins of the alphabets of ordinary languages as deriving historically from pictograms. He is mistaken if he supposes that Egyptian hieroglyphics picture facts or complexes, since its symbols are phonetic, like the letters of the Greek or Roman alphabet. Still, it is true and important to see that the beginnings of language, including Egyptian hieroglyphics, are at worst crudely but at best abstractly pictorial or representational. Language is pictorial despite appearance if the elements of language are pictorial, where at least some elements in the development of at least some languages carry in their sign systems the perceptible appearance of their origin as pictures of facts:

> 4.016   In order to understand the essence of the proposition, consider hieroglyphic writing, which pictures the facts it describes.
>
> And from it came the alphabet without the essence of the representation being lost.

In the final analysis, it is immaterial for Wittgenstein whether or not ordinary language appears pictorial. The transcendental reasoning Wittgenstein offers in support of the conditions that must be satisfied in order for the determinate meaningfulness of expressions in ordinary language to be logically possible implies that appearances notwithstanding all language and any logically possible language is in reality as distinct from appearance a picturing of the facts of the world. The traces of picturing in certain languages and in the origins of language signs are merely clues to and vestiges of the real underlying pictorial essence of language. The transcendental proof of the picture theory is that there is no other way to account for the determinate meaningfulness of language. Language at the deepest level of logical analysis in the transcendent order of imperceptible propositional symbols is meaningful because it pictures facts.

The next most important development in Wittgenstein's picture theory is the practical application of the saying-showing distinction introduced in 2.171–2.174. Wittgenstein holds that the proposition expresses its sense by showing a fact and saying that the fact exists. The distinction between what can be said and what can only be shown in a proposition has the greatest consequences for Wittgenstein's philosophical semantics, and for his rejection of the traditional problems of philosophy:

> 4.021   The proposition is a picture of reality, for I know the state of affairs presented by it, if I understand the proposition. And I understand the proposition, without its sense having been explained to me.

> 4.022   The proposition *shows* its sense.
>
> The proposition *shows* how things stand, *if* it is true. And it *says,* that they do so stand.

Wittgenstein has already argued that pictures cannot express but only show forth their logical forms. But what is logical form, and how is it revealed? Wittgenstein addresses these questions by referring to a proposition's articulation into a definite logical structure with a definite logical form or mathematical multiplicity. These, at the deepest level of logical atomist analysis in the transcendental order of symbols, must be precisely the same as that of any fact the proposition is capable of expressing. The logical form of a fact or proposition, and of a proposition as itself a fact, is the mathematical multiplicity or number of distinct parts into which the two are articulated when completely analyzed. The picture and the fact it pictures must display a one-one element-for-element correlation of simple names for simple objects in their most basic structures. Wittgenstein argues:

4.032　The proposition is a picture of its state of affairs, only in so far as it is logically articulated.

(Even the proposition "ambulo" is composite, for its stem gives a different sense with another termination, or its termination with another stem.)

4.04　In the proposition there must be exactly as many things distinguishable as there are in the state of affairs, which it represents.

They must both possess the same logical (mathematical) multiplicity (cf. Hertz's Mechanics, on Dynamic Models).

4.041　This mathematical multiplicity naturally cannot in its turn be represented. One cannot get outside it in the representation.

The inflected Latin sentence 'Ambulo' ('I walk') has precisely the right logical or mathematical multiplicity to represent the state of affairs which is such that I walk, even though it looks superficially to have no separate component linguistic parts pictorially to represent the application of a predicate to a subject. Wittgenstein rightly replies that the sentence has after all the required multiplicity, because the verb stem that expresses the predicate accepts numerous alternative suffixes to represent the necessary declensions for all the possible subjects to which the predicate can attach. Wittgenstein repeats the pronouncement of 2.172 and 2.174, that a picture, in this case a proposition, cannot, on pain of indefinite regress and the absurdity of standing outside itself in order to depict a fact about itself, represent, describe, or express its own mathematical multiplicity. A proposition cannot say what mathematical multiplicity it has, but can only show it, presenting its logical articulation under analysis and in the transcendental order of symbols into a definite number of elements, by which they can be counted. The theme is continued in these later passages:

4.12　Propositions can represent the whole reality, but they cannot represent what they must have in common with reality in order to be able to represent it—the logical form.

To be able to represent the logical form, we should have to be able to put ourselves with the propositions outside logic, that is outside the world.

4.121　Propositions cannot represent the logical form: this mirrors itself in the propositions.

That which mirrors itself in language, language cannot represent.

> That which expresses *itself* in language, *we* cannot express by language.
>
> The propositions *show* the logical form of reality.
>
> They exhibit it.

4.1211   Thus a proposition *"fa"* shows that in its sense the object *a* occurs, two propositions *"fa"* and *"ga"* that they are both about the same object.

If two propositions contradict one another, this is shown by their structure; similarly if one follows from another, etc.

4.1212   What *can* be shown *cannot* be said.

At this point, Wittgenstein's remarks about the unsayable showing forth or exhibiting of the logical form of reality in true or false propositions are more or less self-explanatory. We have gathered enough of the elements of the picture theory of meaning to understand what he means in these applications of the saying-showing distinction. Yet it is worthwhile to reflect briefly on the claim in the final sentence of 4.1212. Why does Wittgenstein insist that what *can* be shown *cannot* be said?

This way of putting things turns out to be Wittgenstein's strongest formulation of the saying-showing distinction. What can be shown is what must or can only be shown, and hence what cannot be said. The saying-showing distinction as it applies to a proposition is that a proposition shows its sense and says that what its sense describes exists, that a certain fact obtains. What Wittgenstein has so far enumerated as showable is the logical and representational form, and the most deeply analyzed logical form or mathematical multiplicity of pictures, including propositions, and the facts they picture. That logical and representational form is unsayable by virtue of being showable is clear from the reasons Wittgenstein offers for regarding form as showable. The form or multiplicity of a proposition is itself a part of the proposition, as 2.1513 makes clear. This alone implies the impossibility of a proposition's describing its own form. As Wittgenstein argues in several places, it is impossible for a proposition to express rather than show forth its form, because in order to describe its form a proposition *per impossibile* would have to stand outside itself. If another proposition is given to describe the first proposition's logical form in a kind of hierarchy, then we set off on a vicious indefinite regress in which the proposition's determinate meaning as a function of its logical form is never fully determined.

As the most basic combinations of simple objects are atomic facts, so the most basic combinations of names for simple objects are elementary propositions (*Elementarsätze*). The elementary propositions have the same logical forms as the atomic states of affairs they represent. Whereas an atomic fact is a chain-linked juxtaposition of simple objects in a definite order and belonging to three forms (space, time, and generic color or instantiation of phenomenal property), an elementary proposition that represents an atomic fact is a concatenation of simple names with the same logical structure and logical form. The elementary propositions are logically independent of one another and hence cannot contradict one another. It is for the same reason that the atomic facts are ontically independent, as 1.21 requires, so that any atomic fact can either be the case or not be the case and everything else remain the same:

4.21   The simplest proposition, the elementary proposition, asserts the existence of an atomic fact.

4.211   It is a sign of an elementary proposition, that no elementary proposition can contradict it.

4.22   The elementary proposition consists of names. It is a connexion, a concatenation, of names.

4.221   It is obvious that in the analysis of propositions we must come to elementary propositions, which consist of names in immediate combination.

The question arises here, how the propositional connexion comes to be.

4.2211 Even if the world is infinitely complex, so that every fact consists of an infinite number of atomic facts and every atomic fact is composed of an infinite number of objects, even then there must be objects and atomic facts.

Wittgenstein then explains his notation for names and elementary propositions. The symbolism he adopts unsurprisingly resembles the formulations of standard predicate-quantificational logic or functional calculus. Wittgenstein adopts Frege's thesis that a term has meaning only in the context of a proposition, applying it to the specific case of the occurrence of names concatenated in an elementary proposition:

4.23   The name occurs in the proposition only in the context of the elementary proposition.

4.24   The names are the simple symbols, I indicate them by single letters (x, y, z).

The elementary proposition I write as function of the names, in the form "fx", "$\phi(x,y)$", etc.

Or I indicate it by the letters p, q, r.

The one-one correspondence required by the picturing relation in an exact logical isomorphism of proposition as picture and the facts it pictures takes place at the level of simple names for simple objects. The names are concatenated into elementary propositions, truth functions (conjunctions) of which correspond to concurrences of existent atomic facts reducible to chain-linked juxtapositions of simple objects. The correspondences according to the picture theory at its deepest level of logical atomist analysis in the transcendental order of imperceptible symbols are these:

Simple names	—	Simple objects
Elementary propositions	—	Atomic facts
[(Like-ordered concatenations of names)	—	(Like-ordered juxtapositions of objects)]
Complex propositions	—	Complex facts
[Conjunctions of elementary propositions	—	Concurrences of atomic facts]

We are at last in a position to put together all the separate requirements of the picture theory. Since Wittgenstein proposes to signify the names for simple objects in atomic facts by lowercase letters 'a', 'b', 'c', etc., we can represent the concatenation of names in elementary propositions as abc, or $a^\frown b^\frown c$. The ontic-semantic requirements of Wittgenstein's picture theory of meaning are displayed in the following diagram:

Picturing Facts:

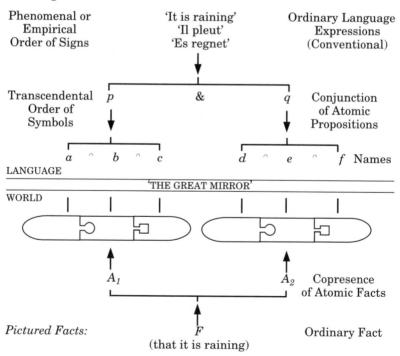

We have followed Wittgenstein's step-by-step development of the picture theory of meaning in all its essentials. The idea of the theory is to explain the determinate meaning of language literally as a picturing of facts. There must be an exact matching of the elements of a picture, including propositions as logical pictures, and the elements of whatever facts the picture can be used to represent. The representation of facts in language, with a few interesting exceptions, does not take place superficially in the conventionally governed perceptible sign systems of language. It is rather at the deepest, most penetrating level of logical atomist structures, where the simple objects of atomic facts are in one-one correspondence with the simple names for simple objects in the elementary propositions, that language pictures facts in the supersensible transcendent symbolic order.

There is an exact mirroring of logically isomorphic structures of identical form or mathematical multiplicity in the reduction of atomic facts as juxtapositions of simple objects in a definite way and according to a determinate logical structure with the analysis of elementary propositions as simple names concatenated in the same definite way and with the same determinate logical structure. The world divides into facts, and facts divide into ontically independent atomic facts. The totality of true thoughts as the description of the world similarly divides into propositions, and these divide into truth functions of logically independent elementary propositions. The reality, finally, is the existence and nonexistence of atomic facts, pictured in language, understood as the set of all true or false elementary propositions, and the total reality is the world. The identically shared logical isomorphisms of facts and pictures as among the facts of the world make possible the determinate meaningfulness of any logically possible language in logically picturing the facts of any logically possible world.

Wittgenstein's confidence in the theory of meaning at the time of the *Tractatus* is understandable if not entirely justified. He is convinced that the picture theory unlocks the secret of the only possible explanation of how language works, not merely in an abstract or ideal setting, but in the human activity of actual everyday linguistic practice in which we make to ourselves pictures of facts. That there can be no other correct account of the determinate meaningfulness of language Wittgenstein believes is entailed by the transcendental argument in support of logical atomism and the picture theory. For language to have meaning, it must be capable of representing facts. To represent facts, language must have something in common with the facts it represents. The perceptible signs of colloquial language as a rule do not share any characteristic features with the facts of the world. The facts into which the world divides must therefore be made up of simple objects correlated with simple names in determinate combinations that constitute elementary propositions. The elementary propositions picture atomic facts in an imperceptible order of symbols that transcends their perceptible appearance in the conventional sign systems of ordinary language. The rigorously reasoned solutions of the picture theory gave Wittgenstein the strength of conviction to believe that there could be no other answer to the fundamental questions he had raised about the logic and semantics of language.[8]

▐ NOTES

1. The remark is amplified in *Tractatus* 4.031: "In the proposition a state of affairs is, as it were, put together for the sake of experiment. One can say, instead of, This proposition has such and such a sense, This proposition represents such and such a state of affairs." The inspiration for the picture theory of meaning is recounted by von Wright in Malcolm 1958, 7–8: "There is a story of how the idea of language as a picture of reality occurred to Wittgenstein. It was in the autumn of 1914, on the East front. Wittgenstein was reading in a magazine about a law-suit in Paris concerning an automobile accident. At the trial a miniature model of the accident was presented before the court. The model here served as a proposition; that is, as a description of a possible state of affairs. It had this function owing to a correspondence between the parts of the model (the miniature-houses, -cars, -people) and things (houses, cars, people) in reality. It now occurred to Wittgenstein that one might reverse the analogy and say that a *proposition* serves as a model or *picture,* by virtue of a similar correspondence between *its* parts and the world. The way in which the parts of the proposition are combined—the *structure* of the proposition—depicts a possible combination of elements in reality, a possible state of affairs." See also von Wright in Malcolm 1958, 7, note 3, where he cautions: "There exist several, somewhat different versions of [the story of how Wittgenstein arrived at the picture theory of meaning]. The story as told here is based on an entry in Wittgenstein's philosophical notebooks in June 1930.—It would be interesting to know whether Wittgenstein's conception of the proposition as a picture is connected in any way with the Introduction to Heinrich Hertz's *Die Prinzipien der Mechanik.* Wittgenstein knew this work and held it in high esteem. There are traces of the impression that it made on him both in the *Tractatus* and in his later writings." Yet another account of the origin of the picture theory of meaning is given by Malcolm 1958, 68–69.

2. See Frege 1970, 70: "This [ambiguity] arises from an imperfection of language, from which even the symbolic language of mathematical analysis is not altogether free; even there combinations of symbols can occur that seem to stand for something but have (at least so far) no reference, e.g. divergent infinite series. This can be avoided, e.g., by means of the special stipulation that divergent infinite series shall stand for the number 0. A logically perfect language (*Begriffsschrift*) should satisfy the conditions, that every proposition grammatically well constructed as a proper name out of signs already introduced shall in fact designate an object, and that no new sign shall be introduced as a proper name without being secured a reference." Russell, Introduction to Wittgenstein's *Tractatus,* 7–8: "In the part of his theory which deals with Symbolism [Wittgenstein] is concerned with the conditions which would have to be fulfilled by a logically perfect language. . . . In practice, language is always more or less vague, so that what we assert is never quite precise. . . . A logically perfect language has rules of syntax which prevent nonsense, and has single symbols which always have a definite and unique meaning. Mr. Wittgenstein is concerned with the conditions for a logically perfect language—not that any language is logically perfect, or that we believe ourselves capable, here and now, of constructing a logically perfect language, but that the whole function of language is to have meaning, and it only fulfills this function in proportion as it approaches to the ideal language which we postulate." This passage obviously reflects yet another important respect in which Russell speaks for himself, and fails to understand Wittgenstein's related but quite different purpose in the *Tractatus* of explaining the meaningfulness of any logically possible ordinary or formal language.

    3. There is an analogy between Platonic 'Ideas' as eternal abstract entities that can be thought about but are not themselves merely mental contents or episodes, and 'ideas' in the philosophically less technical sense of lived-through occurrent mental contents. Similarly, Frege's 'thoughts' or *Gedanken* are not occurrent thought contents, but something more eternal, abstract, and Platonic. A thought in the ordinary sense by contrast is an ephemeral, fleeting psychological event, that, as we sometimes say, flashes through the mind. See the quotations from Frege in note 4 immediately below.

    4. Frege 1977a, 1–30. On 4–5, Frege writes: "So I can say: thoughts are senses of sentences, without wishing to assert that the sense of every sentence is a thought. The thought, in itself imperceptible by the senses, gets clothed in the perceptible garb of a sentence, and thereby we are enabled to grasp it. We say a sentence *expresses* a thought. A thought is something imperceptible: anything the senses can perceive is excluded from the realm of things for which the question of truth arises." In *Die Grundlagen der Arithmetik,* Frege uses the word 'idea' (*Vorstellung*) in the ephemeral psychological sense. See Frege 1950, x, where he first announces his commitment to the 'fundamental principle': "always to separate sharply the psychological from the logical, the subjective from the objective", and then adds: "In compliance with the first principle, I have used the word 'idea' always in the psychological sense, and have distinguished ideas from concepts and from objects." Frege's "Der Gedanke" did not appear until 1918, but he uses the term *'Gedanke'* in much the same way in his earlier writings, including *Begriffsschrift,* which Wittgenstein knew at the time of writing the *Tractatus.*

    5. Bolzano 1972, especially 20–31; 171–80.

    6. Kant 1965, A51/B75. We know that Wittgenstein studied Kant's *Kritik der reinen Vernunft* while a prisoner of war, but we do not know exactly what he thought of it. He was earlier and better acquainted with Schopenhauer's idealist philosophy, in which a similar distinction is drawn between the world of appearance and Will or blind urging as thing-in-itself. The two orders are separated, as Schopenhauer likes to say, invoking the Vedic myth, by the veil of Maya. Schopenhauer regards the distinction between *phenomena* (the world as it appears), and *noumena* (the real world as it is in itself) as the most important achievement of Kant's critical idealism. He writes, 1969, 1, 417–18: *"Kant's greatest merit is the distinction of the phenomenon from the thing-in-itself,* based on the proof that between things and us there always stands the *intellect,* and that on this account they cannot be known according to what they may be in themselves." Schopenhauer also writes in a passage prescient of Wittgenstein's attitude toward the projection of propositions in the transcendental order of symbols into conventional sign systems under the picture theory of meaning, ibid., 239: "if there is absolutely no connexion between what is depicted and the concept indicated by it . . . the sign and the thing signified are connected quite conventionally by positive fixed rule casually introduced." Stenius, 220: "To sum up: it is essential to Wittgenstein's outlook that logical analysis of language as he conceives of it is a kind of 'transcendental deduction' in Kant's sense, the aim of which is to indicate the *a priori* form of experience which is 'shown' by all meaningful language and therefore cannot be 'said'. From this point of view the Tractatus could be called a 'Critique of Pure Language' [phrase attributed to Geach]." See Garver 1994, 91–101.

    7.   Black 1964, 223; Sternfeld 1966, 22–23; Dummett 1981, 49–53; Baker and Hacker 1984a, 279.

    8.   See also Anscombe 1971, 64–97; Ayer, 17–34; Fann 1969, 8–28; Fogelin 1987, 18–26; Griffin 1964, 87–111; Hacker 1989, 56–80; O'Shoughnessy 1953; Peterson 1990; Schulte 1992, 46–60; Stern 1995.

| **The General Form of Proposition**

Wittgenstein delimits the domain of what can be said in a language by establishing the general form of proposition (*allgemeine Form des Satzes*). As with other main parts of the *Tractatus*, Wittgenstein develops the general form of proposition progressively in a series of interconnected remarks about propositions, the logical form of propositions, formal concepts, and procedures for generating a sequence of formal signs that constitute the general form of a formal series. Finally, he combines these requirements to arrive at a formal expression of the formal concept of the general form of proposition as a sequence of formal signs constituting the particular formal series containing all and only the genuine propositions of any language.

The general form of proposition is explained informally and then symbolized as a mathematical operation. Informally, Wittgenstein states in 4.5: "The general form of proposition is: Such and such is the case." The general form of proposition in other words is that by which the existence of a fact or state of affairs is expressed. Wittgenstein formalizes the concept by combining all the elements needed to generate the complete set of propositions of any logically possible language. These include a basis or starting place, an arbitrary choice of an item in the basis, and an operation successively applied to the item. The production of propositions expands at each stage as the operation proceeds, giving further applications of the operation increasingly more possibilities to work with in generating a formal series. By analogy, consider how we might try to specify the set of all even whole numbers. We begin with a basis, the number 2. Then we describe an inductive procedure, by which, beginning with 2, we add 2 to it, and then 2 again to the first product of the operation in a continuing series, and so on, adding 2 to whatever results from the operation at each successive step. Thus, we generate the complete set of all even numbers 2, 4, 6, 8, 10, ...

Wittgenstein would annotate this procedure by enclosing terms for the basis, arbitrary choice of item from the basis, and operation in brackets as: [2,x,+2], or [(inductively expanding) basis,arbitrary item of basis,operation on item]. At the outset, x is the basis 2 itself, and then includes arbitrary selections of items from each of the resulting series, {2,4}; {2,4,6}; etc. Wittgenstein uses a similar device in formalizing the general form of proposition. He defines an induction basis consisting of the set of all elementary propositions. Selections of elementary propositions are then given over to an inductive series-generating operation in the successive joint negation of propositions ('not ____ and not ____'). This commits Wittgenstein to the momentous but logically and philosophically controversial reduction of all propositions to truth functions of the elementary propositions. Using the term '$\bar{p}$' to designate the set of all elementary propositions, '$\bar{\xi}$' as arbitrary selections from the basis, and 'N' as joint negation, Wittgenstein formalizes the general form of proposition in this way:

6   The general form of truth-function is: $[\bar{p},\bar{\xi},N(\bar{\xi})]$.

         This is the general form of proposition.

6.001   This says nothing else than that every proposition is the result of successive applications of the operation N' ($\bar{\xi}$) to the elementary propositions.

6.002   If we are given the general form of the way in which a proposition is constructed, then thereby we are also given the general form of the way in which by an operation out of one proposition another can be created.

6.01   The general form of the operation Ω' ($\bar{v}$) is therefore: $[\bar{\xi},N(\bar{\xi})]'$ ($\bar{v}$) ($= [\bar{v},\bar{\xi},N(\bar{\xi})]$).

         This is the most general form of transition from one proposition to another.

The general form of proposition establishes the fundamental semantic distinctions of Wittgenstein's theory. By defining the set of all genuine propositions as truth functions of the elementary propositions, the general form of proposition draws a sharp distinction between what is sayable within the resources of any logically possible language and whatever falls outside the domain of language as literal nonsense. It is by this division between the meaningful and meaningless that Wittgenstein proposes to eliminate all traditional philosophical problems as pseudoproblems.

The general form of proposition sets definite limits to the expression of thought in any logically possible language by giving an internal demarcation of the set of propositions. As Wittgenstein explains in the preface to the *Tractatus:*

> The book will, therefore, draw a limit to thinking, or rather—
> not to thinking, but to the expression of thoughts; for, in order
> to draw a limit to thinking we should have to be able to think
> both sides of this limit (we should therefore have to be able to
> think what cannot be thought). The limit can, therefore, only
> be drawn in language and what lies on the other side of the
> limit will be simply nonsense. (27)

To define the general form of proposition, Wittgenstein must introduce a basis and an iterative operation to be applied to the basis and successive products. Wittgenstein chooses the set of elementary propositions as the induction basis for the general form of proposition. The picture theory of meaning guarantees that there are precisely as many elementary propositions as there are atomic facts. Because, as 1.21 states, atomic facts are ontically independent from one another, the number of possibilities for a given set of atomic facts to exist or not to exist is determined by a simple combinatorial equation. The total number of combinations of existent or nonexistent atomic facts for n atomic facts is $2n$. The picture theory of meaning implies that this is also the same total number of truth possibilities or true-false combinations for the elementary propositions, by virtue of the exact one-one correspondence of elementary propositions that picture atomic facts. The equivalence holds because, as 5.134 states, the elementary propositions are logically mutually independent in the same way and for the same reason that the atomic facts are ontically mutually independent. In order to exhibit all the factors that enter into the calculation, Wittgenstein adopts a more complex mathematical formula to express the same $2n$ number of possibilities of n existent or nonexistent atomic facts, and true or false elementary propositions:

4.25   If the elementary proposition is true, the atomic fact exists; if it is false the atomic fact does not exist.

4.26   The specification of all true elementary propositions describes the world completely. The world is completely described by the specification of all elementary propositions plus the specification, which of them are true and which false.

4.27   With regard to the existence of n atomic facts there are $Kn = \sum_{v=0}^{n} \binom{n}{v}$ possibilities.

It is possible for all combinations of atomic facts to exist, and the others not to exist.

4.28   To these combinations correspond the same number of possibilities of truth—and falsehood—of n elementary propositions.

If there is a certain number of possibilities for n atomic facts to exist or not to exist, then there must also be precisely the same number of possibilities for the elementary propositions that picture n atomic facts to be true or false. The truth of an elementary proposition corresponds to the existence of the atomic fact it pictures, and the falsehood of an elementary proposition corresponds to the nonexistence of the atomic fact it pictures.

The above formula determines the cardinality or number of members of the set of all elementary propositions, true or false, that constitute the induction basis of Wittgenstein's formulation of the general form of proposition. The value K_n is the sum, Σ, of all possible combinations of truth values, corresponding to the total number of existent or nonexistent atomic facts or true or false elementary propositions, for n atomic facts or elementary propositions, beginning with none where $v = 0$, and ranging through n, in $\sum_{v=0}^{n} \binom{n}{v}$. This is a more complicated but also more informative way of expressing the same quantity as 2^n.[1]

Wittgenstein proposes a graphic way of arraying the possible combinations of truth and falsehood for any set of elementary propositions. Again, no exhaustive listing of the possibilities is attempted, since there are indefinitely many elementary propositions. Wittgenstein is content to exhibit what we now call truth tables that show the $2^1 (= 2)$, $2^2 (= 4)$, and $2^3 (= 8)$ possible 'True' (T) or 'False' (F) truth values respectively for 1, 2, and 3 elementary propositions. The fact that all possible combinations of the truth or falsity of elementary propositions can be presented in a pictorial display is important to Wittgenstein's later applications of the picture theory of meaning and the saying-showing distinction. Wittgenstein concludes that propositions in their essential symbolic forms cannot represent whether they are true or false, but can only show forth their truth values:

4.3   The truth-possibilities of the elementary propositions mean the possibilities of the existence and non-existence of the atomic facts.

4.31   The truth-possibilities can be presented by schemata of the following kind ("T" means "true", "F" "false". The rows of T's and F's under the row of the elementary propositions mean their truth-possibilities in an easily intelligible symbolism).

p	q	r
T	T	T
F	T	T
T	F	T
T	T	F
F	F	T
F	T	F
T	F	F
F	F	F

p	q
T	T
F	T
T	F
F	F

p
T
F

Wittgenstein takes the next important step toward formalizing the general form of proposition by observing that a proposition in its general terms expresses an agreement or disagreement with the truth possibilities of the elementary propositions. In truth table analysis, elementary propositions express (*ausdrücken*) their own truth possibilities, and compound propositions express their truth possibilities as truth operations of the elementary propositions of which they are composed. The reduction of compound to elementary propositions is essential to the general form of proposition. If we begin with the complete set of all elementary propositions as the induction basis, then we should expect to be able to generate every other compound proposition by a truth-functional operation on an appropriate selection of the elementary propositions. We just need to combine the elementary propositions with the right truth operations in order to produce any desired compound proposition, and in general to define the complete set of propositions, elementary and compound:

4.4   A proposition is the expression of agreement and disagreement with the truth-possibilities of the elementary propositions.

4.41   The truth-possibilities of the elementary propositions are the conditions of the truth and falsehood of the propositions.

4.411   It seems probable even at first sight that the introduction of the elementary propositions is fundamental for the comprehension of the other kinds of propositions. Indeed the comprehension of the general propositions depends *palpably* on that of the elementary propositions.

4.42   With regard to the agreement and disagreement of a proposition with the truth-possibilities of n elementary propositions there are $\sum_{k=0}^{K_n}\binom{K_n}{k} = L_n$ possibilities.

Wittgenstein computes the cardinality of the entire set of elementary and compound propositions. "A proposition," he states in 4.1, "presents the existence and non-existence of atomic facts." The number of propositions generated by truth-functional operations on n elementary propositions taken as an induction basis can therefore equivalently be given as the quantity $L_n = 2^{nk}$. This is the total number of propositions forthcoming in the transcendent symbolism of any logically possible language. It is the number of all logically possible truth-functional combinations of all logically possible propositions, considered as expressing agreement or disagreement with two truth possibilities of an arbitrary number of elementary propositions n, for $k = K_n$ $(= 2^n)$ possible combinations of n atomic facts (as explained in 4.25–4.28). Thus, the grand total of all logically meaningful propositions, elementary and compound, generated by the general form of proposition, is a simple mathematical function 2^{2^n} of the total number n of logically possible elementary propositions picturing n logically possible atomic facts.

Can anything more concrete be said about the cardinality of meaningful expressions, the total number of propositions churned out by the truth-functional operations of the general form of proposition? Wittgenstein's formulas are indeterminate in that they all depend on number n, but they do not even approximately specify what number n is supposed to be. Wittgenstein goes so far as to maintain that it is logically meaningless to try to give the number a real value. He seems to allow n to be infinite, when he declares in 4.2211 that "Even if the world is infinitely complex, so that every fact consists of an infinite number of atomic facts and every atomic fact is composed of an infinite number of objects, even then there must be objects and atomic facts." But Wittgenstein also says:

4.1272   So the variable name "x" is the proper sign of the pseudo-concept *object*.

          Wherever the word "object" ("thing", "entity", etc.) is rightly used, it is expressed in logical symbolism by the variable name.

          For example in the proposition "there are two objects which . . .", by "($\exists x, y$) . . .".

          Wherever it is used otherwise, *i.e.* as a proper concept word, there arise senseless [*unsinnig*] pseudo-propositions.

> So one cannot, *e.g.* say "There are objects" as one
> says "There are books". Nor "There are 100 objects"
> or "There are $\aleph_0$ objects".
> And it is senseless [*unsinnig*] to speak of *the*
> *number of all objects* . . .

If we are forced to choose between the apparently conflicting testimony of 4.1272 and 4.2211, in which Wittgenstein ostensibly allows and positively rejects as nonsensical (*unsinnig*) the proposal that there might be infinitely many objects or atomic facts, then we should probably take 4.1272 literally and interpret 4.2211 as a hypothetical with a *per impossibile* condition.

The assertion in 4.2211, unlike 4.1272, is explicitly conditional and arguably counterfactual: "*Even if* the world is infinitely complex . . .". Wittgenstein in 4.2211, moreover, seems to consider the infinite case only to emphasize or further explain the concept of the decomposition of atomic facts into simple objects. He offers an analogy with a situation in which it would be possible to specify that there are $n = \aleph_0$ many atomic facts and the same number of elementary propositions.[2] The point of the passage need not be to take seriously the possibility that we can meaningfully specify the total number of atomic facts or elementary propositions n as infinite, but rather to stress the reducibility of atomic facts into simple objects, *even if,* contrary to what Wittgenstein believes sayable, the atomic facts or simple objects were infinite in number. It might be consistent with Wittgenstein's claim in 4.2211 to hold that it is meaningless to assign any finite or infinite cardinality to the total number of objects, atomic facts, or the elementary propositions that picture them. If it is nonsense to say that the number of atomic facts or elementary propositions n is equal to any of $1,2,3, \ldots ,\aleph_0$, then we cannot make sense of the total number of propositions defined by the general form of proposition. Wittgenstein's 4.1272 unconditionally states that it is nonsense to specify any definite numerical value for n in the combinatorics of the general form of proposition.[3]

It seems preferable, if we are forced to choose between 4.1272 and 4.2211, to accept 4.1272 as Wittgenstein's official position. Wittgenstein maintains that the number n of atomic facts or elementary propositions cannot be given a definite value. Yet if n is variable for no meaningfully specifiable number, then Wittgenstein may be hard pressed to justify the occurrence of n in his combinatorial formulas L_n and K_n, in characterizing the cardinality of possible propositions in any logically possible language. What, if anything, can we learn from Wittgenstein's efforts to derive these combinatorial expressions for the set of all propositions?

Wittgenstein avoids inconsistency because he does not think that the equations for L_n and K_n are meaningful, while such sentences as '$n = 10^{1000}$' or '$n = \aleph_0$' are nonsensical. On the contrary, in 6.2–6.3 he implies that mathematically correct equations like the tautologies of logic to which they reduce are senseless (though not nonsensical; see 4.461–4.4611). The *Tractatus* disallows any attempt to calculate or quantify in real terms the number of simple objects, simple names, atomic facts, elementary, compound, or combined elementary and compound propositions.[4] The formulas, despite being senseless mathematical equations, demonstrate the geometrical increase in the cardinality of truth-functional combinations of any number of elementary propositions. If all propositions are truth functions of the elementary propositions, then Wittgenstein's formulas for L_n and K_n represent or in the picture theory sense show the internal limit of meaningful expression in any logically possible language.

Having established the total number of logically possible propositions relative to the number of atomic facts or elementary propositions, Wittgenstein now introduces a method for ordering the propositions produced by the general form of proposition so that all are included and none excluded. The set of all propositions can be systematically ordered in a series by a proposition-building truth-functional operation applied to the set of all elementary propositions. Wittgenstein uses truth tables as terms for truth-functionally compound propositions that immediately show in their visible sign structures how they are generated from other propositions. By modifying the sign system without sacrificing any of its truth table content, Wittgenstein then offers an equally explicit notation in which truth-functionally compound propositions can be presented in a definite formal series according to their generation by a truth operation systematically applied to any number of elementary propositions. Thus, Wittgenstein satisfies the requirement for the correct formulation of a formal series as a formal concept in 4.1273.

For propositions to be designated by the truth table expression of their truth-operational derivation from elementary propositions, the propositional signs of the logic must include ways of expressing their truth conditions. Wittgenstein maintains:

> 4.44 The sign which arises from the co-ordination of that mark "T" with the truth-possibilities is a propositional sign.

> 4.441 It is clear that to the complex of the signs "F" and "T" no object (or complex of objects) corresponds;

any more than to horizontal and vertical lines or to brackets. There are no "logical objects".

Something analogous holds of course for all signs, which express the same as the schemata of "T" and "F".

4.442   Thus *e.g.*

"

p	q	
T	T	T
F	T	T
T	F	
F	F	T "

is a propositional sign . . . .

If the sequence of the truth-possibilities in the schema is once and for all determined by a rule of combination, then the last column is by itself an expression of the truth conditions. If we write this column as a row the propositional sign becomes: "(TT—T)(p,q)", or more plainly: "(TTFT)(p,q)".

(The number of places in the left-hand bracket is determined by the number of terms in the right-hand bracket.)

It is no accident, and no surprise by now, as Wittgenstein says above in the final parenthetical remark, that the number of terms (4) in '(TTFT)' is determined by the number n of terms (2) in '(p,q)' as 2^n. Wittgenstein rejects Frege's concept of the True and the False as logical objects to which a sentence refers in accounting for its truth value by virtue of its sense.[5] Instead, Wittgenstein proposes to write out '(TTFT)(p,q)' as a way of showing (by special convention) in the perceptible sign system of symbolic logic in which each proposition is formulated the truth operation by which the proposition is produced. Thus, '(TTFT)(p,q)' in Wittgenstein's example is an alternative expression for the proposition, 'If p, then q' (or, 'p only if q', 'Not-p or q', etc., as logically equivalent propositional signs). Writing the proposition in Wittgenstein's fashion makes it possible to express the class of propositions as ordered elements of a formal series in a particular sequence of applications of truth functions to the set of all elementary propositions. This is how it works:

5.1   The truth-functions can be ordered in series . . . .

5.101   The truth-functions of every number of elementary
         propositions can be written in a schema of the
         following kind:

(TTTT)(p,q)   Tautology (if p then p, and if q then q) [$p \supset p$. $q \supset q$]

(FTTT)(p,q)   in words: Not both p and q. [$\sim(p$. $q)$]

(TFTT)(p,q)   ”   ”   If q then p. [$q \supset p$]

(TTFT)(p,q)   ”   ”   If p then q. [$p \supset q$]

(TTTF)(p,q)   ”   ” p or q. [$p \vee q$]

(FFTT)(p,q)   ”   ”   Not q. [$\sim q$]

(FTFT)(p,q)   ”   ”   Not p. [$\sim p$]

(FTTF)(p,q)   ”   ” p or q, but not both. [p . $\sim q : \vee : q$. $\sim p$]

(TFFT)(p,q)   ”   ”   If p then q; and if q then p [$p \equiv q$]

(TFTF)(p,q)   ”   ” p

(TTFF)(p,q)   ”   ” q

(FFFT)(p,q)   ”   ”   Neither p nor q. [$\sim p$. $\sim q$ or $p \mid q$]

(FFTF)(p,q)   ”   ” p and not q. [p . $\sim q$]

(FTFF)(p,q)   ”   ” q and not p. [q . $\sim p$]

(TFFF)(p,q)   ”   ” p and q. [p . q]

(FFFF)(p,q)   ”   ”   Contradiction (p and not p; and q and not q.)
         [p . $\sim p$. $\sim q$. $\sim q$]

If we count the possible compound propositions forthcoming as truth operations of 2 elementary propositions, we find, in confirmation of Wittgenstein's cardinality equations, that there are $2^{2^2} = 16$ combinations (for n, $k = 2$). The series includes all and only the propositions we should expect as truth functions of two elementary propositions. When we go beyond small numbers, things quickly get out of hand. The example in the simplest interesting case illustrates how designating propositions according to Wittgenstein's proposal shows in their perceptible sign system formulation how each is generated as a truth function of elementary propositions. This makes it possible to specify an ordering of their production in a series by means of the truth-functional operation of selective successive joint negation applied to an induction basis consisting of the elementary propositions.

Let us now return to some important distinctions Wittgenstein draws among the propositions in the complete series defined by the general form of proposition. The propositions given as truth functions of the elementary propositions p, q begin with tautology as a construction that is necessarily true by virtue of its logical form, and ends with contradiction or inconsistency as a construction that is necessarily false by virtue of its logical form. Wittgenstein details an elaborate theory of these two extremes of truth-functional combinations. We consider its proper place in the text before proceeding to

Wittgenstein's statement of the general form or proposition, all the parts of which are now in place:

> 4.45   For *n* elementary propositions there are L_n possible groups of truth-conditions.
>
> The groups of truth-conditions which belong to the truth-possibilities of a number of elementary propositions can be ordered in a series.
>
> 4.46   Among the possible groups of truth-conditions there are two extreme cases.
>
> In the one case the proposition is true for all the truth-possibilities of the elementary propositions. We say that the truth-conditions are *tautological*.
>
> In the second case the proposition is false for all the truth-possibilities. The truth-conditions are *self-contradictory*.
>
> In the first case we call the proposition a tautology, in the second case a contradiction.

At the time of working out his thoughts in the *Notebooks 1914–1916,* Wittgenstein experimented with classifying tautology and contradiction as literally nonsensical pseudopropositions. Tautology and contradiction are not pictures of facts, but lack sense because they do not point to any particular state of affairs.[6]

There is an unresolved tension in what Wittgenstein finds it necessary to say about tautology and contradiction. Strictly speaking, since tautology and contradiction do not point to or picture facts, they should be excluded from the category of genuine propositions. Yet to remove them would drastically complicate the elegant constructivism of the general form of proposition, and leave unexplained the fact, as Wittgenstein's truth table analysis plainly shows, that tautology and contradiction are truth-functionally generated along with the other truth-functionally compound propositions.

Wittgenstein strikes an uneasy compromise by acknowledging the peculiarity of tautology and contradiction, while allowing them to count as limiting cases of genuine propositions because they are produced by the same truth-functional operations. Tautology and contradiction, despite being senseless, as Wittgenstein says, are "part of the symbolism." The inclusion of tautology and contradiction as genuine truth-functionally generable propositions further motivates Wittgenstein's distinction between the literal nonsense (*der Unsinn*) that characterizes nonsensical (*unsinnig*) pseudopropositions, and the semantic categorization of senseless (*sinnlos*) propositions applying to tautology and contradiction. Wittgenstein offers this account of the semantic anomaly of tautology and contradiction:

4.461   The proposition shows what it says, the tautology and the contradiction that they say nothing.

The tautology has no truth-conditions, for it is
unconditionally true; and the contradiction is on
no condition true.

Tautology and contradiction are without sense.

(Like the point from which two arrows go out in
opposite directions.)

(I know, *e.g.* nothing about the weather, when I
know that it rains or does not rain.)

4.4611   Tautology and contradiction are, however, not
nonsensical; they are part of the symbolism, in
the same way that "o" is part of the symbolism
of Arithmetic.

4.462   Tautology and contradiction are not pictures
of the reality. They present no possible state of
affairs. For the one allows *every* possible state
of affairs, the other *none*.

In the tautology the conditions of agreement with
the world—the presenting relations—cancel one
another, so that it stands in no presenting relation
to reality.

The fundamental semantic distinction of the *Tractatus* established by the general form of proposition is supposed to demarcate
whatever is part of a correct logical notation from whatever is not.
What belongs most properly to a correct logical notation are the
meaningful propositions that logically picture the logically contingent facts of the world. Tautology and contradiction complicate
the distinction between the meaningful and meaningless for
which Wittgenstein creates a special middle category. Neither
meaningful nor nonsensical, senseless tautologies and contradictions are propositions by courtesy; they come along for the ride
with genuine meaningful propositions as limiting default case
constructions of the symbolism.

Whatever is part of a correct logical notation		*Unsinn* *unsinnig*
sinnlos tautology and contradiction	*Sinn* *sinnvoll* propositions	Whatever is not part of a correct logical notation That which cannot be said but shows itself only in a correct logical notation Whatever lies beyond the limit to the expression of thought in a language

It is by means of this fundamental semantic distinction that
Wittgenstein avoids the traditional philosophical paradoxes, dissolving them as pseudoproblems relegated to the realm of nonsense.

Logical and mathematical form, value in ethics and aesthetics, metaphysics and metalinguistic theory, including Wittgenstein's own logical atomism and picture theory semantics, together
with nonsensical pseudopropositions generally are alike consigned
to the semantic no-man's-land of unsayable *Unsinn*. What remains, according to the theory, are senseless contradictions and
tautologies, and the meaningful scientific propositions constructible within every language, representing contingently possible
existent or nonexistent states of affairs, that picture the world as
a complete structure of facts in logical space. This is the limit of
the sayable or logically meaningful, the other side of which is literal nonsense.

Without withdrawing his characterization of tautology and
contradiction as senseless propositions, Wittgenstein proceeds to
explain why tautology and contradiction should not be regarded
as genuine propositions. They do not picture anything, but are
deviant combinations resulting from genuine proposition-building operations on the same set of primitive symbols that in every
other case produce logically contingent pictures of facts:

> 4.466   To a definite logical combination of signs corre-
> sponds a definite logical combination of their
> meanings; *every arbitrary* combination only
> corresponds to the unconnected signs.
>
> That is, propositions which are true for every state
> of affairs cannot be combinations of signs at all, for
> otherwise there could only correspond to them de-
> finite combinations of objects.
>
> (And to no logical combination corresponds *no*
> combination of the objects.)
>
> Tautology and contradiction are the limiting cases
> of the combinations of symbols, namely their
> dissolution.
>
> 4.4661 Of course the signs are also combined with one
> another in the tautology and contradiction, *i.e.* they
> stand in relations to one another, but these rela-
> tions are meaningless [*bedeutungslos*], unessential
> to the *symbol*.

Wittgenstein is now ready for the first time explicitly to approach the problem of formulating the general form of proposition. Prior to this, he has spoken only of the general form of a
logical operation, considered hypothetically what the cardinality

of propositions must be if we are given a value for the total number of elementary propositions, and explained how all truth-functional combinations of an arbitrary number of elementary propositions can be expressed so as to display their truth-functional method of generation, facilitating the ordering of all propositions in a definite series.

4.5   Now it appears to be possible to give the most
        general form of proposition; *i.e.* to give a description
        of the propositions of some one sign language, so
        that every possible sense can be expressed by a
        symbol, which falls under the description, and so
        that every symbol which falls under the description
        can express a sense, if the meanings of the names
        are chosen accordingly.

        It is clear that in the description of the most gen-
        eral form of proposition *only* what is essential to
        it may be described—otherwise it would not be the
        most general form.

        That there is a general form is proved by the fact
        that there cannot be a proposition whose form could
        not have been foreseen (*i.e.* constructed).

        The general form of proposition is: Such and such is
        the case.

The passage first announces Wittgenstein's project of giving the general form of proposition, and then proposes the mechanism. The set of all elementary propositions serves as the induction basis for a precisely specifiable successive truth-functional operation on selected subsets of the elementary propositions and the products of the induction as they emerge. Wittgenstein maintains that every proposition is constructible as a truth function of some choice from among the elementary propositions. He characterizes the general form of proposition in abstract general terms as the application of some at first unspecified proposition-building operation applied to the set of all elementary propositions:[7]

4.51   Suppose *all* elementary propositions were given
        me: then we can simply ask: what propositions I
        can build out of them. And these are *all* proposi-
        tions and *so* are they limited.

4.52   The propositions are everything which follows
        from the totality of all elementary propositions (of
        course also from the fact that it is the *totality of
        them all*). (So, in some sense, one could say, that
        all propositions are generalizations of the elemen-
        tary propositions.)

4.53   The general propositional form is a variable.

Wittgenstein states that the set of all propositions is produced by a truth-functional operation on the elementary propositions. This conclusion is prefigured by Wittgenstein's discussion of the truth table method of enumerating the series of truth-functionally compound propositions, as in the above roster of sixteen possible propositions, (TTTT)(p,q), (TTTF)(p,q), etc. The identification of a truth operation by which the formal series of all propositions with tautologies and contradictions is generated from the set of all elementary propositions, itself fully constructible from the complete set of all simple names for simple objects, appears as the next step in Wittgenstein's account of the general form of proposition:

5   Propositions are truth-functions of elementary
        propositions.

        (An elementary proposition is a truth-function of
        itself.)

5.01   The elementary propositions are the truth-argu-
        ments of propositions.

With this general conception of the general form of proposition, Wittgenstein turns to address the induction basis of the operation, and the operation to be applied to the induction basis. He first describes his notation for the reiterative application of any operation:

5.2521 The repeated application of an operation to its own
        result I call its successive application ("$O' O' O' a$" is
        the result of the threefold successive application of
        "$O' \xi$" to "a").

        In a similar sense I speak of the successive applica-
        tion of *several* operations to a number of proposi-
        tions.

5.2522 The general term of the formal series a, $O' a$, $O' O'$
        $a, \ldots$ I write thus: "[$a, x, O'x$]." This expression in
        brackets is a variable. The first term of the expres-
        sion is the beginning of the formal series, the sec-
        ond the form of an arbitrary term x of the series, and
        the third the form of that term of the series which
        immediately follows x.

5.2523 The concept of the successive application of an
        operation is equivalent to the concept "and so on".

Wittgenstein explains the generation of a formal series in an ordered sequence of three factors in [$a, x, O' x$]. The leftmost item is the basis, the first term of the series. This is followed by a variable indicating the choice of an arbitrary term of the series at any stage as it is being produced. Finally, the third element is the application of a particular operation to the term. The operation is applied successively to the induction basis and each resulting product of the procedure, which Wittgenstein says goes on indefinitely.

Wittgenstein then considers the relevant case in which a formal series consisting of all propositions is defined by applying truth operations to all selections of terms from the set of elementary propositions:

> 5.3 All propositions are results of truth-operations on the elementary propositions.
>
> The truth-operation is the way in which a truth-function arises from elementary propositions.
>
> According to the nature of truth-operations, in the same way as out of elementary propositions arise their truth-functions, from truth-functions arises a new one. Every truth-operation creates from truth-functions of elementary propositions another truth-function of elementary propositions, *i.e.* a proposition. The result of every truth-operation on the results of truth-operations on elementary propositions is also the result of *one* truth-operation on elementary propositions.
>
> Every proposition is the result of truth-operations on elementary propositions.

As the penultimate step in formalizing the general form of proposition, Wittgenstein maintains that all propositions are the products of reiterative applications of a limited number of truth operations (negation, disjunction, conjunction, or the like) to the elementary propositions as induction basis:

> 5.32 All truth-functions are results of the successive application of a finite number of truth-operations to elementary propositions.

Wittgenstein identifies the general form of proposition as essential to the concept of proposition. By characterizing the logical form of all descriptions of the facts of the world, the general form of proposition, according to the picture theory of meaning, is also the formal logical essence of the world. Wittgenstein believes that only one truth operation or a single general primitive sign is needed in logic, which alone is sufficient to generate all propositions in an iterative application to the set of all elementary propositions:

> 5.471 The general form of proposition is the essence of proposition.

5.4711   To give the essence of proposition means to give the essence of all description, therefore the essence of the world.

5.472   The description of the most general propositional form is the description of the one and only general primitive sign in logic.

Wittgenstein proposes joint negation as the single minimally necessary truth function or truth constant needed in the inductive operations of the general form of proposition in order to generate the complete set of all propositions from the complete set of all elementary propositions. He writes:

5.5   Every truth-function is a result of the successive application of the operation $(- - - - - T)(\xi, \ldots)$ to elementary propositions.

This operation denies all the propositions in the right-hand bracket and I call it the negation of these propositions.

5.501   An expression in brackets whose terms are propositions I indicate—if the order of the terms in the bracket is indifferent—by a sign of the form "$(\bar{\xi})$". "ξ" is a variable whose values are the terms of the expression in brackets, and the line over the variable indicates that it stands for all its values in the bracket.

(Thus, if ξ has the 3 values P, Q, R, then $(\bar{\xi})$ = (P,Q,R).)

To understand Wittgenstein's idea it is necessary to reflect on the special notation he introduces. As Wittgenstein states in 5.474: "The number of necessary fundamental operations depends *only* on our notation." In the following passages he begins to assemble the elements of the notation he will use to formalize the general form of proposition as the inductive application of the single truth-functional operation of joint negation to the set of all elementary propositions in order to generate the complete set of all elementary and compound propositions.

We may proceed by reviewing what Wittgenstein says above about the notation he proposes to use. The term $'(- - - - - T)(\xi, \ldots)'$, as we have seen, is schematic for the truth-functional application of a single truth-functional application $(- - - - - T)$ to a single elementary proposition $(\xi, \ldots)$. The symbol 'ξ' Wittgenstein uses to denote an elementary proposition or selection from the complete set of all elementary propositions. We see that in $(- - - - - T)$ Wittgenstein uses iteration, not to indicate the case where a truth-functional application involves precisely six propositional variables of 2^6 combinations, but, like the dot-dot-dot of a continuing series, to generalize over any indefinite number of truth-functional operations finitely applied to any number of elementary propositions.

The next step for Wittgenstein is to propose a more convenient abbreviation for the cumbersome truth-functional formulation, (- - - - - T)(ξ, ...). For this term he substitutes the expression N($\bar{\xi}$). The interpretation is that 'N' is the joint negation of whatever propositions belong to ($\bar{\xi}$), where $\bar{\xi}$ contains all the elementary propositions ξ:

5.502   Therefore I write instead of "(- - - - - T)(ξ, ...)", "N($\bar{\xi}$)".

N($\bar{\xi}$) is the negation of all the values of the propositional variable ξ.

5.503   As it is obviously easy to express how propositions can be constructed by means of this operation and how propositions are not to be constructed by means of it, this must be capable of exact expression.

5.51   If ξ has only one value, then N($\bar{\xi}$) = ~p (not p), if it has two values then N($\bar{\xi}$) = ~p . ~q (neither p nor q).

5.511   How can the all-embracing logic which mirrors the world use such special catches and manipulations? Only because all these are connected into an infinitely fine network, to the great mirror.

5.514   If a notation is fixed, there is in it a rule according to which all the propositions denying p are constructed, a rule according to which all the propositions asserting p are constructed, a rule according to which all the propositions asserting p or q are constructed, and so on. These rules are equivalent to the symbols and in them their sense is mirrored.

The operator 'N', which Wittgenstein grooms for inclusion in the general form of proposition, is joint negation. Wittgenstein relies on the discoveries of Jean Nicod and H. M. Sheffer that all five standard truth-functional operators (negation, conjunction, disjunction, conditional, and biconditional), can be reduced to the single operation of joint negation. This is commonly symbolized as the Nicod dagger function '↓', where $p{\downarrow}q$ is logically equivalent to ~p & ~q (or, following as Wittgenstein does Whitehead and Russell's notation in the *Principia Mathematica*, ~p . ~q).[8]

Wittgenstein succinctly symbolizes the general form of proposition in 6–6.01 in the cartouche, [$\bar{p},\bar{\xi},$N($\bar{\xi}$)]. As a consequence of the picture theory of meaning, he urges that the method of generating all truth-functionally compound propositions by successive joint negations of elementary propositions described by the formula is the essence not only of proposition but of the world. The general form of proposition is supposed to encompass all and only the genuine propositions of any logically possible language. The method provides an internal description of the bounds of sense, establishing the limits of what can be said and the expression of thought in language from within its borders. Beyond the limit lies nonsense, the meaningless and extralinguistic, and what can only be shown rather than said according to the saying-showing distinction. The general form of proposition divides the propositional from the pseudopropositional, and thereby restricts meaningful thought and language to representational descriptions of facts ultimately reducible in analysis to elementary space-time-color predications, and the world itself to atomic space-time-color facts. It is the principle on the grounds of which Wittgenstein eliminates all traditional philosophical questions and answers as literally meaningless, and banishes the putative theses of philosophy, including the statements of the *Tractatus,* to the semantic void of pseudopropositional nonsense. It is the Kantian principle by which Wittgenstein correspondingly distinguishes between the world and what transcends the world, including the self or metaphysical subject, value, and logical and pictorial form.[9]

With so much of Wittgenstein's early (anti-) philosophy riding on the general form of proposition, we must try to decide whether or not the concept is correct. There are several problems to consider. Wittgenstein's treatment of the general form of proposition begins with a general characterization of formal processes. He maintains that formal concepts and their instances cannot both be introduced as distinct primitive elements of a logical system. The objects belonging to a formal concept presuppose the concept. To present instances of a formal concept is already to present the formal concept, so that both cannot be primitive. We must choose in that case whether we think it is better to enumerate the propositions as primitive elements, or offer a primitive formal concept of proposition from which all propositions can be derived. By specifying a particular formal process, Wittgenstein defines the general form of proposition as a way of introducing the entire class of propositions to logic without attempting the exhaustive enumeration of an indefinitely large set. Wittgenstein explains the problem of choosing primitives in criticizing Russell's logic:

> 4.12721 The formal concept is already given with an object, which falls under it. One cannot, therefore, introduce both, the objects which fall under a formal concept *and* the formal concept itself, as primitive ideas. One cannot, therefore, *e.g.* introduce (as

Russell does) the concept of function and also
special functions as primitive ideas; or the concept
of number and definite numbers.

As an illustration of the definition of a formal concept, Wittgenstein considers the general function, 'b is the successor of a'. He defines the formal concept of a formal series, and explains that it can only properly enter into logic by means of a general operation:

> 4.1273   If we want to express in logical symbolism the
> general proposition "b is a successor of a" we need
> for this an expression for the general term of the
> formal series: aRb, $(\exists x):aRx.xRb$, $(\exists x,y):aRx.xRy.$
> yRb, . . . The general term of a formal series can
> only be expressed by a variable, for the concept
> symbolized by "term of this formal series" is a *formal*
> concept. (This Frege and Russell overlooked; the
> way in which they express general propositions like
> the above is, therefore, false; it contains a vicious
> circle.)
>
> We can determine the general term of the formal
> series by giving its first term and the general form
> of the operation, which generates the following
> term out of the preceding proposition.

To formulate the general proposition that b is the successor of a, we need to formalize all of the particular and general propositions that express numerical succession. There are indeterminately many such propositions that defy complete enumeration: '1 is the successor of 0', '2 is the successor 1', and so on. Wittgenstein merely gestures toward the entire list of successor propositions when he indicates as part of the formal series the items, aRb, $(\exists x):aRx.xRb$, $(\exists x,y):aRx.xRy.yRb$, ... The first, aRb, presents b as the R-related successor of a. But beyond the particular case, we must also include every logical possibility of referring in every possible combination to the R-related successors of a, b, and quantifications of R-successions. We can interpret Wittgenstein's first generalized entry, $(\exists x):aRx.xRb$, as formally expressing the proposition in hybrid English-logic that 'There is or exists $[\exists x]$ a (generalized, variable) object x, such that x is the R-successor of (particular, particularly named) object a, and such that x is the R-successor of (particular, particularly named) object b.' It is significant that Wittgenstein offers a truth-functionally compound generalized formula as the first example to follow the particular succession aRb, which might be $(\exists x):xRb$ or $(\exists x):aRx$, but gives instead their conjunction. In this way, he flaunts efforts at exhaustive systematic enumeration while still conveying an idea of the kinds of elements that must belong to the series and of the series' indefinite continuation by the standard convention, '. . .'.

If we try to present the formal concept of generality by appealing to the general term 'all', then we are caught in much the same vicious circle of which Wittgenstein accuses Frege and Russell. This makes it viciously circular to define the concept 'all' by enumerating all of its instances if a logic also needs to *say* that these are *all* the instances. The correct method instead, according to Wittgenstein, is to introduce the series by means of a variable, in which the first term is turned over to a general operation in order to generate the rest of the series. This is the rationale for defining the general form of proposition by a variable term in the logic of the *Tractatus*.[10] It might be objected that Wittgenstein's general form of proposition commits the same mistake as Russell in trying to give instances of propositions as primitive elements of the logic at the same time that it adduces as primitive the formal concept of proposition in the general form of proposition. The general form of proposition apparently contains elementary propositions as primitive instances of the formal concept of proposition in $\bar{p}$ and $\bar{\xi}$, to which the truth operation of selective joint negation is then applied. Wittgenstein's general form of proposition does not provide an informative definition of the formal concept of proposition, in the sense that we must already know what is meant at least by the concept of an elementary proposition, and we must already have the elementary propositions at our disposal in order to apply the truth operations that produce the set of all propositions. As *Tractatus* 5 says: "(An elementary proposition is a truth-function of itself.)"

This appears to be the same type of vicious circularity Wittgenstein complains about in Frege and Russell. How can the general form of proposition tell us what is meant by the general concept of proposition as a primitive idea of the logic if to understand it we need prior knowledge of the elementary propositions? By analogy, if we try to use the general form of an even number as $[2, x, +2]$ to explain the formal concept or distinguish the set of all even numbers, then we seem to be trapped in the circle of needing to know in advance that '2' in particular is an even number. There are two replies to be made on Wittgenstein's behalf. By including elementary propositions in the general form of proposition, Wittgenstein does not try to introduce primitive instances alongside the presentation of their primitive formal concept, but on the contrary makes the elementary propositions an integral part of the general form of proposition. The definition avoids circularity because elementary propositions are not supposed to be primitive, but are independently constructible as concatenations of the names of simple objects.

The controversy in Wittgenstein's constructivity or finite extensionality thesis in the *Tractatus* is the related problem of whether the general form of proposition is adequate to produce quantified expressions, such as $(\exists x)fx$ (some x's are f's). If selective joint negation of elementary propositions is sufficient for the existential quantifier, then the general form of proposition yields all of monadic predicate-quantificational logic. It is trivial to define the universal quantifier $(x)fx$ or $(\forall x)fx$ (all x's are f's, in alternative notations) as $\sim(\exists x)\sim fx$. The existential quantifier is equivalent in meaning to any of the elementary propositions, as Wittgenstein states in explaining the singularity and generality of the general form of proposition:

> 5.47 It is clear that everything which can be said *beforehand* about the form of *all* propositions at all can be said *on one occasion.*
>
> For all logical operations are already contained in the elementary proposition. For *"fa"* says the same as *"$(\exists x).fx . x = a$".*
>
> Where there is composition, there is argument and function, and where these are, all logical constants already are.
>
> One could say: the one logical constant is that which *all* propositions, according to their nature, have in common with one another.
>
> That however is the general form of proposition.

All logical operations, Wittgenstein maintains, are contained within any arbitrary elementary proposition. We recall that Wittgenstein offers the logical form of an elementary proposition as '*fa*', which says that object a has property f. Wittgenstein claims that from such an elementary proposition it is possible to extract all the minimally necessary logical operations. He gives the derivation as '$(\exists x).fx . x = a$'. This contains the existential quantifier with object variable '$(\exists x)$', the conjunction '.', and the identity predicate (=). (Identity for Wittgenstein is not a property [5.473], and its sign is therefore dispensable in logic [5.533, 6.232]; identity relations cannot be asserted [6.2322].)

Wittgenstein regards it as nonsensical (*unsinnig*) to number the elementary propositions as either finite or infinite. It might then be said that Wittgenstein has no secure foundation from which to maintain that all existentially and universally quantified propositions are truth-functionally forthcoming from successive joint negations of elementary propositions. Wittgenstein would be right to reply that the critic of the general form of proposition has no firm basis from which to claim that joint negation of elementary propositions cannot produce at least the monadic existentially and universally quantified propositions of the logic ('Some x are f' or $(\exists x)fx$) and 'All x are f' or $(\forall x)fx$). Wittgenstein is satisfied to proceed as though an opponent could have no standpoint from which to overturn his transcendental conclusions about the logical requirements of determinate meaningfulness.

Wittgenstein reduces the negative existential $\sim(\exists x).fx$ to joint negation $N(\bar{\xi})$, as sufficient by further selective successive joint negation for deriving the existential and universal quantification of any predication in predicate-quantificational logic:

> 5.52   If the values of ξ are the total values of a function fx for all values of x, then $N(\bar{\xi}) = \sim(\exists x).fx$.
>
> 5.521   I separate the concept *all* from the truth-function.
>
> Frege and Russell have introduced generality in connexion with the logical product or the logical sum. Then it would be difficult to understand the propositions "$(\exists x).fx$" and "$(x).fx$" in which both ideas lie concealed.

Here Wittgenstein offers a reduction of the negative existential $\sim(\exists x).fx$ to the joint negation of all elementary propositions in ξ. To say that nothing has property f by this interpretation is to say by joint negation of the elementary propositions that $\sim fa$, $\sim fb$, $\sim fc$, . . . , for all objects a,b,c, ... If there is an infinite number of objects, then we may need to go further and state that a,b,c, . . . are *all* the objects. Wittgenstein in 4.1273 objects to any such procedure as leading to vicious circularity in Frege's and Russell's definitions of formal concepts. If we try such a gambit we are ensnared in the circularity of explaining the meaning of ordinary language quantifiers like 'all' and 'some' by appeal to the proposition that a,b,c, . . . are *all* the objects. The logic of the *Tractatus* is subject to such an objection only in light of the claim that there might be $\aleph_0$ infinitely many objects (or elementary propositions). But Wittgenstein, as a consequence of the picture theory of meaning, disregards any attempt to consider the number of simple objects or elementary propositions as logically meaningless.

Wittgenstein seems to have anticipated a similar objection to the general form of proposition. He insists in 4.1272 that "it is senseless [nonsensical, *unsinnig*] to speak of the *number of all objects*," and he rejects questions about whether a generalization includes all objects as logically meaningless. Likewise, he adds:

> 4.128   The logical forms are *anumerical*.

> Therefore there are in logic no pre-eminent num-
> bers, and therefore there is no philosophical
> monism or dualism, etc.

A critic can attack the general form of proposition only by arguing that the theory is inadequate if there are infinitely many objects. The objection would then be that the truth-functional operation of joint negation in the general form of proposition applied to the set of all elementary propositions is not powerful enough to construct a proposition equivalent in meaning to the universal $(\forall x)fx$. Otherwise, beyond the limits of what a language can legitimately say, the exhaustive finite expansion *fa, fb, fc, . . . , fz,* shows that everything has property *f.* But while negation and quantifier signs enter into some reducibly sayable propositions, they do not belong to the transcendental order of symbols. In the *Tractatus* logic, only conjunctions of elementary propositions representing existent atomic facts are minimally needed to picture the world, to which whatever is sayable can be logically reduced.

This is why in 4.442 Wittgenstein first shows the truth table evaluation that comes out False as leaving a blank space in the corresponding row, for which he only later and as the implementation of a specific convention substitutes an 'F'. Wittgenstein for the same reason does not need negation in the logically correct notation of any logically possible language. All the logic requires is the conjunction of elementary propositions to show a concurrence or copresence of atomic facts, the totality of which (which also cannot be said), in the words of 1.12, "determines both what is the case, and also all that is not the case." To account for what is not the case, we can then, as in the conventional sign system of ordinary logic, introduce the negation sign, '~'. But we do not need to acknowledge negation or any other logical operator as part of the real order of things, nor of logical signs as representing objects, complexes, or facts. Wittgenstein explains this consequence of the picture theory of meaning:

> 4.062 Can we not make ourselves understood by means
> of false propositions as hitherto with true ones, so
> long as we know that they are meant to be false?
> No! For a proposition is true, if what we assert by
> means of it is the case; and if by "*p*" we mean *~p,*
> and what we mean is the case, then "*p*" in the new
> conception is true and not false.

> 4.0621 That, however, the signs "*p*" and "*~p*" *can* say the
> same thing is important, for it shows that the sign
> "~" corresponds to nothing in reality.
>
> That negation occurs in a proposition, is no charac-
> teristic of its sense $(\sim\sim p = p)$.

> The propositions "*p*" and "*~p*" have opposite senses,
> but to them corresponds one and the same reality.

The absence of negation as an inessential truth function in the *Tractatus* logic does not vitiate the vital role of joint negation in the general form of proposition. The transcendental symbolism that interrelates sayable fact-describing propositions in Wittgenstein's logic gets by without negation only because negation is already deeply integrated into the proposition-building inductive truth-functional operations of the general form of proposition. Wittgenstein later makes similar remarks about the reducibility and nonobjecthood of logical constants generally, taking as his example the universal and existential quantifiers.[11] He writes:

> 5.44 Truth-functions are not material functions.
>
> If *e.g.* an affirmation can be produced by repeated denial, is the denial—in any sense—contained in the affirmation?
>
> Does "*~~p*" deny *~p*, or does it affirm *p*; or both?
>
> The proposition "*~~p*" does not treat of denial as an object, but the possibility of denial is already prejudged in affirmation.
>
> And if there was an object called "*~*", then "*~~p*" would have to say something other than "*p*". For the one proposition would then treat of *~*, the other would not.
>
> 5.441 This disappearance of the apparent logical constants also occurs if "*~(∃x).~fx*" says the same as "*(x).fx*", or "*(∃x). fx . x = a*" the same as "*fa*".

The expressions of logic that are logically equivalent to predicate-quantificational propositions are logically reducible to the elementary propositions *fa, fb, fc,* etc., construed as functions of the simple names (4.24). There is no intelligible objection to such a reduction, because there is no sayable proposition that makes reference to the universe of discourse as a whole, to give determinate meaning to the requirement that the universal quantifier in $(\forall x).fx$ expresses more than *fa* & *fb* & *fc* & . . . , by *saying* that *in addition, a,b,c, . . . are all* the objects. This, according to the *Tractatus* picture theory, is unsayable nonsense. Insofar as the sentence pretends to explain the meaning of the universal $(\forall x).fx$ as something other than a convenient sign for the proposition *fa* & *fb* & *fc* & . . . , the proposal is viciously circular.

Turning from monadic to polyadic predicate-quantificational logic, a potentially more serious objection arises. Robert J. Fogelin argues that there is a "fundamental error in the logic of the *Tractatus.*"[12] The error is supposed to be that the general form of proposition is logically incapable of generating mixed multiple quantifications by means of the joint negation operator N. Fogelin lists eight quantified formulas, and maintains that Wittgenstein's general form of proposition is able at best to generate only four, leaving the mixed multiple quantifications in particular out of the series that the formula is supposed to define. The propositions are these:

(1) $(\forall x)(\forall y)fxy$ (5) $(\forall x)(\forall y)\text{-}fxy$

(2) $(\exists x)(\exists y)fxy$ (6) $(\exists x)(\exists y)\text{-}fxy$

(3) $(\forall x)(\exists y)fxy$ (7) $(\forall x)(\exists y)\text{-}fxy$

(4) $(\exists x)(\forall y)fxy$ (8) $(\exists x)(\forall y)\text{-}fxy$

The general form of proposition is capable of generating forms (1), (2), (5), and (6), Fogelin admits, but not (3), (4), (7), or (8). Fogelin begins by explaining how Wittgenstein's general form of proposition is intended to produce dyadic predicate-quantificational formulas:

> To construct such multiply-general propositions we let ξ have as its values the values of the function fxy for all values of x and y, i.e., faa, fab, fac, etc. Since $N(fxy)$ gives the joint denial of all those propositions that are the values of the propositional function fxy, it is evident we have produced a proposition equivalent to $[\text{-}(\exists x)(\exists y)fxy]$'.[13]

Fogelin then concludes: "if we begin with the functions fxy or $\text{-}fxy$ and apply the operator N directly to them, four members of the family of multiply-general propositions can be generated, four of them cannot."[14] It is incredible, though obviously not impossible, to imagine that Wittgenstein, with his command of symbolic logic and criticism of the shortcomings of highly sophisticated logical systems like those of Frege and Whitehead and Russell, could have overlooked such a glaring incompleteness in his own efforts to describe a principle as important to his logic as the general form of proposition.

Wittgenstein's general form of proposition on reflection seems perfectly adequate to generate the mixed multiple quantifications about which Fogelin is concerned. It is true that beginning only with fxy (or $\text{-}fxy$, which we can directly obtain from fxy by negation), we can only generate the four homogeneous quantifications in (1), (2), (5), and (6). But why suppose as Fogelin does that Wittgenstein has only fxy or $\text{-}fxy$ to work with? Along with fully variable function fxy that emerges in the output of the general form or proposition when N is successively applied to ξ, we also have such function-constant constructions as *faa, fba,* etc. Now assume that we jointly negate these formulas in a particular sequence to produce:

~faa, ~fab, ~fac, . . .; ~fba, ~fbb, ~fbc, . . .; ~fca, ~fcb, ~fcc, . . .; . . .

By Fogelin's description of Wittgenstein's method, which is correct as far as it goes, we obtain from this the further partially quantified sequence:

~(∃y)fay, ~(∃y)fby, ~(∃y)fcy, . . .

Applying Fogelin's interpretation of joint negation in Wittgenstein's general form of proposition to the above series, there results: *~(∃x)~(∃y)fxy*. This in turn is equivalent by quantifier duality to *(∀x)(∃y)fxy*, which is none other than mixed multiple dyadic quantification (3). Negating this by another application of Wittgenstein's N operator gives us *~(∀x)(∃y)fxy*, from which by duality it follows first that *(∃x)~(∃y)fxy*, and then *(∃x)(∀y)~fxy*, which is mixed multiple quantification (8). To produce (7) and (4), we proceed in similar fashion, starting with the sequence obtained from the above by first using N to negate each item:

faa, fab, fac, . . .; fba, fbb, fbc, . . .; fca, fcb, fcc, . . .; . . .

From this we obtain:

~(∃y)~fay, ~(∃y)~fby, ~(∃y)~fcy, . . .

By the same operation again: *~(∃x)~(∃y)~fxy*. This can then be simplified by quantifier duality to yield *(∀x)(∃y)~fxy*, which is mixed multiple quantification (7) from Fogelin's list. To negate this by Wittgenstein's operator N gives us *~(∀x)(∃y)~fxy*, and by the same process, we obtain first *(∃x)~(∃y)~fxy*, and then *(∃x)(∀y)fxy*, which is mixed multiple quantification (4). Fogelin, in conclusion, does not seem to understand the full flexibility of Wittgenstein's general form of proposition, and discovers only the limitations he wrongly imposes on it.[15]

Finally, Wittgenstein's logic in the *Tractatus* is not subject to Gödel's limiting metatheorems. Gödel proves that all standard first-order logics with arithmetic are either syntactically inconsistent or deductively incomplete, because in any such system it is possible to construct true but formally unprovable sentences.[16] The *Tractatus* by contrast describes an untyped logic, in which the right ordering of syntax items in a logically correct sign or transcendent symbol system is guaranteed by the picture theory.[17] The only genuine propositions picture logically contingent facts, while tautology and contradiction show under truth table analysis that they are respectively logically true and logically false. A picture cannot say anything about itself, for then it would need to include a fact-structure larger than itself, including both a logical self-portrait and a representation of the property it purports to predicate or deny. Wittgenstein's semantics and general form of proposition prohibit the construction of self-referential sentences that say of themselves that they are unprovable, which prevents Gödel's theorem from delimiting the theory's transcendent logic.[18]

We would need a very powerful logic, such as Whitehead and Russell's *Principia Mathematica,* the target of Gödel's proof, in order to formulate Gödel sentences.[19] Wittgenstein's logic involves conjunction alone as the only formal operation by which the world can be completely described. The logic at base is therefore not even fully propositional, let alone irreducibly predicate-quantificational, let alone, as Gödel's proof requires, irreducibly predicate-quantificational with a classical infinitary arithmetic involving identity, addition, and multiplication. The identity sign, needed by Gödel's proof for the reflexive numerical coding of syntax, is superfluous in a correct logical notation, according to 5.533 and 6.232. The presumed function of the identity sign is fulfilled instead by what the correct use of names in a proposition shows about the identity or nonidentity of corresponding objects, recalling that by 4.1212 what *can* be shown *cannot* be said.[20] Wittgenstein regards sign systems with irreducible negation, quantifiers, or identity, as logically incorrect languages, opening themselves unnecessarily to logical troubles by trying to say what cannot be said.[21] In this way, Wittgenstein anticipates and develops a nonclassical logic that avoids the kind of difficulties later posed by Gödel's 1931 theorems.[22]

I NOTES

1. Black 1964, 215: "K_n : has the value 2^n." Wittgenstein may use the complicated integral-sum formula in 4.27 because he finds it more informative in displaying the values that enter into the calculation of the possible combinations of atomic facts.
2. Wittgenstein uses Georg Cantor's symbol '$\aleph_0$' to designate the first order of infinity. This is the cardinality, for example, of the infinite number of positive integers 1,2,3, ... Cantor 1966, 278–81; Cantor 1952; Huntington 1917, 63–80.
3. Wittgenstein's term is *'unsinnig'*. This should be translated as 'nonsensical', not 'senseless' (*sinnlos*), as the Ogden edition has it. See Wittgenstein's discussion of the distinction between *sinnlos* and *unsinnig* in 4.461–4.4611.
4. See 6.54. Wittgenstein's attitude toward the *Tractatus* as a heuristic ladder of nonsensical pseudopropositions is examined in chapter 6.
5. Frege 1970, 63: "We are therefore driven into accepting the *truth value* of a sentence as constituting its reference. By the truth

value of a sentence I understand the circumstance that it is true or false. There are no further truth values. For brevity I call the one the True, and the other the False. Every declarative sentence concerned with the reference of its words is therefore to be regarded as a proper name, and its reference, if it has one, is either the True or the False. These two objects are recognized, if only implicitly, by everybody who judges something to be true—and so even by a sceptic."

6. See Wittgenstein *Notebooks* 5.6.15; 6.6.15: "In order for a proposition to be capable of being true it must also be capable of being false. Why does tautology say nothing? Because every possibility is admitted in it in advance. . . . One cannot say of a tautology that it is true, for it is *made so as to be true.*" Compare Wittgenstein's remarks in his "Notes Dictated to G. E. Moore in Norway," from a meeting with Wittgenstein in April 1914, reprinted in *Notebooks,* appendix 2. Wittgenstein maintains, 108: "For so-called *proof* of a logical proposition does not prove its *truth* (logical propositions are neither true nor false) but proves *that* it is a logical proposition (= is a tautology)." Wittgenstein's *Notebooks* must be taken with a grain of salt in trying to understand his settled philosophical positions, as the editors warn in their preface, v: "It should not be used without more ado as evidence for particular interpretations of the *Tractatus.*" Wittgenstein seems to have changed his mind fundamentally about the nature of tautology and contradiction between 1914, 1915, and the time of the *Prototractatus* and *Tractatus* in 1918.

7. In 4.53, Wittgenstein proclaims that the general form of proposition must satisfy his adequacy requirements in 4.1273 for a formal concept defined as a variable formal series. See also 2.2522 and 5.521.

8. Sheffer 1913. Nicod 1917. Russell in his introduction to Wittgenstein's *Tractatus* 13–14 writes: "It has been shown by Dr. Sheffer (*Trans. Am. Math. Soc.,* Vol. XIV, pp. 481–488) that all truth-functions of a given set of propositions can be constructed out of either of the two functions 'not-p or not-q' or 'not-p and not-q'. Wittgenstein makes use of the latter, assuming a knowledge of Dr. Sheffer's work." The Sheffer stroke, however, is defined as disjoint negation, and the Nicod dagger function as joint negation—in effect, Wittgenstein's N-operator. Wittgenstein in 5.1311 assimilates the Sheffer stroke as the notation for joint negation, more properly represented by the Nicod dagger.

9. This aspect of Wittgenstein's philosophical semantics in the *Tractatus,* as several commentators have observed, is reminiscent of Kant's delimitation of the bounds of sense in the *Critique of Pure Reason.* Pears 1987, 1, 3–4: "The simplest general characterization of [Wittgenstein's] philosophy is that it is critical in the Kantian sense of that word. Kant offered a critique of thought and Wittgenstein offers a critique of the expression of thought in language. . . . Philosophy must draw the line that limits the legitimate uses of the intellect, including its own rather special brand of thought." Stenius, 214–20.

10. See Black 1964, 203–5.

11. 4.0312: "My fundamental thought is that the 'logical constants' do not represent. That the *logic* of the facts cannot be represented."

12. Fogelin 1987, 78.

13. Ibid.

14. Ibid., 79.

15. See further discussion of the limitations of Wittgenstein's N operator in Geach 1981; 1982; Fogelin 1982; Soames 1983. My proposal for recovering mixed multiple quantifications in polyadic predicate-quantification logic by Wittgenstein's general form of proposition is similar to that suggested to Fogelin by Robert Stalnaker in Fogelin 1976, 71–72, eliminated from the second edition.

16. Gödel 1931.

17. 3.331–3.333. See also Wittgenstein *Notebooks,* appendix 1 ("Notes on Logic"), 105–6: "No proposition can say anything about itself, because the symbol of the proposition cannot be contained in itself; this must be the basis of the theory of logical types. . . . A proposition cannot occur in itself. This is the fundamental truth of the theory of types." Wittgenstein's dissatisfaction with Russell's theory of types is indicated already in his letter to Russell (R9), 1974b, January 1913, 19: "I think that there cannot be different Types of things! In other words whatever can be symbolized by a simple proper name must belong to one type. And further: every theory of types must be rendered superfluous by a proper theory of the symbolism." Russell's theory of types is explained in chapter 6. The idea is to avoid certain paradoxes in logic by stratifying all syntax items into particular orders (0 for objects, 1 for properties of objects, 2 for properties of properties, etc.), and then restricting well-formed syntax combinations so that only higher types of order $n+1$ can apply to lower types of order n.

18. Black 1964, 225: "Since the world could be completely described in a language containing only primitive negation-free propositions, the presence of negation in any language we use merely shows that *we* have chosen a more indirect form of representation." But on 181 Black writes: "[4.0621] . . . means simply that the negation sign is not a *name*—that negation is not an object. It does not mean that the negation sign does no work and could be dispensed with." The distinction I have emphasized is that negation is essential for the general form of proposition, but not for the logic of propositions, where the general form of proposition as the mathematical expression of a formal concept is not itself a proposition.

19. The title of Gödel's 1931 paper refers to *Principia Mathematica* 'and related systems' (*und verwandte Systeme*). Among the limitations of Wittgenstein's logic that preserves it against Gödel's theorem is that the *Tractatus* does not allow intensional contexts, such as those required for Gödel sentences and Gödel numbering functions of the form $g(\lceil . . . \rceil) = n$. These contexts are intensional because they do not accept intersubstitutions *salva veritate* of logically equivalent expressions with different syntax-item-for-syntax-item Gödel numbers. An obvious example is where $((p \vee \sim p) \equiv (p \supset p))$ & $g(\lceil p \vee \sim p \rceil) \neq g(\lceil p \supset p \rceil)$. See Auerbach 1985 for a different explanation of the intensionality of Gödel's theorem. Nor does it avail to claim that Gödel constructions belong to a metalanguage about the *Tractatus* logic, since Wittgenstein's picture theory forbids object- and metalanguage stratifications just as it forbids hierarchical types or syntax orderings.

20. Gödel's proof gets around Russell's type theory restrictions by arithmetizing the syntax of logic. A sentence with code number G is constructed that says (of itself) that the sentence with code number G is unprovable. Wittgenstein's picture theory of meaning also disallows Gödel's indirect mode of self-non-application. The Gödel sentence requires an unprovability predicate, which Gödel originally expresses as '*Bew*' for the German '*unbeweisbar*' (unprovable). A sentence is constructed within which the sentence we obtain by substituting the corresponding syntax for the Gödel-coded number G is said to have the property of being unprovable: $\overline{Bew}(sub(G))$ & $g(\ulcorner\overline{Bew}(sub(G))\urcorner) = G$. The objection Wittgenstein might raise is that according to the picture theory, the predicate '$\overline{Bew}$' cannot occur because it does not represent anything. Whether or not a proposition is provable is not something that can be said, because it can be shown, as Wittgenstein affirms in 6.112–6.1221. He also writes in 6.1265: "Logic can always be conceived to be such that every proposition is its own proof"; and in 6.127: "All propositions of logic are of equal rank; there are not some which are essentially primitive and others deduced from these. Every tautology itself shows that it is a tautology." When we put this together with 4.1212, that "What *can* be shown *cannot* be said", we see that the picture theory forbids Gödel sentence constructions. An additional though possibly less serious problem concerns the extent to which Gödel requires the identity sign ('=') in specifying that the arithmetical code of the unprovable sentence, since we know from 5.473, 5.533, 6.232, and 6.2322 that Wittgenstein regards the identity sign as having no proper place in a correct logical notation. Fogelin 1987 claims that Gödel's proof defeats the *Tractatus* logic, 82: "I consider Wittgenstein's account of the status of logical propositions central to the vision of the *Tractatus*. That this vision eventually proved incapable of realization does not diminish its significance. Indeed, the theorems of Gödel and Church are important precisely because they deny an idea of great profundity." Wittgenstein was unimpressed by Gödel's proof even after he had abandoned the picture theory of meaning. See Wittgenstein 1983, 118–22.

21. See Presburger 1930; Jacquette 1991. Presburger's subarithmetic avoids Gödel's incompleteness results and is deductively as well as descriptively complete. The fact that Presburger's subarithmetic with addition but without multiplication is demonstrably complete points to the role of infinity assumptions as essential to a classical arithmetic. The reason is that multiplication is otherwise fully reducible to addition in the finite case. Whitehead and Russell's *Principia Mathematica* assumes an extralogical axiom of infinity in order to guarantee its application to classical arithmetic. Whitehead and Russell 1925–27, 2, 183: "Infin ax. = : $\alpha \in$ NC induct. $\supset$. $\exists!\alpha$ Df. This assumption, like the multiplicative axiom, will be adduced as a hypothesis whenever it is relevant. It seems plain that there is nothing in logic to necessitate its truth or falsehood, and that it can only be legitimately believed or disbelieved on empirical grounds." Wittgenstein criticizes the axiom of infinity in 5.535. Russell in his introduction to the *Tractatus* accordingly seems far from the mark when he writes, 21: "There are some respects, in which, as it seems to me, Mr. Wittgenstein's theory stands in need of greater technical development. This applies in particular to his theory of number (6.02 ff.) which, as it stands, is only capable of dealing with finite numbers. No logic can be considered adequate until it has been shown to be capable of dealing with transfinite numbers. I do not think there is anything in Mr. Wittgenstein's system to make it impossible for him to fill this lacuna."

22. See also Anscombe, 113–39; Black 1964, 212–90; Caruthers 1989; Finch, 115–33; Fogelin 1987, 39–85; Hackstaff 1966; Kenny 1973, 19–102; Leblanc 1972; Maslow 1961, 95–136; Miller 1995.

Transcendence of the Metaphysical Subject

The general form of proposition has unexpected consequences for psychology. Wittgenstein argues that the logic of propositions entails the extraworldly transcendence of propositional attitudes, psychological states, and the self, soul, or metaphysical subject. The transcendence of the metaphysical subject leads Wittgenstein to acknowledge the unsayable insights of a transcendent solipsism, as opposed to a more prosaic empiricist skepticism about the existence of other minds.

There are two categories of propositions. The picture theory of meaning recognizes meaningful propositions as logical pictures of facts, and admits senseless tautologies and contradictions only as limiting cases. *Tractatus* 5 maintains that all propositions are truth functions of the elementary propositions, and that even the elementary propositions are truth functions of themselves. The general form of proposition is supposed to comprehend all (and only) the propositions of any logically possible language by the truth-functional operation of selective joint negation. But there also seem to be non-truth-functional contexts in which propositions are constructed out of other propositions. So-called propositional attitudes purport to express a subject's psychological states of belief, doubt, hope, fear, and the like, toward a proposition or state of affairs.

If we begin with the proposition 'It is raining', then we can build up more complex propositions by plugging the proposition into propositional attitude contexts. By this method we obtain, among many others, 'Hans believes that it is raining', 'Kurt doubts that it is raining', 'Hermine hopes that it is raining', 'Gretl fears that it is raining'. Such sentences appear to describe a subject's psychological state of belief, doubt, hope, fear, in assuming a propositional attitude toward the proposition or state of affairs that it is raining. The truth or falsehood of these sentences is not a truth function of the truth or falsehood of the embedded proposition, 'It is raining', because whether it is true or false that it is raining, Hans might still either believe or not believe, Kurt doubt or not doubt, Hermine hope or not hope, and Gretl fear or not fear that it is raining. There is in other words no truth function from the truth value of 'It is raining' to the truth value of 'Hans believes that it is raining'. The non-truth-functionality of propositional attitudes challenges the adequacy of the general form of proposition to define all propositions by purely truth-functional operations, and thereby to express, as Wittgenstein's logic requires in 5.471–5.4711, the essence of proposition and of the world.[1]

Wittgenstein responds to the problem by eliminating propositional attitudes as logically meaningless. He proposes an analysis whereby subject terms and relational psychological attitude predicates are deleted from correct expressions of meaning in colloquial references to psychological states. Rejecting propositional attitude contexts as a distinct category of genuine non-truth-functional propositions removes them as counterexamples to the general form of proposition while it establishes the extraworldly transcendence of the metaphysical subject.

The general form of proposition implies that a proposition occurring within another proposition must fall within the scope of a truth-functional operator, like the joint negation operator N:

> 5.54   In the general propositional form, propositions
> occur in a proposition only as bases of the truth-
> operations.

Wittgenstein acknowledges the existence of non-truth-functional proposition-building contexts that seem to contradict the general form of proposition. These are the sentences Russell refers to as propositional attitudes, including the belief, doubt, hope, fear, and other psychological states a subject might assume toward a proposition. The subject, A, in this model, appears to stand in an external psychological relation to a proposition, p, by thinking it or thinking something about it, as in Thinks(A,p):

> 5.541   At first sight it appears as if there were also a
> different way in which one proposition could occur
> in another.
>
> Especially in certain propositional forms of psychol-
> ogy, like "A thinks, that p is the case", or "A thinks
> p", etc.

Here it appears superficially as if the proposition p
stood to the object A in a kind of relation.

(And in modern epistemology (Russell, Moore, etc.)
those propositions have been conceived in this way.)

The relational theory is a plausible explanation of judgment.
The idea that thinking subjects are related to propositions by their
psychological attitudes is a natural way to understand intentional
states. Yet the relational account contradicts Wittgenstein's picture
theory of meaning and the general form of proposition, because a
sentence of the form Thinks(A,p) expresses a proposition that is not
a truth function of proposition p.

Consider a propositional attitude context of the most general
sort. Where ψ is any propositional attitude (thinks, believes,
doubts, hopes, fears, etc.), A any thinking subject and p any
proposition, then the truth or falsehood of $\psi(A,p)$ does not truth-
functionally depend on whether or not p is true or false, and is
therefore not a truth function of p. From the fact that it is (or is
not) raining it does not follow that I believe, doubt, hope, or fear
that it is (or is not) raining, or that I think anything whatsoever
about it. If there are logically irreducible propositional attitude
contexts for non-truth-functional propositions of the form
$\psi(A, [\_\_])$, completed by plugging propositions into the blank
space, then there are genuine propositions that are not truth
functions of the elementary propositions.

Wittgenstein's solution is to analyze propositional attitudes
away. He argues that propositional attitude contexts do not occur
in a correct logical notation, and concludes that propositional attitude contexts merely appear superficially to involve a coordination of a fact with an object, the thinker as object and the fact
about which the thinker is supposed to have a psychological attitude. He claims that putative propositional attitude contexts
have instead the logical form of non-propositional-attitude coordinations of facts by means of coordinations of their objects. He
tries to avoid the propositional attitude objection to the general
form of proposition by this reduction:

5.542   But it is clear that "A believes that p", "A thinks p",
         "A says p", are of the form "'p' says p": and here we
         have no co-ordination of a fact and an object, but a
         co-ordination of facts by means of a co-ordination of
         their objects.

The proposal is that propositional attitude contexts are ines-
sential to the underlying symbolism of a correct logical notation.
In giving "'p' says p" as the logical form alike of "A believes that p",
"A thinks p", "A says p", the subject term 'A' for whoever believes,

thinks, or says, vanishes, and the propositional attitude or transitive psychological state terms 'believes', 'thinks', etc., are replaced by the universal semantic term 'says'. This term also disappears under the picture theory of meaning, where 'p' by picturing p shows and so by 4.1212 cannot say that 'p' says that p.

Wittgenstein says that 'A believes that p', 'A thinks p', 'A says p', and, in 5.5422, 'A judges p' are *all of the same form*. Does this mean that there is no formal logical distinction between believing and doubting a proposition? Whether p is believed or doubted seems to be an ordinary fact of the world involving distinct psychological occurrences. A subject's having a particular propositional attitude appears to be a fact of the sort Wittgenstein regards as describable, about which things can legitimately be said. According to the *Tractatus,* all this is an illusion. Wittgenstein remarks in 5.541, with emphasis: "*At first sight it appears as if* there were also a different [non-truth-functional] way in which one proposition could occur in another," and "*Here it appears superficially as if* the proposition p stood to the object A in a kind of relation." Propositional attitudes leave the facts of the world just as they are; whether proposition p is believed or doubted does nothing to alter the fact that p. If propositional attitude contexts, like 'A believes that p' and 'A doubts that p', are identical in underlying symbolic logical structure, having the same form, 'p' says $p,$ then the two 'superficial' elements of the construction disappear as superfluous under picture theory analysis. A subject's belief or doubt about p is not a fact of the world to be pictured in a genuine proposition. The subject and the subject's psychological states of believing, doubting, and the like, are eliminated when propositional attitude sentences are properly analyzed.

The principle by which Wittgenstein abolishes colloquial terms for subjects and their propositional attitudes is introduced as an interpretation of Occam's razor. The only need for a term in language is to name an object or picture a fact. Unnecessary signs in a formal symbolism are logically meaningless and as such fail to designate any possible entity:

> 3.328 If a sign is *not necessary* then it is meaningless.
> That is the meaning of Occam's razor.

> 5.47321 Occam's razor is, of course, not an arbitrary rule nor one justified by its practical success. It simply says that *unnecessary* elements in a symbolism mean nothing.
>
> Signs which serve *one* purpose are logically equivalent, signs which serve *no* purpose are logically meaningless.

If, according to the picture theory, putative subject term 'A' and propositional attitude or psychological state term 'ψ' are not absolutely needed in expressing the sense that is supposed to be communicated by propositional attitude context ψ(A, [__]), then ψ(A,p) is logically meaningless. When a sentence of the form ψ(A,p) is analyzed according to the picture theory, the essence of what the sentence tries to express is reducible to another sentence of the form 'p' says that p, or simply 'p'.

Wittgenstein concludes that the logic of non-truth-functional propositional attitudes involves a correlation of the elements of signs with the elements of what they signify, rather than an expression of a particular attitudinal relation between a subject and a proposition. What occurs when, as we would otherwise like to say, a subject thinks a proposition or thinks something about a proposition, is the use of a sign for the proposition. The correlation of sign and fact is all that psychological sentences (mistakenly) try to convey. If the showing forth of identical logical form between sign and fact signified can be accomplished without using psychological subject terms, then subject terms and propositional attitude or psychological state terms are inessential to language, and hence, by Wittgenstein's application of Occam's razor, logically meaningless. Wittgenstein eliminates propositional attitude contexts as counterexamples to the general form of proposition, and rejects attempts to describe the self, soul, or subject and its psychological states as nonsense.[2]

Wittgenstein does not deny that thinking occurs. In 3.11, thinking the sense of a proposition is understood as the method of directionally projecting facts onto other logically isomorphic facts. The thought is a picture of reality, according to 3–3.1, and facts are pictured by thoughts in the projection of sense. But where if anywhere in the world does thought occur, and where if anywhere in the world is the thinking psychological subject? Does thought reside within or outside the world of facts? We may speculate that the pictorial form of representation in a proposition, holding as a coordination of facts by means of a coordination of their elements, also occurs as a mental state or neurophysiological event in the brain and nervous system. In a letter to Russell from Cassino, dated 19 August 1919, Wittgenstein writes: "I don't know *what* the constituents of a thought are but I know *that* it must have such constituents which correspond to the words of Language. Again the kind of relation of the constituents of thought and of the pictured fact is irrelevant. It would be a matter of psychology to find out."[3] Thoughts, like propositions, are pictures of facts by virtue of their logical isomorphism with the deep logical structures of the facts they represent. The logical form of a thought according to Wittgenstein is that which a mental or neurophysiological picturing shares with the facts it pictures. From a logical point of view, a thought is exactly like a linguistic propositional symbol, with the same underlying logical form, 'p' *says that p*. The subject and the subject's propositional attitudes toward the pictured fact are excluded as inessential to meaning.

All judgments about proposition p are reducible to the formula 'p' says that p. Propositional attitudes have no deeper logical structure reflecting a relation between a thinking subject and a proposition. Wittgenstein states that despite appearances such sentences do not involve the coordination of a fact (constituted or represented by the fact-picturing fact 'p') and an object (subject A). There is rather a coordination of facts (the fact-picturing fact 'p' and the fact p pictured by 'p') by means of a coordination of their objects (concatenations of simple names in elementary propositions, and juxtapositions of the simple objects to which the names refer in corresponding atomic facts).

To understand Wittgenstein's position, we must reconsider the distinction between perceptible sign and imperceptible symbol. What looks to be the fact that subject A believes or doubts that p is merely the fact that a propositional sign 'p' that says p is instantiated in thought. Although the picture theory requires that there be such constituents, the medium by virtue of which a psychological occurrence pictures facts is not a topic for logic or philosophical semantics, but for psychology as an empirical science. When, as we say, A believes or doubts that p, a mental or psychological event takes place that serves as a logical picture 'p' expressing the fact that p. Such an event can have a causal influence on the future course of world events. Whether I believe or doubt that my credit card is overdrawn can make a difference in what I do. But this is a matter of causal interconnectedness between facts, and not a difference relevant to pure logic in philosophical semantics. In addition to the picturing of p by 'p', there is no believing or doubting, and no subject that believes or doubts, as facts or objects belonging to the world.[4]

Propositional attitude is epiphenomenal. Wittgenstein regards it as a necessary consequence of his eliminative treatment of propositional attitude contexts that there can be no sayable distinctions between belief, doubt, hope, fear, love, hate, or expectation. The facts about which belief, doubt, and other propositional attitudes are assumed can be described, as can the mental state or neurophysiology associated with the occurrence of thinking. But the existence of a metaphysical subject, and the subject's belief or doubt, are not among the sayable describable world-constituting facts. The one-one coordination of picturing-fact and pictured-fact by means of one-one coordinations of their elements does away with the intuitive justification for propositional attitude contexts as distinct forms of facts involving genuine propositions irreducible to purely extensional operations in truth-functional contexts.[5] Wittgenstein's application of Occam's razor eliminates thinking subjects and propositional attitudes from the things and facts of the world only if he is correct in analyzing the real underlying symbolic logical form of $\psi(A,p)$ as 'p' says that p, for such colloquial expressions as 'A believes that p', 'A doubts that p', 'A hopes that p', 'A fears that p'. If the subject and the subject's psychology belong to the world, then the deep logical form of propositional attitude contexts must also include terms for thinkers and attitudes. How can we determine whether subject sign 'A' and propositional attitude sign 'ψ' in propositional attitude context $\psi(A,p)$ are necessary or superfluous? What considerations might lead us to accept Wittgenstein's reduction of 'superficial' subject and attitude signs to uncover the real underlying logical structure of putative propositional attitudes by replacing $\psi(A,p)$ with p or 'p' says that p? Why should we give up reference to the subject and the subject's intentional states in the logical analysis of ordinary language statements that appear to describe propositional attitudes?

We make to ourselves pictures of facts. We do so by thinking the sense of a proposition in projecting a fact onto another logically isomorphic facts by which it is pictured. If thinking the sense of a proposition were itself among the facts of the world, then there would be an infinite regress of thinking facts that would preclude the determinate meaningfulness of language. Thinking as a projection from picture to pictured fact gives meaning to propositional sign 'p'. But if thinking is itself a fact, q, then the meaning of 'p' is not fixed unless or until the meaning of 'q' is fixed. If the occurrence of q is a fact by which the determinate meaning of 'p' is explained, then Wittgenstein's semantics must also provide an interpretation for proposition 'q'. The meaning of 'q' is fixed according to the picture theory in the same way only by thinking the sense of propositional sign 'q' to project that fact onto the fact that q. If this thinking is itself a fact, r, then the meaning of 'q' is not fixed unless or until the meaning of 'r' is fixed. And so on, indefinitely. The result is that the meaning of proposition 'p' cannot be fixed if a subject's thinking the sense of '*p*' is itself among the facts of the world. If the point of a general philosophical semantics is to explain the possibility of the determinate meaningfulness of language, then the theory cannot allow such indefinite semantic regress.

If the world is to be the same object of distinct epistemic attitudes, then it must remain unaltered by the thoughts thinking subjects may have concerning it, to preserve its referential identity. It must be the very same world about which a thinker is able alternatively to believe or disbelieve, and morally or aesthetically approve or disapprove. The epistemic, moral, and aesthetic attitudes of thinkers toward the world are thus epiphenomenal thoughts that transcend and are not included as a part or among the facts of any logically possible world. Suppose the world contains only three facts, *p*, *q*, *r*. I can believe or doubt, approve or disapprove of all or any one of these facts, and thus believe or doubt, approve or disapprove of the world. Now suppose that the world also contains the fact of my belief. Then the world contains facts *p*, *q*, *r*, plus my belief, *b*. In that case, I do not merely believe *p*, *q*, *r*, but *p*, *q*, *r*, *b*. The trouble in part is that belief *b* cannot be about *p*, *q*, *r*, *b*, for then impossibly it would have to contain within itself a complete picture of itself with all its own internal logical structure, along with pictures of *p*, *q*, and *r*. The picture theory forbids self-referential picturing by requiring exact logical isomorphisms between picturing and pictured facts (3.332; 4.442). If *p*, *q*, *r*, *b* is the world I believe in, rather than *p*, *q*, *r*, moreover, then I cannot doubt the same thing. If I doubt the existence of the world, and if psychological states are part of the world, then presumably I doubt *d* the existence of a different world, *p*, *q*, *r*, *d*. If propositional attitudes are among the facts of the world, then I cannot, for example, alternatively believe or doubt the same world's existence. Propositional attitudes must therefore stand outside the world of facts in order to regard them and assume different attitudes about them from a vantage point with the necessary logical distance. Belief, doubt, hope, fear, and other propositional attitudes appear superficially to be facts of the world, on a par with other facts, including facts about the psychological states of thinking subjects. Wittgenstein's picture theory implies that despite appearances to the contrary propositional attitudes cannot possibly be numbered among the facts of the world.[6]

The most interesting conclusion of Wittgenstein's elimination of propositional attitude contexts is that the self or soul, understood in popular psychology as an agent of will and subject of experience, does not exist:

> 5.5421   This shows that there is no such thing as the soul—
> the subject, etc.— as it is conceived in contempo-
> rary superficial psychology.
>
> A composite soul would not be a soul any longer.

The first and simplest, but not necessarily most informative, reconstruction of this argument is that the self, soul, or subject as we ordinarily think of it does not exist because, then, *per impossibile,* it would have to be something composite (*zusammengesetzt,* literally put or set together). To follow Wittgenstein's objection, we need to understand what he means by the concept of the subject or soul 'as it is conceived in contemporary superficial psychology', and why he thinks that the soul cannot be composite.

How *is* the soul or subject conceived in contemporary superficial psychology? Wittgenstein names no names and mentions no particular theories. It is pointless to begin by supposing that the soul or subject is whatever we ordinarily mean by these words, since, until we have seen the argument, we have no reason to suppose our ordinary concept faulty. Who in philosophy, psychology, or out on the street thinks that the soul is composite? Some philosophers and psychologists say yes; others no. Wittgenstein accuses traditional psychology of being unknowingly committed to an inconsistent concept whereby the self, soul, or subject is both absolutely simple and complex. The traditional idea of the psychological subject is mistaken because it regards the soul as an essentially unitary thinking entity in the world. The metaphysics of logical atomism implies that anything unitary must be simple, while the picture theory requires thought in picturing facts and by implication the subject of thought to possess the same internal complexity as the facts it pictures.

"A composite soul," says 5.5421, "would not be a soul any longer." Why does Wittgenstein maintain that the self, soul, or subject, contrary to the assumptions of superficial psychology, must be absolutely simple? The concept of the subject as an essentially unified thing is a requirement of many theories of mind, notably of Descartes's substance dualism and Kant's doctrine of the transcendental unity of apperception.[7] Wittgenstein seems to accept the essential unity of the soul as an analytic truth, which he takes as the basis for a dilemma against superficial psychology. If the soul as thinking subject belongs to the world, then it must either be an atomic fact (*Sachverhalt*), an ordinary fact (*Tatsache*), a simple object, or complex entity. Ordinary facts and complex entities have no essential unity, but according to logical atomism are constituted by and reducible to copresences of logically independent atomic facts. The soul as an essential unity, as a result, cannot be a complex fact or entity. If, on the other hand, the soul is an atomic fact or simple object, then it lacks the necessary internal articulation of structure, the logical form or mathematical multiplicity, necessary for its thoughts to picture facts. The soul as thinker of thoughts, therefore, cannot be a simple object or atomic fact. The only alternative, which Wittgenstein embraces, is that the self, soul, or subject as an essential unity transcends the world of facts, and is not the structurally complex thinker of thoughts known to superficial empirical psychology or phenomenology.[8]

The contradiction inherent in the idea of the subject as a unitary entity with sufficient internal structure to represent the facts of the world in thought and language is revealed only against the background of Wittgenstein's logical atomism and picture theory of meaning. Traditional psychology and metaphysics are blithely unaware of the inconsistency because they lack an adequate understanding of the logic of language. The composite soul as thinking entity in the world of facts would no longer be an essentially unified soul in the required sense. If it were composite by virtue of having the internal logical isomorphism or identical mathematical multiplicity with the facts it pictures, then it could not be essentially unitary. As an ephemeral ensemble of ontically independent atomic facts, by hypothesis, it would lack the essential interdependence of parts presupposed by the traditional concept of the thinking subject in 'contemporary superficial psychology'.

If the self, soul, or subject cannot be part of the world, then it must be transcendent. Wittgenstein, in company especially with Kant and Schopenhauer, concludes that the metaphysical subject transcends the world:[9]

5.621 The world and life are one.

5.63   I am my world. (The microcosm.)

5.631 The thinking, presenting subject; there is no such thing.

If I wrote a book "The world as I found it", I should also have therein to report on my body and say which members obey my will and which do not, etc. This then would be a method of showing that in an important sense there is no subject: that is to say, of it alone in this book mention could *not* be made.

5.632 The subject does not belong to the world but it is a limit of the world.

Wittgenstein seems to adopt a subjectivist viewpoint. He says that the world and life are one and the subject is the (I am my) world. He maintains that the subject is not part of the world, and, unlike the body and its parts, is not among the facts of the world to be discovered, but is rather a limit of the world. What do these assertions mean, and how are they supposed to follow from Wittgenstein's rejection of propositional attitude contexts as counterexamples to the general form of proposition?

Wittgenstein is correct to infer that if subject terms are logically meaningless because they are logically unnecessary in a correct logical notation, and if an essentially unified self, soul, or subject cannot be either a complex (not essentially unified) nor an atomic fact nor simple object (not complex enough to picture the facts of the world in thought), then the soul or psychological subject as traditionally conceived is not a part of the world it transcends. The subject is rather a limit (*eine Grenze*) of the world, a single point of logical contact and epistemic access, like a hotel detective at the keyhole, spying on the world from outside. It is from this standpoint that the subject projects facts directionally onto logically isomorphic facts with the requisite mathematical multiplicity to picture the world of facts in thought and language. Wittgenstein explains the relation of the metaphysical subject to the world of experience by means of an analogy about the relation between the eye and the visual field:

> 5.633 *Where in* the world is a metaphysical subject to be noted?
>
> You say that this case is altogether like that of the eye and the field of sight. But you do *not* really see the eye.
>
> And from nothing *in the field of sight* can it be concluded that it is seen from an eye.
>
> 5.6331 For the field of sight has not a form like this:

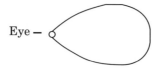

Wittgenstein describes the transcendent subject as a limit of the world. In a similar way, the eye transcends but is a limit point of contact that gives access to the visual field. Even in a mirror, the eye sees itself only reflectively, as the transcendent subject may acquire some indirect notion of itself by self-reflection. Yet in the visual field as in the field of consciousness and of the self's experience of the world generally, the eye and the subject are not directly encountered, but are rather the transcendent ground for the possibility of any visual impression or psychological occurrence that lies outside them to behold.

Wittgenstein continues the analogy by remarking the logical contingency of every fact and every existence in the world and the insight that anything we see might be different than it happens to appear:

> 5.634   This is connected with the fact that no part of our experience is also a priori.
>
> Everything we see could also be otherwise.
>
> Everything we can describe at all could also be otherwise.
>
> There is no order of things a priori.

If the self were a part of the world, as in traditional superficial psychology, then there would be at least some logically necessary truths about the world—namely, a priori knowledge of the existence of the self whenever thought occurs, as in Descartes's *Cogito, ergo sum* (I think, therefore I am). Yet it is a consequence of the picture theory of meaning that anything seen, any fact of the world expressed in thought or language, can be otherwise than it is—the world is only whatever *happens* to be the case.[10]

If I cannot describe the world except as my world (and what else can I describe but my experience?), then there is no a priori experience, including especially the self's experience of its own thinking. If we suppose with Descartes that the world contains the self as thinking entity, then we mistakenly transform at least some logically contingent facts in and about the world into logically necessary or impossible facts that Wittgenstein insists must be excluded from the world by a correct theory of meaning. From Wittgenstein's standpoint, though he does not mention Descartes, it is clear that the rationalist project of establishing the necessary existence of the self or ego in the world of facts, and then deducing the consequences that must follow as a priori truths about the world, is doomed to failure. The rationalist program for an absolutely certain foundationalist epistemology is radically misconceived because of its failure to understand the logic that connects thought and language with the world.[11]

Wittgenstein is now in a position to consider the problem of solipsism. The term 'solipsism' denotes the nonexistence or inability to know the existence of minds other than one's own. Solipsism can be the claim that there definitely exist no other minds, that I cannot know whether there are any other minds, or that I have good reason positively to doubt the existence of other minds, all to varying degrees of epistemic certainty. Wittgenstein, as we might expect, pronounces solipsism offered as a positive philosophical doctrine to be unsayable nonsense. The possibility that there are no other minds or that I cannot know whether there are other minds arises only in the context of the traditional concept of the self, soul, or subject as an essentially unified thinking thing within the world. It is only from this perspective that I can then ask whether there are many such things or only one, and whether I can know that there is more than one, or definitely know that there is no more than one. The questions and attempts to answer them, despite appearances, according to Wittgenstein, are logically meaningless.

What solipsism attempts to say, or what it so to speak would like to be able to say, Wittgenstein nevertheless accepts as a further consequence of the transcendence of the self as an extraworldly limit of the world. Wittgenstein writes:

> 5.6 *The limits of my language* mean the limits of my world.
>
> 5.61 Logic fills the world: the limits of the world are also its limits.
>
> We cannot therefore say in logic: This and this there is in the world, that there is not.
>
> For that would apparently presuppose that we exclude certain possibilities, and this cannot be the case since otherwise logic must get outside the limits of the world: that is, if it could consider these limits from the other side also.
>
> What we cannot think, that we cannot think: we cannot therefore *say* what we cannot think.

Here the *Tractatus* fulfills the promise of its preface to draw a limit to thinking by drawing an internal limit to the expression of thought. The distinction between what can and cannot be thought is bounded from the inside by the general form of proposition. What is thinkable is the class of genuine propositions forthcoming from the reiterative application of joint negation to the set of all elementary propositions. The picture theory of meaning guarantees that the limits of the world and the limits of language precisely coincide. The boundary of logical space is established by the requirements of adequately picturing the facts of the world in thought and language. Logic fills the world and defines its possibilities. The metaphysical subject is excluded as inessential to picturing facts. The subject's extraworldly transcendence thereby seems to entail a kind of solipsism. Wittgenstein continues:

5.62   This remark provides a key to the question, to what extent solipsism is a truth.

In fact, what solipsism *means,* is quite correct, only it cannot be *said,* but it shows itself.

That the world is *my* world, shows itself in the fact that the limits of the language (*the* language which I understand) mean the limits of *my* world.

The insight of solipsism is shown rather than said. The limits of language and world defined by the general form of proposition imply the transcendence of the metaphysical subject at the world's limit. The subject experiences the world, but does not encounter itself or any other subject as a part of the world. There is only the content of what the self thinks, the world the self experiences through its keyhole, the world as my world (or yours), with no other selves, souls, or subjects to be discerned anywhere in reality, where acquaintance with reality occurs only at a single limit point of access to the world:

5.64   Here we see that solipsism strictly carried out coincides with pure realism. The I in solipsism shrinks to an extensionless point and there remains the reality co-ordinated with it.

5.641   There is therefore really a sense in which in philosophy we can talk of a non-psychological I.

The I occurs in philosophy through the fact that the "world is my world".

The philosophical I is not the man, not the human body or the human soul of which psychology treats, but the metaphysical subject, the limit—not a part of the world.

Although solipsism as a metaphysical thesis cannot meaningfully be stated, it tries unsuccessfully to say something philosophically profound. Solipsism is not the positive proposition that I alone exist. Wittgenstein explains that in the literal sense, the self, soul, or subject does not exist either as a simple object or as an atomic or complex of facts or things in the world. I cannot exist alone in the world if I do not exist in the world at all. The conclusion that the I transcends the world, and that this is shown by the correct analysis of the logical form of pseudopropositions that pretend to predicate psychological states of subjects, that the I is no part of the world, makes the world circumscribed by the limits of my language my world. There is no other.[12]

Wittgenstein states that the I shrinks to the single transcendent point of access at the world's limit. What remains is pure realism, the facts of the world experienced by the transcendent metaphysical subject. Wittgenstein offers this account of solipsism as coincident with pure realism as a further consequence of the picture theory of meaning conclusion that there can be no a priori order of things. If the subject intrudes into the world of facts, then there is something a priori knowable about the contents of the world, as in Descartes's *Cogito,* that the necessary existence of the subject as belonging to the world can be known a priori from the occurrence of any thought, even under the most extreme logically possible basis for doubt. Yet there is nothing a priori knowable about the world as experienced from the limit access point of the transcendent metaphysical subject. Everything thinkable that can legitimately be described in the propositions of a logically possible language according to the picture theory of meaning can either be the case or not be the case. There are no logically necessary facts in the world, and hence no a priori knowable facts. This too unsayably implies an unsayable solipsism, in that the subject cannot be part of the world, but must transcend the world of contingent existent or nonexistent facts to which it has epistemic access only at a single limit that is not within and does not constitute any part of the world.[13]

Wittgenstein does not follow conventional solipsism in doubting or denying that other human beings have minds in the sense of experiencing thoughts in real time as fact-picturing mental or neurophysiological events. He would reject what by parity might be called contemporary superficial solipsism, just as he rejects contemporary superficial psychology. Wittgenstein's solipsism is rather a solipsism of the subject's logically unique extraworldly transcendence. Thus he has no trouble saying in 2.1 (emphasis added) not merely as a figure of speech, "*We* make to *ourselves* pictures of facts." But why is the world my world? Why are there not as many different metaphysical subjects understood as transcendent limits of the world as there are living persons? Why does Wittgenstein not allow heuristic talk of other transcendent subjects to show an equally unsayable truth by denying instead of affirming transcendent solipsism? Why does Wittgenstein not offer an analogical argument for the existence of other transcendent metaphysical subjects associated like the solipsist's with a living, properly functioning brain? The only explanation is that Wittgenstein's concept of transcendence precludes the application of identity principles by which things in the world of facts are individuated. This makes it nonsense to consider the possibility of there being more than one distinct transcendent subject. The world may be 'my' world, but it is not mine as opposed to yours.

The world does not belong to any particular personal empirical subject of superficial psychology, but to the impersonal undifferentiated extraworldly transcendent subject, the metaphysical, not the phenomenological 'I', at the limit of the world.[14]

In the course of defending the general form of proposition against counterexamples involving non-truth-functional propositional attitude contexts, Wittgenstein preserves the logic of the *Tractatus*. But he does much more. He presents an argument for the elimination of the subject and its propositional attitudes from the world, refutes the traditional conception of the subject as an essentially unified thinking entity in empirical psychology, proves the extraworldly transcendence of the metaphysical subject, offers a devastating critique of Cartesian epistemic foundationalism, and presents a picture theory interpretation of the unsayable pure realism of solipsism. The subject is not alone in the world, because the subject is not in the world at all; the self is a transcendent limit of the world, an ontic and epistemic singularity. The picture theory of meaning through the general form of proposition thus leads by a surprising series of twists and turns to the metaphysical isolation of a transcendent solipsism.[15]

I N O T E S

1. In an earlier draft of the *Tractatus,* Wittgenstein's elimination of propositional attitude contexts (and criticism of Russell's relational theory of judgment) in 5.54–5.5423, originally came immediately after the statement of the general form of proposition, as *Prototractatus* 6.001–6.0051. Wittgenstein 1971, 196–201.

2. The reduction of all propositional attitude contexts to the form '*p*' says that *p* makes even iterated propositional attitudes formally indistinguishable. The following sentences have precisely the same logical form in which subject and psychological state terms disappear under picture theory analysis: A believes that B doubts that *p;* A doubts that B believes that *p;* B believes that A doubts that *p;* B doubts that A believes that *p.* See Rosenberg 1968, 357: "The most obvious shortcoming of the Tractarian thesis, however, lies in Wittgenstein's complete inability to give an account of iterated *oratio obliqua* [on the grounds that] . . . Pierre says that Karl says that Johann loves Gretchen cannot be shown, because '. . . a formal fact cannot itself stand in semantic relations to other facts.'" Wittgenstein's analysis deletes all subject and psychological state terms as logically meaningless. This provides only a disappointing sense-preserving reduction of the sort Rosenberg seems to expect. Wittgenstein denies that sentences purporting to express propositional attitudes have any meaning to be preserved beyond that expressed by the genuine propositions they contain.

3. Wittgenstein 1974b, Letter (R37) to Russell 19.8.19. Wittgenstein adds: "Does a Gedanke consist of words? No! But of psychical constituents that have the same sort of relation to reality as words. What those constituents are I don't know."

4. Wittgenstein explains the irrelevance of causal connection to logic and philosophical semantics in 5.135–5.1362.

5. The importance of Wittgenstein's picture theory semantics in the elimination of propositional attitude contexts by absorption of their logical form is emphasized by Pears 1977, 189–95. Anscombe, 87–90, argues that Wittgenstein's "'*p*' says *p*" is significant, because it expresses a contingent fact about the use of signs. She refers to 3.1432: "We must not say, 'The complex sign "*aRb*" says "*a* stands in relation *R* to *b*"'; but we must say, 'That "*a*" stands in a certain relation to "*b*" says *that aRb*'." Yet 5.542 contains a metalinguistic pseudoproposition that strictly cannot be said but only shown. See also Cohen 1974, 442–44.

6. This argument, which seems to support Wittgenstein's conclusions, but which he nowhere explicitly presents as such, is related to Kant's refutation of ontological proofs for the existence of God in *The Critique of Pure Reason*. See A599/B627–A600/B628: "A hundred real thalers do not contain the least coin more than a hundred possible thalers. For as the latter signify the concept, and the former the object, should the former contain more than the latter, my concept would not, in that case, express the whole object, and would not therefore be an adequate concept of it. My financial position is, however, affected very differently by a hundred real thalers than it is by the mere concept of them (that is, of their possibility). For the object, as it actually exists, is not analytically contained in my concept, but is added to my concept (which is a determination of my state) synthetically; and yet the conceived hundred thalers are not themselves in the least increased through thus acquiring existence outside my concept. By whatever and by however many predicates we may think a thing—even if we completely determine it—we do not make the least addition to the thing when we further declare that this thing *is*. Otherwise, it would not be exactly the same thing that exists, but something more than we had thought in the concept, and we could not, therefore, say that the exact object of my concept exists."

7. Descartes, *Meditations on First Philosophy*, V. Kant, *Critique of Pure Reason*, A106–31; B129–43.

8. Anscombe, 88: "it is evident [Wittgenstein] is arguing: You can't explain the mind as 'the judging subject' in 'A judges *p*', *because* 'A judges *p*' is of the form "'*p*" says *p*'; so that way you will only reach a complex, and a composite mind would not be a mind."

9. *Notebooks* contains rehearsals for many of these passages, some of them verbatim or nearly so. See, for example, Wittgenstein's remarks in the entries for 23.5.15; 24.7.16; 4.8.16; 5.8.16; 7.8.16; 11.8.16; 12.8.16; 12.10.16. These remarks, along with Wittgenstein's reflections on ethics and aesthetics that are not carried over into the *Tractatus,* are often said to show signs of Schopenhauer's influence on his thinking at this time. The metaphor of the eye in its visual field is taken directly from Schopenhauer 1969, 2, 287: "That which precedes knowledge as its condition, whereby that knowledge first of all became possible, and hence its own basis, cannot be immediately grasped by knowledge, just as the eye cannot see itself." Also, p. 491: "But the I or ego is the dark point in consciousness, just as on the retina the precise point of entry of the optic nerve is blind, the brain itself is wholly insensible, the body of the sun is dark, and the eye sees everything except itself."

10. Descartes, *Meditations* II.

11. Wittgenstein in 6.37 reduces necessary truth to tautology and necessary falsehood to contradiction. Logic and logical form transcend the world as literal nonsense that can only be shown and never said. In epistemology, insofar as he takes any notice of it, Wittgenstein is therefore an empiricist. It is only in the transcendental deduction of the logical requirements of thought, language, and the world, required in order for thought and language meaningfully to represent the facts of the world, that Wittgenstein presents philosophical pseudopropositions that look to be necessary conclusions akin to tautology and contradiction. In 6.54, he dismisses even these along with his entire semantic theory as nonsense.

12. Hintikka 1958 offers a different interpretation of the passages in 5.62–5.641. See Pears 1987, 1, 153–90.

13. It is tempting to see a personal preoccupation as well as a more abstract theoretical interest in Wittgenstein's remarks about solipsism. The problem has deep resonances in Wittgenstein's wartime experiences and lifelong sense of loneliness and social alienation. We are reminded of Wittgenstein's possibly ironic first sentence of the *Tractatus* preface, 27, that "This book will perhaps only be understood by those who have themselves already thought the thoughts which are expressed in it—or similar thoughts." How many persons can Wittgenstein imagine to have anticipated the peculiar complicated thoughts of the *Tractatus?* Could he have realistically supposed that the description would apply to anyone but himself, or that he was writing the book for anyone but himself?

14. This interpretation fits the account of Wittgenstein's early philosophy as influenced by Kantian and Schopenhauerian transcendentalism. Kant's theory of the self-in-itself, the counterpart of the thing-in-itself for the transcendental unity of apperception, and Schopenhauer's distinction between the world as appearance and undifferentiated unindividuated Will as thing-in-itself, are the obvious precursors of Wittgenstein's concept of the transcendent metaphysical subject.

15. See also Ayer, 28–30; Black 1964, 308–10; Cook 1972; 1994, 55–68; Finch, 152–58; Fogelin 1987, 74–77, 93–95; Hacker 1989, 81–107; Huby 1969; Manser 1970; Morrison 1968; Schulte 1992, 64–66; Stenius, 220–22.

CHAPTER
F   I   V   E | **Ethics and Aesthetics as Important Nonsense**

As implications of the general form of proposition and the transcendence of the metaphysical subject, Wittgenstein offers three conclusions about moral and aesthetic value. Moral and aesthetic value like the metaphysical subject transcend the world of facts, ethics and aesthetics are identified as one, and sentences about ethics and aesthetics are unsayable nonsense. By this Wittgenstein does not diminish but rather exalts the importance of moral and aesthetic value by contrast with the mundane world of facts.

The *Tractatus* discussion of the transcendence of value is previewed in a remarkable passage of the *Notebooks* for 2 August 1916. Wittgenstein writes:

> The world is then, in itself, neither good nor evil.
>
> For it must not matter, for the existence of ethics, whether there is life in the world or not. And it is clear that a world in which there is only dead matter is neither good nor evil; therefore, the world of living beings can in itself be neither good nor evil.
>
> Good and evil enter only through the *subject*. And the subject does not belong to the world, rather it is a boundary of the world.

The entry contains two distinct but closely related arguments in support of the same position. One concerns the intuitive amorality of an imaginable lifeless world, and the other the dependence of ethics on the extraworldly metaphysical subject. The arguments each seek to prove the transcendence of ethics.

These inferences are the prelude to Wittgenstein's *Tractatus* discussion of value. Wittgenstein places ethics and aesthetics as one outside the world, by which all attempts to express value are relegated to the extrasemantic category of literal nonsense.[1] Value thereby joins representational form, logical form, the metaphysical subject, and whatever cannot be said but only shown. This includes, as Wittgenstein later adds, the mystical, *das Mystische,* interpreted as religious or spiritual experience of the world considered as a whole or from the standpoint of eternity, *sub specie aeterni.*[2] Moral and aesthetic value transcends the world because the metaphysical subject as the source of all moral and aesthetic judgment transcends the world. The elimination of propositional attitude sentences as logically meaningless also excludes value statements, and thereby banishes value from the world. The general form of proposition makes ethics and aesthetics, including attempts at value judgments in theory and practice, literally nonsensical.[3]

The *Notebooks* arguments are interesting in their own right, and call for careful examination as shedding light on Wittgenstein's subsequent opinions about ethics. In the *Notebooks,* unlike the *Tractatus,* Wittgenstein seems to be offering straightforward deductive proofs for the transcendence of ethics. This is indicated by the choice of an informal inferential framework in Wittgenstein's use of the terms 'For' and 'therefore', and by the derivational structure of his reasoning in the passage. It is a style of presenting philosophical ideas that is largely absent from the *Tractatus,* which assumes a more oracular tone, albeit with occasional justificatory remarks elliptically linking theme to theme. This is consistent with the central *Tractatus* teaching that philosophical problems are pseudoproblems and philosophical assertions pseudopropositions, a stance Wittgenstein approaches but does not fully articulate in the *Notebooks.*[4] The *Notebooks* arguments can be read as preparatory studies for Wittgenstein's *Tractatus* claims about the exclusion of value from the world of fact. They clarify concepts connected with Wittgenstein's even more epigrammatic statement of the transcendence thesis in the *Tractatus,* where he shuns the *Notebooks'* explicit 'syllogistic' demonstration.

There are several difficulties in the *Notebooks* proofs. Although Wittgenstein excludes moral value from the world of facts, he appears in the first argument to maintain as a fact about an imaginable world consisting only of lifeless matter that it lacks value. He speaks of 'the existence of ethics' (itself a puzzling phrase) as he otherwise speaks of the existence or nonexistence of ordinary states of affairs. From this, it might be said that Wittgenstein ought to allow facts about moral values to obtain in some worlds, potentially making values and the instantiation of values an integral part of the world. If this is not permitted, it is difficult to see how the argument is supposed to work. The major premise of the first argument, that the existence of ethics does not depend on whether or not the world is inhabited by life, is problematic. The assumption seems to contradict the minor premise that a world consisting only of dead matter is neither good nor evil. It may even involve the argument in vicious circularity, since it seems to presage the conclusion that ethics transcends the world. Yet if moral value is outside the world of contingent facts in which life happens or happens not to exist, why is a lifeless world in particular, *as opposed to* an inhabited world, neither good nor evil? What is the force of Wittgenstein's qualification that the world 'in itself' is neither good nor evil? What is the relation between the transcendence of the metaphysical subject and the transcendence of ethics and ethical value? How are the contingent facts of the existence of living things connected with the transcendence of the metaphysical subject and the transcendence of ethics?

Wittgenstein's first *Notebooks* proof for the transcendence of ethics incorporates three distinct claims about the ontology of ethics and its relation to the world. The inference trades on the nature of ethics as logically independent of whether a world is contingently inhabited or lifeless, and the intuitive amorality of an imaginable lifeless world devoid of conscious subjects. The argument can be reconstructed in this way:

1. The existence of ethics is logically independent of whether or not the world is inhabited by living things.

2. A world uninhabited by living things is neither good nor evil.

---

3. The world in itself can be neither good nor evil; ethics transcends the natural world. (1,2)

This is a close transcription of Wittgenstein's first *Notebooks* argument. But the proof is deductively incomplete in this form, and invites some of the criticisms mentioned above. The inference can be expanded by making explicit three assumptions that seem to be presupposed by Wittgenstein's argument, together with their conclusions. The added premises are indicated as the Kantian, Logical-ontic independence, and Consciousness theses.

[0. The existence of ethics (as a system of moral values) must apply, if at all, to every logically possible world, and not merely accidentally to the contingencies of the actual or any particular logically possible world.] (Kantian thesis)

---

1.   The existence of ethics is logically independent of whether or not the world is inhabited by living things.   (0)

[1a.   If the existence of ethics is logically independent of whether or not the world is inhabited by living things, then the world in itself, regardless of whether it happens to be inhabited or lifeless, is (exclusively), if moral (good or evil), logically necessarily moral, and otherwise, if amoral (neither good nor evil), logically necessarily amoral.]
                      (Logical-ontic independence thesis)

[1b.   The world in itself, regardless of whether it happens to be inhabited or lifeless, is (exclusively), if moral, logically necessarily moral, and otherwise, if amoral, logically necessarily amoral.]   (1,1a)

[1c.   Value is value for consciousness; a world is good or evil only if it contains conscious beings capable of experiencing good or evil as such.]
                      (Consciousness thesis)

2'.   A (logically possible) world uninhabited by living things (and hence by no conscious beings) is amoral.   (1c)

[2a.   Not every logically possible world is moral.]   (2')

3'.   The world in itself can be (is logically necessarily) amoral (neither good nor evil); ethics transcends the world.   (1b,2a)

It is possible to justify Wittgenstein's assumption in (1) that the existence of ethics is logically independent of whether or not the world is inhabited by living things. The claim derives from the more general Kantian thesis in [0] that the principles of morals are logically independent of empirical contingency.[5] Right and wrong in themselves or in the abstract do not depend on the state of the world. But whether a priori standards of right and wrong are satisfied by or instantiated in the world, as Kant would probably agree, depends very much on the facts and circumstances that happen to obtain.

The assumption might be defended on the non-Wittgensteinian grounds that ethics considered as a philosophical theory must hold for every logically possible world, regardless of the facts of any particular world. This proposal is prompted by Wittgenstein's strange use of the expression 'the existence of ethics'. The phrase calls attention to the peculiar ontic status of ethics. Ethics is not a physical object or complex, and is therefore removed from the vagaries of logically possible worlds by virtue of its abstract propositional or theoretical nature. The interpretation cannot be sustained without qualification, because Wittgenstein rejects the intelligibility of theoretical or philosophical ethics or metaethics in the customary sense, as a further consequence of value's transcendence.

It may therefore be preferable to think of the Kantian thesis as upholding the logical independence of the existence of ethics from world contingencies in more appropriately neutral terms as a system of moral values. This formula avoids explicit commitment to theoretical or philosophical ethics in the sense objectionable to the saying-showing distinction. Yet it preserves something of the flavor of thetic abstraction in which Wittgenstein often tries heuristically to communicate what strictly cannot be said. The idea is that a system of values applies conditionally, if at all, to any logically possible world, but is satisfied by or instantiated in a particular world only if the contingent facts and circumstances of the world meet the requisite criteria. The 'existence' of ethics is independent of the world of facts in something like but not exactly in the sense of an abstract theory, which is close enough to the spirit of Kant's deontology to deserve labeling as a Kantian thesis.[6]

The Logical-ontic independence thesis in [1a] may be more controversial. It relates the claim that the existence of ethics is logically independent of whether or not the world is inhabited by living things to the conclusion that the world *in itself* is logically necessarily (exclusively) either good or evil or neither good nor evil. The thesis seems indispensable if there is to be any connection between the logical independence of ethics and the habitation of the world by living things, and the assumption that the world in itself is either moral or amoral. There is an easy defense of the argument if the phrase 'in itself' is understood in the essentialist sense expected by the Kantian thesis. On this interpretation, the premise says no more than that the world is essentially either moral or amoral, despite its accidental habitation or nonhabitation by living things. If the world in itself has value, then presumably its value must hold independently of its contingent states of affairs, which is to say essentially or necessarily, so that the same system of values holds universally for every logically possible world.

The essential morality or amorality of the world depends by definition, respectively, on whether all logically possible worlds are moral, or whether any are amoral. Wittgenstein identifies life as a necessary condition for the world's morality, and maintains that a world uninhabited by living things is neither good nor evil. It seems natural to suppose that he has in mind something like the popular view by which the instantiation of moral value presupposes the existence of animal consciousness to experience the world, notably through pleasure or pain, or in attitudes of judgment, as good or evil.[7] Otherwise there is no special reason for regarding the instantiation of good or evil as contingent in particular on life. Plants and bacteria are alive but amoral, and it seems natural to suppose that their existence in a logically possible world by itself does not imply the instantiation of moral value. The third added assumption in the expanded version of Wittgenstein's argument implements this line of reasoning by introducing the Consciousness thesis in [1c], from which there follows in (2') a variation of premise (2) from the original reconstruction.

The subconclusion in (2') that a logically possible world uninhabited by living things and hence by no conscious beings is neither good nor evil supports the proposition in [2a] that not every logically possible world is good or evil. If not every logically possible world is good or evil, then by [1c] it follows in (3') that the world in itself (essentially) is logically necessarily neither good nor evil. There are some moral and some amoral worlds, depending as a necessary but not sufficient condition on whether or not they contain living conscious beings. The possibility of amoral worlds proves that the world is not essentially moral. If the world in itself is neither good nor evil, but is a potential object of moral valuation, then ethics transcends the world.

This version of Wittgenstein's first *Notebooks* argument for the transcendence of ethics avoids the inconsistency and circularity objections. There is no contradiction in supposing that ethics as a system of values is logically independent of contingent world circumstances such as a world's being inhabited or lifeless, and that the instantiation of moral values in a world, its being good or evil rather than neither good nor evil, depends (among other things) on whether or not the world happens to contain living conscious subjects. Nor is there a circularity in the argument that ethical value in the sense of instantiating good or evil transcends the world, as a consequence of the assumption that ethics in the sense of a system of values is logically independent of whatever biological-psychological contingencies happen to obtain.

The difficulty in Wittgenstein's proof lies rather in its attempt to derive conclusions about the transcendence of ethics as the instantiation of ethical value from assumptions about the transcendence of ethics as a system of values. Wittgenstein presumably wants to allow that ethics as it is contingently instantiated in the actual world through the existence of life, and more relevantly, of conscious psychological subjects, is transcendent as an instantiation of value, and not merely as an abstract value system. Wittgenstein makes what may seem to be an unwarranted elision from one relatively innocuous sense of the transcendence or logical independence of ethics from world habitation contingencies to another philosophically much more loaded and contentious sense. It is in managing the logical inference between these two senses of transcendence without equivocation that the Logical-ontic independence thesis comes into play. It is supposed to relate the logical independence of abstract ethical theory to the transcendence of real world instantiations of moral value. The fallacy of equivocation is bracketed in this way only by concealing a double meaning in a single proposition, the truth or plausibility of which must be assured to guarantee the soundness of Wittgenstein's inference.

The evaluation of Wittgenstein's first *Notebooks* argument thus boils down in this reconstruction to the question of whether assumption [1a] is acceptable. The condition that ethics in the sense of an abstract value system is logically independent of whether or not the world is inhabited by living things may be correct. But the proposition that the world is (exclusively) logically necessarily good or evil if good or evil, and otherwise logically necessarily neither good nor evil, is not obviously true. The best way to see this is to consider that, given the nature of an abstract value system, the antecedent of the conditional in [1a] is more likely to be widely acknowledged as holding necessarily regardless of the contingencies that obtain in any logically possible world for any ethical system, but that the truth of the consequent logically depends on the content of the values in question.

The assumption that the world in itself is, if moral, logically necessarily moral, and, if amoral, logically necessarily amoral, is (despite the fact that Wittgenstein would resist this terminology) a philosophically loaded metaethical (pseudo-) proposition, the acceptability of which presupposes the acceptability of the particular content of the moral philosophy adopted. To give just one example, most consequentialists, as opposed to deontologists, would probably reject the thesis that the world is logically necessarily moral if contingently it happens to be moral, and oppositely if contingently it happens to be amoral. The world may happen to be moral for the consequentialist because contingently it happens to contain not only living conscious subjects but living conscious subjects capable of pleasure or pain. Other logically possible worlds need not satisfy this condition, if in those worlds

there are conscious but pain- and pleasure-insensitive psychological subjects, *even if* it remains necessarily true that every
value system, at least as ordinarily conceived, is logically independent of whether or not the world is inhabited by living things.
A consequentialist value system implies that choosing to maxi-
mize happiness over unhappiness as predictable effects of causally possible alternative actions is always morally preferable to
any contrary choice. Values, if they apply at all, apply universally
and necessarily, even for nonactual worlds uninhabited by living
subjects in the previously explained conditional sense that they
would be instantiated *if* the world contained moral agents capable of choice and beings capable of happiness or unhappiness.
But in those nonactual worlds no ethical value in the relevant
sense of an instantiation of the values prescribed by the system
obtains. We might at first imagine that Wittgenstein in absolut-
ist fashion could object that there is only one correct system of
values, or that moral pluralism is confined to the limits of certain
deontic preferences. But Wittgenstein cannot uphold substantive
commitment to particular ethical values as a positive philosophical thesis without contradicting his main conclusion that value
judgments are nonsensical pseudopropositions. Nor can he admit
as meaningful attempts to offer such reasonings on behalf of particular moral systems.

An analogy from outside of traditional moral philosophy may
be helpful in understanding the force of this criticism of the Logical-ontic independence thesis. Conceptual analyses are supposed
par excellence, if true, to be logically necessarily true. The standard example, 'All bachelors are unmarried male adults', is presumably logically necessarily true, or true regardless of the
particular contingencies that obtain or fail to obtain in any particular logically possible world. The sense in which the analysis is
necessarily true is the conditional one by which, *if* any world contains a bachelor, *then* it thereby contains an unmarried male
adult. It does not follow that every logically possible world contains bachelors, nor, if a world happens to contain bachelors, that
it then logically necessarily contains bachelors, or, if it happens
to fail to contain bachelors, that it then logically necessarily fails
to contain bachelors. The objection similarly casts doubt on the
cogency of the Logical-ontic independence thesis. Yet if the interpretation of Wittgenstein's reference to 'the existence of ethics'
entailed by the Kantian thesis in terms of a system of values is
wrong, and Wittgenstein intends by this phrase the real-world
instantiation of ethical value or particular ethical values, then

the inconsistency and circularity problems return with a vengeance. The dilemma seems fatal for Wittgenstein's first proof of the transcendence of ethics, and so we turn to the second.

The second *Notebooks* argument seeks to prove the transcendence of ethics from the transcendence of the metaphysical subject, together with the assumption that good and evil 'enter' the world only 'through' the subject. As before, the most direct though incomplete reformulation of the inference requires only a few steps. The argument says in effect:

1.   The (contingently existent) metaphysical subject is a necessary condition for (the instantiation of) ethics in (ethical value of) the world.

2.   The metaphysical subject transcends the natural world.

---

3.   Ethics transcends the natural world.   (1,2)

The argument lacks conviction without a principle relating the transcendence of the metaphysical subject to the transcendence of ethics. The mere fact, as Wittgenstein puts it, that ethics 'enters' only 'through' the transcendent subject by itself does not unquestionably entail that ethics itself is transcendent. A counterexample similar to that of the previous discussion can be given. If we stipulate that artworks and artifacts generally also enter the natural world only through or by means of the transcendent metaphysical subject, it does not immediately follow by analogy that artworks and artifacts transcend the natural world in the same way as values. Even if they are not purely physical objects by virtue of their derivative intentionality, artworks and purposive human-made objects generally are also part and parcel of the phenomenal world. They belong to the same causal nexus as other naturally occurring entities, and cannot reasonably be considered transcendent in the strong sense of being altogether excluded from the world of facts.

This objection does not refute Wittgenstein's argument from the transcendence of the subject. But it indicates the importance of supplying the missing premises that might carry the inference from the explicit assumptions that ethics enters the world only through the metaphysical subject and that the metaphysical subject transcends the natural world. What is it about the transcendence of the subject as the source of ethical valuation that for Wittgenstein implies the transcendence of ethics?

One possibility is that by instantiating ethics or an ethical evaluation the metaphysical subject superadds something to the world that otherwise would not obtain. The world of facts is complete in and of itself, with or without value attributions. The superaddition of ethical value occasioned by the transcendent subject's transcendent value attitudes might then also transcend the facts of the world. Take away the transcendent subject, and with it the moral values that enter by way of a subject's regarding the world as good or evil, and the world itself remains unchanged. Ethics in this sense is epiphenomenal. It makes no contribution to the structure of facts in logical space that constitutes the world.[8] The facts remain as they are, logically independently of whether there happen to be psychological subjects on the scene capable of regarding the facts as good or evil. As Wittgenstein would undoubtedly agree, the existence or nonexistence of complex biological systems including intelligent animals makes a great difference to the totality of facts by which the world is constituted. But metaphysical subjects in addition to intelligent animals considered as biological entities do not exist as part of the world, and there are no facts about the metaphysical subject that enter into the totality of world-constituting facts.[9]

It is possible in this way to propose the following addition to the more schematic reconstruction of Wittgenstein's second argument for the transcendence of ethics. The Subject thesis in (1) states that the subject is a necessary condition for the instantiation of ethics in or ethical evaluation of the world. This is Wittgenstein's assertion in the second last sentence of the *Notebooks* passage, when he states: "Good and evil enter only through the *subject.*" For convenience, Wittgenstein's reason for positing the transcendence of the metaphysical subject is referred to simply as Occam's razor argument in (2). The bridge from the transcendence of necessary conditions for the instantiation of a property to the transcendence of the instantiation is supported by two supplementary principles. These premises formulate how Wittgenstein might have understood the transmission of transcendence from necessary conditions to whatever they condition by property instantiations that are not world-constitutive facts. The principles are introduced as the Condition-fact and Fact-instantiation transcendence theses in [2a] and [2b]. The same conclusion is forthcoming as before in (3), via the intermediate conclusion in [2c]. This establishes that ethics in the sense of an instantiation of ethical value is not entirely conditioned by world-constitutive facts. We now have:

1.   The metaphysical subject is a necessary condition
        for the instantiation of ethics in (ethical value of)
        the world.   (Subject thesis)

2.   The metaphysical subject transcends the natural
        world.   (Occam's razor argument)

[2a.   If the instantiation of a property in or of the world
      has among its necessary conditions a requirement
      that transcends the natural world, then the instan-
      tiation of that property is not entirely conditioned
      by world-constitutive facts.]
          (Condition-fact transcendence thesis)

[2b.   Instantiations of properties in or of the world that
      are not entirely conditioned by world-constitutive
      facts are themselves not world-constitutive facts,
      but transcend the natural world.]
          (Fact-instantiation transcendence thesis)

[2c.   The instantiation of ethics in (ethical valuation of)
      the world is not entirely conditioned by world-
      constitutive facts.]   (1,2,2a)

3.   Ethics transcends the natural world.   (2b,2c)

This version of the inference offers a sympathetic conjecture about Wittgenstein's reasoning in the second *Notebooks* argument. It is in keeping with the semantic theory and transcendence metaphysics of his philosophy, and portrays the inference as a credible rationale for the conclusion in the second part of Wittgenstein's remarks on the transcendence of value.

The assumptions in [2a] and [2b], and the intermediate derivation in [2c], provide an answer to the problem of the apparent nontranscendence of artworks and artifacts. Explicating Wittgenstein's main assumption in terms of the (partial) transcendence or nontranscendence of the conditions for instantiating properties makes possible a more sophisticated reply than the principle that whatever enters the world only by or through the transcendence of subject is thereby transcendent. The reconstruction avoids the counterexample by implying that if artworks and artifacts have properties that are instantiated by the agency of a transcendent metaphysical subject as ground or necessary condition, then artworks and artifacts are also for that reason and to that extent transcendent. Artworks and artifacts are physical objects constituted like other complexes as structures of facts, but their value transcends the world. This is not to say that artworks and artifacts considered as physical objects are transcendent, but rather their beauty, utility, and other values. As such, the transcendence of artworks and artifacts is comparable to the good or evil value of world-constitutive states of affairs that transcend the world through the moral valuations conditioned by the transcendent metaphysical subject, and to intelligent animals that do not transcend the world as biological entities, but by instantiating the transcendent metaphysical subject.[10]

The Subject thesis in (1) is relatively unproblematic. The conclusion of Wittgenstein's Occam's razor argument in step (2), concerning the subject's transcendence, might be independently supported, even if Wittgenstein's reasons connected with the implications of the general form of proposition are inconclusive. An alternative defense of the Subject thesis might begin with Humean skepticism about the existence of the self as invisible and inscrutable to empirical introspection,[11] or a Strawsonian or Parfitesque no-ownership theory of self motivated by the failure of satisfactory personal identity criteria,[12] or Nagelian considerations based on the interpretation of split-brain phenomena.[13] From any such starting point it may be possible to chart a route to a revisionary formulation of Kant's transcendental unity of apperception,[14] or a Schopenhauerian variation of transcendent Will as descriptively unknowable thing-in-itself.[15] If the subject's transcendence can be accepted on grounds other than those inextricably linked to Wittgenstein's logical atomism and picture theory of meaning, then a version of Wittgenstein's second *Notebooks* argument for the transcendence of ethics from the transcendence of the metaphysical subject might be upheld, even if the semantic machinery of the early philosophy is rejected.[16]

The proof purports to effect a transition from the transcendence of subject to the transcendence of the subject's ethical valuations, and hence to the transcendence of ethics. The inference is authorized by means of the Condition-fact transcendence thesis in [2a] and Fact-instantiation thesis in [2b]. The Condition-fact transcendence thesis stands as an analytic truth by virtue of the meaning of an instantiation's collective necessary conditions. The Fact-instantiation thesis makes a more substantive claim in requiring that instantiations of properties in or of the world that are not entirely conditioned by world-constitutive facts about the world that they transcend. This too might be regarded as an analytic statement about the transcendent ontic status of instantiations that have at least some transcendent necessary conditions. But there is a difficulty. Wittgenstein in *Tractatus* 2.172 maintains that representational form is not describable as a world-constitutive fact, but shows itself only in pictures of facts. In 6.13, he further declares that logical form is transcendent, which, by the reduction of mathematical to logical form in 6.2–6.23, implies the transcendence of mathematical form. The satisfaction of certain representational, logical, and mathematical forms is evidently a necessary condition for the instantiation of every world-constitutive fact. Cyril Barrett in *Wittgenstein on Ethics and Religious Belief* notes the difference between the transcendence of form and value, when he writes: "The transcendentality of ethical, aesthetic and religious expression is not identical with that of logic and mathematics. They do not mirror the structure of the world. They treat the world as a whole: they transcend the facts of the world."[17] The Fact-instantiation thesis paradoxically seems to entail that all world-constitutive facts, and not merely metaphysical subject and valuational property instantiations, are transcendent. It is incoherent to suppose that world-constitutive facts transcend the world, or, what comes to the same thing, that the world transcends itself.

The problem is tractable, since it results from a loophole in the statement of an added premise in the expansion of Wittgenstein's sketchy presentation of the second argument. What is needed is a principled way to exclude transcendent conditions of representational and logical (including mathematical) form from the assumption. This is readily provided by introducing an exclusionary clause to the effect that

[2b']   Instantiations of properties in or of the world that are not entirely conditioned by world-constitutive facts (other than conditions reducible to representational or logical form) are themselves not world-constitutive facts, but transcend the natural world.
(Revised fact-instantiation transcendence thesis)

The amended thesis in [2b'] need not be considered ad hoc. It formulates more precisely the intent of the implicit assumption attributed to Wittgenstein concerning the transcendence of instantiations of properties dependent specifically on transcendent *subjective* conditions. Alternatively, the concept of *condition* can be more restrictively defined to exclude logical or mathematical form as conditioning the instantiation of properties. The distinction might be approved on the grounds that agreement with representational and logical form is presupposed by all immanent phenomena in every logically possible world, and hence does not contribute substantive conditions to the instantiation of any particular property.

Wittgenstein's second *Notebooks* proof for the transcendence of ethics in this reconstruction, if not absolutely compelling, is at least sufficiently plausible to merit serious consideration. The logic seems impeccable, the assumptions believable, and the central claim on which the argument turns, that the metaphysical subject as the ground of ethical valuation is transcendent, and that the subject's transcendence is transmitted to subjective valuation and so to value, is independently supportable in several ways without commitment to Wittgenstein's logical atomism and picture theory semantics. The preliminary examination of Wittgenstein's *Notebooks* arguments now makes it possible to trace the development of his ideas about the transcendence of value in the *Tractatus*.

It is interesting to contrast Wittgenstein's arguments in the *Tractatus* with another approach he might otherwise have been expected to take. Wittgenstein might have tried to demonstrate the transcendence of value by offering an argument parallel to his treatment of the transcendence of the subject, and of the empirical thinking subject's propositional attitudes and psychological states. We can imagine him beginning with linguistic contexts purporting to express moral or aesthetic value, like the putative propositional attitude or epistemic and emotive value contexts he discusses in 5.54–5.5422. Had Wittgenstein followed such a strategy in the *Tractatus* presentation of value, he might have considered non-truth-functional proposition-building contexts like these:

It is (morally or aesthetically) good that [__]
It is (morally or aesthetically) bad (or wrong) that [__]

The contexts are completed by introducing a proposition to produce a larger proposition that is truth-functionally independent of the truth or falsehood of the proposition it contains. We see this when we fill in the blank with such propositions as 'John married Susan' or 'Picasso painted *Guernica*'. This seeming proposition-building operation is decidedly non-truth-functional, by which it appears to pose the same threat to the general form of proposition as propositional attitude contexts like 'A believes (doubts, hopes, fears) that [__]'. Wittgenstein might then have invoked an Occam's razor style reductive argument against non-truth-functional value contexts as against non-truth-functional propositional attitude contexts. Why does he not do so?

One possibility is that the ordinary language construction, 'It is (morally or aesthetically) good that *p*', does not make explicit reference to a subject. This factor could conceivably be made part of the deep analysis of the sentence. Then we have an automatic reduction of what appears to be objective to overtly subjective value. The construction in that case gets translated as something like, 'A judges that it is (morally or aesthetically) good that *p*'. If such a reduction could be carried out, then, in the analysis of A's judgment, Wittgenstein would arrive at the same conclusion as in 5.542, namely, that 'It is (morally or aesthetically) good that *p*' and 'It is (morally or aesthetically) bad (or wrong) that p' are alike of the logical form 'p' says that p. The metaphysical subject A and the moral or aesthetic subject's moral or aesthetic attitudes disappear from the analysis, and so by Occam's razor the terms that purport to refer to them are logically meaningless. The moral or aesthetic subject is thereby logically unnecessary, along with their semantically epiphenomenal psychological states, in the same way as the epistemic or emotive subject of 'contemporary superficial psychology', as opposed to the metaphysical subject that transcends the world. That Wittgenstein does not attempt this parallel strategy in proving the transcendence of value is noteworthy. There is no definite clue in the text, but it is reasonable to speculate that Wittgenstein would regard such a reduction of value to individual judgments and attitudes in the imposition of subject term A and value judgment attitude υ in $\upsilon(A,p)$ as too subjective a way of interpreting the logical form of ordinary language value statements that seems to have the more objective form, $V(p)$ (equally unsayable in a correct logical symbolism). What Wittgenstein offers instead is different both from the argument we might have expected as an outgrowth of the *Notebooks* syllogisms, and from the *Tractatus* analysis of propositional attitude contexts.

Among the *Tractatus* transcendentalia, Wittgenstein includes all pictorial, representational, logical-mathematical form, the metaphysical subject or philosophical 'I', and propositional attitudes or psychological states. Now he adds coalescent moral-aesthetic value as transcending the world of facts.[18] The *Tractatus* states:

> 6.41   The sense of the world must lie outside the world. In the world everything is as it is and happens as it does happen. *In* it there is no value—and if there were, it would be of no value.
>
>   If there is a value which is of value, it must lie outside all happening and being-so. For all happening and being-so is accidental.
>
>   What makes it non-accidental cannot lie *in* the world, for otherwise this would again be accidental.
>
>   It must lie outside the world.
>
> 6.42   Hence also there can be no ethical propositions.
>
>   Propositions cannot express anything higher.
>
> 6.421   It is clear that ethics cannot be expressed.
>
>   Ethics is transcendental.
>
>   (Ethics and aesthetics are one.)

A brief comparison of the *Notebooks* and *Tractatus* arguments reveals significant similarities and a few outstanding but ideologically inconsequential differences. Both sets of remarks proclaim the transcendence of value. The *Notebooks* passage, unlike the *Tractatus,* does not use the words 'sense of the world' or 'transcendental', but refers to the 'world in itself' and the extraworldliness of ethics. It is only elsewhere in the *Notebooks,* in a suite of reflections about the nature of happiness and the variety of moral attitudes that might be assumed toward the world, that Wittgenstein speaks explicitly of the transcendence of ethics.[19]

The *Tractatus* generalizes the first *Notebooks* argument in two ways. First, the *Tractatus* refers to the extraworldliness of value generally, without mentioning ethics in particular until specific application is made in 6.42–6.421. Second, the extraworldliness of value in the *Tractatus* is contrasted with the accidents of world-constitutive facts, without mentioning the existence of life as a particular contingency of world affairs relative to which value is nonaccidental and by virtue of which value must therefore lie outside the world. Experimenting with the particular case concerning good and evil in his *Notebooks* may have led Wittgenstein to more general conclusions about value exhibited in the *Tractatus.*

Wittgenstein locates undifferentiated value outside the world. Then he explains the semantic implications of transcendence for the ineffability of ethics and the pseudopropositional status of efforts to express ethical value. Finally, he concludes with the intriguing identification of ethics and aesthetics as one.[20] The semantic dimensions of transcendent value are implicit in the *Notebooks,* but clearly spelled out in the *Tractatus* transcendence arguments. The *Tractatus* discussion of transcendence on the other hand does not draw directly on the transcendence of the metaphysical subject as transmitting transcendence to value by contributing to the transcendental ground of subjective valuation, as in the second *Notebooks* argument. The *Tractatus* develops Wittgenstein's concept of the transcendence of the subject even more fully than the *Notebooks,* but leaves the connection between the subject's transcendence and the transcendence of value obscure.[21]

What does Wittgenstein mean by identifying ethics and aesthetics as one? They are not identical merely because both are transcendent, unsayable, and nondiscursive.[22] The same is true of pictorial form, logical and mathematical form, and sheer nonsense like "There is only one 1" (4.1272) or "Socrates is identical" (5.473, 5.4733). Wittgenstein does not lump all of these together as one in the realm of *Unsinn* in the way that he specifically identifies ethics and aesthetics. We can be reasonably certain that Wittgenstein does not mean anything so quotidian as that morality reduces in practice to the duty to create, preserve, and appreciate beauty, or that the life of the artist is the fulfillment of a moral obligation. The *Notebooks* entries for July and August 1917, in which these parts of the *Tractatus* are first drafted, testify to Wittgenstein's reflections on Schopenhauer's idealist metaphysics, ethics, and aesthetics. Wittgenstein's difficult parenthetical pronouncement of 6.421, in which ethics and aesthetics are identified as one, might be understood by considering Schopenhauer's doctrine that aesthetic genius implies a moral duty to place knowing above willing and to perfect natural forms in art.[23] Schopenhauer's hints at an identification of ethics and aesthetics in turn go back to Plato's Pythagorean concept of justice as a harmony of the parts of the soul, and Socrates' image of the moral wrongdoer as 'unmusical'.[24]

Wittgenstein understood the *Tractatus* as an unconventional contribution to ethics. The saying-showing distinction is supposed to mark the boundary to the expression of thought in any logically possible language, from which value is necessarily excluded. Wittgenstein explains the normative subtext of his logical-philosophical treatise in a letter to Ludwig von Ficker:

> The sense of the book is an ethical one. I once wanted to include in the preface a sentence which actually is not now in it but which I will write out for you here since it will perhaps be a key (to the book) for you. I wanted, then, to write: my work consists of two parts: of that which is under consideration here and of all that I have *not* written. And it is precisely this second part that is the important one.[25]

It is the nonfactual, nonobjective, and normative that remains when the world is completely, meaningfully, scientifically, described that is Wittgenstein's primary concern. The complex logical-semantic apparatus of the text serves only to mark the distinction between the sayable and what is leftover as unsayable, and to delegate the sayable to the mundane sciences. The transcendent subjective aspect of the world is strictly unsayable, and concerning it Wittgenstein can only revert to silence. The world in and of itself is valueless, neither good nor evil, beautiful nor ugly. The world has, as a matter of fact, none of the indeterminately many in-between shades in the spectrum of moral-aesthetic values. There is no theoretical task for ethics or aesthetics; there is only the transcendence of ethical-aesthetic attitudes that color the world in the subjective ethical-aesthetic experience of facts.

The world considered as good or beautiful or the opposite, though a nonfactual aspect inexpressible in a genuine proposition, is nevertheless of the utmost importance to Wittgenstein. Value belongs to the showing side of the saying-showing dichotomy, without which, for Wittgenstein, our understanding of the world and human experience of the world is incomplete.[26] "The world of the happy person," Wittgenstein contends, "is quite another than that of the unhappy" (6.43). By this he means to speak not of a plurality of worlds constituted as distinct structures of facts, but of the same objective world in contrasting subjective aspects. "The world and life are one" (5.621), he writes; nevertheless, "The world is independent of my will" (6.373). Again, in 6.43, Wittgenstein portrays the dual aspect of objective world and the subjective valuational will when he claims: "If good or bad willing changes the world, it can only change the limits of the world, not the facts; not the things that can be expressed in language." The objectivity of world-constitutive facts and subjectivity of world-transcendent values recalls not only Schopenhauer's idealist distinction between the world as Will and phenomenal appearance or representation, but also Galileo's and John Locke's realist division between objective primary and subjective secondary qualities.[27]

The transcendence of value, like philosophical pseudopropositions generally for Wittgenstein, on the whole changes nothing. The thesis leaves everything as it is, having sharpened our understanding and helped us to avoid conceptual confusion.[28] We can expect that the same kinds of world occurrences will elicit feelings of moral approval or disapproval, and motivate the same kinds of actions intended to conform to or challenge the same kinds of ethical standards in social interactions and moral decision-making. Wittgenstein does not imagine that transcendence implies an ethical nihilism, whereby value is degraded in importance because of its transcendence of the natural world. On the contrary, we know from his letter to von Ficker that by identifying limits to the meaningfulness of language Wittgenstein intends to set the transcendent and unsayable in bold relief as the more important nonfactual aspect of the world.[29] It is the sayable and describable that is 'accidental' in his terminology, that is exclusively concerned with the contingent facts of the world, the contents of which are of scientific importance only, and hence, for Wittgenstein, of negligible philosophical interest.[30]

To conclude that value transcends the world makes an important addition to our understanding both of value and the world. But it is rather in a negative sense that the thesis has the potential to shape our interpretation of the nature of ethics and aesthetics. Its primary implication is that there is no theoretical task for ethics, and therefore no philosophical discipline in the category of what is commonly called metaethics. This is in keeping with Wittgenstein's leveling of the presumed hierarchy of traditional philosophical domains, eliminating metaphilosophy, metamathematics, and metaphysics. There is only a single flatland dimension of moral and aesthetic attitudes toward states of the world, including facts about what people do. Beyond this, according to Wittgenstein, there is no prospect for meaningful speculation about moral or aesthetic value. Ethics and aesthetics considered as one are literal nonsense according to the picture theory of meaning and general form of proposition. But for Wittgenstein value in moral and aesthetic judgment is humanly important, even among the most important, nonsense.

The transcendence of value implies that it is pointless to formulate ethical or aesthetic theories and defend one against the others. The consequentialism-deontology debate, to take a conspicuous example, is altogether a pseudoproblem if the point of offering arguments for one in refutation of an opponent is to arrive at a true moral philosophy or to get at the truth of how moral agents should act and think about the morality of their actions. Truth is irrelevant to ethics, and to value generally. Consequentialism and deontology alike are literally nonsensical in purporting to say what is unsayable. The values that are supposed to be communicated by these putative discursive ethical theories at most show themselves in uses of valuational language, in particular modes of conduct, and in world-constitutive facts involving actions conditioned by the transcendent subject that indicate the transcendental value psychological subjects place on states of affairs in the world through the attitudes that motivate their behavior. Wittgenstein's own resolute moral standpoint and passionate involvement in the arts, as patron and craftsman of music, literature, sculpture, and architecture, and in the artistry of his philosophical writing, the high standards of virtue, personal and artistic honesty and authenticity of expression he demanded of himself and others, is mute testimony to the importance he attached to the meaningless nonsense of ethics and aesthetics.

The deeper philosophical problem raised by Wittgenstein's arguments for the transcendence of ethics is whether it is intelligible to adopt the stance that value statements are nonsense. The intuitive rejoinder for anyone not already persuaded by Wittgenstein's conclusions is that Wittgenstein himself inconsistently engages in metaethics in order to maintain that there can be no meaningful propositions of ethics or metaethics.

There are several ways in which Wittgenstein might reply to such a charge. The best answer to the inconsistency objection is to treat it as a particular instance of the global problem of how Wittgenstein is able to communicate so much of what is officially supposed to be unsayable according to the *Tractatus*. Does Wittgenstein contradict himself by introducing any of the logical, semantic, or metaphysical topics of the *Tractatus,* in explaining the basic principles of his logical atomism, picture theory of meaning, and general form of proposition? It appears on the contrary that Wittgenstein regards his philosophical pseudopropositions as enabling the reader to arrive at a correct view of the limits of meaningful expression in language.

The only inconsistency to arise on this interpretation requires the heuristic role of Wittgenstein's philosophical pseudopropositions to be meaningful in order to help us see that they are meaningless. Wittgenstein easily avoids the objection by appealing to the saying-showing distinction in claiming that the effect of his philosophical pseudopropositions, including those about the meaninglessness of ethics and metaethics, is achieved by showing rather than saying. Wittgenstein's strategy is analogous to the logical structure of an argumentum reductio ad absurdum, where the idea is not to assume and draw inferences from propositions hypothetically as though they were true in order to demonstrate that they are false, but rather to make use of pseudopropositions hypothetically as though they were meaningful in order to show (in the picture theory sense) that they are meaningless pseudopropositions.

Wittgenstein's conclusion that there can be no meaningful ethics or metaethics is itself in one sense a meaningless pseudoproposition of meaningless metaethics. The difference is that Wittgenstein expressly denies commitment to such a positive thesis as anything that can or must be propositionally said. On the contrary, Wittgenstein believes that the nonsense of ethics and metaethics is shown by the exclusion of any genuine ethical or metaethical propositions from the general form of proposition. The heuristic import of the superficially metaethical conclusion of the *Tractatus* that there can be no meaningful ethics or metaethics, and that ethics and aesthetics are one, is to provide a temporary and ultimately eliminable aid to the understanding in a strictly unsayable pseudopropositional traditional philosophical idiom. Afterward, having recognized the nonsense of value pseudopropositions and pseudotheories, we no longer need the *Tractatus* pseudopropositions, but can rely instead on an inexpressible grasp of how the general form of proposition reveals the meaninglessness of ethics and aesthetics, and of metaethics and theoretical aesthetics. We are then in a position to discard the *Tractatus* altogether, including its apparently metaethical and meta-aesthetic but officially antimetaethical antimeta-aesthetic philosophy, and its apparently philosophical but officially logically meaningless logical, semantic, metaphysical, and metaphilosophical antiphilosophy and antimetaphilosophy.

Wittgenstein's transcendence thesis achieves an economy of productive philosophical effort, by rechanneling energy from unpromising directions. For those who try to advance a metaethics, and to decide ethical problems as though they admitted answers modeled on the methods of discovering scientific truths, there is only the deflationary activity of remarking the error and explaining the literal nonsense of their misuses of language. Wittgenstein's discussion of 'the right method of philosophy' in 6.53 has special application to the benighted efforts of theoretical ethics and metaethics. The transcendence thesis is of a piece with Wittgenstein's repeated urgings that speculative philosophy acknowledge the wrong turns it has taken, retracing its steps to its more circumscribed limits of proper application as theory of meaning.[31] Wittgenstein regards philosophical ethics and metaethics as so misconceived that puncturing their pretensions and silencing their adherents is at best a nugatory achievement. This is part of what Wittgenstein means in the final sentences of the preface to the *Tractatus,* when he announces that: "I am . . . of the opinion that the problems have in essentials been finally solved. And if I am not mistaken in this, then the value of this work secondly consists in the fact that it shows how little has been done when these problems have been solved."[32] All that might be added to this disclaimer in tempering the bravado of Wittgenstein's first statement is a recognition, not only of how little is done, but of how little needs to be done, in undermining the sandcastle of theoretical ethics and aesthetics.[33]

I NOTES

1. 6.41–6.421. See *Notebooks* 8.1.16.
2. 2.151; 2.172; 2.18; 4.12–4.1211; 4.461; 6.22; 5.541–5.5422; 5.631–5.641; 6.432–6.45; 6.522.
3. 3.3; 4.01; 4.021–4.023; 4.06; 4.2.
4. 4.1272–4.128; 5.534–5.535. See chapter 6.

5. Kant 1959, 5: "Is it not of the utmost necessity to construct a pure moral philosophy which is completely freed from everything which may be only empirical and thus belong to anthropology? That there must be such a philosophy is self-evident from the common idea of duty and moral laws. . . . [Everyone] must concede that the ground of obligation here must not be sought in the nature of man or in the circumstances in which he is placed, but sought a priori solely in the concepts of pure reason, and that every other precept which rests on principles of mere experience, so far as it leans in the least on empirical grounds (perhaps only in regard to the motive involved), may be called a practical rule but never a moral law. Thus not only are moral laws together with their principles essentially different from all practical knowledge in which there is anything empirical, but all moral philosophy rests solely on its pure part."

6. Wittgenstein's first *Notebooks* argument for the transcendence of ethics can be reconstructed without explicit Kantian overtones by allowing assumption (1) to stand on its own, underived from any more general principle. Yet Wittgenstein's statement that the existence of ethics is logically independent of whether or not the world is inhabited by living things seems to presuppose more fundamental reasoning. The identification of a Kantian thesis as an origin of the independence of the existence of ethics from the occurrence of life has the advantage of linking Wittgenstein's work to the critical idealist tradition through well-documented connections with Schopenhauer. See Tilghman 1991; Griffiths 1974.

7. The idea is carried to an extreme in Brentano's value theory. Brentano claims that, since consciousness is intrinsically good, whereas evil requires consciousness, there can be no absolute evil. Brentano 1969, 1973. Chisholm 1986. The complex meaning Wittgenstein attaches to the concept of life is indicated in *Notebooks* 24.7.16: "The World and Life are one. Physiological life is of course not 'Life'. And neither is psychological life. Life is the world. Ethics does not treat of the world. Ethics must be a condition of the world, like logic. Ethics and aesthetics are one." See *Tractatus* 5.621.

8. 1.13–2.011; 2.013.

9. 5.542; 5.631–5.641. *Notebooks* 2.8.16–12.8.16.

10. The derivative intentionality of art and artifacts is described in similar terms by Margolis 1980; 1984; 1986.

11. Hume 1978. The classic empiricist statement of skepticism about the existence of self appears on 252: "For my part, when I enter most intimately into what I call *myself,* I always stumble on some particular perception or other, of heat or cold, light or shade, love or hatred, pain or pleasure. I never can catch *myself* at any time without a perception, and never can observe any thing but the perception."

12. Strawson 1959. Parfit 1984.

13. Nagel 1971.

15. Kant, *Critique of Pure Reason,* A106–31; B129–43.4. See Johnston 1989, esp. 74–78, 92–94, on the 'ineffability of value'. The influence of Weininger's 1903 and 1918 on Wittgenstein's doctrine of the transcendence of value is discussed by Haller, 90–99.

16. The extent to which Wittgenstein's transcendence of ethics translates from the early philosophy to the later period after he had rejected logical atomism and the picture theory of meaning is important to understanding the development of his thought as a whole. The role of the saying-showing distinction between sense and nonsense and the transcendence of extraworldly subjectivity is taken over in the later period of Wittgenstein's philosophy by his concept of the plurality of language games. Wittgenstein 1968 §77: "'Anything—and nothing—is right.'—And this is the position you are in if you look for definitions corresponding to our concepts in aesthetics or ethics. In such a difficulty always ask yourself: How did we *learn* the meaning of this word ('good' for instance)? From what sort of examples? in what language-games? Then it will be easier for you to see that the word must have a family of meanings."

17. Barrett 1991, 30; see also 60–63. *Notebooks* 24.7.16: "Ethics does not treat of the world. Ethics must be a condition of the world, like logic." *Tractatus* 6.13: "Logic is not a theory but a reflexion of the world. Logic is transcendental."

18. 5.5421. 5.641: "The philosophical I is not the man, not the human body or the human soul of which psychology treats, but the metaphysical subject, the limit—not a part of the world." See also 5.631–5.633.

19. *Notebooks* 11.6.16–8.7.16; 21.7.16–1.8.16; 13.8.16; 20.10.16–21.10.16.

20. Ethics is identified with aesthetics in the final statement of *Notebooks* 24.7.16. See also, in connection with Wittgenstein's extension of the relation between ethics and happiness, his remark for 21.10.16, that "the beautiful *is* what makes happy."

21. There is a distance of many intervening pages between *Tractatus* 5.5421, in the last passage of which Wittgenstein explicitly mentions the transcendence of the metaphysical subject, and 6.41, where Wittgenstein discusses the transcendence of value. The *Tractatus* makes no attempt to connect the two ideas or explicitly to prove the transcendence of value by the transcendence of the metaphysical subject. The *Notebooks* by contrast present the two sets of remarks immediately after one another in what looks to be the continuation of a single line of thought.

22. The majority of commentators on the *Tractatus* do not hazard interpretations of Wittgenstein's reasoning in 6.421. Black, for example, offers no interpretation or concordance, nor does he even include mention of the final parenthetical identification of ethics and aesthetics in the passage.

23. See Jacquette 1996a, 1–36.

24. Plato, *Republic* 410a7–412a6.

25. Wittgenstein 1967b, 143 (editor's appendix). It is intriguing to consider that Wittgenstein, impressed by the discursive limits of his own peculiarly intense moral and aesthetic experience, may have concluded, not à la Hume that there is a *psychological* explanation of how passion can overwhelm and interfere with reason and the verbal expression of value, but rather that there is a deeper *logical-semantic* explanation for the speechlessness and inadequacy of attempts to express values. To do justice to the nondiscursiveness of value, Wittgenstein offers the complicated logical-semantic machinery of the *Tractatus* primarily for the purpose of marking the distinction between fact and value as precisely and unequivocally as possible.

26. See Black 1964, 370. Black castigates Wittgenstein's transcendence doctrine as "irredeemable nonsense," which he distinguishes from the nonsense that arises merely from trying to say what can only be

shown. If the analysis proposed here is correct, then there is no difficulty in the idea that a transcendent ethics might show itself in a variety of ways in the world of facts. For example, in *Notebooks* 8.7.16, Wittgenstein, perhaps reflecting on his recent experiences as an artillery officer in World War I, maintains: "Fear in face of death is the best sign of a false, i.e. a bad, life."

27. Wittgenstein's thesis of the transcendence of value is also related to the so-called 'is-ought' distinction. See Hume's discussion of an inferential version of the distinction in attempts to derive statements of moral value from statements of fact in *Treatise,* 469, and Moore's 1903 formulation of the 'naturalistic fallacy' concerning attempts to define the good in terms of natural properties involving matters of fact, esp. 10, 13–14. Wittgenstein's transcendence thesis also reinforces Aristotle's observation in *Nicomachean Ethics* 1094b11–1095a2, that ethical matters do not admit of rigorous demonstration, and that "it is the mark of an educated man to look for precision in each class of things just so far as the nature of the subject admits." Joachim 1951, 1–18 and 31–47, on the analysis of book 1, chapter 6.

28. 4.112–4.115.

29. 4.113. See also *Notebooks* 7.30.16: "What is the objective mark of the happy, harmonious life? Here it is again clear that there cannot be any such mark, that can be *described*. This mark cannot be a physical one but only a metaphysical one, a transcendental one. Ethics is transcendental."

30. Wittgenstein acknowledges as much in his letter to von Ficker. This lack of philosophical interest in the scientific description of facts also explains why Wittgenstein, trained as scientist and engineer, to the chagrin of Russell and the logical positivists of the Vienna Circle, has almost nothing to say about epistemology or philosophy of science. Even the late (1969) manuscript *On Certainty* is not so much an attempt to develop a theory of empirical knowledge as a study of philosophical grammar surrounding uses of certain epistemic language game terms.

31. The question naturally arises whether in offering philosophical reflections on the transcendence of value Wittgenstein is not also engaging in theoretical ethics or metaethics, in violation of the saying-showing distinction. To this objection Wittgenstein can only reply that in doing so he is admittedly uttering literal nonsense, though with a mitigating heuristic purpose. After setting things right in this way, there is no need for him to speak as though there could be a genuine value theory. This is in sharp contrast with those who accept the possibility of a theoretical or philosophical ethics or metaethics, and are committed to its continued use. There is a rhetorical point in Wittgenstein's using the mistaken pseudolanguage of theoretical ethics to help arrive at a correct concept of significance by which ethical talk can then be understood as meaningless. After the exercise is complete, the pseudopropositions of ethics like the rest of the *Tractatus* ladder are cast away as philosophically unnecessary.

32. Wittgenstein, *Tractatus,* preface, 29.

33. See also Anscombe, 171–73; Barrett 1991; Barrett, Paton, and Blocker 1967; Finch, 167–80; Jacquette 1997a; Janik and Toulmin, 120–201; Johnston 1989; Kelly 1995; Pears 1987, 1, 153–90; Schulte 1992, 71–76; Tanner 1966; Walker 1968.

CHAPTER
S I X | Philosophical Pseudoproblems

The picture theory of meaning avoids many classical philosophical problems. The *Tractatus* logic is not subject to standard self-referential paradoxes like the Liar or Russell's, because the picture theory forbids any sentence in a correct logical symbolism from saying anything about itself. The most nagging conceptual puzzles about the nature of mind in its relation to body, the immortality of the soul, solipsism, freedom of will, and the principles of ethics and aesthetics are eliminated as nonsense by the general form of proposition and the extraworldly transcendence of the metaphysical subject and the extraworldly transcendence of value.

The history of philosophy has been a mistake. Its questions cannot be intelligibly asked or answered. Philosophers suffer from the delusion that they are involved in meaningful inquiry. Wittgenstein believes that when properly analyzed all philosophical discourse is literally nonsensical, *unsinnig*. The only genuine propositions to be found in any logically correct language are those that express true or false factual statements, ultimately reducible to conjunctions of atomic space-time-color predications of the form 'Red here now', 'Blue there then'. The range of meaningful thoughts and expressions is limited internally by the boundary of thought and language defined by the general form of proposition. What passes for meaningful philosophical discourse, including the sentences of the *Tractatus,* is beyond the pale of what can meaningfully be said in any logically possible language. The apparent engagement of thought with traditional philosophical problems is logically meaningless, a tangled web of nonsensical pseudopropositions (*Scheinsätze*) about nonsensical philosophical pseudoproblems.

The *Tractatus* is not so much another contribution to philosophy, on a par though in doctrinal disagreement with the great systems of the past. Wittgenstein offers a refinement of (pseudo-) philosophical methods aimed at ending philosophy as traditionally conceived by silencing its nonsensical questions. Philosophical problems disappear into the semantic outland of nonsense, and with them all of traditional philosophy. Wittgenstein then turns the attack on his own labors in articulating the metaphysics of logical atomism and the picture theory of meaning. The *Tractatus* implies its own meaninglessness, a result Wittgenstein willingly embraces. When Wittgenstein pulls the rug out from under traditional philosophy in the concluding passages of the *Tractatus,* he does as much to his own pseudopropositional exposition. Working through the development of logical atomism and the picture theory of meaning with their consequences nevertheless serves an important heuristic purpose, by nonpropositionally communicating an understanding of the logic of language through which the problems of philosophy can at last be put to rest. After this, having assimilated insight into the limits of thought, language, and the world, we can discard philosophy, including the meaningless pronouncements of the *Tractatus,* and trade its confusions in for more practical concerns, in the appreciation and cultivation of value in theoretical silence, and in the only productive uses of language in the expression of everyday nonphilosophical thought and the advancement of empirical science.

An overview of Wittgenstein's dismissal of philosophical problems as pseudoproblems provides a framework for understanding the details of his conclusions. Wittgenstein traces philosophical pseudoproblems and philosophical pseudopropositions to the sign-symbol distinction. He lays the groundwork for a picture theory diagnosis of the origin and avoidance of the traditional problems of philosophy in the fact that the same perceptible linguistic sign can be used equivocally:

3.32   The sign is the part of the symbol perceptible by the senses.

3.321   Two different symbols can therefore have the sign (the written sign or the sound sign) in common—they then signify in different ways.

3.322   It can never indicate the common characteristic of two objects that we symbolize them with the same signs but by different *methods of symbolizing.* For the sign is arbitrary. We could therefore equally well choose two different signs and where then would be what was common in the symbolization.

Wittgenstein illustrates the difficulty posed by the conventionality of signs in semantic confusions that pervade traditional philosophy. Analysis must look beyond the arbitrary application of signs to the methods of symbolizing facts, where philosophical problems do not arise. Wittgenstein offers the example of multiple uses of the term 'is' as subject-predicate copula, identity, and existence predicate. The pseudoproblems that result are due to the accident that some modern European languages permit the verb of being to serve all three roles. But this latitude is not encountered in every language, nor in what is essential to language in the transcendent order of imperceptible symbols:

> 3.333 In the language of everyday life it very
> often happens that the same word signifies
> in two different ways—and therefore belongs
> to two different symbols—or that two words,
> which signify in different ways, are apparently
> applied in the same way in the proposition.
>
> Thus the word "is" appears as the copula, as the
> sign of equality, and as the expression of exis-
> tence; "to exist" as an intransitive verb like "to
> go"; "identical" as an adjective; we speak of *some-
> thing* but also of the fact of *something* happening.
>
> (In the proposition "Green is green"—where the
> first word is a proper name and the last an adjec-
> tive—these words have not merely different
> meanings but they are *different symbols*.)

A typical example of this kind of equivocation occurs in the logical howler of trying to prove the existence of God by the deduction: (1) God *is* by definition the creator of the universe (in the copula of predication sense); therefore, God *is* (in the existence sense). The problem is avoided by distinguishing between these two meanings of the verb and disqualifying the inference from one sense to the other.

Many sign-symbol confusions in philosophical (pseudo-) discourse are less easy to uncover or disentangle. Wittgenstein writes: `

> 3.324 Thus there easily arise the most fundamental con-
> fusions (of which the whole of philosophy is full).
>
> 3.325 In order to avoid these errors, we must employ a
> symbolism which excludes them, by not applying
> the same sign in different symbols and by not
> applying signs in the same way which signify in
> different ways. A symbolism, that is to say, which
> obeys the rules of *logical* grammar—of logical
> syntax.

(The logical symbolism of Frege and Russell is such
a language, which, however, does still not exclude
all errors.)

If semantic analysis is to avoid philosophical babble, we
must adopt a correct logical symbolism unencumbered by the
equivocations of conventional sign systems in ordinary language.
The propositions of colloquial language may be, as Wittgenstein
says in 5.5563, "just as they are, logically completely in order."
But this is true only of essential symbolic and not of superficial
logical sign-system structures. "Words are like the film on deep
water," Wittgenstein writes in *Notebooks* 30.5.15.

The equivocations permitted by the same sign conventionally
representing different symbols makes ordinary language a
logician's nightmare. They are the source of philosophical
difficulties that Wittgenstein believes cannot arise in the transcendent order of symbols. Frege and Russell also recognize the
limitations of ordinary language, and propose as a solution to replace logically faulty everyday discourse for scientific purposes
with a more exact and unequivocal ideal language or *Begriffsschrift*. Frege and Russell define logical analysis as the substitution
of reformulations of disordered ordinary language expressions in an
ideal logical notation. For Wittgenstein, by contrast, logical analysis is a transcendental archaeology of the logical structures underlying the conventions of ordinary language. Wittgenstein sees
no need to find an ideal replacement for ordinary language, since
if ordinary language were not already logically completely in order as a meaningful expression of facts, there would be no possibility of exchanging it for a more exact symbolization.

Wittgenstein is dissatisfied with the logic of Frege and Whitehead and Russell, and complains about the inadequacy of their
formalisms. The picture theory of meaning supports criticisms of
their use of identity (5.533, 6.232), the assertion sign ('⊢') (*Ur-
teilsstrich*) to indicate logical theoremhood (4.442), type theory
(3.331–3.333; 5.251–5.252; 6.123), the axiom of infinity (5.535),
and axiom of reducibility (6.1232–6.1233). Wittgenstein nevertheless credits Russell with the perception that the surface logic
of a proposition must often be distinguished from its real, deeper,
underlying logic:

4.0031 All philosophy is "Critique of language" (but not
at all in Mauthner's sense). Russell's merit is to
have shown that the apparent logical form of the
proposition need not be its real form.

The *Tractatus* does not try to replace everyday language with an ideal formalism. Wittgenstein wants to understand the logic of language as we actually use it. By explaining the necessary conditions for any language, he claims to discover the concept or essence of language. His starting place is the anthropological fact that we make to ourselves pictures of facts. The problem of understanding the determinate meaningfulness of language cannot be addressed by setting ordinary language aside as though it had no meaning and developing an ideal language instead. Inquiry into the nature of language necessarily leads Wittgenstein beyond the realm of perceptible signs of particular languages to what is essential to the concept of language in the transcendent order of imperceptible symbols. The logically correct symbolism posited by the *Tractatus* picture theory as a requirement for the possibility of the determinate meaningfulness of language in some ways resembles the formal logical systems of Frege and Russell. Wittgenstein's logic of symbols by contrast exists all along as hidden beneath or transcending ordinary language signs.[1]

Philosophical confusions arise through equivocation. The logic that underlies the accidental appearance of linguistic sign-systems is unequivocal. Language in the transcendent order is free of the logical errors that occur as the result of ambiguous expressions in traditional philosophical discourse. What are popularly called philosophical problems are not substantive difficulties to be solved or resolved by meaningful philosophical theories. Philosophical problems are meaningless pseudoproblems that disappear when we arrive at an understanding of the requirements of the logically correct symbolism underlying any logically possible language. If we think of philosophy as the quest to discover a certain set of propositions that will satisfy our intellectual curiosity about a special subject matter or answer deeper yearnings about the meaning of life, then we are afflicted with an entirely mistaken expectation. There are no philosophical problems, no genuine philosophical propositions that could possibly provide meaningfully true or false answers to meaningful philosophical questions. By adopting a correct view of the logic of language that excludes all philosophical discourse as nonsense we can avoid being troubled by philosophical puzzles. It is only in this way that we can hope to resolve philosophical 'problems', by recognizing that there are no such problems, and that philosophical 'propositions' are nonsensical pseudopropositions involving logically meaningless abuses of language.

The elimination of philosophical problems as pseudoproblems can be understood by comparison with the strategy Wittgenstein adopts in his criticism of Russell's type theory. The theory of types is offered in *Principia Mathematica* as a solution to various forms of the Liar paradox, including the set theoretical version to which Russell lends his name. The Liar and the Russell paradox are self-non-applicational constructions, in which a sentence explicitly denies the self-attribution of a logical or semantic property the sentence must have in order for the self-denial to be true. The Liar paradox formulates a proposition that says of itself that it lies or is false. If the sentence is true, then it is false, since it says of itself that it is false; if the sentence is false, then it is true, since then it falsely says of itself that it is false. The Russell paradox similarly defines the set of all sets that are not members of themselves, from which it seems to follow that the set of all sets that are not members of themselves is itself a member of itself if and only if it is not a member of itself.[2]

Russell sought to avoid the paradox by imposing a simple theory of types. Terms are stratified in an ascending ordered hierarchy of types; object terms have type 0, predicate terms that apply to objects (as in 'This apple is red') have type 1 or are first-order, predicates of predicates (as in 'Redness is a color') have type 2 or are second-order, and so on, indefinitely. Russell stipulates that no term of any type can be applied to any other term of the same or higher type, but that for any terms in any well-formed proposition of the logic, only a predicate term of type $n+1$ can be applied to a predicate or object term of type n. This avoids the Liar and Russell paradoxes, which are formulated in symbolic logic by means of sentences containing predicates that purport to express formal logical, semantic, or set theoretical self-non-applications.[3]

Wittgenstein rejects Russell's theory of types. He claims that what type theory tries unsuccessfully to accomplish by restricting logically permissible syntax combinations within logic is automatically guaranteed by the picture theory's requirements for adequate formal representation. Types are unnecessary, and therefore logically meaningless, according to Wittgenstein's interpretation of Occam's razor. The pseudoproblems of the Liar and Russell paradox are avoided in a correct logical symbolism by the need for an exact logical isomorphism or mathematical multiplicity of symbol and fact. Wittgenstein's explanation of Occam's razor which he applies to the elimination of propositional attitude contexts and the psychological subject first occurs in 3.328, as part of his refutation of Russell's theory of types. Wittgenstein maintains that the syntax of a correct logical notation must function correctly on its own, without the intervention of an explication of a symbol's meaning:

> 3.33   In logical syntax the meaning of a sign ought never
> to play a rôle; it must admit of being established
> without mention being thereby made of the *meaning* of a sign; it ought to presuppose *only* the description of the expressions.

The adequate description of an expression according to the picture theory must always share with it a certain logical isomorphism, which when completely analyzed exhibits its purely formal logical meaning. This makes the effort to give a further explication of meaning in what is standardly called a metalanguage superfluous. Wittgenstein objects to Russell's theory of types because it requires this sort of explanation of the meaning of typed expressions, by giving the type-orderings of type-indexed expressions F^1a^0, $G^2(F^1a^0)$, and the like.

The attempt to make a propositional sign say something about itself violates the requirements of exact logical isomorphism between symbol and what is symbolized. The conditions for a correct logical symbolism preclude the possibility of propositional signs denying semantic properties of themselves, as in the case of 'paradoxical' self-non-applications. The picture theory of meaning makes Russell's theory of types unnecessary by implying that a representationally correct formalism cannot contain picturing facts capable of picturing themselves for purposes of predicating or denying properties of themselves. A picture could only say something about itself, Wittgenstein likes to say, by standing outside itself. There is no room within the logical structure of a proposition for the proposition to picture itself—it would need to be bigger than itself in order to say anything about itself. The problematic syntax combinations known as the Liar paradox and Russell paradox that Russell tries to avoid by type theory cannot occur in a correct logical symbolism.[4]

Wittgenstein explains how Russell's paradox disappears under the picture theory of meaning when we adopt the standpoint of a logically correct symbolism in a representationally adequate formal logic. Wittgenstein clarifies his criticism of Russell's paradox and Russell's theory of types respectively as a philosophical pseudoproblem and pseudosolution. The logical impossibility of a proposition with the necessary logical structure containing within itself its own representation is decisive in discounting both Russell's paradox as a logically meaningful philosophical problem and the theory of types as a logically meaningful solution. Wittgenstein adds:

> 3.331 From this observation we get a further view—into Russell's *Theory of Types*. Russell's error is shown by the fact that in drawing up his symbolic rules he has to speak about the things his signs mean.
>
> 3.332 No proposition can say anything about itself, because the propositional sign cannot be contained in itself (that is the "whole theory of types").
>
> 3.333 A function cannot be its own argument, because the functional sign already contains the prototype of its own argument and it cannot contain itself.
>
> If, for example, we suppose that the function $F(fx)$ could be its own argument, then there would be a proposition "$F(F(fx))$", and in this the outer function F and the inner function F must have different meanings; for the inner has the form $\phi(fx)$, the outer the form $\psi(\phi(fx))$. Common to both functions is only the letter "F", which by itself signifies nothing.
>
> This is at once clear, if instead of "$F(F(u))$" we write "$(\exists\phi) : F(\phi u). \phi u = Fu$".
>
> Herewith Russell's paradox vanishes.

Wittgenstein uses an elegant formal device to demonstrate the impossibility of Liar or Russell paradoxes. The logical structure of functions on objects and functions on functions, in picture theory terms, shows even to casual inspection that no proposition in the required picture theory sense can literally contain itself as argument, or otherwise designate, refer to, or attribute to or deny properties of itself in the notation. The function $F(fx)$ cannot be its own argument, for if it were, then, taking the function as its own argument and inserting the function $F(fx)$ in the fx argument place, we obtain the manifestly different proposition $F(F(fx))$.[5] Here, as Wittgenstein observes, the outermost function term 'F' and the innermost function term 'F' would need to have different meanings. This is the very sort of equivocation in the meaning of logical terms that cannot arise in a correct logical symbolism. Wittgenstein employs metavariables to show that the innermost application of the function term would need to be different from the outermost, because the first has the form $\phi(fx)$, and the second the form $\psi(\phi(fx))$. If the forms are different, then their meanings according to the picture theory are most definitely different. The two functions in that case are not correctly symbolized, but misleadingly designated by an identical sign, 'F', which, as Wittgenstein rightly notes, "by itself signifies nothing." Russell's paradox vanishes, in the same way that the picture theory of meaning disposes of all traditional philosophical problems as pseudoproblems. The theory of types is unnecessary as a solution to the paradox, because there is no paradox to be solved.[6]

In explaining the concept of thought as an applied propositional sign, Wittgenstein generalizes on the nonexistence of philosophical problems and the nonsense of attempts to ask and answer philosophical questions. Philosophy is deprived of its centuries-old subject matter in just a few poignant passages:

> 4.003 Most propositions and questions, that have been written about philosophical matters, are not false, but senseless [*unsinnig*]. We cannot, therefore, answer questions of this kind at all, but only state their senselessness [*Unsinnigkeit*]. Most questions and propositions of the philosophers result from the fact that we do not understand the logic of our language.
>
> (They are of the same kind as the question whether the Good is more or less identical than the Beautiful.)
>
> And so it is not to be wondered that the deepest problems are really *no* problems.

The attempt to state philosophical problems or solutions is as meaningless as the pseudopropositional excesses of metaphysical idealism that tough-minded critics like Frege and Russell ridicule. Wittgenstein concludes that even the most scientifically oriented philosophers are mistaken in their efforts to articulate philosophical problems and solutions, though their use of formal logic and superficially lucid prose may make their particular style of nonsense more difficult to detect.

There are no philosophical problems, and no philosophical propositions to serve as philosophical solutions. Philosophy consists of pseudoproblems, of meaningless formulations that masquerade as genuine questions and meaningless formulations that masquerade as genuine answers. Philosophers pretend to make sense in discussing the logical paradoxes, the existence of abstract entities, the metaphysics of substance and causation, God, the nature of the soul, freedom of will, knowledge and skepticism, ethics and aesthetics, and the meaning of life. The analysis of philosophical concepts seems to result in a connected series of propositions drafted on the model of scientific hypotheses and theories, to be defended by arguments and tested by criticism according to the standards of good reasoning. All this Wittgenstein rejects as literal nonsense, dismissing the concepts of philosophy as pseudoconcepts (*Scheinbegriffe*). The proper use of language, the only meaningful expression of thought, is in the logical picturing of existent or nonexistent facts. If philosophy is excluded from the meaningful development of theory by virtue of its limitation to pseudoconcepts and pseudopropositions about philosophical pseudoproblems, then it remains to say what value if any philosophy might have. This Wittgenstein now proceeds to explain:

> 4.111 Philosophy is not one of the natural sciences.
>
> (The word "philosophy" must mean something which stands above or below, but not beside the natural sciences.)
>
> 4.112 The object of philosophy is the logical clarification of thoughts.
>
> Philosophy is not a theory but an activity.
>
> A philosophical work consists essentially of elucidations.
>
> The result of philosophy is not a number of "philosophical propositions", but to make propositions clear.
>
> Philosophy should make clear and delimit sharply the thoughts which otherwise are, as it were, opaque and blurred.

Philosophy, Wittgenstein says in 4.0031, is critique of language. The Kantian or Schopenhauerian flavor of Wittgenstein's transcendental deduction of logical atomism and the picture theory of meaning has already been remarked. The other Kantian element of Wittgenstein's early philosophy is the demarcation of a definite limit to the possibilities of meaning in thought and language, the boundary between what can be said and what is nonsense or can only be shown, between the facts of the world and whatever transcends the world of facts. This is akin to Kant's distinction between reason and faith, and to the task of the *Critique of Pure Reason* to determine the limits of knowledge attainable by pure reason alone as opposed to reason informed by intuition or sense experience, and as distinct from what lies beyond the bounds of sense.[7]

Wittgenstein describes the proper role of philosophy as the activity of clarifying the meaning, scope, and limits of language, rather than as a system of propositions like those meaningfully advanced in the empirical sciences. Wittgenstein's elucidations of meaning in the *Tractatus* thereby qualify as philosophy. What remains are heuristic pseudoconcepts in nonsensical logical, semantic, and philosophical pseudopropositions. Despite the efforts of metaphysics, the picture theory of meaning implies that the world as a whole cannot be represented in thought or language. To grasp a nonrepresentational sense of the world in its entirety imaginatively as though from the outside or beyond, looking down at it from above as an object of contemplation, Wittgenstein says, is the mystical:

6.44　Not *how* the world is, is the mystical, but *that* it is.

6.45　The contemplation of the world sub specie aeterni is its contemplation as a limited whole.

　　　The feeling of the world as a limited whole is the mystical feeling.

The temptation to offer a philosophical theory to satisfy the sense of mystery that accompanies our contemplation of the world as a whole, *sub specie aeterni,* is to be resisted as a powerful source of philosophical pseudoproblems. Wittgenstein denies the adequacy of philosophy to explain the ultimate nature of existence. The question cannot be meaningfully asked or answered. We must abandon the search for philosophical knowledge, for there is none to be had. To give up philosophical questions and the urge for their solution as logically meaningless, with a full appreciation of why there can be no such meaningful questions or answers, is all the philosophical satisfaction we have any right to expect. We can only try to answer nonphilosophical questions, and recognize when we are done that there is nothing more to be said. The quieting of desire for philosophical explanation is the best Wittgenstein believes we can do in confronting the deepest (pseudo-) problems of philosophy:

6.5　For an answer which cannot be expressed the question too cannot be expressed.

　　　The riddle does not exist.

　　　If a question can be put at all, then it *can* also be answered.

6.51　Scepticism is *not* irrefutable, but palpably senseless [*unsinnig*], if it would doubt where a question cannot be asked.

　　　For doubt can only exist where there is a question; a question only where there is an answer, and this only where something can be *said*.

6.52　We feel that even if *all possible* scientific questions be answered, the problems of life have still not been touched at all. Of course there is then no question left, and just this is the answer.

Wittgenstein then turns to the lofty topic of the meaning of life. The questions here, contrary to the speculative tradition in philosophy, are one and all logically meaningless. We can seek no answers, but must try to be satisfied with the insight that there is nothing worthwhile to be known or said about such things. This attitude is shown by persons who have arrived at an inexpressible understanding of the whole in mystical experience, and are unable to put their hard-won insights into words. What cannot be said shows itself instead in action, in philosophy reconceived as the activity of clarification, and in limiting expression to genuine propositions about ordinary nonphilosophical matters of fact:

> 6.521 The solution of the problem of life is seen in the vanishing of the problem.
>
> (Is not this the reason why men to whom after long doubting the sense of life became clear, could not then say wherein this sense consisted?)
>
> 6.522 There is indeed the inexpressible. This *shows* itself; it is the mystical.

The implications for teaching philosophy are humbling. As an activity of clarifying thoughts, proper philosophical pedagogy is limited to saying what is sayable and rejecting all attempts to say whatever is logically unsayable as nonsense. Wittgenstein anticipates the objection that such an exercise would not appear to be teaching philosophy. He replies that nevertheless it is the only philosophical practice justified by the logic of propositions. To teach philosophy according to the picture theory of meaning is to guide students in the correct expression of nonphilosophical thoughts, and to disabuse them of the expectation that there are substantive philosophical doctrines to discover or learn, to explain that there are no philosophical questions or philosophical answers, no philosophical truths:

> 6.53 The right method of philosophy would be this. To say nothing except what can be said, *i.e.* the propositions of natural science, *i.e.* something that has nothing to do with philosophy: and then always, when someone else wished to say something metaphysical, to demonstrate to him that he had given no meaning to certain signs in his propositions. This method would be unsatisfying to the other—he would not have the feeling that we were teaching him philosophy—but it would be the only strictly correct method.

In the final passages of the text, Wittgenstein turns the critique of language against the pseudopropositions of the *Tractatus*.

The famous image of the ladder in 6.54 gives a heuristic justification to the literal nonsense we have endured. It has not all been for nothing, even though the sentences we have struggled over are meaningless and do not constitute a legitimate philosophical theory of the world, thought, or language, or of any of the other themes developed along the way. We have arrived at wisdom about the transcendental logic of language, of ideas that we see now are officially inexpressible, unsayable, meaningless, nonsensical. We ascend the ladder as the understanding proceeds from pseudoproposition to pseudoproposition, rung to rung. Then, with a grasp of the limitations of the world and meaning in thought and language, we look back to see that the ladder itself was only a useful prop to help us arrive at this point, and we are at length compelled to cast it aside as no longer needed:

> 6.54 My propositions are elucidatory in this way: he who
> understands me finally recognizes them as senseless
> [*unsinnig*], when he has climbed out through them,
> on them, over them. (He must so to speak throw
> away the ladder, after he has climbed up on it.)
>
> He must surmount these propositions; then he sees
> the world rightly.

The last dramatic and oft-quoted sentence of the *Tractatus* is as impressive for what it shows as for what we know by now it cannot say, in the empty white space of the page and the absence of further commentary:

> 7 Whereof one cannot speak, thereof one must be
> silent.

Here Wittgenstein's treatise abruptly ends. The problems of philosophy are rejected as pseudoproblems, and all efforts to answer them are dismissed as pseudopropositions. Wittgenstein accordingly stops doing philosophy, not only in the book, but in his personal life. Having concluded that there is nothing sufficiently interesting left to do, Wittgenstein withdraws from the practice, teaching, and writing of philosophy.[8] He leaves himself little choice but to waive traditional philosophical pursuits for more practical concerns. He turns to unassuming service, teaching grade school and working in a monk's garden, and later to art. The minor uninteresting role that remains to philosophy when its pseudoproblems have been discounted he believes he has already undertaken as far as his abilities allow in writing the *Tractatus*.[9]

These are powerful (anti-) philosophical conclusions. But are they correct? The transcendent is inscrutable, yet Wittgenstein by the general form of proposition consigns many different kinds of things to nonsense, to what can only be shown and not said. The most enlightening ideas of philosophy join logic, logical, pictorial, and representational form, the metaphysical subject, ethical-aesthetic value considered as one, and arrant gibberish. In the subcategory of philosophy alone Wittgenstein places together as meaningless nonsense what he himself refers to in the preface to the *Tractatus* as "the great works of Frege and the writings of my friend Bertrand Russell," to which, he says, "I owe in large measure the stimulation of my thoughts" (29), along with the worst excesses of metaphysical idealism represented by such confectionary neo-Hegelian slogans as 'Identity negates itself in the cradle of the infinite'. What are we to think about the implication that all philosophy alike is pseudopropositional?

One objection to Wittgenstein's exiling so much of importance to the realm of literal nonsense is that we should still be entitled at least to use language as Wittgenstein does in the *Tractatus* to construct our own ladders. By such means we might consider, for example, the epistemic, moral, and aesthetic attitudes that can or should be adopted toward the world of facts. What mystic sages understand about the unspeakable meaning of life might be arrived at by less spiritual philosophical methods in a continuation of philosophical traditions within the framework of Wittgenstein's logical atomism and picture theory of meaning. When we are done, we can discard the heuristic fruits of efforts to work through philosophical problems philosophically. Why should the rest of the world stop doing philosophy precisely when Wittgenstein decides to at the end of the *Tractatus?*

Wittgenstein, in his letter to von Ficker, indicates his interest in the unwritten and unsayable importance of value. The practical philosophical questions concern such things as whether it is always wrong to steal or kill. To say that the sentence 'It is morally wrong to steal' is literal nonsense is unconvincing, since at one level we know perfectly well what such sentences mean. A semantics that classifies the statement as nonsense does not settle the problem of what we ought to do, whether we ought or ought not to steal. It is one thing to walk away from philosophical pseudoproblems like whether or not there are universals or the soul is immortal as nonsensical and ultimately incapable of meaningful answer. It is quite another matter to respond to the question whether we should acquiesce to heinous institutional evil with a shrug of the shoulders and a refusal to consider the issue seriously on the grounds that it is nothing more than a nonsensical philosophical pseudoproblem. If the problems of traditional philosophy cannot be settled as definitely and straightforwardly as the problems of mathematics and empirical science, that may only show that they are different kinds of problems, not that they are pseudoproblems.

The picture theory of meaning might explain the logically necessary conditions for representing facts in factual language. But why should Wittgenstein regard its requirements as sufficient for all of language, marking the limitations of meaningful expression in any logically possible language to the exclusion of all philosophical discourse as pseudopropositional? Why should we agree with Wittgenstein that all meaningful language is only and exclusively fact-representational? Consider Wittgenstein's rejection of pseudopropositions about the self and psychological states, including judgments of moral and aesthetic value. The transcendence of the self or soul by which all such discourse is deemed nonsense is implied by Occam's razor. Yet the subject's propositional attitudes are shown to be unnecessary at most only for the specifically representational function of fact-picturing language. The argument does not prove anything more unless we already agree with Wittgenstein that all language is essentially descriptive, fact-picturing or fact-representing. If by 'meaning' we mean nothing beyond the true or false picturing of logically contingent facts (with tautology and contradiction thrown in as limiting cases), then of course it is a foregone conclusion that talk about the self, soul, or subject, psychological states, value, and matters of philosophical inquiry generally are all logically meaningless. But is language meaningful only in picturing facts? Why is it meaningless to speak about transcendent logical and representational form, the metaphysical subject, and value? Does not Wittgenstein do so at length, and do we not understand well enough what he says?[10]

Wittgenstein might defend his narrowly focused view of meaning by asking us to reconsider the alternatives. He might recall his application of Frege's doctrine of contextual semantic holism in 3.142, that "Only facts can express a sense, a class of names cannot," and in 3.3, that "Only the proposition has sense; only in the context of a proposition has a name meaning." It must be so if language is to avoid the inherent ambiguities of the same signs used conventionally to denote different things. If terms by themselves have no meaning, but only in the context of a descriptive proposition, and if the explanation of the sense of a proposition can be explained only as a picture of facts, then we are driven back despite ourselves to the pictorial representation of facts in meaningful propositions, and hence to the logical representational limits of the picture theory of meaning. Terms must be articulated into a definite logical structure in order to convey determinate meaning. The only possible relation is the picturing or representing of facts by other logically isomorphic facts.

It follows, if Wittgenstein's transcendental reasoning is sound, that there can be no describable, and hence no thinkable, alternative to the picture theory of meaning. All thinking and all logically meaningful language is a true or false picturing of facts. This is the quasi-Kantian limit to thought and its expression in language that Wittgenstein proposes to draw from within its bounds as the critique of language that reveals the necessary conditions by which thought and language are logically possible. It is on the strength of this argument, that there is no alternative to the picture theory of meaning, and that the picture theory of meaning excludes all fact-nonrepresentational appearances of thought or language as logically meaningless and literally nonsensical, that Wittgenstein regards the concepts, problems, and propositions of philosophy as pseudoconcepts, pseudoproblems, and pseudopropositions.[11]

I N O T E S

1. Haller, 57–73.
2. Black 1964, 145–47.
3. The Liar paradox can be written as $ZZ \equiv \sim ZZ$, where $Z = \lambda x[\sim(xx)]$, given the equivalence $(\forall y)(\lambda x[\ldots x \ldots] y \equiv (\ldots y \ldots))$ (the 'λ' operator converts a proposition into a predicate term for a complex property). The Russell paradox can be written as $R' \in R \equiv R' \notin R$, where $R = \{x \mid x \in x\}$ (or, equivalently, $= \{x \mid \in(xx)\}$), and $R' = \{x \mid x \notin x\} (= \{x \mid \notin (xx)\})$. In both formulations, a term is applied to another instance of the same type term (ZZ, $\sim ZZ$, $\sim(xx)$, $\in(xx)$, $\notin(xx)$). Russell's type theory forbids all such constructions as logically improperly formed and hence not constructible in his logic, thereby avoiding the paradoxes.
4. Wittgenstein 1974b, letter to Russell (R9), January 1913, 19. See also Wittgenstein's critique of the theory of types in *Notebooks*, "Notes on Logic," appendix 1, pp. 105–6, and "Notes Dictated to G. E. Moore in Norway," appendix 2, 108–10.
5. Wittgenstein could not interpret $F(F(fx))$ as a function, but only as the partial expression of a successive operation. The distinction between function and operation is explained in *Tractatus* 5.25.
6. Griffin 1964, 19–25; Kenny 1973, 41–51; Bradley, 156–61.
7. The first part of 4.0031 adds the qualification: "All philosophy is 'Critique of language' (but not at all in Mauthner's sense)." Fritz Mauthner's strict nominalist critique of language is examined in relation to Wittgenstein's remark by Janik and Toulmin, 119–33, 165–68, 178–82, 196–99. Also Haller, 52–62, 70–73.
8. See von Wright in Malcolm 1958, 11: "The author of the *Tractatus* thought he had solved all philosophical problems. It was consistent with this view that he should give up philosophy." Fann 1978, 41: "After the publication of the *Tractatus* Wittgenstein abandoned philosophy to

become an elementary-school teacher in an Austrian village. This course of action was quite consistent with his contention in the *Tractatus* that all essential philosophical problems were solved. Ramsey reported, '[Wittgenstein] says that he himself will do nothing more not because he is bored but because his mind is no longer flexible. He says no one can do more than 5 or 10 years good work at philosophy (his work took 7).' [From [Ramsey's] letter to his mother dated September 20th, 1923. Included in [F. A.] von Hayek's *Unfinished [Draft of a] Sketch [of a Biography of Wittgenstein]* (unpublished, 1953)]."

9. Wittgenstein, preface to the *Tractatus*, 29: "Here I am conscious that I have fallen far short of the possible. Simply because my powers are insufficient to cope with the task.—May others come and do it better."

10. Russell considers a similar criticism in his introduction to the *Tractatus*, 22: "What causes hesitation ['in accepting Mr. Wittgenstein's position'] is the fact that, after all, Mr. Wittgenstein manages to say a good deal about what cannot be said, thus suggesting to the sceptical reader that possibly there may be some loophole through a hierarchy of languages, or by some other exit." Priest 1995, 203: "In working out the details of his project Wittgenstein is forced, time and time again, to make statements on the far side of the boundary [between meaningful thought and nonsense]. The problem is like a time-bomb hidden in the machinery of the *Tractatus*, which finally detonates at the penultimate proposition in the book, producing stunned silence."

11. See also Hamburg 1953; McGuinness 1966; Priest 1995, 202–11; Schulte 1992, 41–46; Shields 1993; Wisan 1956; Worthington 1988.

PART TWO

Signs and Sources of Transition

When you have thought for some
time about a problem of your own,
you may come to see that it is closely
related to what has been discussed
before, only you will want to present
that problem in a different way.
These thoughts which seem so
important to you now, will one day
seem like a bag of old, rusty nails, no
use for anything at all.
—Wittgenstein, quoted in M.O'C. Drury,
"Conversations with Wittgenstein"

Wittgenstein used to say that the
Tractatus was not *all* wrong: it was
not like a bag of junk professing to be
a clock, but like a clock that did not
tell you the right time.
—G. E. M. Anscombe, *An Introduction to
Wittgenstein's Tractatus,* 78

Some Remarks on Logical Form

[162]   Every proposition has a content and a form. We get the picture of the pure form if we abstract from the meaning of the single words, or symbols (so far as they have independent meanings). That is to say, if we substitute variables for the constants of the proposition. The rules of syntax which applied to the constants must apply to the variables also. By syntax in this general sense of the word I mean the rules which tell us in which connections only a word gives sense, thus excluding nonsensical structures. The syntax of ordinary language, as is well known, is not quite adequate for this purpose. It does not in all cases prevent the construction of nonsensical pseudopropositions (constructions such as "red is higher than green" or "the Real, though it is an *in itself,* must also be able to become a *for myself*", etc.).

If we try to analyse any given propositions we shall find in general that they are logical sums, products or other truth-functions of simpler propositions. But our analysis, if carried far enough, must come to the point where it reaches propositional forms which are not themselves composed of simpler propositional forms. We must eventually reach the ultimate connection of the terms, the immediate connection which cannot be broken without [163] destroying the propositional form as such. The propositions which represent this ultimate connection of terms I

"Some Remarks on Logical Form" originally appeared in the *Aristotelian Society Supplementary Volume 9, Knowledge, Experience and Realism,* (London: Harrison and Sons, Ltd., 1929), pp. 162–71, and is reprinted by permission of the editor of the Aristotelian Society (1996). The original pagination is indicated in brackets.

call, after B. Russell, atomic propositions. They, then, are the kernels of every proposition, *they* contain the material, and all the rest is only a development of this material. It is to them we have to look for the subject matter of propositions. It is the task of the theory of knowledge to find them and to understand their construction out of the words or symbols. This task is very difficult, and Philosophy has hardly yet begun to tackle it at some points. What method have we for tackling it? The idea is to express in an appropriate symbolism what in ordinary language leads to endless misunderstandings. That is to say, where ordinary language disguises logical structure, where it allows the formation of pseudopropositions, where it uses one term in an infinity of different meanings, we must replace it by a symbolism which gives a clear picture of the logical structure, excludes pseudopropositions, and uses its terms unambiguously. Now we can only substitute a clear symbolism for the unprecise one by inspecting the phenomena which we want to describe, thus trying to understand their logical multiplicity. That is to say, we can only arrive at a correct analysis by, what might be called, the logical investigation of the phenomena themselves, *i.e.,* in a certain sense *a posteriori,* and not by conjecturing about *a priori* possibilities. One is often tempted to ask from an *a priori* standpoint: What, after all, *can* be the only forms of atomic propositions, and to answer, *e.g.,* subject-predicate and relational propositions with two or more terms further, perhaps, propositions relating predicates and relations to one another, and so on. But this, I believe, is mere playing with words. An atomic form cannot be foreseen. And it would be surprising if the actual [164] phenomena had nothing more to teach us about their structure. To such conjectures about the structure of atomic propositions, we are led by our ordinary language, which uses the subject-predicate and the relational form. But in this our language is misleading: I will try to explain this by a simile. Let us imagine two parallel planes, I and II. On plane I figures are drawn, say, ellipses and rectangles of different sizes and shapes, and it is our task to produce images of these figures on plane II. Then we can imagine two ways, amongst others, of doing this. We can, first, lay down a law of projection—say that of orthogonal projection or any other—and then proceed to project all figures from I into II, according to this law. Or, secondly, we could proceed thus: We lay down the rule that every ellipse on plane I is to appear as a circle in plane II, and every rectangle as a square in II. Such a way of representation may be convenient for us if for some reason we prefer to draw only circles and squares on plane II. Of course, from these images the exact shapes of the original figures on plane I cannot be immediately inferred. We can only gather from them that the original was an ellipse or a rectangle. In order to get in a single instance at the determinate shape of the original we would have to know the individual method by which, *e.g.*, a particular ellipse is projected into the circle before me. The case of ordinary language is quite analogous. If the facts of reality are the ellipses and rectangles on plane I the subject-predicate and relational forms correspond to the circles and squares in plane II. These forms are the norms of our particular language into which we project in *ever so many different* ways *ever so many different* logical forms. And for this very reason we can draw no conclusions—except very vague ones—from the use of these [165] norms as to the actual logical form of the phenomena described. Such forms as "This paper is boring", "The weather is fine", "I am lazy", which have nothing whatever in common with one another, present themselves as subject-predicate propositions, *i.e.*, apparently as propositions of the same form.

If, now, we try to get at an actual analysis, we find logical forms which have very little similarity with the norms of ordinary language. We meet with the forms of space and time and with the whole manifold of spatial and temporal objects, as colours, sounds, etc., etc., with their gradations, continuous transitions, and combinations in various proportions, all of which we cannot seize by our ordinary means of expression. And here I wish to make my first definite remark on the logical analysis of actual phenomena: it is this, that for their representation numbers (rational and irrational) must enter into the structure of the atomic propositions themselves. I will illustrate this by an example. Imagine a system of rectangular axes, as it were, cross wires, drawn in our field of vision and an arbitrary scale fixed. It is clear that we then can describe the shape and position of every patch of colour in our visual field by means of statements of numbers which have their significance relative to the system of co-ordinates and the unit chosen. Again, it is clear that this description will have the right logical multiplicity, and that a description which has a smaller multiplicity will not do. A simple example would be the representation of a patch P by the expression "[6—9, 3—8]" and of a proposition [166]

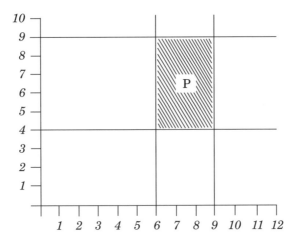

about it, *e.g.*, P is red, by the symbol "[6−9, 3−8]R", where "R" is yet an unanalysed term ("6−9" and "3−8" stand for the continuous interval between the respective numbers). The system of coordinates here is part of the mode of expression; it is part of the method of projection by which reality is projected into our symbolism. The relation of a patch lying between two others can be expressed analogously by the use of apparent variables. I need not say that this analysis does not in any way pretend to be complete. I have made no mention in it of time, and the use of two-dimensional space is not justified even in the case of monocular vision. I only wish to point out the direction in which, I believe, the analysis of visual phenomena is to be looked for, and that in this analysis we meet with logical forms quite different from those which ordinary language leads us to expect. The occurrence of numbers in the forms of atomic propositions is, in my opinion, not merely a feature of a special symbolism, but an essential and, consequently, unavoidable feature of the representation. And numbers will have to enter these forms when—as we should say in ordinary language—we are [167] dealing with properties which admit of gradation, *i.e.*, properties as the length of an interval, the pitch of a tone, the brightness or redness of a shade of colour, etc. It is a characteristic of these properties that one degree of them excludes any other. One shade of colour cannot simultaneously have two different degrees of brightness or redness, a tone not two different strengths, etc. And the important point here is that these remarks do not express an experience but are in some sense tautologies. Every one of us knows that in ordinary life. If someone asks us "What is the temperature outside?" and we said "Eighty degrees", and now he were to ask us again, "And is it ninety degrees?" we should answer, "I told you it was eighty." We take the statement of a degree (of temperature, for instance) to be a *complete* description which needs no supplementation. Thus, when asked, we say what the time is, and not also what it isn't.

One might think — and I thought so not long ago — that a statement expressing the degree of a quality could be analysed into a logical product of single statements of quantity and a completing supplementary statement. As I could describe the contents of my pocket by saying "It contains a penny, a shilling, two keys, and nothing else". This "and nothing else" is the supplementary statement which completes the description. But this will not do as an analysis of a statement of degree. For let us call the unit of, say, brightness b and let $E(b)$ be the statement that the entity E possesses this brightness, then the proposition $E(2b)$, which says that E has two degrees of brightness, should be analysable into the logical product $E(b)$ & $E(b)$, but this is equal to $E(b)$; if, on the other hand, we try to distinguish between the units and consequently write $E(2b) = E(b') $ & $ E(b'')$, we assume [168] two different units of brightness; and then, if an entity possesses one unit, the question could arise, which of the two — b' or b'' — it is; which is obviously absurd.

I maintain that the statement which attributes a degree to a quality cannot further be analysed, and, moreover, that the relation of difference of degree is an internal relation and that it is therefore represented by an internal relation between the statements which attribute the different degrees. That is to say, the atomic statement must have the same multiplicity as the degree which it attributes, whence it follows that numbers must enter the forms of atomic propositions. The mutual exclusion of unanalysable statements of degree contradicts an opinion which was published by me several years ago and which necessitated that atomic propositions could not exclude one another. I here deliberately say "exclude" and not "contradict", for there is a difference between these two notions, and atomic propositions, although they cannot contradict, may exclude one another. I will try to explain this. There are functions which can give a true proposition only for one value of their argument because — if I may so express myself — there is only room in them for one. Take, for instance, a proposition which asserts the existence of a colour R at a certain time T in a certain place P of our visual field. I will write this proposition "R P T", and abstract for the moment from any consideration of how such a statement is to be further analysed. "B P T", then, says that the colour B is in the place P at the time T, and it will be clear to most of us here, and to all of us in ordinary life, that "R P T & B P T" is some sort of contradiction (and not merely a false proposition). Now if statements of degree were analysable—as I used to think—we could explain this contradiction by saying that the colour R con- [169] tains all degrees of R and none of B and that the colour B contains all degrees of B and none of R. But from the above it follows that no analysis can eliminate statements of degree. How, then, does the mutual exclusion of R P T and B P T operate? I believe it consists in the fact that R P T as well as B P T are in a certain sense *complete*. That which corresponds in reality to the function "( ) P T" leaves room only for one entity—in the same sense, in fact, in which we say that there is room for one person only in a chair. Our symbolism, which allows us to form the sign of the logical product of "R P T" and "B P T", gives here no correct picture of reality.

I have said elsewhere that a proposition "reaches up to reality", and by this I meant that the forms of the entities are contained in the form of the proposition which is about these entities. For the sentence, together with the mode of projection which projects reality into the sentence, determines the logical form of the entities, just as in our simile a picture on plane II, together with its mode of projection, determines the shape of the figure on plane I. This remark, I believe, gives us the key for the explanation of the mutual exclusion of R P T and B P T. For if the proposition contains the form of an entity which it is about, then it is possible that two propositions should collide in this very form. The propositions "Brown now sits in this chair" and "Jones now sits in this chair" each, in a sense, try to set their subject term on the chair. But the logical product of these propositions will put them both there at once, and this leads to a collision, a mutual exclusion of these terms. How does this exclusion represent itself in symbolism? We can write the logical product of the two propositions, p and q, in this way:—[170]

p	q	
T	T	T
T	F	F
F	T	F
F	F	F

What happens if these two propositions are R P T and B P T? In this case the top line "T T T" must disappear, as it represents an impossible combination. The true possibilities here are—

RPT	BPT
T	F
F	T
F	F

That is to say, there *is* no logical product of R P T and B P T in the first sense, and herein lies the exclusion as opposed to a contradiction. The contradiction, if it existed, would have to be written—

RPT	BPT	
T	T	F
T	F	F
F	T	F
F	F	F

but this is nonsense, as the top line, "T T F", gives the proposition a greater logical multiplicity than that of the actual possibilities. It is, of course, a deficiency of our [171] notation that it does not prevent the formation of such nonsensical constructions, and a perfect notation will have to exclude such structures by definite rules of syntax. These will have to tell us that in the case of certain kinds of atomic propositions described in terms of definite symbolic features certain combinations of the T's and F's must be left out. Such rules, however, cannot be laid down until we have actually reached the ultimate analysis of the phenomena in question. This, as we all know, has not yet been achieved.

Critical Interpretation of Wittgenstein's 1929 Essay

Historical Context

"Some Remarks on Logical Form" was written as a paper to be presented before the Annual Joint Session of the Aristotelian Society and Mind Association in Nottingham, England, 12–15 July 1929. At the meeting, Wittgenstein did not read the paper, but chose instead to speak about the concept of infinity. There is unfortunately no record of what he said on the occasion. The essay by then had already been committed to the supplementary volume of the *Proceedings of the Aristotelian Society,* as is customary for invited Aristotelian Society lectures. It could not be withdrawn, as Wittgenstein, having disowned the piece, presumably would have preferred, and was published later that same year.[1]

Wittgenstein had only just recently returned to philosophy after a seven years hiatus. Following the publication of the *Tractatus* in 1922, Wittgenstein, concluding that there were no genuine philosophical problems, and hence nothing for a philosopher as philosopher to do, gave up the field and devoted himself to non-philosophical pursuits. By this action Wittgenstein showed more than the *Tractatus* tried to say that there was no meaningful work for philosophy. In March 1928, upon hearing the lecture "Mathematics, Science and Language" given by the Dutch intuitionist mathematician L. E. J. Brouwer in Vienna, Wittgenstein reportedly decided that perhaps he could again begin to make worthwhile contributions to philosophy. Herbert Feigl, with whom Wittgenstein and Friedrich Waismann attended and afterward heatedly discussed Brouwer's lecture in a nearby café, writes of the incident: "that evening marked the return of Wittgenstein to strong philosophical interest and activities."[2]

When Wittgenstein returned to philosophy, he returned to Cambridge. Moore, whom Wittgenstein had known from his graduate student days at Cambridge, at Keyne's suggestion and with Frank P. Ramsey's recommendation, arranged for Wittgenstein to continue research in philosophy as a postgraduate in Trinity College. For this he was required to obtain a doctoral degree, which he satisfied by submitting a copy of the *Tractatus* and undergoing an oral examination conducted by Russell, Moore, and Ramsey, who was nominally Wittgenstein's dissertation advisor. It is evidence of Wittgenstein's renunciation of worldliness, and of the slight importance he attached to the *Tractatus,* that he had no copy of his own for this purpose, but was able to obtain one through the good offices of Ogden.[3] Wittgenstein was supported at this time by a renewable research fellowship that continued from 1929 through 1935. It was during the first tract of his postdoctoral residence in Cambridge that Wittgenstein composed the essay "Some Remarks on Logical Form." Ray Monk, in *Ludwig Wittgenstein: The Duty of Genius,* describes Wittgenstein's psychology at the time:

> Wittgenstein was, [literary critic F. R.] Leavis recalls, working desperately hard at this time, and was chronically short of sleep. On one occasion, when they were out walking together until after midnight, Wittgenstein was so exhausted that on their way back to Malting House Lane he could hardly walk without the support of Leavis' arm. When they finally reached Frostlake Cottage, Levis implored him to go to bed at once. 'You don't understand', Wittgenstein replied. 'When I'm engaged on a piece of work I'm always afraid I shall die before I've finished it. So I make a fair copy of the day's work and give it to Frank Ramsey for safe-keeping. I haven't made today's copy.' The work that he was then engaged in writing was the paper entitled 'Some Remarks on Logical Form', which has the distinction of being the only piece of philosophical writing he published after the *Tractatus.*[4]

The argument was important to Wittgenstein. At stake was the general form of proposition, logical atomism, and the picture theory of meaning—the *Tractatus* logic, metaphysics, and semantic theory that was supposed to undermine all of philosophy and eliminate philosophical problems as nonsense.

At the time of writing the 1929 essay, Wittgenstein was still fundamentally committed to the early (anti-) philosophy as the only correct explanation of meaning. The task before him was merely one of answering an objection raised by Ramsey about the *Tractatus* 6.3751 treatment of color incompatibility. Ramsey was a gifted young logician and philosopher of mathematics, who had translated the *Tractatus* for the 1922 Routledge & Kegan Paul German-English edition, and for whom Wittgenstein had the greatest philosophical respect. The color incompatibility problem concerns the impossibility of two different colors completely and uniformly occurring in the same place at the same time. The *Tractatus* claims that color incompatibility is reducible to logical contradiction. Color incompatibility as logical impossibility must show itself as a syntactical contradiction (p & $\sim p$) when ordinary language statements about different colors being in the same place at the same time are completely analyzed and their logical structures are exhibited in a truth table. The *Tractatus* nowhere explains how such an analysis is to be carried out, and Ramsey had expressed serious doubts about whether color incompatibility could be understood as contradiction. In the 1929 essay, Wittgenstein addresses some of the most important questions passed over in silence in the *Tractatus*. He confronts the challenge of picture theory analysis, and for the first time offers substantive hints at directions for if not a concrete example of what an analysis, atomic fact, simple object, elementary proposition, and simple name might be like, in the course of trying to solve the color incompatibility problem.

Wittgenstein first believes that Ramsey's difficulty can be met from within the general framework of the picture theory of meaning. The picture theory as formulated in the *Tractatus* does not function quite properly, but needs only minor repair. It is just a matter of applying the representational requirements of propositions as logical pictures in a slightly different way than the *Tractatus* had foreseen, using additional conceptual resources made available by specifying more precisely the true mathematical multiplicity of elementary (or, as the essay now has it, 'atomic') propositions. The occurrence of color with its continuous properties at a definite place within logical space can only be adequately pictured if elementary propositions contain real numbers as part of their logical structures. Wittgenstein argues that the analysis of elementary propositions as containing real number parameters for the occurrence of degrees of particular colors at a particular place and time implies the exclusion of one color by another. Color incompatibility is explained not as ordinary logical contradiction, but as the logical unpicturability of two different degrees of color being in the same place at the same time.

The color incompatibility problem threatens to collapse the semantic edifice of the *Tractatus*. Wittgenstein knows that the picture theory and general form of proposition must be rejected if he cannot answer Ramsey's objection, and in the 1929 essay he attempts a sustained reply. The essay, unlike most of Wittgenstein's terse sometimes unconnected apothegms, is written in exemplary expository philosophical prose. It is the only time that Wittgenstein, whose sartorial signature was the casual sport jacket and open-collar button-down shirt, so to speak, put on a tie (or at least tried it on at home before the mirror). At first, he must have been satisfied with the result. He completed the paper for publication, and seems to have been prepared to offer it to the Aristotelian Society – Mind meeting. Then something happened. Wittgenstein, turning the problem over and over again, must have had second thoughts, and began to find weaknesses in the argument. It was shortly thereafter that he came to the conclusion that the essay was inadequate, even radically mistaken. Wittgenstein refused to read the 1929 essay in Nottingham, and decided instead to talk about infinity. G. E. M. Anscombe reports that Wittgenstein described "Some Remarks on Logical Form" as "weak and uncharacteristic." Yet this does not diminish the essay's importance or that of the historical facts surrounding its rejection in understanding the development of Wittgenstein's thought—quite the contrary.[5]

We must ask why Wittgenstein became dissatisfied with his solutions to the color incompatibility problem, and how his thinking at this time may have contributed to the transition from the early to the later philosophy. Wittgenstein's disapproval of "Some Remarks on Logical Form" is chronicled by Monk:

> It is a mark of how quickly [Wittgenstein's] thought was developing at this time, however, that almost as soon as he had sent [the 1929 essay] off to be printed he disowned it as worthless, and, at the meeting of which it supposedly forms part of the proceedings, read something quite different—a paper on the concept of infinity in mathematics, which has, consequently, been lost to posterity.[6]

The essay and the fact that Wittgenstein chose not to read it are clues to Wittgenstein's thinking at this critical time of transition between the early philosophy of the *Tractatus* and the later period of the *Philosophical Investigations*. Wittgenstein's disavowal of the 1929 essay is an essential piece of the puzzle in interpreting the metamorphosis in Wittgenstein's thought as he turns from logical atomism and the picture theory of meaning to the development of a very different approach to the meaning of language and the purpose and limits of philosophy. Monk understands the significance of Wittgenstein's 1929 essay in its historical context when he observes:

> 'Some Remarks on Logical Form' is nonetheless interesting as a record of a transitory phase in the development of Wittgenstein's philosophy — a phase in which the logical edifice

of the *Tractatus,* though crumbling, had not yet been demolished altogether. The paper can be seen as an attempt to answer criticisms made by Frank Ramsey of Wittgenstein's discussion of color-exclusion in the *Tractatus.*[7]

▌ Two Methods of Projecting Meaning

Wittgenstein begins the 1929 essay with a reference to the *Tractatus* distinction between a proposition's logical form and content. When the logical form of a representationally adequate proposition is completely analyzed, it must be as richly and intricately articulated with precisely the right logical form and mathematical multiplicity as the facts it logically pictures.

Logical form is abstracted from a proposition's meaning by substituting variables for meaningful constants, to which the same rules of logical syntax apply. The rules determine the meaning of a term in context. They do not simply refer to the terms of ordinary language, because these, according to Wittgenstein, are notoriously inadequate in excluding the construction of nonsensical syntax combinations. Wittgenstein takes a playful swipe at the meaninglessness of existentialist philosophy, remarking on the nonsense of its characteristic pronouncements about the Real, as an *in itself* also becoming a *for myself.* This is a prime example of the sort of philosophical pseudoproposition Wittgenstein denounces in the *Tractatus,* which he now concludes is as meaningless as the more obviously nonsensical construction 'Red is higher than green'.

Philosophical semantics has simple foundations. Wittgenstein reaffirms his *Tractatus* commitment to the reduction of propositions to truth functions of elementary or what he now calls atomic propositions, explicitly adopting the terminology of Russell's 1917–18 "Lectures on Logical Atomism." Logical analysis is the project of uncovering the underlying logical structure of any meaningful proposition as a truth function of elementary propositions. Wittgenstein recognizes that: "This task is very difficult, and Philosophy has hardly yet begun to tackle it at some points" (163). The problem is to give a complete logical atomist picture theory reduction of propositions in ordinary language. It is an enterprise the *Tractatus* does not venture to consider as a practical exercise, the possibility of which Wittgenstein mentions only in the most general terms as presupposed by the determinate meaningfulness of language.

What method should be adopted to analyze propositions in ordinary language? Wittgenstein goes beyond the *Tractatus* in asking how a picture theory analysis is supposed to work. He describes the purpose of analysis as the replacement of ordinary language that disguises logical structure, involves equivocal expressions, and permits the formulation of pseudopropositions, with "a symbolism which gives a clear picture of the logical structure, excludes pseudopropositions, and uses its terms unambiguously" (163). Wittgenstein disallows a priori efforts to give adequate formalisms in place of the superficially deceptive grammatical constructions of ordinary language. "Now we can only substitute a clear symbolism for the unprecise one," he maintains, "by inspecting the phenomena we want to describe, thus trying to understand their logical multiplicity" (163). We must look to the world, to the facts we want to represent in thought and language, in order to know what logical forms they require. Wittgenstein explains:

> we can only arrive at a correct analysis by, what might be called, the logical investigation of the phenomena themselves, *i.e.*, in a certain sense *a posteriori,* and not by conjecturing about *a priori* possibilities. One is often tempted to ask from an *a priori* standpoint: What, after all, *can* be the only forms of atomic propositions, and to answer, *e.g.,* subject-predicate and relational propositions with two or more terms further, perhaps, propositions relating predicates and relations to one another, and so on. But this, I believe, is mere playing with words. An atomic form cannot be foreseen. (163)

The idea is to substitute a logically correct symbolism to give a more perspicuous expression of the meanings concealed in the vernacular. This approach does not contradict the *Tractatus* 5.5563 thesis that "All propositions of our colloquial language are actually, just as they are, logically completely in order." It is rather a question of how best to gain access to the actual as opposed to the superficial and misleading merely apparent logical order of propositions in ordinary language. The subject-predicate and relational linguistic forms of ordinary language do not necessarily belong to the deep logical structure especially of elementary or atomic propositions in a logically correct symbolism.

The analysis of meaning can only be accomplished by examining the phenomena to be pictured, in a logical analysis of the facts themselves. The logician must determine their formal expressions with the requisite logical isomorphisms in a logically correct symbolism, and then map these back into ordinary language

formulations. There are at least two ways in which such a semantic mapping can proceed. The choice depends on where the mapping begins and where it ends up in depicting the exact relation
between the facts of the world and their adequate expression in
thought and language. We can try to identity the rules of projection
by which the facts of reality are represented in ordinary discourse,
or we can work backward from the representation of facts in ordinary language until we arrive at a logically correct symbolism.

Wittgenstein distinguishes between two methods of semantic analysis by means of an analogy with two ways of geometri-
cally projecting figures from one plane onto another. This evokes
the *Tractatus* 3.11 concept of the perceptible sign of a proposition
as the projection of a possible state of affairs, and of the method of
projection as thinking the sense of the proposition. Wittgenstein
presents the geometrical techniques as a 'simile' for two modes of
semantic projection from transcendent logical symbol to ordinary
language sign:

> Let us imagine two parallel planes, I and II. On plane I
> figures are drawn, say, ellipses and rectangles of different
> sizes and shapes, and it is our task to produce images of
> these figures on plane II. Then we can imagine two ways,
> among others, of doing this. We can, first, lay down a law of
> projection—say that of orthogonal projection or any other—
> and then proceed to project all figures from I into II, accord-
> ing to this law. Or, secondly, we could proceed thus: We lay
> down the rule that every ellipse on plane I is to appear as a
> circle in plane II, and every rectangle as a square in II. Such
> a way of representation may be convenient for us if for some
> reason we prefer to draw only circles and squares on plane
> II. Of course, from these images the exact shapes of the origi-
> nal figures on plane I cannot be immediately inferred. We
> can only gather from them that the original was an ellipse or
> a rectangle. In order to get in a single instance the determi-
> nate shape of the original we would have to know the indi-
> vidual method by which, *e.g.*, a particular ellipse is projected
> into the circle before me. (164)

The advantages and disadvantages of each geometrical
method apply in the semantic analogy. The first method is impractical, virtually impossible to follow in practice, but fully informative with respect to the exact structures of facts projected
into and hence analyzable from thought and language. The
method requires knowledge of the laws of projection by which
facts are mapped onto the elements of thought and language.
This information is so obscured by the complicated natural history of linguistic evolution as to be inaccessible to analysis. The
second method Wittgenstein says is more practical, but propor-

tionately less informative. Without knowing the laws of projection, we can only offer correlations of facts and thoughts from which we cannot determine the logical structures of facts projected into colloquial thought or language. Wittgenstein interprets the parable for the problem of giving a complete picture theory analysis of propositions in ordinary language:

> The case of ordinary language is quite analogous. If the facts of reality are the ellipses and rectangles on plane I the subject-predicate and relational forms correspond to the circles and squares in plane II. These forms are the norms of our particular language into which we project in *ever so many different* ways *ever so many different* logical forms. And for this very reason we can draw no conclusions—except very vague ones—from the use of these norms as to the actual logical form of the phenomena described. Such forms as "This paper is boring", "The weather is fine", "I am lazy", which have nothing whatever in common with one another, present themselves as subject-predicate propositions, *i.e.*, apparently as propositions of the same form. (164–65)

If we want the convenience of drawing only circles and squares in plane 2, then we should adopt the second correlation method. Whatever is curved in plane 1 is projected as a circle in plane 2, and whatever is polygonal is projected as a square. This constitutes a simplified correlation of projected shapes. The method by definition provides no exact recovery of the shapes of figures in plane 1 from the circles and squares of plane 2. It offers at most a vague idea based on crude approximations.

The dilemma is pervasive. The convenience of having to draw only circles and squares at the expense of information about the logical structures of the facts they represent is like the simplicity of using only subject-predicate and relational forms in formalizing the superficial logical structures of ordinary language. The price of convenience and a more limited palette of logical forms is the oversimplification and uninformativeness inherent in the mere correlation of picturing and pictured facts. The second method of projection and analysis disguises the real underlying logical structures of facts projected into ordinary thought and language. The propositions Wittgenstein mentions as apparently of the same logical form have nothing to do with one another. The picture theory implies that they must therefore have different transcendent symbolic logical structures. To see them as such, we would need to know the exact laws by which they are projected into the everyday idiom, and not their mere correlation with a particular set of logical forms. There are indefinitely many ways of projecting facts into language. Without access to the unknown laws of projection, subject-predicate and relational forms, even as they appear in the syntax of formal symbolic logic, might be only a procrustean bed for many different logical structures, just as the squares and circles in Wittgenstein's geometrical analogy have to do duty for any polygon and any ellipse.

What then is to be done? Which of the two a posteriori methods of projecting and analyzing logical structures is to be preferred in offering a picture theory analysis of the logical form of propositions in everyday discourse? Wittgenstein appears to leave the issue undecided, having pointed out the incommensurable difficulties of each approach without trying to defend one over the other. Yet it is clear he regards the second mere correlation method as hopeless in trying to understand the transcendent logical forms of facts, thoughts, and propositions. He has already said that we must consult the phenomena to be represented in thought and language if we want to understand the real logical structures of a logically correct symbolism needed to picture a given set of facts. To begin with ordinary language expressions and attempt to work backward to the logical structure of facts without knowledge of the laws of projection is futile, particularly where there are indefinitely many possibilities and no principles by which to choose. We must begin by trying to understand the real structure of a fact and consider how we might ideally express its form and content in a logically correct symbolism. From this we may glean certain of the laws of projection by which some facts can be projected into more rigorous unequivocal logical structures, in a weakened compromise version of Wittgenstein's first method of semantic projection and analysis. Limited knowledge of the symbolic logical forms arrived at in this way can finally be stipulatively one-many correlated with ordinary language expressions, without knowing the specific laws of projection, in a strengthened compromise application of the second method of semantic projection and analysis.

▌Logical Analysis of Phenomena

In comparing these two methods of analyzing the expression of facts in thought and language, Wittgenstein goes beyond but does not retract or revise any part of the *Tractatus*. The 1929 essay begins by expanding on matters about which the *Tractatus* is silent, agnostic, or which it regards as philosophically irrelevant.

The *Tractatus* implies the possibility of giving a complete logical atomist picture theory analysis of all thought and language. But it offers no practical advice about how such an analysis might be achieved. When he returns to the problem in "Some Remarks on Logical Form," Wittgenstein proposes for the first time to apply the principles of logical analysis in concrete terms. He concludes that we must attempt an a posteriori 'logical investigation' of simple facts, using the tools of an unambiguous logical symbolism to clarify and refine the expression of their properties, and then correlating the resulting formulations with the grammatical forms of ordinary language. Wittgenstein contrasts the complicated logical structures of facts with the comparatively oversimplified forms of everyday discourse in which they are typically expressed:

> If, now, we try to get at an actual analysis, we find logical forms which have very little similarity with the norms of ordinary language. We meet with the forms of space and time with the whole manifold of spacial and temporal objects, as colours, sounds, etc., etc., with their gradations, continuous transitions, and combinations in various proportions, all of which we cannot seize by our ordinary means of expression. (165)

In the *Tractatus*, Wittgenstein has no need to identify the laws of projection. All he requires is a sound transcendental argument to establish that such laws must exist. It is only when he considers the facts to be pictured in a correct logical symbolism that Wittgenstein sees the practical limitations of analyzing colloquial language without access to the impenetrable laws of semantic projection by which it pictures facts.

What does Wittgenstein hope to accomplish by turning from the expression of facts in ordinary thought and language to the facts themselves? The transcendental argument begins with the determinate meanings conveyed by ordinary language and concludes that there must be logical atoms in one-one object-name mirroring relations at the foundations of analysis. The obscurities of natural language make top-down analysis a practical impossibility. If we cannot read off transcendental logical structures from surface grammar, then we may have no alternative but to consult the facts themselves in order to determine bottom-up the features of their logical forms as we might need to represent them in the most perspicuous logical symbolism. Wittgenstein concludes that we must take as data for this method of logical analysis the perceptible mathematical structures of space, time, and generic color facts.

Wittgenstein's first discovery in the logical investigation of facts marks a significant departure from the *Tractatus*. He maintains that real numbers must enter into the logical structure of elementary propositions in order to account for and adequately picture the "gradations, continuous transitions, and combinations in various proportions" of generic color. There are continuous proportionate real-numbered gradations, transitions, and combinations in the range of shades of hues, brightnesses, and saturations of ordinary visual colors. The same is presumably true of any type of phenomenal quality. But whereas the *Tractatus* had assumed that values of degree could be reductively analyzed by logical operations on the elementary propositions, Wittgenstein now thinks that real numbers are a logically irreducible part of the logical form of elementary propositions. He states:

> here I wish to make my first definite remark on the logical analysis of actual phenomena: it is this, that for their representation numbers (rational and irrational) must enter into the structure of the atomic propositions themselves. (165)

The reason to include rational and irrational real numbers in the logical structures of elementary propositions is that without them the facts of the world cannot be adequately pictured. Wittgenstein shows this by means of the grid diagram (166) that illustrates the occurrence of color P in a two-dimensional spatial area described by numerical coordinates.

The example is simplified in several ways. Time is unrepresented, as Wittgenstein acknowledges, adding that two-dimensional graphics are insufficient even for the mathematically adequate logical depiction of monocular vision. We can nevertheless think of the grid as showing the abstract occurrence of color in a region of space at a single time-slice. The most obvious simplification of this logical picture of a simple (if not yet atomic) fact is that the extension of color is whole-number coordinated.[8] Realistically, we should expect even our best descriptions of space-color or space-time-color facts to be less digital, more fuzzy and analog, a matter of approximation to projected ideal boundaries that we can never fix with absolute certainty. Yet if we have even the tiniest square or circle of spatiotemporal area occupied by color, then we already have in the mathematical multiplicity of its complete and adequate description, among others, the irrationals $\sqrt{2}$ and π. Wittgenstein takes a bold step forward from the *Tractatus* in admitting that the real world of facts has the logical multiplicity of the continuum of rational and irrational real numbers:

> Imagine a system of rectangular axes, as it were, cross wires, drawn in our field of vision and an arbitrary scale fixed. It is clear that we then can describe the shape and position of

every patch of colour in our visual field by means of statements of numbers which have their significance relative to the system of co-ordinates and the unit chosen. Again, it is clear that this description will have the right logical multiplicity, and that a description which has a smaller multiplicity will not do. (165)

The grid is a simplified logical picture of a simple fact. If atomic facts involve the occurrence of color in a spatiotemporal area, then the smallest increments of the area to be described, the finest conceivable gridwork for atomic facts, must have the logical form and mathematical multiplicity of the continuum. Wittgenstein reaches this conclusion shortly after hearing Brouwer's lecture on infinity, and at the Aristotelian Society – Mind meeting, where he was supposed to present the paper on logical form, he chose instead to talk about infinity. Although these facts might be coincidental, they more likely reflect Wittgenstein's interest in the concept of infinity and continuous quality as a more promising solution to the color incompatibility problem. Wittgenstein next declares real numbers an essential part of the logical form of all phenomenal qualities:

> I only wish to point out the direction in which, I believe, the analysis of visual phenomena is to be looked for, and that in this analysis we meet with logical forms quite different from those which ordinary language leads us to expect. The occurrence of numbers in the forms of atomic propositions is, in my opinion, not merely a feature of a special symbolism, but an essential and, consequently, unavoidable feature of the representation. And numbers will have to enter these forms when—as we should say in ordinary language—we are dealing with properties which admit of gradation, *i.e.*, properties as the length of an interval, the pitch of a tone, the brightness or redness of a shade of colour, etc. (166–67)

The grid is a logical picture of the space-color fact with the same logical form. "The system of co-ordinates here is part of the mode of expression," Wittgenstein writes, "it is part of the method of projection by which the reality is projected into our symbolism" (166). If the grid as an adequate logical picture contains real-numbered color expanses, then any logically equivalent linguistic proposition on analysis must also possess a logical form with the identical real-numbered mathematical multiplicity.

Wittgenstein concludes that the diagram, to the extent that it accurately pictures a space-color fact, proves the need for real numbers in the logical forms of elementary propositions. Whole-numbered descriptions necessarily lack the mathematical multiplicity required to picture the continuous grain of real world facts projected onto the plane of thoughts or into a correct logical symbolism. The recognition of real numbers as belonging to the logical structures of atomic propositions enables Wittgenstein to tinker with the picture theory in minor ways to solve the color incompatibility problem. Where the *Tractatus* offers no practical guidance about the right method of logical analysis, "Some Remarks on Logical Form" takes the first step forward by offering a preliminary clarification of its purpose and procedure, and maintaining the need for real number factors as internal to the logical structures of atomic propositions. The corrections to the *Tractatus* logic Wittgenstein advances in the essay are proposed within the framework and for the sake of preserving logical atomism and a new and improved picture theory of meaning.

Wittgenstein interposes his own thought and mode of expression in describing these phenomena. To suppose that Wittgenstein in characterizing the world as a basis for picture theory analysis is somehow in direct contact with real facts unmediated by their representation in thought and language must appear philosophically naive from a Kantian perspective. Wittgenstein has already gone beyond his early transcendentalism by insisting that logical analysis begin with an a posteriori logical investigation. He maintains that on close inspection there are discernible mathematical features of simple facts that must enter into their representation, that are not reflected in the syntactical structures of ordinary language. An elementary proposition is not simply of the form $a^\frown b^\frown c$, but something more like $.5a^\frown.321b^\frown.775777\ldots c$.

The Color Incompatibility Problem

The presence of real numbers in the logical forms of elementary propositions is not a chance disclosure, but a conclusion deliberately offered to solve the color incompatibility problem. To understand how Wittgenstein relates real-numbered continuities, gradients, transitions, and proportions of phenomenal qualities to the analysis of color incompatibility in "Some Remarks on Logical Form," we must consider Ramsey's objections to the *Tractatus* theory.

The *Tractatus* logic, as has been mentioned, reduces every impossibility to logical impossibility. Wittgenstein accordingly tries to explain color incompatibility as a consequence of the principle of noncontradiction:

6.375   As there is only a *logical* necessity, so there is only a *logical* impossibility.

6.3751 For two colours, *e.g.* to be at one place in the visual field, is impossible, logically impossible, for it is excluded by the logical structure of colour.

> Let us consider how this contradiction presents itself in physics. Somewhat as follows: That a particle cannot at the same time have two velocities, *i.e.* that at the same time it cannot be in two places, *i.e.* that particles in different places at the same time cannot be identical.

> (It is clear that the logical product of two elementary propositions can neither be a tautology nor a contradiction. The assertion that a point in the visual field has two different colours at the same time, is a contradiction.)

The general form of proposition is capable of generating only one category of impossibility. There is only the logical impossibility of deep symbolic syntactical contradiction, inconsistency, or the negation of tautology. Where a fact or proposition is impossible, Wittgenstein in the *Tractatus* is committed to the existence of an outright logical contradiction at some, possibly the deepest, level of analysis. The *Tractatus* explanation of color incompatibility is that color predications that seem to imply the occurrence of two different colors in the same place at the same time are logically syntactically contradictory when completely analyzed in a correct logical symbolism.[9]

In 6.3751, Wittgenstein believes that the color incompatibility problem poses no special problem for the *Tractatus*. The general form of proposition divides all language into meaningful propositions and senseless tautologies and contradictions, excluding everything else as nonsense. There is only one kind or category of impossibility, which is logical impossibility understood as syntactical contradiction. To assert that it is impossible for two colors simultaneously to appear in the exact same place in the visual field is therefore to say that a construction purporting to express such an occurrence exhibits syntactical contradiction at some level of analysis. Whatever prohibits such a possibility and makes the imagined expression a contradiction is what Wittgenstein alludes to but does not elaborate as "the logical structure of color."

The thesis is by no means self-evident, but is essential to Wittgenstein's logic. There seems intuitively to be nothing syntactically contradictory about color incompatibility. Similar examples have inspired some philosophers to distinguish alternative varieties of impossibility, including logical, causal, and, with respect to problems like color incompatibility, conceptual or metaphysical impossibility. The color incompatibility problem threatens the underlying logic of Wittgenstein's logical atomism and picture theory of meaning in the *Tractatus* because it potentially undermines the general form of proposition. If there are impossible propositions that are not syntactical contradictions, then the general form of proposition does not adequately distinguish between the meaningful, senseless, and nonsensical. If these distinctions begin to erode, then Wittgenstein can no longer confidently dismiss philosophical problems as nonsensical, but may need to reconsider them as possessing another logical modality and as belonging to another category of genuine propositions than those demarcated by the general form of proposition. With this, the *Tractatus* loses its grip on the fundamental semantic distinction between what can be said and what can only be shown, and with it the well-defined limit to thought in language on which the elimination of traditional philosophical problems depends.

Among other objections to Wittgenstein's logical atomism, Ramsey, in his 1923 *Mind* "Review of 'Tractatus'," raises the difficulty of explaining color incompatibility as a contradiction. Ramsey argues in a passage worth quoting at length:

> It is a principle of Mr. Wittgenstein's, and, if true, is a very important discovery, that every genuine proposition asserts something possible, but not necessary. This follows from his account of a proposition as the expression of agreement and disagreement with truth-possibilities of independent elementary propositions, so that the only necessity is that of tautology, the only impossibility that of contradiction. There is great difficulty in holding this; for Mr. Wittgenstein admits that a point in the visual field *cannot* be both red and blue; and, indeed, otherwise, since he thinks induction has no logical basis, we should have no reason for thinking that we may not come upon a visual point which is both red and blue. Hence he says that 'This is both red and blue' is a contradiction. This implies that the apparently simple concepts red, blue (supposing us to mean by those words absolutely specific shades) are really complex and formally incompatible. He tries to show how this may be, by analysing them in terms of vibrations. But even supposing that the physicist thus provides an analysis of what we mean by 'red', Mr. Wittgenstein is only reducing the difficulty to that of the *necessary* properties of space, time, and matter or the ether. He explicitly makes it depend on the *impossibility* of a particle being in two places at the same time. These necessary properties of space and time are hardly capable of a further re-

duction of this kind. For example, considering between in point of time as regards my experiences; if B is between A and D, and C between B and D, then C must be between A and D; but it is hard to see how this can be a formal tautology.[10]

Ramsey's criticism begins to unravel the tightly knit fabric of Wittgenstein's logic. If there are types of impossibility other than logical impossibility that are not reducible to outright contradiction, then the picture theory of meaning is false. In that case, there is more to impossibility than logical form exhibiting itself in syntactically contradictory expressions under truth table analysis, and content as well as pure logical form must also be a determinant of nonlogical impossibility. Wittgenstein refers to the "logical structure" of color, but, as Ramsey observes, these remarks suggest only a reduction of color incompatibility to the incompatibility of simultaneous occupation of different parts of space by the same material object. Yet it is as difficult to understand how the incompatibility of simultaneous spatial occupation by different complexes is supposed to be decided by pure logic as a disguised syntactical contradiction, as it is in the case of color incompatibility.

Wittgenstein in the *Tractatus* does not assert, as Ramsey maintains, that color incompatibility is 'reducible' to the impossibility of a physical particle occupying two places at the same time. He seems rather to be offering an analogy when he begins by saying: "Let us consider how this contradiction presents itself in physics . . ." It is possible that Wittgenstein accepts or wants the picture theory to be compatible with a materialist theory that reduces all generic color to microphysical interactions. In either case, Ramsey is surely right to complain that the same explanatory difficulty of accounting for the metaphysical incompatibilities of color qualities equally affects physics. Whether Wittgenstein intends his observations as reduction or analogy, he has no persuasive basis for eliminating doubts about the existence of nonlogical impossibility that threaten the general form of proposition and the picture theory of meaning.

After commenting on the need for real numbers in the logical forms of elementary propositions, the following sentence of the 1929 essay about the real number gradations of color properties marks the beginning of Wittgenstein's attempt to answer Ramsey's objections about the color incompatibility problem. Wittgenstein continues:

> It is a characteristic of these properties [that admit of gradation] that one degree of them excludes any other. One shade

of colour cannot simultaneously have two different degrees of brightness or redness, a tone not two different strengths, etc. And the important point here is that these remarks do not express an experience but are in some sense tautologies. Every one of us knows that in ordinary life. If someone asks us "What is the temperature outside?" and we said "Eighty degrees", and now we were to ask again, "And is it ninety degrees?" we should answer, "I told you it was eighty." We take the statement of a degree (of temperature, for instance) to be a *complete* description which needs no supplementation. Thus, when asked, we say what the time is, and not also what it isn't. (167)

The answer was not as obvious in the *Tractatus*. There, consistently with the picture theory, Wittgenstein could do no more than indicate that a logical contradiction of unspecified content must occur at an unidentified level of analysis. Wittgenstein takes advantage of the description of space-color facts as requiring real number gradations to account for the expanse of color within a real number coordinated grid area as a simplified logical picture of real world color facts to advance what seems at first at least to be a substantially different solution to the color incompatibility problem.

The differences between the *Tractatus* and "Some Remarks on Logical Form" on the question of color incompatibility are not as pronounced as they might at first appear. Wittgenstein is still convinced that color incompatibility is a consequence of what are "in some sense tautologies." The cautionary phrase "in some sense" may suggest a slight departure from the *Tractatus* logic, which acknowledges tautologies and contradictions only in the univocal truth table sense determined by the general form of proposition. The focal point of the 1929 argument is Wittgenstein's claim that by admitting real numbers into the logical structures of atomic facts and the elementary propositions with the right mathematical multiplicity to picture them, we are in a better position to conclude as a characteristic specifically of these kinds of propositions that they are simultaneously mutually exclusive.

Wittgenstein now insists that color incompatibility precludes the occurrence of more than one generic color or phenomenal quality of any continuous degree in a single place at a single time. As evidence for the mutual exclusion of such qualities, Wittgenstein cites ordinary reasoning about temperature and time. If we are told that the temperature outdoors is eighty degrees, we do not need to ask whether it is not also ninety degrees. If we give the time, we do not also need to say what time it is not. These examples seem correct enough as they stand. But they do not constitute a solution to the color incompatibility problem, as opposed to further instances of color incompatibility that collectively stand in need of a satisfactory explanation. The principle by which color incompatibility is 'explained' in the 1929 essay seems to be the assumption that no two qualities can occur at the same place at the same time. To claim that two or more temperatures or times cannot simultaneously be coinstantiated is an application of the same unargued *Tractatus* assertion that physical particles cannot have two velocities at the same time. We want to know why it is supposed to be a characteristic specifically of qualities that admit of degree to exclude one another from the same place at the same time. It is no answer to compile additional examples in which the exclusion of one gradient quality by another is intuitively obvious. In all of these instances we need to understand the deeper logic of their incompatibility, and to see whether the explanation agrees with or contradicts the picture theory and general form or proposition. If quality exclusion is a matter of tautology "in some sense," we need to know more precisely in what sense this is supposed to be true.

Instead of addressing these fundamental questions, Wittgenstein argues against the reducibility of real number factors within the logical structures of atomic facts and elementary propositions. He notes how his current thinking has changed from the position he had taken in the *Tractatus*. He rejects the *Tractatus* reduction of the numerical value of degrees of generic color dimensions to conjunctions of elementary propositions together with a clause asserting their totality or closure:

> One might think—and I thought so not long ago—that a statement expressing the degree of a quality could be analyzed into a logical product of single statements of quantity and a completing supplementary statement. As I could describe the contents of my pocket by saying "It contains a penny, a shilling, two keys, and nothing else". This "and nothing else" is the supplementary statement which completes the description. But this will not do as an analysis of a statement of degree. For let us call the unit of, say, brightness b and let $E(b)$ be the statement that the entity E possesses this brightness, then the proposition $E(2b)$, which says that E has two degrees of brightness, should be analyzable into the logical product $E(b)$ & $E(b)$, but this is equal to $E(b)$; if, on the other hand, we try to distinguish between the units and consequently write $E(2b) = E(b')$ & $E(b'')$, we assume two different units of brightness; and then, if an entity possesses one unit, the question could arise, which of the two— b' or b'' — it is; which is obviously absurd. (167–68)

The *Tractatus* reduces number to the exponent of an iterated logical operation. This is Wittgenstein's diluted but from his perspective philosophically more correct form of the logicism or reduction of all mathematics to logic that Frege and Whitehead and Russell had independently strived to attain in the *Grundgesetze der Arithmetik* and *Principia Mathematica*. In the *Tractatus*, Wittgenstein similarly states:

> 6.021   A number is the exponent of an operation.
>
> 6.022   The concept number is nothing else than that which is common to all numbers, the general form of number.
>
> The concept number is the variable number.
>
> And the concept of equality of numbers is the general form of all special equalities of numbers.
>
> 6.03   The general form of the cardinal number is: $[0, \xi, \xi + 1]$.

We might naturally wonder, then, why numbers would need to be added as primitive components in the logical structures of elementary propositions. Why could they not simply be reduced to the exponents of iterations of logical operations, in an application that shows forth their number rather than something that must be said? Why should it not be as Wittgenstein argues with respect to Russell's Axiom of Infinity, earlier in the *Tractatus:*

> 5.453   All numbers in logic must be capable of justification.
>
> Or rather it must become plain that there are no numbers in logic.
>
> There are no pre-eminent numbers.
>
> 5.535   So all problems disappear which are connected with such pseudo-propositions.
>
> This is the place to solve all the problems which arise through Russell's "Axiom of Infinity".
>
> What the axiom of infinity is meant to say would be expressed in language by the fact that there is an infinite number of names with different meanings.[11]

We cannot overlook Wittgenstein's conditional characterization of what the Axiom of Infinity "is meant to say," as something literally nonsensical, and what "would be expressed" if an infinity of logical terms were required, merely by their presence and showing forth a logical form with an infinitary mathematical multiplicity. With this careful wording Wittgenstein does not commit himself to the idea of infinity, let alone to the nondenumerable higher-order infinity of the continuum. But if he is prepared to do so in "Some Remarks on Logical Form," why does he not simply regard real numbers as reducing to a showing forth of the infinitary logical form required of whatever atomic propositions are logically capable of representing the continuous and transitional gradients of whatever qualities admit of degree?

The answer is given in Wittgenstein's 1929 essay. Although previously Wittgenstein believed that such a reduction could be carried out, he now insists that the numerical degree of the gradient quality of any space-time-color fact is logically primitive. We cannot reduce n degrees of quality to n conjunctions of elementary propositions in which are shown the number of iterations of truth-functional operations. The *Tractatus* reduction fails on truth-functional grounds:

> I maintain that the statement which attributes a degree to a quality cannot further be analyzed, and, moreover, that the relation of difference of degree is an internal relation and that it is therefore represented by an internal relation between the statements which attribute the different degrees. That is to say, the atomic statement must have the same multiplicity as the degree which it attributes, whence it follows that numbers must enter the forms of atomic propositions. (168)

The only alternative is for real numbers to belong to the logical forms of atomic propositions in order to account for the continuous gradations in features like length, pitch, and brightness. This makes it possible to characterize the logical structure of color in such a way as to solve the color incompatibility problem within the general *Tractatus* framework:

> There are functions which can give a truth proposition only for one value of their argument because—if I may so express myself—there is only room in them for one. Take, for instance, a proposition which asserts the existence of a colour R at a certain time T in a certain place P of our visual field. I will write this proposition "R P T", and abstract for the moment any consideration of how such a statement is to be further analysed. "B P T", then, says that the colour B is in the place P at the time T, and it will be clear to most of us here, and to all of us in ordinary life, that "R P T & B P T" is some sort of contradiction (and not merely a false proposition). (168)

Wittgenstein blames ordinary language and standard logical symbolisms for permitting the formulation of such conjunctions as 'Red-here-now and blue-here-now' or R P T & B P T. He proposes to explain color exclusion by means of the 'completeness' of space-time-color predications that prevents more than one generic color from satisfying the sentence function '( )-here-now' or

'( ) P T'. But he does not say what a refined propositional symbolism would do to inhibit the function from being completed by more than one color quality term:

> But from the above it follows that no analysis can eliminate statements of degree. How, then, does the mutual exclusion of R P T and B P T operate? I believe it consists in the fact that R P T and B P T are in a certain sense *complete*. That which corresponds in reality to the function "( ) P T" leaves room only for one entity—in the same sense, in fact, in which we say that there is room for one person only in a chair. Our symbolism, which allows us to form the sign of the logical product of "R P T" and "B P T", gives here no correct picture of reality. (169)

The lack of room in logical space for more than one color to occupy a single place at a single time recalls the physics analogy of the *Tractatus,* concerning the impossibility of a single material particle being in different places at the same time. The reference to this earlier example might be understood as an attempt to defend the *Tractatus* concept of color incompatibility, after reconciling it to the new insight that real numbers as signs of continuous degree are essential to the internal logical structures of elementary propositions. As evidence that Wittgenstein in this connection maintains a link with his early theory, he draws on the *Tractatus* (3.42, 4.023, 6.124) image of the logical scaffolding of the world, and the thesis (2.1511) that a proposition in picturing a fact "reaches up to reality":

> This remark, I believe, gives the key for the explanation of the mutual exclusion of R P T and B P T. For if the proposition contains the form of an entity which it is about, then it is possible that two propositions should collide in this very form. The propositions "Brown now sits in this chair" and "Jones now sits in this chair" each, in a sense, try to set their subject term on the chair. But the logical product of these propositions will put them both there at once, and this leads to a collision, a mutual exclusion of these terms. (169)

There are also differences between the *Tractatus* and "Some Remarks on Logical Form" approaches to the color incompatibility problem. Wittgenstein has already stated that the mutual exclusion of colors simultaneously from a single place in the visual field is "some sort of contradiction," as the consequence of what are "in some sense tautologies." Yet according to the general form of proposition, there is only one sort of contradiction and one sense of tautology. The color incompatibility problem is the problem of determining the kind of impossibility by which colors exclude one another from the same time and place, in view of the implausibility of regarding color incompatibility as logical impossibility with the form of syntactical contradiction. To say that the impossibility of colors simultaneously occupying the same place is analogous to the inability of a particle occurring simultaneously in two different places, to the completeness of space-time-color predications that allow room for only one color to satisfy the function '( ) P T', or by which two persons cannot sit in the same chair at the same time, is no help in this regard. The question can equally be raised in what precise sense of 'impossibility' it is supposed to be impossible for a particle to be in two places at once, for the function '( ) P T' to be completed by more than one quality, or for two persons to be simultaneously seated in the same (narrow) chair, since these also do not appear to be straightforward instances of logical impossibility interpreted as syntactical contradiction.

Rather than offering a deep analysis to expose the logical contradiction in any of these cases, Wittgenstein proposes that impossible conjunctions of space-time-color predications cannot be represented in a correct logical symbolism, as shown by special truth tables. This is a more striking departure from the *Tractatus* picture theory of meaning, because Wittgenstein in the 1929 essay sees the need to distinguish between logical contradiction and property exclusion in a way the *Tractatus* would not have allowed. He admits that color incompatibility is not simply logical impossibility in the sense of syntactical contradiction, but is instead a matter of continuous gradient property exclusion in a new logical category. It is useful to refer again to the series of truth tables in Wittgenstein's essay (169–70), in which he displays the revision of standard truth table analysis required by the color incompatibility problem.

The truth-functional logic of conjunction is inadequate for gradient property exclusion. Wittgenstein, by offering an alternative truth table for color incompatibility, structurally different from the logic of truth-functional connections, concedes that at least some conjunctions involving color predications cannot be correctly interpreted by the usual definition. The implications of Wittgenstein's substitution of the revised truth table for his rethinking of the color incompatibility problem are extensive, leading to the rejection of logical atomism, the picture theory of meaning, and the general form of proposition.

▌Contradiction and
▌Quality Exclusion

The distinction between syntactical contradiction and quality exclusion acknowledges a logical anomaly. The fact that both R P T and B P T are genuine propositions, but that R P T & B P T requires its own special truth matrix, that their logic does not conform to the general definition of conjunction, indicates that the *Tractatus* oversimplifies the analysis of logical form in one of its most central doctrines. Nor do these ad hoc tailored truth tables tell us anything we did not already know. They merely restate a symbolized version of the color incompatibility problem without illuminating it. The 'true' possibilities for color combination are those represented by the revised table, in which the first line of truth value assignments is eliminated. But by virtue of what notion of possibility are these combinations excluded as impossible or as other than 'true' possibilities? What are the logical foundations of quality exclusion?

The sense is that Wittgenstein has not resolved the problem at all, but merely made adjustments for it in one pictorial method of representing logical form. The theoretical repercussions of this dodge for the general form of proposition, and the showing forth of logical form under the picture theory of meaning, are easily important and far-reaching enough to have caused Wittgenstein to begin to question the integrity of the *Tractatus* logic and semantics. This could be so particularly if he thought that the solution of the 1929 essay was the only possible way to salvage logical atomism and the picture theory, and then came to see that the 1929 solution was also fundamentally mistaken. Wittgenstein may have understood that color incompatibility is logically at odds with the *Tractatus* thesis that atomic facts are mutually ontically independent and elementary propositions mutually logically independent. If color incompatibility entails that phenomenal qualities are excluded from occurring in the same place at the same time in anything like the sense of a logical tautology or by virtue of involving anything like a logical contradiction, then it is hard to see how atomic facts and elementary propositions can be ontically and logically independent, as *Tractatus* 1.21, 4.211, and 5.134 require.

The picture theory of meaning, in coping with the color incompatibility problem, implies that 'Red-here-now' must be logically independent of and yet logically exclude if not contradict 'Blue-here-now'. This is itself a contradiction in Wittgenstein's semantics. What is gained by Wittgenstein's replacement of the standard truth table for conjunction with a modified truth table for quality exclusion? The conjunction R P T & B P T has no truth table representation for the case in which R P T is true and B P T is true. It disappears from the standard truth table when it is shortened by an entire row in order to picture the logical structure of color incompatibility. What does its disappearance signify? The sawed-off truth table is Wittgenstein's 1929 way of showing that there is no possible state of affairs in which R P T and B P T are true. By the distinction of 4.461–4.4611, this should mean that it is not just senseless, as in the case of normal contradictions, but altogether nonsensical to think about or try to express incompatible space-time-color facts, since their conjunction has no logical picture. Yet Wittgenstein gives no reason for regarding color incompatible conjunctions as nonsensical (pseudo-) propositions. The conjunction R P T & B P T follows easily enough from selective joint negation by the general form of proposition from the elementary propositions R P T and B P T, and Wittgenstein's truth table treats it as a contradiction.[12] If the conjunction is always false, then it should be senseless rather than nonsensical, and should be represented as a limiting case in truth table analysis. Wittgenstein briefly considers such a definition, but then withdraws it as "nonsense," arguing that it purports to exhibit "a greater logical multiplicity than that of the actual possibilities." Although R P T & B P T can never be true, R P T can be true and B P T can be true. If R P T is true, then B P T is false, and conversely. The color terms 'R' and 'B' function in the context '( ) P T' with something like the truth-functional force of negation. Space-time-color predications in the elementary propositions R P T and B P T effectively contradict one another, and are in that sense by no means logically independent.

Wittgenstein's solution in the 1929 essay implies that logic by itself cannot determine whether the four-rowed traditional truth table for propositional conjunction or the three-rowed revised table for property nonexclusion is appropriate for any arbitrary conjunction. 'Red-here-now & Blue-here-now' calls for the three-rowed table. The original four-rowed version will not do, because it lacks the requisite logical form or mathematical multiplicity to express the exclusion of R P T and B P T, where elementary propositions R P T and R P T cannot both be true. There is no valid logical inference from R P T & B P T to (R P T & ~R P T) ∨ (B P T & ~B P T). But 'Red-here-now & Blue-there-then' (or 'Blue-here-then' or 'Blue-there-now') on the contrary are correctly evaluated only by the four-rowed table. The three-rowed table lacks the requisite logical form or mathematical multiplicity to express the truth of R P T & B P T', where the elementary propositions R P T and R P T' are true. Yet R P T & B P T and R P T & B P T' are logically isomorphic. Wittgenstein in *Notebooks* 22.8.14 and *Tractatus* 5.473 insists that logic must take care of itself. We are not to intervene or assist logic in providing the transcendental ground of fact, thought, and language. The logic of the *Tractatus,* as Wittgenstein realizes shortly before he is to deliver the 1929 essay to a philosophical audience, is too seriously flawed to survive the corrections needed to express color incompatibility as a kind of tautology.

Wittgenstein concludes the 1929 essay on this note:

> It is, of course, a deficiency of our notation that it does not prevent the formation of such nonsensical constructions [R P T & B P T], and a perfect notation will have to exclude such structures by definite rules of syntax. These will have to tell us that in the case of certain kinds of atomic propositions described in terms of definite symbolic features certain combinations of the T's and F's must be left out. Such rules, however, cannot be laid down until we have actually reached the ultimate analysis of the phenomena in question. This, as we all know, has not yet been achieved. (170–71)

It would be but a short step from the conclusion of this essay to the recognition that, according to Wittgenstein's own methodology, it is not until the logic of propositions is understood that a successful analysis of the phenomena can be undertaken, since the latter knowledge as a posteriori is estranged from the project of pure semantics. The issue looks back to Wittgenstein's methodological consideration of two ways of projecting facts into the planes of thought and language. Wittgenstein may have seen that he was caught in a vicious circle of needing to discover a posteriori truths about the world of phenomena in order to determine how the logical analysis of color predications should go, and needing to understand how the logical analysis of color predications works in order to investigate a posteriori problems about the world of phenomena. Wittgenstein says as part of the claim that logic takes care of itself that we should never have to look at the world to determine questions of logic. In the *Tractatus* he clearly makes known:

> 5.551 Our fundamental principle is that every question which can be decided at all by logic can be decided off-hand.
>
> (And if we get into a situation where we need to answer such a problem by looking at the world, this shows that we are on a fundamentally wrong track.)

The final sentence of Wittgenstein's 1929 essay reminds us that the complete logical analysis of even so much as a single ordinary thought or proposition remains an unfinished task for philosophy. His discussion in the essay is offered in the spirit of taking the important first step, following the requirements for an actual analysis established in the most abstract terms by the *Tractatus.* Yet before these advance efforts could be announced at the Aristotelian Society – Mind Association meeting, Wittgenstein decided that the project was doomed.

Considerations of this global methodological kind, or specific dissatisfaction with the picture theory's implications for the color incompatibility problem, together with the philosophy of logic to which he remained loyal through the later unpublished works, caused Wittgenstein to abandon the early semantic philosophy for a radically different approach.[13] The color incompatibility problem in Ramsey's influential criticisms and the failure and repudiation of his own attempt to solve the problem in a way consistent with the early theory in "Some Remarks on Logical Form" paved the way for Wittgenstein's later philosophical inquiries and criticisms of logical atomism and the picture theory.

The first sign of Wittgenstein's new attitude toward the color incompatibility problem appears in his 1933 lectures at Cambridge, recorded in the *Blue Book.* Wittgenstein now speaks of quality exclusion as logically impossible because of a grammatical rule:

> 'The colours green and blue can't be in the same place simultaneously' . . . is a grammatical rule and states a logical impossibility.[14]

The problem arises again in *Philosophical Remarks,* where Wittgenstein takes a similar approach but reaches an importantly different conclusion than in "Some Remarks on Logical Form." In these later unpublished logical-mathematical aphorisms, composed during 1934–35, Wittgenstein states:

> It must be possible for the contradiction to show itself entirely in the symbolism, for if I say of a patch that it is red and green, it is certainly at most only one of these two, and the contradiction must be contained in the *sense* of the two propositions. That two colours won't fit at the same time in the same place must be contained in their form and the form of space.[15]

> The proposition $f(g) \cdot f(r)$ isn't nonsense, since not *all* truth possibilities disappear, even if they are all rejected. We can, however, say that the '·' has a different meaning here, since '$x \cdot y$' usually means (*TFFF*); here, on the other hand, it means (*FFF*). And something analogous holds for '$x \lor y$', etc.[16]

> This is how it is, what I said in the *Tractatus* doesn't exhaust
> the grammatical rules for 'and', 'not', 'or' etc.; there are rules
> for the truth functions which also deal with the elementary
> part of the proposition.[17]

With these admissions, the logic of the *Tractatus* crumbles. The interdependence of Wittgenstein's logic, ontology, semantics, and antiphilosophy assures that the logic's failure overthrows the picture theory of meaning. The semantic distinction between saying and showing and between sense, nonsense, and the senseless established by the general form of proposition, are also undone, though it is through these that philosophical problems are supposed to be eliminated as logically meaningless pseudoproblems. The demolition begins in 1929, at whatever moment Wittgenstein resolved that he would not read "Some Remarks on Logical Form" to the Aristotelian Society – Mind Association meeting, and continued quickly as Wittgenstein came to reject virtually every major conclusion of the early philosophy.

Problems in the logic of color predications are not just symptoms of fundamental difficulties in the *Tractatus*. They are the disease itself that is fatal to Wittgenstein's logical atomism and picture theory of meaning. A logically correct true or false description of the world, the contingent facts into which the world divides, or what we may also think of as the legitimate domain of significant assertion or of propositions in the true sense, is pervaded by color predications. If the logic of color or phenomenal quality generally is not the logic of tautology, then the logical foundations of the *Tractatus* are thoroughly misconceived. Wittgenstein must have understood these disastrous implications of the color incompatibility problem sometime before July 1929.

Wittgenstein's Philosophy at the Turning Point

We are at last in a position to appreciate the importance of Wittgenstein's unavailing attempts to solve the color incompatibility problem in the 1929 paper, and of his decision not to present it. We must try to reconstruct Wittgenstein's objections to logical atomism and the picture theory implied by the failure of the *Tractatus* and the 1929 essay to explain color incompatibility as overtures to the later philosophy.

The standard but probably apocryphal account is that the scales fell from Wittgenstein's eyes during a train ride with his friend the Italian economist Piero Sraffa. Sraffa supposedly asked Wittgenstein about the logical form of a sweeping motion

187 I Critical Interpretation

of the fingers under the chin in a Neapolitan gesture of contempt. This episode is often told as a companion piece to Wittgenstein's reading the report of a Paris court trial, in which toy cars and dolls were used to model the facts of the case, as suggesting the picture theory of meaning. Yet the Sraffa anecdote is baffling as an explanation of why Wittgenstein gave up his early philosophy. Why, we must ask, did Wittgenstein not simply interpret Sraffa's gesture as a meaningless literally nonsensical showing forth of value, an evaluation (something evidently negative and deroga- tory), for which a logical form as obtains in the case of meaningful expressions is not to be expected? Such a response would have understood Sraffa's gesture as more ethical-aesthetic grist for the picture theory mill. But Wittgenstein reportedly sees the ges- ture as significant, and is chagrined by what he assumes is the picture theory's inability to specify its logical form.[18]

Wittgenstein's abandonment of the picture theory seems to have been largely due to Ramsey's criticisms of the *Tractatus* treatment of color incompatibility. In coming to terms with the logical difficulties of quality exclusion and its implications for the *Tractatus*, in the course of preparing what he must have hoped would amount to a minor revision in the 1929 essay, Wittgen- stein recognized the defects of the early philosophy and at once disowned and declined to present the results of his first steps to- ward a *Tractatus*-type analysis. It may not be possible to resolve all the related historical questions, but I believe as others have also suggested that there is strong textual and circumstantial evidence for the hypothesis that Wittgenstein's later philosophy was stimulated by the realization that logical atomism and the picture theory are incapable of explaining color incompatibility, and that the general form of proposition does not establish the logic of quality exclusion. This awareness was reinforced by the attempt and assessment of the failure to mend the theory by an appeal to real numbers for degrees of continuous properties as irreducibly part of the logical infrastructures of elementary propositions and the atomic facts they are supposed to picture in "Some Remarks on Logical Form."

Any of these criticisms might have revealed to Wittgenstein deeper difficulties in the *Tractatus* treatment of the color incom- patibility problem than the 1929 essay could possibly repair. The concept of color incompatibility implies the material inadequacy of the general form of proposition, and with it the rupture of the saying-showing distinction between sense, nonsense, and the senseless that is vital to Wittgenstein's expulsion of philosophi- cal pseudoconcepts, pseudoproblems, and pseudopropositions.

The color incompatibility problem presents a direct challenge to what is perhaps the most important presupposition of Wittgenstein's philosophy of logic, that logic takes care of itself. If there is a difficulty in the logic of color predications, then the logical foundations of Wittgenstein's theory are in jeopardy. Color incompatibility seems to be more than a mere empirical limitation. But it proves impossible in Wittgenstein's theory to explain as a variety of logical necessity, if this is understood in the sense of tautology. The color incompatibility problem implies that the atomic facts and elementary propositions of Wittgenstein's early philosophy must at the same time be ontically or logically independent and sometimes logically exclusionary. That R P T contradicts or is logically incompatible with B P T contradicts or is incompatible with their logical independence, even if the relation is renamed 'exclusion', and even if the combination R P T & B P T is deemed nonsense by the disappearance of the first row in the standard truth table for conjunction.[19]

If Wittgenstein's struggles with the color incompatibility problem led him to a more penetrating investigation of the pragmatics of meaning, then his reflections about these difficulties may have put him in such a frame of mind that he was prepared for Sraffa's question about the meaning or logical form of the Neapolitan gesture to open up a new path of inquiry in radical departure from his previous method of analysis. The gesture may then have served as a mental triggering, in somewhat the way that Newton's study of planetary motion and local gravitation in Galileo's physics prepared him to adopt a theory of universal gravitation when he witnessed a falling apple in the tale popularized by Voltaire.[20]

There is nothing left of logical atomism and the picture theory of meaning if the color incompatibility problem is not more satisfactorily solved than in *Tractatus* 6.375–6.3751. The inclusion of real numbers in the logical structures of atomic propositions required for the logical isomorphism between pictures and real world facts only makes the difficulties in logical atomism and the picture theory more glaring. The color incompatibility problem, Ramsey's criticisms of the *Tractatus* solution, the attempt and failure to solve, and the exercise of working more carefully through the color incompatibility problem while writing the 1929 essay, provoked a crisis of what until that point had been Wittgenstein's absolute assurance that he had adequately explained the workings of language and exposed the nonsense of philosophy. The color incompatibility problem leaves Wittgenstein's early philosophy in shambles and forces him to begin all over again rethinking the problem of language and its implications for philosophy.[21]

∎ N O T E S

1. See von Wright in Malcolm 1958, 13–14.

2. Monk, 249, quotes Nedo and Ranchetti 1983, 223.

3. Von Wright, editor's introduction, Wittgenstein 1973, 12: "When Wittgenstein submitted the *Tractatus* as a Ph.D. dissertation after his return to Cambridge in 1929, Ogden helped him to obtain a free copy of the book from the publishers. Wittgenstein, in a short note, expressed his gratitude."

4. Monk, 272. See introduction, note 20, above.

5. Anscombe relates in a note attached to the first reprinting of "Some Remarks on Logical Form," in Copi and Beard 1966, 31n. 1: "Wittgenstein disowned the following essay. He told me that he had returned to Cambridge thinking he would be able to do philosophy again, but after a time he dried up and had no ideas. Then came the invitation to write a paper for the Aristotelian Society, and he thought he would accept and try to write something, just to see whether anything came out that way. He described what he wrote as quite worthless. When the time of the meeting came he had recovered his capacity to think and told his audience that he would talk about something quite different, which he did: namely infinity. . . . In a letter to the editor of *Mind* [Gilbert Ryle] Wittgenstein referred to this essay and called it 'weak'; and when Professor J. W. Scott asked him for a summary of it for his *Index to the Proceedings of the Aristotelian Society,* Wittgenstein wrote back begging him not to include any summary of it. . . . Again, in this letter, which is lost, Wittgenstein referred to the essay as 'weak and uncharacteristic'. I have consented to the reprint of the essay because I suppose that it will certainly be reprinted some time, and if that is to happen there had better be a statement indicating how little value can be set upon it as information about Wittgenstein's ideas." The letter appears in Wittgenstein 1933. That Wittgenstein generally appreciated and placed value on such gestures as refusing to present a paper after rejecting its ideas is indicated by his remarks recorded by Drury in Rhees 1984, 109: "I told Wittgenstein that my friend James, who had been working on his Ph.D. thesis for a year, had decided in the end that he had nothing original to say and would therefore not submit his thesis or obtain his degree. WITTGENSTEIN: For that action alone they should give him his Ph.D. degree."

6. Monk, 272–73.

7. Ibid., 273. Wittgenstein 1974b, Letter to Russell (R54), July 1929, 99: "Dear Russell, On Saturday the 13th I will read a paper to the Aristotelian Society in Nottingham and I would like to ask you if you could possibly manage to come there, as your presence would improve the discussion *immensely* and perhaps would be the only thing making it worth while at all. My paper (the one *written* for the meeting) is 'Some remarks on logical form', but I intend to read something else to them about generality and infinity in mathematics which, I believe, will be greater fun*.—I fear that whatever one says to them will either fall flat or arouse *irrelevant* troubles in their minds and questions and therefore

I would be much obliged to you if you came, in order—as I said—to make the discussion worth while. Yours ever L. Wittgenstein [*though it may be all Chinese to them.]" The editor notes, ibid.: "Russell's Appointments Diary does not show that he went to Nottingham." See also Moore's report of the events connected with Wittgenstein's participation in the Aristotelian Society – Mind meeting, mentioned in Cavell 1962, 67–68. Cavell refers to Moore 1954–55.

8. "Some Remarks on Logical Form," 165–66: "A simple example would be the representation of a patch P by the expression '[6——9, 3——8]' and of a proposition about it, *e.g.,* P is red, by the symbol '[6——9, 3——8] R', where 'R' is yet an unanalyzed term ('6——9' and '3——8' stand for the continuous interval between the respective numbers)."

9. *Notebooks,* 16.8.16: "A point cannot be red and green at the same time: at first sight there seems no need for this to be a logical impossibility. But the very language of physics reduces it to a kinetic impossibility. We see that there is a difference of structure between red and green. And then physics arranges them in a series. And then we see how here the true structure of the objects is brought to light. The fact that a particle cannot be in two places at the same time does look more like a logical impossibility. If we ask why, for example, then straight away comes the thought: Well, we should call particles that were in two places different, and this in its turn all seems to follow from the structure of space and of particles."

10. Ramsey 1923; rpt., Copi and Beard, 17–18. See Black, 367–69. Allaire 1958.

11. Whitehead and Russell's 1925–27 axiom of infinity is discussed above in chapter 3, note 20.

12. The formula for generating R P T & B P T by joint negation from the elementary propositions R P T and B P T according to the general form of proposition can be indicated in Nicod dagger function notation simply as: (R P T ⊦ R P T) ⊦ (B P T ⊦ B P T).

13. The continuity of Wittgenstein's attitude toward logic is indicated by his remark in *Philosophical Investigations* §97: "Thought is surrounded by a halo.—Its essence, logic, presents an order, in fact the *a priori* order of the world: that is, the order of *possibilities,* which must be common to both world and thought. But this order, it seems, must be *utterly simple.* It is *prior* to all experience, must run through all experience; no empirical cloudiness or uncertainty must be allowed to affect—it must rather be of the purest crystal. But this crystal does not appear as an abstraction; but as something concrete, indeed, as the most concrete, as it were the *hardest* thing there is (*Tractatus Logico-Philosophicus* No. 5.5563)."

14. Wittgenstein 1958, 56.

15. Wittgenstein 1975, 107. See also 105–9.

16. Ibid., 107.

17. Ibid. Wittgenstein's later ideas on color, inspired by his reading of Goethe's *Farbenlehre,* are collected in his 1977. See Wittgenstein 1974, 210–11: "The proposition 'this place is now red' (or 'this circle is now red') can be called an elementary proposition if this means that it is neither a truth function of other propositions nor defined as such. . . . But from 'a is now red' there follows 'a is now not green' and so elementary propositions in this sense aren't independent of each other like the elementary propositions in the calculus I once described—a calculus to which, misled as I was by a false notion of reduction, I thought that the whole use of propositions must be reducible." Waismann 1979 evidently understood Wittgenstein to believe that color predications are elementary propositions, as indicated in his restatement of Wittgenstein's early logical atomism in "Theses," appendix B, 249–53. Waismann on 241 repeats a version of the *Tractatus* solution to the color incompatibility problem.

18. Malcolm 1958, 69: "One day (they [Wittgenstein and Sraffa] were riding, I think, on a train) when Wittgenstein was insisting that a proposition and that which it describes must have the same 'logical form', the same 'logical multiplicity', Sraffa made a gesture, familiar to Neapolitans as meaning something like disgust or contempt, of brushing the underneath of his chin with an outward sweep of the finger-tips of one hand. And he asked: 'What is the logical form of *that?*' Sraffa's example produced in Wittgenstein the feeling that there was an absurdity in the insistence that a proposition and what it describes must have the same 'form'. This broke the hold on him of the conception that a proposition must literally be a 'picture' of the reality it describes." Malcolm adds in a note: "Professor G. H. von Wright informs me that Wittgenstein related this incident to him somewhat differently: the question at issue, according to Wittgenstein, was whether every proposition must have a 'grammar', and Sraffa asked Wittgenstein what the 'grammar' of that gesture was. In describing the incident to von Wright, Wittgenstein did not mention the phrases 'logical form' or 'logical multiplicity'."

19. Wittgenstein acknowledges the dilemma in a conversation with Waismann and Moritz Schlick in Vienna on 2 January 1930. Waismann 1979, 73–74: "I want to explain my views on elementary propositions and first I want to say what I used to believe and what seems right to me now. I used to have two conceptions of an elementary proposition, one of which seems correct to me, while I was completely wrong in holding the other. . . . I had the idea that elementary propositions must be independent of one another. . . . In holding this I was wrong, and the following is what is wrong with it. I laid down rules for the syntactical use of logical *constants,* for example '$p \cdot q$', and did not think that these rules might have something to do with the inner structure of propositions. What was wrong about my conception was that I believed that the syntax of logical constants could be laid down without paying any attention to the inner connection of propositions. That is not how things actually are. I cannot, for example, say that red and blue are at one point simultaneously. Here no logical product can be constructed. Rather, the rules for the logical constants form only a part of a more comprehensive syntax about which I did not yet know anything at the time."

20. Wittgenstein 1968a, x: "since beginning to occupy myself with philosophy again, sixteen years ago, I have been forced to recognize grave mistakes in what I wrote in that first book [the *Tractatus*]. I was helped to realize these mistakes—to a degree which I myself am hardly able to estimate—by the criticism which my ideas encountered from Frank Ramsey, with whom I discussed them in innumerable conversations during the last two years of his life. Even more than to this—always certain and forcible—criticism I am indebted to that which a teacher of this university, Mr. P. Sraffa, for many years unceasingly practised on my thoughts. I am indebted to *this* stimulus for the most consequential ideas of this book."

21. See also Ackermann 1988, 135–40; Austin 1980; Baker 1988, 112–66; Black 1964, 367–69; Fann 1969, 41–54; Hacker 1989, 108–12; Jacquette 1990a; Kenny 1973, 103–19; Stern 1991

Philosophical Grammar in the Later Philosophy

The complexity of philosophy is not in its matter, but in our tangled understanding.

—WITTGENSTEIN, PHILOSOPHICAL REMARKS §2

In disowning "Some Remarks on Logical Form," Wittgenstein also disowns the *Tractatus*. Logical atomism, the picture theory of meaning, and general form of proposition cannot be sustained in light of the color incompatibility problem. The three interconnected interdependent logical, metaphysical, and semantic components of the early philosophy fall apart if any one of them is untenable. Wittgenstein tries to salvage a modified *Tractatus* logic in the 1929 essay. When he decides that the effort has failed, he is not long in understanding its sweeping consequences for his overall project of doing away with philosophy by explaining the meaning of language.[1]

The realization that the *Tractatus* could not be made to work must have been not only disappointing but liberating. The success of the *Tractatus* would have implied the end of philosophy; its failure released Wittgenstein's philosophical energies in new directions with the twofold purpose of undertaking both a critical and constructive task. For in detaching himself from the *Tractatus,* Wittgenstein does not free himself of the questions that had prompted his elaboration of the early philosophy in the first place. Now he must start over again. As though he were designing and building a project in mechanical engineering, Wittgenstein identifies the source of error to determine what went wrong in the *Tractatus* prototype. He uses the knowledge gained to avoid the same mistakes in rethinking the nature of language and its implications for philosophy. Wittgenstein's later philosophy is an interplay between his self-criticisms of the *Tractatus* and his continuing efforts to address the same set of problems in a different way, chastened by the defeat of the early philosophy.[2]

What does not change but is fundamental to Wittgenstein's thought in the early, transitional, and later periods is the insight that philosophical problems arise only through the misunderstanding of language. The problem is to replace a compelling but faulty theory with a correct account. When he searches out the source of error in the *Tractatus,* Wittgenstein places the blame on a single disastrous oversight: the early theory's virtual neglect of the concept of naming as the most basic linguistic activity. The *Tractatus* says that names are simple, primitive signs, that by themselves lack sense but have meaning contextually in an elementary proposition by designating simple objects similarly ordered in the logically isomorphic structures of the atomic facts that elementary propositions picture. But the *Tractatus* does not try to explain how names name, how the naming or use of a name takes place, or, in other words, how the designation of objects infuses meaning into thought and language at the deepest level of logical analysis.

In the *Tractatus* Wittgenstein tries to prove by transcendental argument that there must be simple names for simple objects. The picture theory does not imply 'naming' in the vulgar sense by which Adam and Eve name the animals they encounter strolling through the Garden of Eden. It is enough to know that there must be names, that names are simple, that they have meaning only in the context of a proposition, and that in the elementary propositions in which they occur they stand in one-one correspondence with simple objects in the atomic facts pictured by elementary propositions. Formal philosophical semantics requires only the existence of logical isomorphisms in which the structures of world and language are abstractly correlated. How naming occurs in the transcendental order of imperceptible symbols is a pseudoquestion that cannot sensibly be asked or answered. If we know that there must be simple objects, and that simple objects must be named by simple names with identical matching space-time-color forms in the elementary propositions that picture atomic facts, then the simple names concatenated in elementary propositions name whatever simple objects are linked together in the atomic facts they picture. Thus, the *Tractatus* declares:

> 4.0311 One name stands for one thing, and another for another thing, and they are connected together. And so the whole, like a living picture, presents the atomic fact.

> 4.0312 The possibility of propositions is based upon the principle of the representation of objects by signs.
>
> My fundamental thought is that the "logical constants" do not represent. That the *logic* of the facts cannot be represented.

A name 'stands for' an object. The question of how names refer to objects or what a name's standing for an object consists in does not interest Wittgenstein in the *Tractatus*. Logic must take care of itself; the naming of objects in the transcendent order of imperceptible symbols cannot depend on our intervention, to which in any case we have no epistemic or direct linguistic access.

In the transition period, Wittgenstein is no longer satisfied with the transcendental conclusion that there must be simple names that somehow name simple objects. To understand the logic of quality exclusion in addressing the color incompatibility problem, Wittgenstein decides that semantic analysis must begin with an a posteriori logical investigation of the phenomena. The question of how particular names name particular objects arises only when top-down transcendental argument gives way to the logical investigation of real fact structures as the program of logical analysis. Wittgenstein then asks in more practical terms for the first time how the facts of the world might actually be pictured from the ground up. In retrospect, the concept of naming as the most basic semantic relation should have been one of the central topics for the picture theory of meaning. Yet the need to explain how names name the objects with which they are supposed transcendentally to be one-one correlated is entirely overlooked by Wittgenstein until the faulty application of the theory to the color incompatibility problem forces him to reconsider the theory's foundations.

The problem of naming which the *Tractatus* takes for granted is that of explaining the semantics of name-object correlations well enough to determine in principle which names go with which objects. The transcendental argument concludes that there must be names, but it does not explain how particular names name particular objects. The picturing of atomic facts in language according to the *Tractatus* and "Some Remarks on Logical Form" looks something like this:

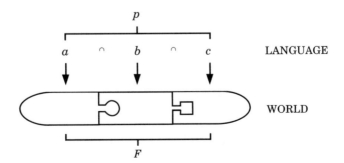

How does the naming of simple objects work? There is supposed to be a one-one correspondence between juxtapositions of
simple objects ordered in a determinate structure of space-time-
color forms, and concatenations of simple names for simple objects of the same forms ordered in an identical structure. The
correlation of space-time-color forms and the thesis that terms
have meaning only contextually within a proposition implies that
if p logically pictures atomic fact F, then 'a' names object o_1 rather
than o_2, o_3, or any other object in any fact other than F, 'b' names
o_2 rather than o_1, o_3, or any other object, and 'c' names o_3 rather
than o_1, o_2, or any other object.

Things are more complicated if the picturing of particular
atomic facts by particular elementary propositions is not presupposed, and we must try to imagine matching elementary propositions to atomic facts on the basis of whether a simple name in an
elementary proposition names a simple object in one atomic fact
rather than another. How does the picture theory adjudicate
even in principle between such picturing correspondences as indicated in the following diagram, where the elementary proposition p appears by virtue of its logically isomorphic structure
alone to have equal title to represent either or both atomic facts
$F1$ and $F2$, and where simple names a, b, and c, concatenated
into the logical structure of elementary proposition p appear by
virtue of their space-time-color forms alone to have equal title respectively to name either or both objects o_1 or o_4, o_2 or o_5, o_3 or o_6,
in atomic facts $F1$ and $F2$?

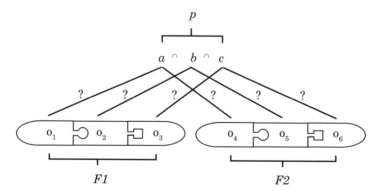

The problem is not the directionality of projection from name
to object rather than from object to name. Wittgenstein claims
that propositions as logical pictures are themselves facts, which
means that elementary propositions in order to picture atomic
facts must be composed of simple names that are at the same

time themselves simple objects. Picturing is an exact one-one correlation of (picturing) fact with (pictured) fact and (naming) object with (named) object. Thought establishes lines of projection from fact to picture by thinking the sense of a proposition, whereby the simple objects that constitute atomic facts are transcendentally "named" in what 5.511 calls "the great mirror." We can therefore suppose that intentionality sweeps downward through picturing propositions from the highest levels of propositional meaning in colloquial sign systems to the truth-functions of elementary propositions by which they are analyzed in the transcendental order of symbols, through the picturing of atomic facts by elementary propositions, and finally to the naming of simple objects by simple names.

The *Tractatus* says only that one-one naming correspondences must exist. But the meanings of logical pictures are not fixed, and the determinate meaning of language is not adequately accounted for, unless analysis in principle specifies the naming of particular simple objects by particular simple names. It is precisely this requirement that the *Tractatus* in its top-down transcendental outlook takes for granted. The picture theory as a result provides no ultimate semantic grounding for the meaning of any of the propositions it is supposed to explain. If we cannot know which particular objects names name, then the exact meaning of any proposition built up by concatenation of names into elementary propositions is undetermined, as is the meaning of any compound proposition constructed by the general form of proposition as a truth function of elementary propositions. The picture theory is caught in a vicious circle. The naming of a particular simple object by a particular simple name is undetermined unless the picturing of a particular atomic fact by a particular elementary proposition is determined. But equally the picturing of a particular atomic fact by a particular elementary proposition is undetermined unless the naming of particular simple objects by particular simple names is determined. In the *Tractatus*, Wittgenstein maintains there is no need to correlate particular simple names with particular simple objects:

> 5.526 One can describe the world completely by completely generalized propositions, *i.e.* without from the outset co-ordinating any name with a definite object.
>
> In order then to arrive at the customary way of expression we need simply say after an expression "there is one and only one *x*, which . . . .": and this *x* is *a*.

If Wittgenstein cannot solve the color incompatibility problem except from an empiricist perspective, and if he cannot avoid
the naming problem once he adopts an empiricist standpoint,
then the color incompatibility problem forces Wittgenstein either
to solve the naming problem or abandon the picture theory of
meaning. When he decides that the naming problem cannot be
solved, Wittgenstein draws the only possible conclusion, which is
to reject the picture theory. It is finally the naming problem, by
way of the color incompatibility problem, that refutes Wittgenstein's early philosophy. And it is the concept of naming and the
attempt to work out a more satisfactory account of how the naming of things in language actually takes place in real language
that holds center stage in Wittgenstein's later philosophy.

After 1929, Wittgenstein begins to appreciate naming as the
most important semantic relation, the foundation of meaning in
thought and language. In *Philosophical Investigations* §§26, 49,
he speaks of naming as a 'preparation' for propositional meaning
in the description of facts. Wittgenstein systematically dis-
mantles the *Tractatus* presuppositions about naming and related
components of the early theory, and offers constructively in its
place a positive account which he sees as the only possible alternative. Thus, *Philosophical Investigations* §38 speaks derisively
of "the conception of naming as an occult process," which is just
how the *Tractatus* regards naming, or rather epitomizes how the
Tractatus simply ignores the problem of naming. Wittgenstein's
appreciation of naming and his attempt to advance a preferred
solution are the unifying motif of what otherwise appears to be a
disconnected series of philosophical reflections on a wide range of
topics in the later writings. Wittgenstein's new way of thinking
about naming and meaning in thought and language is not easily
paraphrased, but claims our attention in the following chapters
as it drives Wittgenstein's inquiry throughout the *Philosophical
Investigations*.[3]

The opening sentence of Wittgenstein's *Blue Book*, the first
recorded philosophical question of his 1933 lectures at Cambridge, signals his awakening interest in the problem of naming.
Wittgenstein asks, simply: "What is the meaning of a word?" (1).
His answer occupies most of the *Philosophical Investigations*, for
which *The Blue and Brown Books* are preliminary studies. The
fact as Frege held that names have meaning only in the context of
a proposition does not imply that a philosophical semantics can
avoid the need to explain the meanings of individual names. We
have not explained the meaning of a proposition if we can only do
so in terms of the unknown meanings of the names it contains.

The problem Wittgenstein now confronts is to explain naming as it would occur at the deepest level of logical analysis, where what makes a term a *name* is something it must share in common even with ordinary names that conventionally designate composite things in colloquial speech. Wittgenstein's approach is to begin with ordinary naming in ordinary language, and inquire into the necessary and sufficient conditions of naming as it actually occurs. Yet ordinary language conceals rather than reveals its logical forms by its obscurity and labyrinthine ambiguity, as Frege, Russell, and Wittgenstein frequently complain. What is Wittgenstein's alternative to descending into the murky depths of natural language?

Wittgenstein describes the new method he has invented for the philosophical study of meaning and the meaningfulness of language in pragmatic terms in the next immediately following *Blue Book* entry:

> Let us attack this question by asking, first, what is an explanation of the meaning of a word; what does the explanation of a word look like?
>
> The way this question helps us is analogous to the way the question "how do we measure a length?" helps us to understand the problem "what is length?"
>
> The questions "What is length?", "What is meaning?", "What is the number one?" etc., produce in us a mental cramp. We feel that we can't point to anything in reply to them and yet ought to point to something. (We are up against one of the great sources of philosophical bewilderment: a substantive makes us look for a thing that corresponds to it.) (1)

If we want to understand the meaning of words for purposes of philosophical semantics, we must inquire into the way we explain the meanings of particular words. This preliminary task gives philosophical semantics a pragmatic cast. Wittgenstein claims that we are paralyzed if we try to answer the problem of naming by associating a corresponding object or thing with a term. If that is the kind of account we desire, then we have no idea even how to begin to conduct a search for an adequate explanation of meaning. Instead, Wittgenstein advocates a practical approach to the problems of philosophical semantics. The method is analogous to the explanation of the concept of length by way of investigating the way in which we actually measure particular lengths, the things we do and the activities connected with the measurement of length in which we engage. Wittgenstein continues:

> Asking first "What's an explanation of meaning?" has two advantages. You in a sense bring the question "what is

meaning?" down to earth. For, surely, to understand the meaning of "meaning" you ought also to understand the meaning of
"explanation of meaning". Roughly: "let's ask what the explanation of meaning is, for whatever that explains will be the
meaning." Studying the grammar of the expression "explanation of meaning" will teach you something about the grammar of the word "meaning" and will cure you of the temptation
to look about you for some object which you might call "the
meaning". (1)

The meaning of a word, as we ordinarily think of it, is easy
enough to explain. It is whatever the word stands for, whatever
thing it names; whether complex things, events or occurrences,
concepts, properties, propositions, numbers, sets, persons, or the
like. Simple names, if there are any, name simple objects, if there
are any. The *Tractatus* implies that in the transcendental order of
symbols all names are simple and as such can only name simple
objects in a completely analyzed logically correct logical picturing.
Whatever may appear to be a complex name or name for a complex entity in ordinary language is supposed to be analyzable in
meaning as a complex description of a complex of increasingly
simpler facts. The analysis of meaning eventually reaches conjunctions of elementary propositions representing atomic facts, at
which point the only remaining objects available for naming are
the simple objects chain-linked together in the logical structures
of corresponding atomic facts.

In the transitional and later period Wittgenstein rejects this
answer. The color incompatibility problem shows that the picture
theory in its superstructure is wrong, and Wittgenstein is committed to discovering exactly how it fails at its semantic foundations. He now believes that we must try to understand naming
and 'the meaning of a word' if we are to understand the construction of propositions out of combinations of names. The *Blue Book*
states that the only way to do this is to inquire into what name
users actually do in explaining to others the meanings of particular names, in the course of which we will thereby explain all there
is to know about the concept of meaning. It is the same pragmatic
method by which we arrive at the concept of length by investigating the activity of measuring length, the ways in which and the
things we do when we measure lengths. By analogy, we can only
approach the problem of meaning, or more specifically the problem of naming, by asking how we actually name things, the practices by which we use names to name things and explain the
meanings of names.

This, Wittgenstein says, brings the inquiry down to earth.
We begin with the concrete activity of language use in explaining

the meanings of names. As such, we avoid being stymied in the effort merely to associate corresponding things with singular terms. The mere pairing up of linguistic signs or names and the things to which they refer does not by itself explain naming, as the failure of logical atomism and the picture theory demonstrates. The only fruitful approach is to begin from an empirical anthropological standpoint, with roughly the same theoretical orientation in philosophical semantics that Wittgenstein assumes when in *Tractatus* 2.1 he maintains that we make to ourselves pictures of facts. The early philosophy in the *Tractatus* develops the logic of *pictures*. The transitional period of "Some Remarks on Logical Form" criticizes the poverty of logical reductionism and proposes a rededication to the project of analysis through a logical investigation of the formal structures of *facts*. The posttransitional later philosophy in *The Blue and Brown Books* and *Philosophical Investigations* looks beyond both facts and pictures to the practical philosophical anthropological study of the human *activity* of naming.

The decision to begin with the explanations we give when we actually use and communicate the meanings of names in naming things does not yet constitute a method for investigating the complex phenomena of ordinary language. The vagueness, ambiguity, and equivocation of everyday linguistic practice remain an obstacle to understanding the logic of language in the same way now, just as Wittgenstein had observed in the *Tractatus*. The methodological innovation of Wittgenstein's later philosophy by which he proposes to overcome the obscurity of everyday thought and language to reveal the nontranscendental semantics of naming is the description and critical study of language games.[4]

| NOTES

1. Kenny 1973, 103–19. Hacker 1989, 108–45, speaks of Wittgenstein's period of "Disintegration and Reconstruction." Baker 1988, 116–29, refers to these events as the "Demolition and Reconstruction" of Wittgenstein's early philosophy.

2. This is not to say that Wittgenstein afterward regarded the *Tractatus* as philosophically uninteresting. In the preface to *Philosophical Investigations,* Wittgenstein writes, vi: "Four years ago I had occasion to re-read my first book (the *Tractatus Logico-Philosophicus*) and to explain its ideas to someone. It suddenly seemed to me that I should publish those old thoughts and the new ones together: that the latter could be seen in the right light only by contrast with and against the background of my old way of thinking." See Malcolm 1958, 69: "Wittgenstein frequently said to me disparaging things about the *Tractatus.* I am sure, however, that he still regarded it as an important work. For one thing, he was greatly concerned in the *Investigations* to refute the errors

of the former book. Also he told me once that he really thought that in the *Tractatus* he had provided a perfect account of a view that is the *only* alternative to the viewpoint of his later work."

    3. I fully agree with Malcolm's wise words of caution in his 1963, 96: "An attempt to summarize the *Investigations* would be neither successful nor useful." Yet, like Malcolm, while reaching different conclusions, I shall try to do so anyway.

    4. See also Caruthers 1989, 108–46; Fogelin 1987, 143; Hallett 1977, 98–139; Hanfling 1989, 31–54; Kenny 1973, 80, 139–58; Rundle 1990, 23–39.

| **Language Games**

Language games are simplified fictional language use scenarios. Wittgenstein uses language games to investigate aspects of collo- quial speech and writing, abstracted from the real world com- plexities in which they are embedded, in order to highlight features that would otherwise be indistinguishable.

Wittgenstein adapts the concept of a language game from his friend the Cambridge economist Piero Sraffa, who used similar models of economic phenomena.[1] Wittgenstein introduces the concept of a language game in the *Blue Book,* where it comple- ments his method of explaining meaning by describing how we explain the meanings of particular names. Wittgenstein com- bines the idea of a language game as the actual activity by which children learn language and as a philosophical device for clarify- ing meaning:

> I shall in the future again and again draw your attention to
> what I shall call language games. These are ways of using
> signs simpler than those in which we use the signs of our
> highly complicated everyday language. Language games are
> the forms of language with which a child begins to make use
> of words. The study of language games is the study of primi-
> tive forms of language or primitive languages. If we want to
> study the problems of truth and falsehood, of the agreement
> and disagreement of propositions with reality, of the nature
> of assertion, assumption, and question, we shall with great
> advantage look at primitive forms of language in which these
> forms of thinking appear without the confusing background
> of highly complicated processes of thought. When we look at
> such simple forms of language the mental mist which seems
> to enshroud our ordinary use of language disappears. We see
> activities, reactions, which are clear-cut and transparent. On
> the other hand we recognize in these simple processes forms

of language not separated by a break from our more complicated ones. We see that we can build up the complicated
forms from the primitive ones by gradually adding new
forms. (17)

The activities by which we explain the meanings of names to
one another are our only access to the concept of meaning. The
real world is too complicated for a complete description of what we
actually do in explaining the meanings of words. But we can understand the essential principles by concentrating on simplified
toy models of actual language use more easily grasped in imaginary language games.

This is Wittgenstein's method in the *Philosophical Investigations*. He begins his examination of an extensive series of language games with a quotation from St. Augustine's *Confessions:*

> 1. "When they (my elders) named [*appellabant*] some object,
> and accordingly moved towards something, I saw this and I
> grasped that the thing was called by the sound they uttered
> when they meant to point it out. Their intention was shewn
> by their bodily movements, as it were the natural language
> of all peoples: the expression of the face, the play of the eyes,
> the movement of other parts of the body, and the tone of
> voice which expresses our state of mind in seeking, having,
> rejecting, or avoiding something. . . ." (Augustine, *Confes-
> sions,* I. 8.) [editor's translation from the Latin].
>   These words, it seems to me, give us a particular picture of
> the essence of human language. It is this: the individual words
> in language name objects—sentences are combinations of such
> names.—In this picture of language we find the roots of the
> following idea: Every word has a meaning. This meaning is
> correlated with the word. It is the object for which the word
> stands. (§1)

Augustine describes how persons already conversant in a
language taught him the meanings of names. They spoke a word
and pointed or moved toward it, Augustine says, and after repeated efforts, he grasped the connection. This is the very sort of
account of an attempt to explain meaning to which Wittgenstein
in the first paragraphs of the *Blue Book* says we must turn in order to understand the concept of meaning.

The picture of the essence of human language Wittgenstein
claims to find in the *Confessions* is remarkably like that of the
Tractatus. In criticizing Augustine, Wittgenstein is criticizing
many of his own picture theory presuppositions about the reference of names. Augustine reports that the meanings of words
were explained to him as the objects correlated with names, which
could then be combined into sentences. The meaning of a name is

communicated by body movements. What Augustine's elders actually did in explaining to him the meaning of a name, he says,
was to move toward an object while uttering a sound or speaking
its name. Augustine then associated name with object and came
to understand the object designated by a name as its meaning.
This is a behavioral ostensive explanation of naming and the
meanings of names. Wittgenstein finds the picture attractive but
inadequate to the facts of language. The first difficulty in Augustine's description, construed as an explanation of the meaning of
singular terms, is that it does not take account of the enormous
variety of distinct linguistic functions of words. Wittgenstein
remarks:

> Augustine does not speak of there being any difference be-
> tween kinds of word. If you describe the learning of language
> in this way you are, I believe, thinking primarily of nouns
> like "table", "chair", "bread", and of people's names, and only
> secondarily of the names of certain actions and properties;
> and of the remaining kinds of word as something that will
> take care of itself. (§1)

The commentary that follows quickly draws us into a densely
interwoven fabric of philosophical remarks about a series of
fictional linguistic transactions Wittgenstein is about to denote as
language games. Wittgenstein illustrates the limitations of
Augustine's reductive doctrine of the meaning of words by introducing a language game. He imagines sending someone on a shopping errand, with a piece of paper to be presented to the
shopkeeper marked with a request for a specific number of a
specific kind of object:

> Now I think of the following use of language: I send someone
> shopping. I give him a slip marked "five red apples". He
> takes the slip to the shopkeeper, who opens a drawer
> marked "apples"; then he looks up the word "red" in a table
> and finds a colour sample opposite it; then he says the series
> of cardinal numbers—I assume that he knows them by
> heart—up to the word "five" and for each number he takes
> an apple of the same colour as the sample out of the
> drawer.—It is in this and similar ways that one operates
> with words.—"But how does he know where and how he is to
> look up the word 'red' and what he is to do with the word
> 'five'?"—Well, I assume that he *acts* as I have described. Ex-
> planations come to an end somewhere.—But what is the
> meaning of the word "five"?—No such thing was in question
> here, only how the word "five" is used. (§1)

Are we to think of the three words in 'five red apples' as names
whose meanings are objects? What happens in the language game

Wittgenstein describes? Wittgenstein wants us to inquire into how the words actually function in the sentence, and not to settle for easy answers if they are incorrect.

Does the word 'five' name an object? The standard reply is that the word names the abstract object the number five, a particular abstract entity in a particular location on the number line. But is this what the slip to the grocer requests? Does the writer of the order, the messenger, or the shopkeeper use the word 'five' as a name the meaning of which is the abstract entity exactly between the whole numbers four and six on the number line? How does the word 'five' function in their transaction? The word appears to work perfectly well without any reference to an object, concrete or abstract, without naming anything at all; it is just the particular number of things requested by the order. The occurrence of the word contextually in 'five red apples' and the presentation of the words conventionally in the practice of marketing gives the word its meaning. It is understood to involve something like a one-one correlation, in this case, the terms in a recital of the numbers from one to five accompanied by the selection of a single object of the required kind. As we might also say, 'five' does not name an object as its meaning in Wittgenstein's scenario, but gives an instruction for a process of counting the things needed to fill an order.

The same is true of 'red' and 'apples'. Philosophers like to think of predicates as designating properties—'red' is the name of the property red or redness. But is that the function of the word in the shopping list? Must red be named as an object where red or redness is the meaning of the word 'red' in order for the shopper to request, the errands person to deliver the request, or obtain from the shopkeeper a correctly filled order for five red apples? The shopkeeper, as Wittgenstein describes his activity, merely consults a color chart and finds a color sample marked 'red' (the shopkeeper can count, but doesn't know his colors), which the shopkeeper then uses for visual comparison to select five objects from the bin marked 'apples'. The writer, messenger, and intended agent of the communiqué at no point name, try to name, or need to associate a definite object with any of the terms 'five', 'red', or 'apples'. 'Apples' might seem to come the closest in naming an object and having that object as its meaning, since apples are obviously objects. Yet here too the term does not refer to any particular apples, since the instructions are satisfied by any five apples, provided they are red. The writer does not need to name the particular five red apples he wants for the order to be correctly understood. The shopkeeper opens a drawer marked with the general term 'Apples' and proceeds to fill the order, armed with the color sample and his ability to count. But the apples are not individually named, and the shopkeeper need not name or know the names of the apples, nor need he refer to the apples individually by name or interpret the list as designating any five particular apples.

If the terms in the shopping list 'five red apples' functioned as names, Wittgenstein implies, the shopkeeper would have to deliver to the errands person a shopping bag containing a five (the number five or an instance thereof), a red (redness or the color red), and (which?) apples. Wittgenstein trusts us to appreciate the absurdity of such an interpretation, having merely described the facts of an everyday market transaction. The terms 'five', 'red', and 'apples' are not names, and so the sentence (a request or command) 'five red apples' is a sentence that is not composed of names. Wittgenstein similarly would have scoffed at any such counterexample to the *Tractatus* semantics when his thinking was still firmly in the grip of logical atomism and the picture theory. There he would have discounted these objections as involving only superficial colloquial conventions of expression that do not reveal their true logical forms in the perceptible order of signs, but only in the imperceptible transcendental order of symbols considered independently of their signs.

There is arguably some philosophical significance even in Wittgenstein's choice of an imperative or command in the shopping list sentence 'five red apples', rather than a categorical or declarative proposition like 'Red here now'. The two are sufficiently similar in their superficial grammatical structures that Wittgenstein may have chosen 'five red apples' for just that reason as the closest thing suitable for a simplified practical application. An economic exchange requires and provides the pragmatic test of correct communication and understanding of meaning. A command is a command, and not another thing; it has a unique function as one of a special kind of language tool. To argue that, despite appearances, every sentence, including categorical assertions, questions, commands, and expressions of propositional attitude, must have the same underlying logical form and perform the same semantic function of stating a fact, strikes Wittgenstein in the later period as insufficient for understanding the meaning of all language.

Wittgenstein's first language game demonstrates an important conclusion. It shows, contrary to Augustine's semantic reductivism, that the communication and understanding of language does not necessarily involve a combination of names associated with objects as their meanings. Wittgenstein next considers an even more simplified language game, in which a builder calls out the names of building materials to an assistant as they are needed in a certain order, as a way of coordinating their labor:

> 2. That philosophical concept of meaning has its place in a primitive idea of the way language functions. But one can also say that it is the idea of a language more primitive than ours.
>
> Let us imagine a language for which the description given by Augustine is right. The language is meant to serve for communication between a builder A and an assistant B. A is building with building-stones: there are blocks, pillars, slabs and beams. B has to pass the stones, and that in the order in which A needs them. For this purpose they use a language consisting of the words "block", "pillar", "slab", "beam". A calls them out;— B brings the stone which he has learnt to bring at such-and-such a call.—Conceive this as a complete primitive language.

The builder and assistant's language game is simple enough to satisfy Augustine's oversimplified description of language. This is how some languages work. Yet Wittgenstein, considering the diversity of ways in which we explain the meanings of words, finds the naming of objects to be only a fraction of the many uses and functions of words:

> 3. Augustine, we might say, does describe a system of communication; only not everything that we call language is this system. And one has to say this in many cases where the question arises "Is this an appropriate description or not?" The answer is: "Yes, it is appropriate, but only for this narrowly circumscribed region, not for the whole of what you were claiming to describe."
>
> It is as if someone were to say: "A game consists in moving objects about on a surface according to certain rules..."—and we replied: You seem to be thinking of board games, but there are others. You can make your definition correct by expressly restricting it to those games.

As in the *Blue Book,* Wittgenstein includes as language games primitive languages, language teaching activities, languages and the extralinguistic actions into which their use is intertwined, and linguistic thought experiments for exploring the semantics of language. For convenience he refers to each game by the paragraph number in which it is introduced, adding more interesting complications and variations:

> 7. In the practice of the use of language (2) one party calls out the words, the other acts on them. In instruction in the language the following process will occur: the learner *names* the objects; that is, he utters the word when the teacher

points to the stone.—And there will be this still simpler exercise: the pupil repeats the words after the teacher—both of
these being processes resembling language.

We can also think of the whole process of using words in (2)
as one of those games by means of which children learn their
native language. I will call these games "language-games" and
will sometimes speak of a primitive language as a language-
game.

And the processes of naming the stones and of repeating
words after someone might also be called language-games.
Think of much of the use of words in games like ring-a-ring-a-
roses.

I shall also call the whole, consisting of language and the
actions into which it is woven, the "language-game".

The concept of a language game has a definite pragmatic bent.
Language games are linguistic activities with a purpose, however
urgent or frivolous, and cannot be understood apart from what
the players are trying to accomplish. Language games offer Wittgenstein an innovative method of exploring the properties of language in their most pure and simplified forms. He builds in more
and more realistic features of actual language use until he is prepared at last to consider all human language uses with the pur-
poseful activities in which they are interwoven as language
games.

In §8, Wittgenstein modifies the language game of §2 by allowing the builder and his assistant to use demonstratives 'this',
'that', 'here', and 'there' in more sophisticated sentences than
'Slab!' or 'Pillar!', including 'This slab there!' and even 'This—
there!'. Here is further evidence of the inadequacy of interpreting
every constituent of a meaningful sentence as a singular term
designating an object. Wittgenstein remarks:

> 38. But what, for example, is the word "this" the name of in
> language-game (8) or the word "that" in the ostensive
> definition "that is called...."?—If you do not want to produce
> confusion you will do best not to call these words names at
> all.—Yet, strange to say, the word "this" has been called the
> only *genuine* name; so that anything else we call a name was
> one only in an inexact, approximate sense.
>
> This queer conception springs from a tendency to sublime
> the logic of our language—as one might put it. The proper
> answer to it is: we call very different things "names"; the word
> "name" is used to characterize many different kinds of use of
> a word, related to one another in many different ways;—but
> the kind of use that "this" has is not among them...

I shall not work through all of Wittgenstein's variations of
the basic language game between the builder and the builder's
assistant. The general point Wittgenstein makes in different

ways is that not all single words function as names, and not all terms have meaning by virtue of naming objects.

Philosophical semantics must do justice to the diversity of ways in which names are actually used. Meaning, Wittgenstein seems to think, could not be expressed at all if ordinary language users were predominantly using something so semantically fundamental as names. This is Wittgenstein's first criticism of what he takes to be Augustine's semantic reductivism. We must pay attention to how language users explain the meanings of words. But we should do so from the standpoint of a particular set of philosophical questions, modeling selected features for study in language games, and trying to deduce from descriptions of the explanations of naming the pragmatic conditions of meaning.

Wittgenstein is impressed by the multiplicity of language tools for the expression of many different kinds of meanings. He encourages us to:

> 11. Think of the tools in a tool-box: there is a hammer, pliers, a saw, a screw-driver, a rule, a glue-pot, nails and screws.— The functions of words are as diverse as the functions of these objects. (And in both cases there are similarities.)
>
> Of course, what confuses us is the uniform appearance of words when we hear them spoken or meet them in script and print. For their *application* is not presented to us so clearly. Especially when we are doing philosophy!
>
> 12. It is like looking into the cabin of a locomotive. We see handles all looking more or less alike. (Naturally, since they are all supposed to be handled.) But one is the handle of a crank which can be moved continuously (it regulates the opening of a valve); another is the handle of a switch, which has only two effective positions, it is either off or on; a third is the handle of a brake-lever, the harder one pulls on it, the harder it brakes; a fourth, the handle of a pump: it has an effect only so long as it is moved to and fro.

The natural variety of language tools, despite their similar appearances as words, contradicts the semantic reductivism of the *Tractatus,* and defies attempts to identify a single common essence by which all terms function in a language. Wittgenstein argues:

> 14. Imagine someone's saying: "*All* tools serve to modify something. Thus the hammer modifies the position of the nail, the saw the shape of the board, and so on."—And what is modified by the rule, the glue-pot, the nails?—"Our knowledge of a thing's length, the temperature of the glue, and the solidity of the box."—Would anything be gained by this assimilation of expressions?—

Wittgenstein now views the attempt to explain language in terms of a single set of structures as misdirected. It is not that the *Tractatus* hit upon the wrong reduction, but that the idea of trying to reduce the wide variety of different language tools to a single function like picturing, representing, or mirroring the facts of the world is inherently inadequate. Semantic reductivism can appear to succeed only by the greatest distortion of the diversity of ways of expressing meaning in ordinary language. Such an account lacks application, as does the attempt to reduce the multiple functions of distinct kinds of tools to that of 'modifying something', where we must stretch the meaning of the concept past the point of usefulness to include even such 'modifications' as changes in our knowledge of the length of something by the use of a tape rule.

Wittgenstein's choice of a quotation from Augustine's *Confessions* is appropriate as the opening paragraph for his later work in semantics. The *Philosophical Investigations* offers soul-searching confessions of its own, as testimony to Wittgenstein's later disaffection for the semantic reductivism of his philosophy:

> 114. (*Tractatus Logico-Philosophicus*, 4.5): "The general form of proposition is: This is how things are."—That is the kind of proposition that one repeats to oneself countless times. One thinks that one is tracing the outline of the thing's nature over and over again, and one is merely tracing round the frame through which we look at it.

> 115. A *picture* held us captive. And we could not get outside it, for it lay in our language and language seemed to repeat it to us inexorably.

Wittgenstein in the later period seems to believe that all we need to do is look in order to see the truth about language. When Wittgenstein looks at language use in the world and in philosophically interesting language games, what does he see?

> 37. What is the relation between name and thing named?— Well, what *is* it? Look at language-game (2) or at another one: there you can see the sort of thing this relation consists in. This relation may also consist, among many other things, in the fact that hearing the name calls before our mind the picture of what is named; and it also consists, among other things, in the name's being written on the thing named or being pronounced when that thing is pointed at.

There is no single answer to the problem of naming. Meaning is more various and complex than the single semantic relation of picturing. The methods by which something is named are as diverse as the practices of naming, of using different language tools with different functions for the expression of different meanings. It is these practices in language games that we must consider if we are to understand meaning:

> ... This is connected with the conception of naming as, so to speak, an occult process. Naming appears as a *queer* connexion of a word with an object.—And you really get such a queer connexion when the philosopher tries to bring out *the* relation between name and thing by staring at an object in front of him and repeating a name or even the word "this" innumerable times. For philosophical problems arise when language *goes on holiday*. And *here* we may indeed fancy naming to be some remarkable act of mind, as it were a baptism of an object. And we can also say the word "this" *to* the object, as it were *address* the object as "this"—a queer use of this word, which doubtless only occurs in doing philosophy. (§38)

The modification of the 'slab' language game by adding the demonstratives 'this', 'that', 'here', and 'there' in language game (8) illustrates the variety of language tools in ordinary discourse. Wittgenstein remarks that demonstratives are not names nor are they reducible to names, but constitute a distinct category of singular referring terms. The impulse to reduce the variety of language tools to a single form Wittgenstein calls the "tendency to sublime the logic of our language," or to try to see in its functional diversity a single set of semantic principles by virtue of which meaning is expressed by a single logic overarching the many different modes of meaning within ordinary language.

This is quite a different conclusion from that which Wittgenstein describes as the *Tractatus* subliming of the logic of language. By this he means the semantic reduction of all meaningful language to truth functions of elementary propositions consisting of concatenations of simple names whose meanings are simple objects. The *Philosophical Investigations* by contrast has a broader appreciation for the diversity of types of language games in which words and names are differently used. From his anthropological study of stylized language use in language games, Wittgenstein in the later period no longer expects a unified reductive account to explain the meanings of all terms by a single principle.[2]

As we move from microlinguistic to macrolinguistic language games, as in proceeding from the microeconomic to macroeconomic models on which Wittgenstein's language games method is based, we find increasing confirmation of the complexities of language games. From this perspective we can only hope to extract general principles about the diverse functioning of many different kinds of terms in language in many different kinds of cultural activities described by many different kinds of language games. We come away from the exercise with a firm sense of the multiplicity of different language uses. This should convince us that language cannot be understood entirely on its own apart from the ways in which people actually communicate. Language is not an abstract entity in a transcendental order beyond experience, but a human activity involving linguistic signs in many different kinds of information exchange in complexly related interpersonal transactions.

It follows at once that the *Tractatus* picture theory is wrongheaded in its assumptions about the adequate explanation of meaning. How indeed could *picturing* be transcendental in the first place, how could *mirroring* be imperceptible? A picture depicts and a mirror reflects a *visible* image or likeness. In developing language games as an alternative method to the transcendental reasoning of the early philosophy, Wittgenstein adopts a mode of inquiry that permits him to do justice to the complexities of ordinary language, while abstracting and simplifying certain aspects for detailed philosophical study without the confusions and distractions of real-life linguistic activity.

What can language games tell us about how meanings are communicated and how languages are taught? If Augustine has not described the meaning of all language, he may nevertheless have accurately portrayed the workings of language in a specific case involving some names for some objects. If we can explain at least some meaning by a refinement of Augustine's anecdotal account of how he acquired language through the explanations of meanings he received literally at the hands and by the body language of others, "the natural language of all peoples," then perhaps the remaining parts of language that do not function strictly as names or constructions out of names, in Wittgenstein's words, might "take care of itself." Does Augustine's explanation hold true for at least a fragment of ordinary language use, to give us a foothold in philosophical semantics by a plausible natural history of how some language involving the naming of objects is taught?

Wittgenstein's answer is to reject Augustine's description of how meanings were transmitted to him as a child as philosophically inadequate even for its limited application in teaching the meanings of names by associating their use with particular objects. The behavioral or body language explanation takes us only so far, and presupposes what any such interpretation must finally explain. Wittgenstein begins by recounting the view of

naming as in some sense a preparation for more complicated
meaning and more sophisticated expression in a language in the
use of propositions for the description of facts:

> 26. One thinks that learning language consists in giving
> names to objects. Viz, to human beings, to shapes, to colours,
> to pains, to moods, to numbers, etc. To repeat—naming is
> something like attaching a label to a thing. One can say that
> this is preparatory to the use of a word. But *what* is it a
> preparation *for?*

Wittgenstein observes that there is no direct route from the
naming of objects to what we may want to say about them. He
emphasizes the plurality of language games with different uses
of sentences consisting of single words or names. Naming things
may be a preparation for description in the limited sense that we
cannot describe something unless we have named it, though even
this is disputable, and depends in any case on which of any number of different things we mean by the word 'name'. Naming by
itself does not enable us to describe, or like builder A and assistant B to construct, more complex propositional meanings merely
by putting names together like the building blocks required in a
language of commands for 'Slab!'—'Pillar!'—'Pillar!'—'Beam!'.
Nor for that matter is there just one kind of language game of
describing or talking about things once we have named them.
Wittgenstein writes:

> 27. "We name things and then we can talk about them: can
> refer to them in talk."—As if what we did next were given
> with the mere act of naming. As if there were only one thing
> called "talking about a thing". Whereas in fact we do the
> most various things with our sentences. Think of exclama-
> tions alone, with their completely different functions.
>
> > Water!
> > Away!
> > Ow!
> > Help!
> > Fine!
> > No!
>
> Are you inclined still to call these words "names of objects"?
> In languages (2) and (8) there was no such thing as asking
> something's name. This, with its correlate, ostensive definition,
> is, we might say, a language-game on its own. That is really to
> say: we are brought up, trained, to ask: "What is that called?"—
> upon which the name is given. And there is also a language-
> game of inventing a name for something, and hence of saying,
> "This is . . . ." and then using the new name. (Thus, for ex-
> ample, children give names to their dolls and then talk about

them and to them. Think in this connexion how singular is
the use of a person's name to *call* him!)

The trouble with Augustine's ostensive body language account of meaning is that the movement of a body part in conjunction with the utterance of a particular sound, no matter how
often and how regular their association, underdetermines the
object to be named, even in the limited application of such a
model to the explanation of the meanings of names by their correspondence with particular objects. Wittgenstein illustrates the
problem in several ways, considering the standard indicative
definition of things by body motion in pointing toward a thing
and giving its name. He argues:

> 28. Now one can ostensively define a proper name, the name
> of a colour, the name of a material, a numeral, the name of a
> point of the compass, and so on. The definition of the number
> two, "That is called 'two'"—pointing to two nuts—is perfectly
> exact.—But how can two be defined like that? The person
> one gives the definition to doesn't know what one wants to
> call "two"; he will suppose that "two" is the name given to
> *this* group of nuts!—He *may* suppose this; but perhaps he
> does not. He might make the opposite mistake; when I want
> to assign a name to this group of nuts, he might understand
> it as a numeral. And he might equally well take the name of
> a person, of which I give an ostensive definition, as that of a
> colour, of a race, or even of a point of the compass. That is to
> say: an ostensive definition can be variously interpreted in
> *every* case.

Wittgenstein does not doubt that meaning can be conveyed
by pointing at things and uttering their names. The question is
only whether it is the motion accompanied by verbal behavior
alone that explains the meaning of a name. What does pointing to
an object and saying its name, 'Elizabeth' (or 'five' or 'red' or
'apples'), perhaps repeatedly and with emphasis, a special tone of
voice, and significant beckoning with the eyes, accomplish? Wittgenstein concludes that it is not merely pointing or body movement and verbal behavior by themselves that serve to explain the
meaning of a word, because these can always be differently understood. What is it in the first place to point to something, and
under what conditions can a desire or intent to assign to or communicate the meaning of a name be correctly attributed to a language game player?

Wittgenstein's critique of the ostensive behavioral theory of
naming in Augustine's *Confessions* has two parts. Body movement in pointing toward something while uttering a sound or in-
scribing a sign logically underdetermines the reference of a

name. Pure behavioral ostension alone cannot be the complete account of how the explanation of meaning takes place even when the meaning of a name is in fact communicated ostensively. Wittgenstein demonstrates this with a number of examples, beginning with the attempt above to explain to someone the meaning of the number word 'two' by pointing to two nuts. The explanation is perfectly exact; that is not the problem. The difficulty is understanding how and in light of what kinds of facts the definition functions as it typically does to explain the meaning of the word. Why do we not usually misunderstand the name as naming the particular collection of two objects ostended rather than the abstract number two? How are we able to grasp the sense of what is being offered as a definition of a number of things rather than of their color or substance or the space they occupy?

The answer is that ostensive definition works only when a certain framework of conventions for the explanation of meaning is presupposed by both the explainer and explainee. Wittgenstein argues that a context is required in which the functioning of ostension in the attempt to explain meaning is already understood:

> 30. So one might say: the ostensive definition explains the use—the meaning—of the word when the overall role of the word in language is clear. Thus if I know that someone means to explain a colour-word to me the ostensive definition "That is called 'sepia'" will help me to understand the word.—And you can say this, so long as you do not forget that all sorts of problems attach to the words "to know" or "to be clear".
>
> One has already to know (or be able to do) something in order to be capable of asking a thing's name. But what does one have to know?

An act of bodily behavioral ostension by itself does not explain meaning. If I know in advance that by pointing to something someone intends to explain the meaning of a special color word, the exact meaning of which I do not yet know, then pointing to a color sample can be used to explain the word. I may even be able to get by with considerably less knowledge of the explainer's intentions. If I share other beliefs and expectations, I can sometimes deduce from pointing to several differently shaped objects of the same color that the explainer is trying to communicate a color name rather than the name of a shape or the name of a particular material substance or location in space. Wittgenstein concludes that ostension is not a self-sufficient explanation of the meaning of words, but presupposes a background of knowledge or ability to act in certain ways:

32. Someone coming into a strange country will sometimes learn the language of the inhabitants from ostensive definitions that they give him; and he will often have to *guess* the meaning of these definitions; and will guess sometimes right, sometimes wrong.

And now, I think, we can say: Augustine describes the learning of human language as if the child came into a strange country and did not understand the language of the country; that is, as if it already had a language, only not this one. Or again: as if the child could already *think*, only not yet speak. And "think" would here mean something like "talk to itself".

The problem is clarified by comparison with the situation of a person who already understands a language but must learn a new language in a foreign place by making good and lucky guesses about the intended referents of ostensive definitions as the natives point to objects and pronounce their names. Wittgenstein says that Augustine's picture of how the meanings of words was explained to him as a child is reasonable only if we assume that he could already speak another language whereby he understands the convention of pointing out objects as the meanings of names. Learning the meaning of a name by ostension would then amount only to translating the new terminology into a previously assimilated natural language, or into a preexisting internal language of thought. The child would otherwise have no clue from the pointing and intoning of sound alone that there is such a thing as a name, or that an object is being pointed at as the meaning of a name instantiated by the sound, let alone what particular object is supposed to be associated with the name.[3]

We do not notice the limitation in Augustine's description because we also share the background knowledge of how pointing and pronouncing a name are typically used to explain its meaning. This is a language game we all know how to play. By themselves the movement of a finger in space and the disturbance of the air by uttering a sound have none of these implications. The tendency to take the cultural conditions for granted makes it appear as though Augustine has adequately described how he was taught the meanings of words when he refers to actions that we would also understand as attempts at ostensive definition. Wittgenstein brings out the background presuppositions of Augustine's account of naming by taking partial inventory of the potential for underdetermination of meaning in pointing as the most common type of pure behavioral ostension. He considers:

33. Suppose, however, someone were to object: "It is not true that you must already be master of a language in order to

> understand an ostensive definition: all you need—of course!
> —is to know or guess what the person giving the explanation
> is pointing to. That is, whether for example to the shape of the
> object, or to its colour, or to its number, and so on."—And
> what does 'pointing to the shape', 'pointing to the colour' con-
> sist in? Point to a piece of paper.—And now point to its
> shape—now to its colour—now to its number (that sounds
> queer).—How did you do it?—You will say that you 'meant' a
> different thing each time you pointed. And if I ask how that is
> done, you will say you concentrated your attention on the col-
> our, the shape, etc. But I ask again: how is *that* done?
> . . . You sometimes attend to the colour by putting your
> hand up to keep the outline from view; or by not looking at the
> outline of the thing; sometimes by staring at the object and
> trying to remember where you saw that colour before.
> You attend to the shape, sometimes by tracing it, sometimes
> by screwing up your eyes so as not to see the colour clearly, and
> in many other ways. I want to say: This is the sort of thing that
> happens *while* one 'directs one's attention to this or that'. But it
> isn't these things by themselves that make us say someone is
> attending to the shape, the colour, and so on . . .

As a thought experiment, we are asked to point to the shape
of an object, and then to its color. When we try the experiment,
Wittgenstein asks, what if anything do we do? What in particular
do we do in pointing to the shape of an object that is different
from pointing to its color? How, as he later adds, do we point to its
number? We might outline the shape of an object by tracing its
form with a movement of the finger, but any such gesture could
equally be interpreted as pointing to its color or number. There is
nothing intrinsically explanatory about body movement and accompanying verbal behavior. Something more than pure behavioral ostension is required if the explanation of meaning by
behavioral ostension is to work.

If body movement alone does not adequately explain the
meanings of words, then it is natural to reconsider the mental
states of language users who try to explain or must have linguistic meanings explained to them. Wittgenstein finds eye movement and feeling just as inconclusive by themselves in trying to
understand the ostensive meaning of a name:

> 34. But suppose someone said: "I always do the same thing
> when I attend to the shape: my eye follows the outline and I
> feel . . .". And suppose this person to give someone else the
> ostensive definition "That is called a 'circle'", pointing to a
> circular object and having all these experiences—cannot his
> hearer still interpret the definition differently, even though
> he sees the other's eyes following the outline, and even
> though he feels what the other feels? That is to say: this 'in-
> terpretation' may also consist in how he now makes use of

the word; in what he points to, for example, when told: "Point to a circle".—For neither the expression "to intend the definition in such-and-such a way" nor the expression "to interpret the definition in such-and-such a way" stands for a process which accompanies the giving and hearing of the definition.

The next step involves a shift from body to mind. The inclusion of a characteristic accompanying psychological process in addition to a purely behavioral body motion is a natural way to enhance the ostensive explanation of meaning. But the appeal to a subject's mental states is also inadequate in determining meaning or explaining the meaning of a word. The explainee can still misinterpret the intended object of the explainer's ostension despite sharing the same feelings or characteristic experiences or while undergoing precisely the same psychological processes:

> 35. There are, of course, what can be called "characteristic experiences" of pointing to (e.g.) the shape. For example, following the outline with one's finger or with one's eyes as one points.—But *this* does not happen in all cases in which I 'mean the shape', and no more does any other one characteristic process occur in all these cases.—Besides, even if something of the sort did occur in all cases, it would still depend on the circumstances—that is, on what happened before and after the pointing—whether we should say "He pointed to the shape and not to the colour".

The eye movements and psychological experiences that sometimes occur when we ostensively name an object are neither necessary nor sufficient in determining or explaining meaning. Wittgenstein maintains that in judging what an explainer of the meaning of a word intends to convey by ostension, the explainee must resort to factors external both to the act of ostension, its accompanying psychological experiences, and other special conventions by which the exact meaning of a word is supposed to be communicated. We must additionally take into consideration the circumstances of what transpires before and after the ostension in a wider context of occurrences, in order to identify the intended object.

Thus, we have yet to nail down the requirements for the explanation of meaning by ostension. Wittgenstein takes the opportunity once again to emphasize the variety of different meanings of phrases that can apply in such explanations, and therefore to the futility of trying to determine by body movement or characteristic psychological state alone what someone means by pointing. There are nuances of intended meaning that do not seem readily determined by characteristic experiences shared by or communicated between language users in explaining the meanings of words. Wittgenstein asks rhetorically in §35: "But do you also know of an experience characteristic of pointing to a piece in a game *as a piece in a game?*" The naming of a game piece is something we easily do when we designate the king in chess as having a certain function in the game beyond being a particular piece of wood with a particular shape, size, and color. From this standpoint, too, it seems unpromising to account for how we explain meaning by supplementing body movement with characteristically accompanying psychological experiences or mental states.

Wittgenstein contrasts the behavioral ostensive account of naming he attributes to Augustine with efforts to determine meaning by thought. The opposition of body and mind sets the stage for further discussion of philosophical psychology as it relates to the problem of naming in philosophical semantics:

> 36. And we do here what we do in a host of similar cases: because we cannot specify any *one* bodily action which we call pointing to the shape (as opposed, for example, to the colour), we say that a *spiritual* [mental, intellectual] activity corresponds to these words.
>
> Where our language suggests a body and there is none: there, we should like to say, is a *spirit.*[4]

If naming cannot be adequately explained by body movement, with or without characteristic motions or psychological states, it might yet be thought to function by means of a private psychological ostension or internal private mental pointing to an object as the meaning of a name. We shall return to Wittgenstein's rejection of this alternative in his difficult and frequently misunderstood private language argument. Along the way, we must first introduce the remaining essential concepts of Wittgenstein's later philosophy. The investigation of language games presides over Wittgenstein's deliberations about the problem of meaning after 1930, as the practical philosophical method that replaces his earlier transcendental reasoning in discovering the semantics of language and its implications for philosophy.[5]

I NOTES

1. Fann 1969, 45–50; Sraffa 1960.
2. Rhees 1959–60. See also Rankin 1967.
3. This is related to Quine's discussion of the problems of radical translation for field linguistics. See Quine 1960, pp. 27, 54, 72–79, 206, 221.
4. The English equivalents 'mental, intellectual' in brackets in the translation of §36 are supplied by the translator, and do not appear

in the original German text. They are legitimate variations for a language that has no straightforward equivalent of the word 'mind', but may also indicate contemporary uneasiness with or embarrassment about Wittgenstein's use of the more Cartesian-sounding terms *'geistige'* and *'Geist'*, italicized for emphasis in Wittgenstein's typescript in the bilingual edition of the *Philosophical Investigations,* which he contrasts here with 'Körper' (body).

    5. See also Baker and Hacker 1980, 1, 29–162, 163–314; Cook 1994, 101–18; Fann 1969, 63–81; Hanfling, 127–51; Hervey 1961; Hilmy 1987; Kenny 1973, 159–77; Pears 1971, 105–26; Pears 1987, 2, 271–80; Pole 1958, 1–28; Schulte 1992, 97–106; Schulte 1993, 11–23; Sellars 1954; Smart 1957.

CHAPTER
N I N E | **Critique of Logical Atomism**

The great mistake of the *Tractatus* is its assumption that names can only designate simple objects, that this is the one and only proper linguistic function of singular terms. Wittgenstein accordingly next turns his instrumentalist attack on the logical atomism of the early philosophy and the picture theory doctrine that all meaning reduces to truth-functions of elementary propositions construed as concatenations of simple names in one-one correspondence with simple objects.

Wittgenstein in the *Philosophical Investigations* subjects this idea to the most careful scrutiny. He concludes that the concepts of simplicity, reducibility, and analyzability are just as diverse, multitextured, and relative in application to the particular pragmatic contexts of particular language games as are the individual words or sentences or any of the other language tools, the irreducible differences among which he has already described. The concept of simple names and simple objects is rejected on the grounds that simplicity is not something universal, absolute, and independent of the pragmatic natural language game contexts to which they belong and which they are supposed to help explain. There are no absolutely simple names or absolutely simple objects to provide the reductive account of meaning entailed by logical atomism and the picture theory of meaning.

Wittgenstein begins the critique of logical atomism by calling attention to some of the arguments that might be given against what in everyday discourse are commonly called 'names'. If we are committed, as are Frege, Russell, and the early Wittgenstein, to the extensionalist view that names can only name existent objects, then we must admit that names cannot name complex objects, since then there can be no meaningful sentences in which the complexes that names name are described as no longer existing. Wittgenstein recounts a version of his own earlier reasoning about the necessity for simple objects as the only proper referents of names:

> 39. But why does it occur to one to want to make precisely this word into a name, when it evidently is *not* a name? — That is just the reason. For one is tempted to make an objection against what is ordinarily called a name. It can be put like this: *a name ought really to signify a simple.* And for this one might perhaps give the following reasons: The word "Excalibur", say, is a proper name in the ordinary sense. The sword Excalibur consists of parts combined in a particular way. If they are combined differently Excalibur does not exist. But it is clear that the sentence "Excalibur has a sharp blade" makes *sense* whether Excalibur is still whole or is broken up. But if "Excalibur" is the name of an object, this object no longer exists when Excalibur is broken in pieces; and as no object would then correspond to the name it would have no meaning. But then the sentence "Excalibur has a sharp blade" would contain a word that had no meaning, and hence the sentence would be nonsense. But it does make sense; so there must always be something corresponding to the words of which it consists. So the word "Excalibur" must disappear when the sense is analysed and its place be taken by words which name simples. It will be reasonable to call these words the real names.

The argument is that a name has meaning only if its object exists. But any composite referent can cease to exist even though it continues to make sense to speak of it, for example, as having ceased to exist. From this it seems to follow that names can only properly name simple necessarily existent objects. This is why Wittgenstein in the *Tractatus* concludes that simple names designate the same set of simple objects in every logically possible world.

Wittgenstein in the *Philosophical Investigations* now refutes this argument by pointing out that names can continue to function in certain language games even when the composite objects they name no longer exist. The example goes back to a modification of language game (2), in which Wittgenstein has builder A mark his tools with identifying signs, which assistant B brings when builder A calls for them by name. Wittgenstein regards this language game as a paradigm case of the way in which names literally attach to objects:

> 15. The word "to signify" is perhaps used in the most straightforward way when the object signified is marked with the sign. Suppose that the tools A uses in building bear

certain marks. When A shews his assistant such a mark, he brings the tool that has that mark on it.

It is in this and more or less similar ways that a name means and is given to a thing. — It will often prove useful in philosophy to say to ourselves: naming something is like attaching a label to a thing.

By projecting a number of different language games that might be played using names inscribed on broken tools, Wittgenstein underscores the point that we need not suppose that words necessarily cease to function as names even when the composite objects they ostensibly name cease to exist as complete entities. Wittgenstein's later more broadly conceived instrumentalism moves beyond extensionalism by denying that names function only by designating existent objects. He develops the example in this way:

> 41. In §15 we introduced proper names into language (8). Now suppose that the tool with the name "N" is broken. Not knowing this, A gives B the sign "N". Has this sign meaning now or not? — What is B to do when he is given it? — We have not settled anything about this. One might ask: what *will* he do? Well, perhaps he will stand there at a loss, or shew A the pieces. Here one *might* say: "N" has become meaningless; and this expression would mean that the sign "N" no longer had a use in our language-game (unless we gave it a new one). "N" might also become meaningless because, for whatever reason, the tool was given another name and the sign "N" no longer used in the language-game. — But we could also imagine a convention whereby B has to shake his head in reply if A gives him the sign belonging to a tool that is broken. — In this way the command "N" might be said to be given a place in the language-game even when the tool no longer exists, and the sign "N" to have meaning even when its bearer ceases to exist.

Wittgenstein grants only that the meanings of names are sometimes, but significantly not always, defined by their use in a language, and that their meaning is sometimes, but significantly not always, definable by correspondence with or ostension of the objects the names designate. Admitting exceptions as Wittgenstein now does contradicts the semantic reductivism or sublimated logic of the early philosophy:

> 43. For a *large* class of cases — though not for all — in which we employ the word "meaning" it can be defined thus: the meaning of a word is its use in the language.
>
> And the *meaning* of a name is sometimes explained by pointing to its *bearer*.

This does not preclude the possibility of specialized language games in which genuine names name simple existent objects only. The language game of describing facts presented in the *Tractatus* might be such a possible language game. But the language game of describing atomic facts as combinations of simple objects each of which is designated by a simple name is only one among many possibilities, and does not necessarily have privileged semantic precedence over other kinds of language games in which names function quite differently. Wittgenstein breaks the grip of the logical atomist picture theory of meaning when he concludes that it does not explain the meaning of all language:

> 44. We said that the sentence "Excalibur has a sharp blade" made sense even when Excalibur was broken in pieces. Now this is so because in this language-game a name is also used in the absence of its bearer. But we can imagine a language-game with names (that is, with signs which we should certainly include among names) in which they are used only in the presence of the bearer; and so could *always* be replaced by a demonstrative pronoun and the gesture of pointing.

Wittgenstein now turns directly to the question of whether names designate only simple objects, as the logical atomist picture theory of the *Tractatus* requires. He refers to an argument given by Socrates in Plato's *Theaetetus,* that only substances or "that which exists in its own right" can truly be named, where only metaphysically "primary elements" exist in their own right, and that every other meaningful expression is essentially a "composition of names." This is the same reasoning that supports Russell's simple 'individuals' in his "Lectures on Logical Atomism," and Wittgenstein's simple objects in the logical atomism of the *Tractatus:*

> 46. What lies behind the idea that names really signify simples?—Socrates says in the Theaetetus: "If I make no mistake, I have heard some people say this: there is no definition of the primary elements—so to speak—out of which we and everything else are composed; for everything that exists in its own right can only be *named,* no other determination is possible, neither that it *is* nor that it *is not.* . . . But what exists in its own right has to be . . . named without any other determination. In consequence it is impossible to give an account of any primary element; for it, nothing is possible but the bare name; its name is all it has. But just as what consists of these primary elements is itself complex, so the names of the elements become descriptive language by being compounded together. For the essence of speech is the composition of names."[1]

Both Russell's 'individuals' and my 'objects' (*Tractatus Logico-Philosophicus*) were such primary elements.

Socrates' thesis is persuasive but not entirely convincing to Wittgenstein, once his confidence in the transcendental necessity of the *Tractatus* semantics has been shaken by color incompatibility and the problem of naming. In his later pluralistic approach to the distinctions among language tools, Wittgenstein understands the terms 'simple', 'simplicity', 'complex', and 'complexity' nonreductively as functioning differently in particular language games. He rejects the concepts of absolute simplicity and absolute complexity in metaphysics and semantics. He illustrates the slipperiness of these predicates relative to the interests of those describing the logical structures of language and the world in several categories of ordinary discourse:

> 47. But what are the simple constituent parts of which reality is composed?—What are the simple constituent parts of a chair?—The bits of wood of which it is made? Or the molecules, or the atoms?—"Simple" means: not composite. And here the point is: in what sense 'composite'? It makes no sense at all to speak absolutely of the 'simple parts of a chair' .
> . . .
> If I tell someone without any further explanation: "What I see before me now is composite", he will have the right to ask: "What do you mean by 'composite'? For there are all sorts of things that that can mean!"—The question "Is what you see composite?" makes good sense if it is already established what kind of complexity—that is, which particular use of the word— is in question. If it had been laid down that the visual image of a tree was to be called "composite" if one saw not just a single trunk, but also branches, then the question "Is the visual image of this tree simple or composite?", and the question "What are its simple component parts?", would have a clear sense—a clear use . . . .
> But isn't a chessboard, for instance, obviously, and absolutely, composite?—You are probably thinking of the composition out of thirty-two white and thirty-two black squares. But could we not also say, for instance, that it was composed of the colours black and white and the schema of squares? And if there are quite different ways of looking at it, do you still want to say that the chessboard is absolutely 'composite'?—Asking "Is this object composite?" *outside* a particular language-game is like what a boy once did, who had to say whether the verbs in certain sentences were in the active or passive voice, and who racked his brains over the question whether the verb "to sleep" meant something active or passive.
> We use the word "composite" (and therefore the word "simple") in an enormous number of different and differently related ways. (Is the colour of a square on a chessboard simple, or does it consist of pure white and pure yellow? And is white simple, or

does it consist of the colours of the rainbow?—Is this length of 2 cm. simple, or does it consist of two parts, each 1 cm. long? But why not one of one bit 3 cm. long, and one bit 1 cm. long measured in the opposite direction?)

To the *philosophical* question: "Is the visual image of this tree composite, and what are its component parts?" the correct answer is: "That depends on what you understand by 'composite'." (And that is of course not an answer but a rejection of the question.)

The main point Wittgenstein now sees, by contrast with his presuppositions in the *Tractatus,* is that the question of an object's simplicity or complexity cannot meaningfully be asked independently of its application in a particular language game. The simplicity or complexity of objects must be relativized to the specific language games in which they are named.

Wittgenstein next considers Socrates' conclusion that only indestructible objects can be named. The *Tractatus* also accepted this result as a requirement of logical atomism, holding that simple objects are the unchanging underlying substance of every logically possible world. Wittgenstein restates the argument in quotations as the thought of an imaginary interlocutor in his ongoing philosophical soliloquy:

> 55. "What the names in language signify must be indestructible; for it must be possible to describe the state of affairs in which everything destructible is destroyed. And this description will contain words; and what corresponds to these cannot then be destroyed, for otherwise the words would have no meaning." I must not saw off the branch on which I am sitting.
>
> One might, of course, object at once that this description would have to except itself from the destruction.—But what corresponds to the separate words of the description and so cannot be destroyed if it is true, is what gives the words their meaning—is that without which they would have no meaning.—In a sense, however, this man is surely what corresponds to his name. But he is destructible, and his name does not lose its meaning when the bearer is destroyed.—An example of something corresponding to the name, and without which it would have no meaning, is a paradigm that is used in connexion with the name in the language-game.

Wittgenstein appeals to the commonsense observation that people can be named despite being destructible. He hints that not everything composite can be destroyed, because a description of the destruction of all composite things is itself composite and therefore destructible. Such a description is not itself destroyed if it exists as a true description of the destruction of all composites. It follows, contrary to logical atomism, that there can be no true description of the destruction of everything that is destructible. Yet if there is even one exception, if it is false because of even the most arcane counterexample that all composite things can be destroyed, then Socrates' argument does not prove that only indestructible simple objects can be named.

The simple objects of the *Tractatus* are instantiations of qualities or qualitylike things, belonging to the forms of space, time, and generic color or coloredness. These are indestructible in the sense that they are abstract and nonspatiotemporal, and hence not subject to the decomposition of ordinary compound objects. Wittgenstein considers contexts in which it seems sensible to ascribe something like the destruction of color instantiations, including its gradual fading at a particular time and place, and its disappearance from memory, whereupon, the name 'red', considered as a simple name for a simple indestructible object, turns out to lose its meaning. The implication Wittgenstein suggests is that once again there is no absolute sense in which objects named by logically simple names need be indestructible even if they are in another sense simple. The language game in which 'red' features may then cease to be played, at which point it drops out of consideration for philosophical semantics:

> 57. "Something red can be destroyed, but red cannot be destroyed, and that is why the meaning of the word 'red' is independent of the existence of the red thing."—Certainly it makes no sense to say that the colour red is torn up or pounded to bits. But don't we say "The red is vanishing"? And don't clutch at the idea of our always being able to bring red before our mind's eye even when there is nothing red any more. That is just as if you chose to say that there would still always be a chemical reaction producing a red flame.—For suppose you cannot remember the colour any more?—When we forget which colour this is the name of, it loses its meaning for us; that is, we are no longer able to play a particular language-game with it. And the situation then is comparable with that in which we have lost a paradigm which was an instrument of our language.

The logical atomist model by which only simple objects are named by simple names has no empirical basis. The source of the idea is an analogy with ordinary composite objects consisting of simpler components. It is to our experience of these, and the everyday language games in which we discuss them, that we must turn in order to understand the concept:

> 59. "A *name* signifies only what is an *element* of reality. What cannot be destroyed; what remains the same in all changes."—But what is that?—Why, it swam before our

minds as we said the sentence! This was the very expression of a quite particular image: of a particular picture which we want to use. For certainly experience does not shew us these elements. We see *component parts* of something composite (of a chair, for instance). We say that the back is part of the chair, but is in turn itself composed of several bits of wood; while a leg is a simple component part. We also see a whole which changes (is destroyed) while its component parts remain unchanged. These are the materials from which we construct that picture of reality.

When we consider the way in which the terms 'simple' and 'composite' are used in actual applications, we are reminded that in our reasoning we do not think about complexes as analyzable into their component parts. Thinking about my car, for example, I do not necessarily think about its chassis, axles, engine block, electrical system, gas tank, and so on. Why, then, should I suppose that my thought and the things I may say about my car should be reducible to or analyzable in terms of the descriptions of its parts? If this, finally, is not a feature of my ordinary thinking, speaking, and writing about composite things, and if such experiences are the only source of my concept, if they define the concept in its pragmatic limitations for the language games in which I participate, why should I suppose that all composites are composed of absolute simples beyond the horizons of perception?

Wittgenstein denies the absolute reducibility of statements about composite things into statements about their parts. He is unwilling to accept a description of the parts of an object as an analysis of a description of the object unless the analysis fits into a context of information and pragmatic interactions with the language users whose discourse the analysis is meant to explain. Wittgenstein considers the problem of analyzing the description of a broom into a description of its component handle and bristles. The passage in its implications for the refutation of logical atomism is worth reproducing in its entirety:

> 60. When I say: "My broom is in the corner",—is this really a statement about the broomstick and the brush? Well, it could at any rate be replaced by a statement giving the position of the stick and the position of the brush. And this statement is surely a further analysed form of the first one.—But why do I call it "further analysed"?—Well, if the broom is there, that surely means that the stick and brush must be there, and in a particular relation to one another; and this was as it were hidden in the sense of the first sentence. Then does someone who says that the broom is in the corner really mean: the broomstick is there, and so is the brush, and the broomstick is fixed in the brush?—If we were to ask anyone if he meant this

he would probably say that he had not thought specially of the broomstick or specially of the brush at all. And that would be the *right* answer, for he meant to speak neither of the stick nor of the brush in particular. Suppose that, instead of saying "Bring me the broom", you said "Bring me the broomstick and the brush which is fitted on to it."!—Isn't the answer: "Do you want the broom? Why do you put it so oddly?"—Is he going to understand the further analysed sentence better?—This sentence, one might say, achieves the same as the ordinary one, but in a more roundabout way.—Imagine a language-game in which someone is ordered to bring certain objects which are composed of several parts, to move them about, or something else of the kind. And two ways of playing it: in one (a) the composite objects (brooms, chairs, tables, etc.) have names . . . ; in the other (b) only the parts are given names and the wholes are described by means of them.—In what sense is an order in the second game an analysed form of an order in the first? Does the former lie concealed in the latter, and is it now brought out by analysis?—True, the broom is taken to pieces when one separates the broomstick and brush; but does it follow that the order to bring the broom also consists of corresponding parts?

It is clear that Wittgenstein understands by the analysis of a thought or expression something that a thinker or language user would recognize as an explication of meaning. If the thinker or language user does not regard a reduction as spelling out the meaning of the thought or expression to be analyzed, then the reduction is not an analysis of meaning in the intended sense.

From the truism that a composite consists of parts, Wittgenstein in the later philosophy is no longer satisfied with the description of the composite as reducible to or analyzable as a description of its components or conjunction of descriptions of its components. This is not to say that a statement about a composite cannot be replaced by a statement or series of statements about its parts. Wittgenstein concludes only that such a substitution of statements should not automatically be regarded as a semantic explication or analysis of the meaning of a thought or expression about the complex. A thinker or language user might not have meant to say anything whatsoever about the parts of a broom, the stick and brush, in entertaining a thought or speaking or writing about the whole object.[2]

Wittgenstein remarks the tendency to suppose that propositions about the parts of a composite must somehow be semantically more fundamental than propositions about the whole, and must therefore constitute an analysis of propositions about the composite when substituted for them. Wittgenstein disputes this natural predisposition by pointing out that it is just as possible for someone to fail to understand the meaning of propositions about the parts of a composite as of the comparatively unanalyzed propositions about the whole. If what we mean by and expect from a genuine semantic analysis is an explication of meaning, if that is the pragmatic criterion by which we are to judge whether or not a substitution of one set of thoughts or statements for another is to count as an analysis, then in principle an analysis could proceed in either direction from whole to parts or parts to whole, or, for that matter, remain at the same level of thoughts or statements about the whole or its parts:

> 63. To say, however, that a sentence in (b) is an 'analysed' form of one in (a) readily seduces us into thinking that the former is the more fundamental form; that it alone shews what is meant by the other, and so on. For example, we think: If you have only the unanalysed form you miss the analysis; but if you know the analysed form that gives you everything.—But can I not say that an aspect of the matter is lost on you in the *latter* case as well as the former?

An analysis in the true sense of the word has a particular function in particular sorts of language games, and must be judged accordingly. To qualify as an analysis, a substitution of thoughts or propositions for others must give an explication of meaning, for which the replacement of thoughts or propositions about a whole composite thing by thoughts or propositions about its constituents is neither necessary nor sufficient.

Wittgenstein summarizes his criticism of the early *Tractatus* concept of analysis as involving the reduction of all meaning to truth functions of concatenations of simple names whose referents are corresponding simple objects. He describes a language game involving predications of colors to particular spatial locations in a chessboard-like grid consisting of nine squares arranged in a large figure. If the squares are numbered from left to right and top to bottom, then the field of color values can be described by such stylized propositions in a symbolism as 'RRBGGGRWW', indicating that squares 1 and 2 are red (R), 3 is black (B), 4, 5, and 6 are green (G), 7 is red (R), and 8 and 9 are white (W). Wittgenstein offers the color square as a parody of logical atomism and the picture theory. Here is a picturing of space-color facts that might be thought to occur at a particular time-slice in a description of some limited part of the world reducible to copresences of atomic facts:

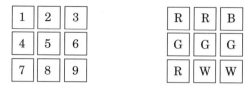

Wittgenstein completes his critique of logical atomism and the picture theory of meaning by combining the two objections we have already considered into a single example based on a modification of the language game described in §48. He describes a similar grid in which the squares are not uniformly colored but divided into differently colored rectangles. This provides an analogue of his objections to the language game relativity of simplicity and complexity. Wittgenstein invites us to imagine that some language users have terms in a language game for combinations of colors in the squares of the grid, but not for the individual colors that make up the top and bottom rectangles of which each square is composed. Then he observes that replacing statements about the squares composed of differently colored rectangles by statements about the rectangles would not provide a semantic analysis in the sense of an adequate explication of the meaning of any statement made about the compositely colored squares. It does not correctly interpret the descriptions offered by and for language users participating in those language games where by hypothesis there is no terminology or corresponding concept for the uniformly colored rectangles that make up the multicolored squares, but only for the squares as multicolored composite wholes. The most to be derived from such an attempt at 'analysis', Wittgenstein maintains, is the replacement of one language game by another distinct though possibly related language game. The substitution of a given language game for another by itself does not constitute semantic analysis in the relevant sense of providing an explication of meaning:

> 64. Let us imagine language (48) altered so that names signify not monochrome squares but rectangles each consisting of two such squares. Let such a rectangle, which is half red half green, be called "U"; a half green half white one, "V"; and so on. Could we not imagine a people who had names for such combinations of colour, but not for the individual colours? Think of the cases where we say: "This arrangement of colours (say the French tricolor) has a quite special character."
>
> In what sense do the symbols of this language-game stand in need of analysis? How far is it it even *possible* to replace this language-game by (48)?—It is just *another* language-game; even though it is related to (48).

The criticisms Wittgenstein gives of his own earlier philosophy appear superficially answerable by invoking the distinction between appearance and reality in the analysis of meaning in ordinary language. Obviously, we do not see in expressions of colloquial discourse like 'five red apples' the deep logical structures attributed to all meaningful thought and language by logical atomism and the picture theory.

Wittgenstein's later objections to the *Tractatus* make sense only on the assumption that sometime during the transition period Wittgenstein forsakes the semantic transcendentalism of the early philosophy. The appeal to language games that model or are based on ordinary language use and that provide counterexamples to the attributions of deep logical structures in the *Tractatus* would be entirely beside the point if Wittgenstein had continued through this time to believe that the perceptible order of signs as we experience them empirically in ordinary thought and language were nothing but a conventional overlay disguising the imperceptible transcendental order of symbols to which a logically correct semantic analysis must aspire.[3]

I NOTES

1. Plato, *Theaetetus* 201c–202d.
2. Malcolm 1986, 1–62.
3. See also Baker 1984; Black 1978; Garver 1994, 237–67; Gier 1981; Hunter 1968; Hunter 1990; Pole 52–60; Schulte 1992, 106–10; Whittaker 1978.

CHAPTER
T E N | **Forms of Life and
Family Resemblance**

Wittgenstein discovers that when we look to actual linguistic practice, we find an overwhelming array of different things we do with names and language games involving names and naming. Wittgenstein does not propose to catalog these phenomena in complete scientific detail; that would be a philosophically uninteresting job for a field linguist. Wittgenstein gestures instead toward the variety of possibilities, sometimes by description and sometimes by lists. Thus, he writes:

> 23. But how many kinds of sentence are there? Say assertion, question, and command?—There are *countless* kinds: countless different kinds of use of what we call "symbols", "words", "sentences". And this multiplicity is not something fixed, given once for all; but new types of language, new language-games, as we may say, come into existence, and others become obsolete and get forgotten. (We can get a *rough picture* of this from the changes in mathematics.)
>
> Here the term "language-*game*" is meant to bring into prominence the fact that the *speaking* of language is part of an activity, or of a form of life.
>
> Review the multiplicity of language-games in the following examples, and in others:
>
> Giving orders, and obeying them—
> Describing the appearance of an object, or giving its
>   measurements—
> Constructing an object from a description (a drawing)—
> Reporting an event—
> Speculating about an event—
> Forming and testing an hypothesis—
> Presenting the results of an experiment in tables and
>   diagrams—
> Making up a story; and reading it—
> Play-acting—

> Singing catches—
> Guessing riddles—
> Making a joke; telling it—
> Solving a problem in practical arithmetic—
> Translating from one language into another—
> Asking, thanking, cursing, greeting, praying.
>
> —It is interesting to compare the multiplicity of the tools in language and of the ways they are used, the multiplicity of kinds of word and sentence, with what logicians have said about the structure of language. (Including the author of the *Tractatus Logico-Philosophicus*).

The important conclusions here are: (i) the plurality of different kinds of words and sentences, contrary to the semantic reductivism of the *Tractatus;* (ii) the organic, historical-cultural nature of language as an evolving body of linguistic practices or language games; (iii) the pragmatic concept of a language game as an activity in a *form of life*.

Wittgenstein describes language as a living thing with a cultural natural history, and therefore as part of a form of life. The theme appears already in *Tractatus* 4.002, where Wittgenstein writes: "Colloquial language is a part of the human organism and is not less complicated than it." But the idea acquires prominence and a special terminology only in the later period with the abandonment of semantic transcendentalism.[1]

Language is a complex human activity involving an irreducible multiplicity of diverse language tools each with a definite linguistic job to do. The tools of language can only be understood *as* tools by understanding their purpose and function, which in turn can only be understood as embedded in a form of life. Words and other linguistic tokens (punctuation, etc.) must be understood in instrumental terms by which they have earned their place in a language game by contributing directly to meaning (builder A) or helping other terms to mean something (helper B).

Wittgenstein's later semantics is in some ways the very antithesis of the *Tractatus* theory. Whereas the *Tractatus* logic and semantics is abstract and transcendental, the *Philosophical Investigations* account of meaning is down to earth. The meanings of signs (etc.) in a language must be understood against a background of interconnected extralinguistic cultural practices. All uses of language, all linguistic practices, are part of the many language games by which we can study their many different purposes as embedded in a culture.

The idea of a form of life as part of the later instrumentalist concept of language is introduced without special fanfare a bit earlier in *Philosophical Investigations,* when Wittgenstein states:

> 19. It is easy to imagine a language consisting only of orders
> and reports in battle.—Or a language consisting only of
> questions and expressions for answering yes or no. And in-
> numerable others.—And to imagine a language is to imagine
> a form of life. . . .

There is scant elaboration of the idea of a *Lebensform*. Wittgenstein uses the term explicitly only three times in the part of
the text written to the completion of what we now have as part 1
of the *Philosophical Investigations,* with two references thereafter in part 2. Later in part 1 he states, anticipating the objection
that his semantic pragmatism is subjectivistic:

> 241. "So you are saying that human agreement decides what
> is true and what is false?"—It is what human beings *say* that
> is true and false; and they agree in the *language* they use.
> That is not agreement in opinions but in form of life.

Part 2 begins with these remarks about the relation between
mastery of a linguistic technique within a form of life as a prerequisite for the psychological state of feeling hopeful:

> One can imagine an animal angry, frightened, unhappy,
> happy, startled. But hopeful? And why not?
> A dog believes his master is at the door. But can he also
> believe his master will come the day after to-morrow?—And
> *what* can he not do here?—How do I do it?—How am I sup-
> posed to answer this?
> Can only those hope who can talk? Only those who have
> mastered the use of a language. That is to say, the phenom-
> ena of hope are modes of this complicated form of life. (If a
> concept refers to a character of human handwriting, it has no
> application to beings that do not write.) (174e)

Finally, Wittgenstein speaks of forms of life in explaining the
cultural background of calculation in mathematics. We break
more or less into the middle of an extended discussion to find
Wittgenstein saying:

> It is no doubt true that you could not calculate with certain sorts
> of paper and ink, if, that is, they were subject to certain queer
> changes—but still the fact that they changed could in turn only
> be got from memory and comparison with other means of calcu-
> lation. And how are these tested in their turn?
> What has to be accepted, the given, is—so one could say—
> *forms of life.* (226e)

This does not offer much exegetical raw material. Wittgenstein is not particularly expansive about what would appear to be
one of the most important concepts in his later philosophy. We are
told only that to imagine a language game is to imagine a form of
life, and that agreement in language is agreement in a form of life.

From this it does not follow that a language or language game is identical with a form of life, and there is room to speculate about the force of the word 'form' in the phrase 'form of life'.

Wittgenstein's concept of a form of life is not intended to be technically rigorous or precise.[2] He has abandoned the quest for that kind of explanation of the workings of language in the later philosophy, which he now sees as part of the misdirected project of philosophical semantics in the *Tractatus*. What stands out in Wittgenstein's treatment of language and language games in the later period is his reliance on an extrasemantic pragmatic or praxeological foundation for the semantics of language use belonging to a form of life.[3]

Wittgenstein frequently reminds us that explanations must come to an end. Explanation is a human activity in which we engage with a definite purpose in real finite time. Language functions without occult processes, as an integral part of the other kinds of transactions in which we are involved as the kind of animals we are, as connected with what we do and may need to do to live. Wittgenstein says in the apple marketing language game, concerning the shopkeeper's use of the words 'five' and 'red': "I assume that he *acts* as I have described. Explanations come to an end somewhere."

This is the epitome of Wittgenstein's later attitude toward meaning, which he announces in the first pages of the *Blue Book* as the project of bringing semantics down to earth. When semantics is brought back down to earth in Wittgenstein's later philosophy, it is grounded in forms of life. In describing an attempt to explain the meaning of the biblical name 'Moses', Wittgenstein similarly declares:

> 87. Suppose I give this explanation: "I take 'Moses' to mean the man, if there was such a man, who led the Israelites out of Egypt, whatever he was called then and whatever he may or may not have done besides." — But similar doubts to those about "Moses" are possible about the words of this explanation (what are you calling "Egypt", whom the "Israelites" etc.?). Nor would these questions come to an end when we got down to words like "red", "dark", "sweet". — "But then how does an explanation help me to understand, if after all it is not the final one? In that case the explanation is never completed; so I still don't understand what he means, and never shall!" — As though an explanation as it were hung in the air unless supported by another one. Whereas an explanation may indeed rest on another one that has been given, but none stands in need of another — unless *we* require it to prevent a misunderstanding. One might say: an explanation

> serves to remove or to avert a misunderstanding—one, that
> is, that would occur but for the explanation; not every one
> that I can imagine . . .

The explanation of meaning cannot continue indefinitely, but must perform its task in relatively brief exchanges between language users. Wittgenstein in the later philosophy is determined that an adequate philosophical semantics should explain the practical workings of everyday linguistic interactions in communicating and understanding meaning. If explanations of meaning must come to an end, then they must terminate in something nonlinguistic. For the meaning of anything within language, anything linguistic or semantic, stands just as much in need of an explanation. It is dynamic action, the way persons interact in the cultural practices that define human life, the forms of life in which they engage and through which they are trained to master linguistic techniques, that Wittgenstein in the later philosophy regards as the extrasemantic praxeological foundations of semantics:

> 432. Every sign *by itself* seems dead. *What* gives it life?—In
> use it is *alive*. Is life breathed into it there?—Or is the *use* its
> life?

A question that naturally comes to mind in considering Wittgenstein's discussion of language games and forms of life is their more exact definition. What is a language game, and how are we to distinguish different language games from one another? Are language games always exclusive, or can they sometimes overlap or be included in one another? What is a form of life? Is there just one form of life for all persons capable at least in principle of understanding one another in a common language, or can a form of life be personal and individual? What, in short, are the identity or necessary and sufficient conditions for the concept of a language game and a form of life?

Wittgenstein argues that these questions ask too much of concepts that by their nature cannot be contained within any neat definition. To illustrate, Wittgenstein examines what he takes to be the futility of trying to reduce the natural variety of distinct games or things called 'games' to any single common essence. He maintains:

> 65. Here we come up against the great question that lies be-
> hind all these considerations.—For someone might object
> against me: "You take the easy way out! You talk about all
> sorts of language-games, but have nowhere said what the
> essence of a language-game, and hence of language, is: what
> is common to all these activities, and what makes them into

language or parts of language. So you let yourself off the very part of the investigation that once gave you yourself most headache, the part about the *general form of proposi-tions* and of language."

And this is true.—Instead of producing something common to all that we call language, I am saying that these phenom-ena have no one thing in common which makes us use the same word for all,—but that they are *related* to one another in many different ways. And it is because of this relationship, or these relationships, that we call them all "language". I will try to explain this.

The semantic reductivism of the early philosophy is rejected. There are concepts so intrinsically complex that their meanings cannot be adequately captured by any single identity condition or set of jointly necessary and sufficient conditions. As in the *Trac-tatus,* where Wittgenstein insists that the deep logical structure of elementary propositions under analysis must have the right logical form or mathematical multiplicity to picture atomic facts, so in the *Philosophical Investigations,* Wittgenstein maintains that the description and explanation of language in its praxeo-logical foundations must have the same degree of complexity and diversity as the facts it explains in order to constitute a correct description of meaning in ordinary language. Hence the need for a simplifying, aspect-enhancing language game strategy for the investigation of philosophical semantics.

What then is the number of language games and forms of life? Wittgenstein maintains explicitly of language games and by im-plication of forms of life that they have no common essence, and that it is pointless to attempt a single definition of the concept in terms of identity conditions or necessary and sufficient properties. The Platonic Form or Idea of a language game or form of life can-not be complex enough to account for either of these concepts. Language games and forms of life have no single set of properties in common. Wittgenstein illustrates the failure of essentialist definitions to identify the essence of the concept of game, and by extension the concept of a language game. The class of things we call 'games' is so diverse and open-ended that we cannot arrive at any common set of distinguishing properties. When we try to ad-vance a unified series of necessary and sufficient conditions, we are immediately beset by counterexamples:

66. Consider for example the proceedings that we call "games". I mean board-games, card-games, ball-games, Olympic games, and so on. What is common to them all?— Don't say: "There *must* be something common, or they would not be called '*games*'"—but *look and see* whether there is

anything common to all.—For if you look at them you will not see something that is common to *all*, but similarities, relationships, and a whole series of them at that. To repeat: don't think, but look!—Look for example at board-games, with their multifarious relationships. Now pass to card-games; here you find many correspondences with the first group, but many common features drop out, and others appear. When we pass next to ball-games, much that is common is retained, but much is lost.—Are they all 'amusing'? Compare chess with noughts and crosses. Or is there always winning and losing, or competition between players? Think of patience. In ball games there is winning and losing; but when a child throws his ball at the wall and catches it again, this feature has disappeared. Look at the parts played by skill and luck; and at the difference between skill in chess and skill in tennis. Think now of games like ring-a-ring-a-roses; here is the element of amusement, but how many other characteristic features have disappeared! And we can go through the many, many other groups of games in the same way; can see how similarities crop up and disappear.

And the result of this examination is: we see a complicated network of similarities overlapping and criss-crossing: sometimes overall similarities, sometimes similarities of detail.

The empiricism of Wittgenstein's later philosophy is evident. Wittgenstein enjoins us to look at the world in order to decide whether or not an essentialist definition of the concept of game is possible. We must consider what are called 'games' in order to know whether the category is of such complexity that its instances can all be adequately corralled in a single set of identity conditions, or whether the concept cannot be fit into such a conceptual straightjacket.

If we do not dogmatically presuppose that all things called games must have a common essence, then when we look more closely we see that the concept of game is not a simple concept that can be sharply defined by a single set of jointly necessary and sufficient conditions. When Wittgenstein looks at the concept of game he discovers a variety of different kinds of games for which no distinguishing set of characteristics seems sufficient to include all games and exclude all nongames. Some similarities are shared by some but not all games, and some of the properties we might naturally think of as belonging exclusively to games are also shared by things that are not games.[4] Instead, Wittgenstein says, the concept of a game is a family resemblance concept. Individuals need not all share a single set of properties in order to be members of the same family, but may have distributed over their respective qualities an overlapping and criss-crossing of attributes; some but not all with the family nose, others but again not all with the family chin. The application to language games is explicit, and the extension for forms of life is clear:[5]

> 67. I can think of no better expression to characterize these similarities than "family resemblances"; for the various resemblances between members of a family: build, features, colour of eyes, gait, temperament, etc. etc. overlap and criss-cross in the same way.—And I shall say: 'games' form a family.
>
> And for instance the kinds of number form a family in the same way. Why do we call something a "number"? Well, perhaps because it has a—direct—relationship with several things that have hitherto been called number; and this can be said to give it an indirect relationship to other things we call the same name. And we extend our concept of number as in spinning a thread we twist fibre on fibre. And the strength of the thread does not reside in the fact that some one fibre runs through its whole length, but in the overlapping of many fibres.
>
> But if someone wished to say: "There is something common to all these constructions—namely the disjunction of all their common properties"—I should reply: Now you are only playing with words. One might as well say: "Something runs through the whole thread—namely the continuous overlapping of those fibres".

The *Philosophical Investigations,* in its efforts to describe and explain the complex meanings of language use in practice, stylistically shares this same twisted overlapping structure, which Wittgenstein says in the preface was "of course, connected with the very nature of the investigation."[6] The book is a metaphor of its teachings, just as the *Tractatus* in its distinctive aphoristic style reflects its austere reductive logic, and presents itself typographically as a ladder of pseudopropositions for the reader to ascend.[7]

Wittgenstein also rejects essentialist definitions that attempt to define concepts as disjunctions of properties. Such definitions afford no understanding of the concept itself. We must wait to see what objects are collected under the concept or are judged as belonging to the concept, and then we must add more clauses to the original cluster of properties as each problem case arises to include in the disjunction. This gives us coverage of the concept, but without understanding the concept's meaning. Wittgenstein finds it pointless in giving an essentialist definition of a concept to begin with a core of properties that appear to hold, for example, for many games, to which ad hoc clauses are then added to cover each special case as it arises. Again, by reference to §14, Wittgenstein is no more satisfied with a disjunctive definition of the concept of game than with the idea of defining the different types of tools in a toolbox by saying that they all serve to 'modify' something. The propositions in both instances say something true about the entities in question, but do not informatively get at the essence that all tools or all games must have in common in order to be tools or games.

It might be objected that there is a third essentialist strategy that Wittgenstein does not consider. The proposal might be seen as an alternative to the problem of finding a single set of jointly necessary and sufficient conditions for a concept or merely stringing together conditions by disjunction on a case-by-case basis. There is yet another mode of analysis by which we can disambiguate the distinct but related meanings of a concept all of which conventionally go by the same concept term. It is a semantic strategy to divide and conquer, as when a dictionary disambiguates distinct lexical meanings conveyed by a single term as sense 1 and sense 2. After the distinct meanings of a systematically ambiguous concept in ordinary language word like 'game' are disambiguated, we may be in a position to define the term as representing a systematically ambiguous concept by means of a principled disjunction that takes into account the term's acquired multiplicity of meanings. Thus, a drug according to the desktop dictionary is (1) a medication; or (2) a narcotic.

Wittgenstein could probably accept the disambiguation ploy as a category of correct definition for certain types of concepts. This admission by itself would not require him to retract his claim that there are also family resemblance concepts that do not lend themselves to adequate definition by reduction to a common essence or disjunction of common essences demarcated by exact identity conditions. Wittgenstein would probably be dissatisfied even with this compromise, on the grounds that the particular concepts in question, language games and forms of life, are by their very nature family resemblance concepts. They are distinctly living, evolving, cultural entities that change their constitution over time. Concepts of dynamic phenomena that gain and lose what may otherwise appear to be distinguishing features in the course of ongoing development are necessarily family resemblance concepts rather than essentialist or systematically ambiguous concepts. Wittgenstein invites us to look by analogy at the changes in mathematics as it has evolved during its continuing history. Mathematics as it is practiced at any given time is a cultural activity, and the concept or definition of mathematics as Wittgenstein understands it realistically could not have occurred to anyone in Euclid's day, nor in other cultures at different times and different places. The difference that disallows both essentialist and disambiguating analyses is that certain dynamic concepts are inherently intrinsically open-ended—they depend for their meaning on an ongoing cultural development that remains in process, and that adds new and drops established conditions as it grows and decays, emerges, evolves, dies out, or is replaced.

We can picture the partially overlapping sharing of properties by objects belonging to a family resemblance concept as Wittgenstein thinks of it in the simplest cases schematically in this way:

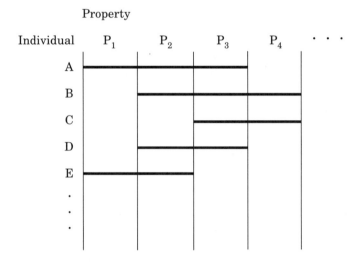

The individuals that fall under a family resemblance concept do so by sharing some properties, but no single essential set of jointly necessary and sufficient properties. The individuals belonging to a family resemblance concept may change unpredictably, because the overlapping and criss-crossing properties that qualify an object for membership in a class of things falling under a family resemblance concept is open-ended, lacking definite boundaries or closure. Properties P_1 through P_5 do not exhaust the ways in which an object might gain membership to the intension of a family resemblance concept, so that individuals A through E represented in the diagram do not define the concept by extension. If the family resemblance concept is 'game', then P_1 might be the property of being played on a board, and A and E might be respectively chess and checkers; P_2 might be the property of implying a winner and loser, and B might be baseball while C might be the unscored game of catch Wittgenstein describes in §65; and so on.

Wittgenstein's interest in family resemblance concepts appears early in the posttransitional period. In the *Blue Book,* he contrasts the idea of a family likeness with what he calls the essentialist "craving for generality." There he states:

> We see activities, reactions, which are clear-cut and transparent. On the other hand we recognize in these simple processes forms of language not separated by a break from our more complicated ones. We see that we can build up the complicated forms from the primitive ones by gradually adding new forms.
>
> Now what makes it difficult for us to take this line of investigation is our craving for generality.
>
> This craving for generality is the resultant of a number of tendencies connected with particular philosophical confusions. There is—
>
> (*a*) The tendency to look for something in common to all the entities which we commonly subsume under a general term.— We are inclined to think that there must be something in common to all games, say, and that this common property is the justification for applying the general term "game" to the various games; whereas games form a *family* the members of which have family likenesses. Some of them have the same nose, others the same eyebrows and others again the same way of walking; and these likenesses overlap.[8]

Wittgenstein next considers an objection about the informativeness or uninformativeness of family resemblance concepts, given their lack of definite boundaries. The epistemic issue concerns the motivation for trying wherever possible to provide essentialist definitions. The complaint is that to classify a collection of entities as belonging to as a family resemblance concept is to admit that we do not understand what the concept means. It is just a way of shirking the laborious task of spelling out an essentialist analysis that is the only possible way to explain the real meaning of a concept:

> 70. "But if the concept 'game' is uncircumscribed like that, you don't really know what you mean by a 'game'."—When I give the description: "The ground was quite covered with plants"—do you want to say I don't know what I am talking about until I can give a definition of a plant?
>
> My meaning would be explained by, say, a drawing and the words "The ground looked roughly like this."—Then were just *this* grass and *these* leaves there, arranged just like this? No, that is not what it means. And I should not accept any picture as exact in *this* sense.

The criticism is answered by observing that we do sometimes know perfectly well what we mean by the use of imprecise concepts. There are situations in which only a deliberately chosen inexact term or phrase will do to correctly express an idea. If we specify the particular plants we meant to say covered the ground, then we err by imposing a false precision on something that is by nature imprecise. There are terms whose function is precisely to express something imprecise about something that is by nature imprecise. Such terms by their very nature cannot be understood as meaning something precise, because what they mean is itself something intrinsically imprecise.

Wittgenstein responds to the related objection that family resemblance concepts are not genuine concepts by opposing the a priori requirement for absolute precision in all concepts with the plain fact that everyday communication works perfectly well by using vague expressions to represent intrinsically vague ideas. Like the injunction to *"look and see"* whether or not all games have something essential in common, Wittgenstein, in his antitranscendental allegiance to the circumstances of actual language use, is content to refute the objection about what we must assume to be required of a philosophically adequate concept with the observation that as a matter of practice we do not always use terms in such a narrowly constrained way:

> 71. One might say that the concept 'game' is a concept with blurred edges. — "But is a blurred concept a concept at all?" — Is an indistinct photograph a picture of a person at all? Is it even always an advantage to replace an indistinct picture by a sharp one? Isn't the indistinct one often exactly what we need?
>
> Frege compares a concept to an area and says that an area with vague boundaries cannot be called an area at all. This presumably means that we cannot do anything with it. — But is it senseless to say: "Stand roughly there"? Suppose that I were standing with someone in a city square and said that. As I say it I do not draw any kind of boundary, but perhaps point with my hand — as if I were indicating a particular *spot*. And this is just how one might explain to someone what a game is. One gives examples and intends them to be taken in a particular way. — I do not, however, mean by this that he is supposed to see in those examples that common thing which I — for some reason — was unable to express; but that he is now to *employ* those examples in a particular way. Here giving examples is not an *indirect* means of explaining — in default of a better. For any general definition can be misunderstood too. The point is that *this* is how we play the game. (I mean the language-game with the word "game".)

The *Tractatus* rejects such sentences as nonsensical pseudo-propositions or inexact colloquial sign-system expressions of perfectly unambiguous meanings in the transcendental order of imperceptible symbols. The *Philosophical Investigations* on the contrary accepts some vague sentences at face value as meaning-ful and standing just as much in need of an adequate explanation of their meaningfulness as the most lucid true or false represen-tations of empirical fact.

There are many different kinds of language tools for many different types of language games, of which exact description is only one. Wittgenstein offers a pictorial analogy to reinforce the point that inexact concepts are sometimes more appropriate than the effort to describe exactly what is inherently vague. The ex-pression of value is singled out as an application for which exact language is often the wrong tool for the job:

> 77. And if we carry this comparison still further it is clear that the degree to which the sharp picture *can* resemble the blurred one depends on the latter's degree of vagueness. For imagine having to sketch a sharply defined picture 'corre-sponding' to a blurred one. In the latter there is a blurred red rectangle: for it you put down a sharply defined one. Of course—several such sharply defined rectangles can be drawn to correspond to the indefinite one.—But if the colours in the original merge without a hint of any outline won't it become a hopeless task to draw a sharp picture corresponding to the blurred one? Won't you then have to say: "Here I might just as well draw a circle or heart as a rectangle, for all the colours merge. Anything—and nothing—is right."—And this is the position you are in if you look for definitions corre-sponding to our concepts in aesthetics or ethics.
>
> In such a difficulty always ask yourself: How did we *learn* the meaning of this word ("good" for instance)? From what sort of examples in what language-games? Then it will be easier for you to see that the word must have a family of meanings.

What is true of the concept of game generally is true of the con-cept of language game in particular, and, by extension, of the concept of a form of life. Wittgenstein reasons as follows:

> 83. Doesn't the analogy between language and games throw light here? We can easily imagine people amusing them-selves in a field by playing with a ball so as to start various existing games, but playing many without finishing them and in between throwing the ball aimlessly into the air, chasing one another with the ball and bombarding one an-other for a joke and so on. And now someone says: The whole time they are playing a ball-game and following definite rules at every throw.
>
> And is there not also the case where we play and—make up the rules as we go along? And there is even one where we alter them—as we go along.

Wittgenstein raises a related difficulty about the implications of family resemblance concepts for understanding logic. The abandonment of neat compartmentalizations of objects belonging to or falling under concepts by means of strict identity requirements or necessary and sufficient conditions appears at first to threaten the rigor of logic in thought and language. He accordingly asks what happens to logic if we admit family resemblance concepts. The reply, which he might equally have given at the time of writing the *Tractatus,* is that the theory of concepts is powerless to add to or take anything away from the rigor of logic. Its workings can only be assessed from the standpoint of what Wittgenstein calls "our real need." By this he apparently means the descriptive and explanatory requirements of understanding the logic of ordinary language. We must look and see what logic is and does, and not impose preconceived requirements on it that need not be satisfied by actual thought and language. To get our priorities straight, we must consider logic as it occurs in linguistic practice in the words and sentences contained in the language games we play. Adopting this standpoint is certain not to disclose discrepancies between family resemblance concepts as they function in colloquial thought and language and the requirements of logic. If ordinary thought and language embody family resemblance concepts, then family resemblance concepts must be compatible with logic understood as the logic of ordinary thought and language. Wittgenstein concludes:

> 108. We see that what we call "sentence" and "language" has not the formal unity that I imagined, but is the family of structures more or less related to one another. — But what becomes of logic now? Its rigour seems to be giving way here. — But in that case doesn't logic altogether disappear? — For how can it lose its rigour? Of course not by our bargaining any of its rigour out of it. — The *preconceived idea* of crystalline purity can only be removed by turning our whole examination round. (One might say: the axis of reference of our examination must be rotated, but about the fixed point of our real need.)
>
> The philosophy of logic speaks of sentences and words in exactly the sense in which we speak of them in ordinary life when we say e.g. "Here is a Chinese sentence", or "No, that only looks like writing; it is actually just an ornament" and so on.

If the concepts of game and instrument or tool are family resemblance rather than essentialist kinds of concepts, if they admit of no definition of identity requirements in terms of jointly necessary and sufficient conditions, then the concept of a form of life is also a family resemblance concept.

Wittgenstein in §19 states that "to imagine a language means to imagine a form of life." He considers an imaginary language consisting only of battlefield orders and reports or of questions and yes-or-no answers. A commitment to the claim that imagining a language means imagining a form of life has implications for the relative exactitude of evolving languages, language games, and forms of life, and hence for whether the corresponding concepts are essentialist or family resemblance. Can the concept of a form of life be more sharply essentialistically defined than the concept of a language game or language tool? The answer may depend on what we understand Wittgenstein to imply when he says that to imagine a language means to imagine a form of life. Presumably, he is not referring to different though perhaps causally or associationally related imaginings as distinct psychological occurrences, but to one and the same imagining considered in two ways. If to imagine a language game is to imagine a form of life, then any fuzzy open-endedness of the dynamic evolving concept of a language game entailed by imagining a language or language game cannot fail to belong to the dynamic evolving concept of the corresponding form of life.[9]

When we look at the densely intertwined linguistic and extra-linguistic practices that constitute what Wittgenstein means by a form of life, we find empirically that it is just as difficult to pin down the concept of a form of life and to distinguish among putatively different but criss-crossing and overlapping forms of life as it is in the case of language games. What is the form of life in which I participate? What shall I include and what shall I exclude from the facts about myself in specifying my form of life? How many different forms of life can I be thought to share with others, socially, professionally, and in other ways, that are relevant to the language games in which I engage? Is membership in a screen star's fan club a form of life or a part if at all of my form of life? Do I share that form of life only with other members of the club, or is part of that form of life something I can also share with outsiders by virtue of overlapping participation in yet another larger form of life? Can I share a form of life with anyone in any of whose language games I can take part, with whom I can share meanings of language or facial expression or natural signs of pleasure or pain? Is there not then a single human form of life in which all personal, historical, and cultural differences are subsumed?

Wittgenstein seems to regard the concepts of tools, games, language tools, language games, and forms of life all alike as family resemblance rather than essentialist concepts. In the nature of the case he does not expect clear-cut answers to these misplaced questions that have application only to essentialist concepts. The reason is the same as before, in the case of family resemblance relations among games, tools, language games, and language tools. The ideas to be considered are all concepts of living, evolving, and therefore conceptually dynamic open-ended categories that change, expanding and contracting their blurry extensions. The concepts are not static, but have a natural history, reflecting the cultural development of human practices as something living, organic, and dynamically evolving. The multiplicity of different kinds of language games that resist incorporation under any single set of necessary and sufficient conditions provide all the evidence Wittgenstein needs to support the claim that language games are family resemblance rather than essentialist concepts.[10]

The contribution the family resemblance concept of a form of life makes to the extrasemantic praxeological foundations of Wittgenstein's later philosophical semantics is twofold. (1) A form of life has the necessary complexity to figure adequately into empirical descriptions and pragmatic explanations of the use of family resemblance concepts in family resemblance language games only if the concept of a form of life is itself a family resemblance concept. (2) The concept of a form of life connects language use in practice with the extrasemantic cultural background and stage-setting of the activities of everyday human practices that ultimately provide the praxeological foundations for the explanation of how and why we express ourselves in language. More than this we do not need to know nor can we possibly discover about the concept of a form of life, and Wittgenstein accordingly says little more about it.[11]

The concept of a form of life as the concept of an open-ended dynamically evolving cultural entity is a family resemblance concept. We ignore the real complexity of the linguistic phenomena we describe in philosophical semantics at peril of descriptive and explanatory inadequacy. Wittgenstein's philosophical alter ego in §65 complains about his method of language games: "You take the easy way out! . . . you let yourself off the very part of the investigation that once gave you yourself most headache, the part about the *general form of propositions* and of language." Now we can see that language games and forms of life are anything but descriptive or explanatory theoretical shortcuts.[12] They alone among the descriptive categories available to philosophical semantics are capable as family resemblance concepts of doing justice to the real complexities of language. Introducing language games and forms of life as family resemblance concepts does not excuse us from difficult theoretical work, but on the contrary sets a heroic task for philosophical semantics in the realistic description of linguistic practices that are as conceptually complex as any other aspect of human culture.[13]

∎ NOTES

1. See Wittgenstein 1968a §27.

2. By this admission we avoid identity and individuation problems connected with Wittgenstein's concept of a form of life.

3. I adopt the term 'praxeological foundation' from Haller's insightful discussions of Wittgenstein's later philosophy of language. Haller 1988, esp. 55 and passim. On Wittgenstein's introduction to American pragmatism through Ramsey's interest in C. S. Peirce's 'pragmaticism', see Fann 1969, 46. Yet we know from his letter to Russell (R2) 22.6.12 that Wittgenstein was familiar with William James's *Varieties of Religious Experience,* and that later when lecturing at Cambridge on philosophical psychology near the end of the war he considered using James's *Principles of Psychology* primarily as a convenient statement of ideas he wanted to criticize. Monk, 477–78; Goodman 1994, 339–54.

4. See Manser 1967.

5. Wittgenstein introduces the concept of family resemblance in his 1958, 17–20, 87, 124. See also Wittgenstein 1967a §§326, 392, 474–76; 1983, 266, 299, 399, 408. An unacknowledged predecessor to Wittgenstein's notion of family resemblance is Dugald Stewart 1818, 262, 271. Gier, 61, connects Wittgenstein's concept of family resemblance with a similar idea in Oswald Spengler, as he links the concept of a form of life with *Lebensphilosophie* in Wilhelm Dilthey, Georg Simmel, and Spengler. See Hallett 1977, 74; and von Wright 1978, 77.

6. Wittgenstein 1968a, Preface, v.

7. See McGinn 1984, 2: "We must avoid the temptation to regard the text as a sort of cipher through which we must penetrate to reveal the linearly ordered argument beneath. It is not that Wittgenstein really has an argument of orthodox form which for some inscrutable reason he chose to present in a disguised fashion."

8. Wittgenstein 1958, 17. Wittgenstein's argument that there is no common essence to the class of things called games is discussed in detail by Suter 1989, 25–38.

9. Garver has argued that Wittgenstein treats forms of life as biologically specific. On this interpretation, there is only one human form of life, by virtue of which all humans can in principle understand one another in some language. I see the attractions of this view, but I am inclined to Haller's criticisms of Garver's position in Haller 1988, 129–36. Garver's essay was originally published as his 1984. See also Garver 1994, 237–67. Note that Wittgenstein explicitly uses the plural *'Lebensformen'* in 1958, 226, in speaking of understanding human modes of calculation only, without considering interspecies comparisons.

10. Wittgenstein does not say that all concepts are family resemblance, so we should not expect a solution to the problem of universals as a dividend of his concept of family resemblance.

11. My conclusions here are largely in agreement with Black 1978.

12. Russell's uncharitable remarks are to be discounted in this light when in his 1929, 216–17, he charges: "The late Wittgenstein . . . seems to have grown tired of serious thinking and to have invented a doctrine which would make such an activity unnecessary." Wittgenstein is said to have made a similar remark, though not as a riposte to Russell's, indicating the feeling was more or less mutual. Malcolm 1958, 68: "in 1946 Wittgenstein had a poor opinion of Russell's contemporary philosophical writings. 'Russell isn't going to kill himself doing philosophy now,' he said with a smile."

13. See also Ackermann, 82–83; Bambrough 1960–61; Campbell 1965; Fogelin 1987, 133–38; Griffin 1974; Hanfling, 64–71; Hodges 1973; Khatchadourian 1957–58; Pompa 1967; Rundle, 40–63; Wennerberg 1967.

CHAPTER
ELEVEN | **Rule-Following**

Games, including language games, are defined and played by following rules. Wittgenstein, having interpreted the problem of understanding meaning in language as involving families of language games with no essential properties but an overlapping and criss-crossing of features, now turns to the question of the rules that govern human activities, including ordinary games, language games, social-institutional transactions, and calculations in mathematics. Wittgenstein is as much interested in the teaching and learning of rules as in the particular content and constitution of rule-governed activities.

Wittgenstein has two main concerns about rules. He wants to show that rules cannot provide alternative absolute foundations for semantic reductivism. Rule-following cannot replace logical atomism and the picture theory in a new but equally univocal essentialist account of meaning. Wittgenstein maintains that rules by themselves cannot provide absolute foundations for language because rules can always be variously interpreted. Rules underdetermine the exact ways in which their instructions are to be carried out except by an indefinite regress of rules for following rules that takes language users beyond the practical limits of language game playing. Second, Wittgenstein relates the function of language game rules to the extrasemantic praxeological foundations of semantics. Individual rules must be understood as serving the purposes of a particular type of human activity; they are followed or infringed only as part of an evolving form of life.

The constitution of language games as rule-governed activities is emphasized by Wittgenstein's comparisons with ordinary games. His favorite example is chess, and the definition of indi-

vidual pieces and the game itself by the rules of play. The problem of explaining different kinds of words in language or of tools
or instruments in a language game is related to the problem of
classifying chess pieces as game tokens. Wittgenstein remarks:

> 17. It will be possible to say: In language (8) we have differ-
> ent *kinds of word*. For the function of the word "slab" and the
> word "block" are more alike than those of "slab" and "d". But
> how we group words into kinds will depend on the aim of the
> classification, — and on our own inclination.
> Think of the different points of view from which one can
> classify tools or chess-men.

The same analogy is given with respect to defining chess
pieces as chess pieces, as embodying a certain pragmatic function
and role in playing the game as defined by its rules. Game tokens
are understood as doing complex things when moved on the
board, such as capturing a bishop or forcing an opponent to expose a queen, rather than merely as particularly shaped samples
of wood, ivory, or bone.

The function of a game piece as of a word in language is a
part of empirical reality, something spatiotemporal rather than
abstract. The words in language games can similarly be understood in terms of their real world functions, the actions they
make possible in the complex network of extralinguistic activities in which they are integrated, by the rules that define their
use and constitute the language games to which they belong. The
chess king is not fully explained as a physical object, but is
defined by its role in the game according to the rules of chess —
not only the rules directly concerned with the king's possible
movements, but the entire system of rules defining the interactions of the king with pawns, rooks, knights, bishops, and queen,
in the interplay of two opponents each trying to achieve a certain
strategic purpose:

> 108. We are talking about the spatial and temporal phenomena
> of language, not about some non-spatial, non-temporal phan-
> tasm. [Note in margin: Only it is possible to be interested in a
> phenomenon in a variety of ways]. But we talk about it as we do
> about the pieces in chess when we are stating the rules of the
> game, not describing their physical properties.
> The question "What is a word really?" is analogous to "What
> is a piece in chess?"

It is not until much later that Wittgenstein finds himself in a
position to answer these questions. The problem of specifying
rules is largely one of distinguishing what is essential from what
is inessential in the practice of game playing and the game's

official statement of rules, where the two need not agree. The analogy between language games and ordinary games like checkers and chess prompts Wittgenstein to ask:

> 562. But how can I decide what is an essential, and what an inessential, accidental, feature of the notation? Is there some reality lying behind the notation, which shapes its grammar?
>
> Let us think of a similar case in a game: in draughts a king is marked by putting one piece on top of another. Now won't one say it is inessential to the game for a king to consist of two pieces?

The expectation here is certainly correct. Wittgenstein notes that the rules of checkers require the crowning of a single piece that advances all the way to an opponent's back row of squares by placing another captured piece on top of it. But when we understand what is essential to the game, this seems gratuitous. We could just as easily indicate the distinction between crowned and uncrowned pieces by a special color, replacement of one type of single token by another, or marking the token by a distinguishing sign. Something of the sort is already done in checkers when more kings need to be crowned than there are captured pieces available from the board. The usual practice is to borrow a piece from the other player until it can be paid back, though this too presupposes that more pieces have already been jumped than kings crowned. In some situations, the players must simply remember that a physically undistinguished token is functioning as a king. But how do we decide which official rules are essential and which are accidental to a game?

Wittgenstein explores the question with respect to what seems to be an inessential but standard use of the king in chess as part of the preparation for play. He describes the functional role of the king in deciding who plays white:

> 563. Let us say that the meaning of a piece is its role in the game.—Now let it be decided by lot which of the players gets white before any game of chess begins. To this end one player holds a king in each closed fist while the other chooses one of the two hands at random. Will it be counted as part of the role of the king in chess that it is used to draw lots in this way?

> 564. So I am inclined to distinguish between the essential and the inessential in a game too. The game, one would like to say, has not only rules but also a *point*.

The decisive factor seems to be whether or not the conventionally approved object is absolutely the only one that can be used to achieve the same purpose, or whether whatever is chosen for that particular function in the game is thereby automatically constituted as an object of the sort defined. The function of the king in moving only one square at a time in any direction and being able to capture an opponent's pieces, of castling with the rook, and being the target whose capture wins the game for an opponent, is evidently the king's essential function. Nothing else could serve in this capacity without thereby being a chess king, regardless of how the piece is shaped or the materials from which it is made, and regardless of whether its function is fulfilled by gameboard tokens or a symbolic code, or even by abstract thoughts or propositions, as when chess is played mentally or through the mail or by computer, or reported by schematic diagrams in the newspaper.

Using the king to decide by lot who is to make the first move on the contrary seems arbitrary and accidental, even if the rules officially specify that it is to be the king that should be used for this purpose. The reason is that there is no compulsion to suppose that no other piece could serve the same function, or, for that matter, that the choice of who is to go first could not also be determined by guessing the hand in which some object other than a chess piece is concealed, drawing straws, or flipping a coin. Nor is there any predilection to suppose that if an object other than the king is used in this way, a pawn or coin or stone, that the object thereby automatically becomes a chess king by serving its rule-defined function, in the way that a coin or a stone could become the king if we lost the original king from the set and had to substitute another object in its place, using the new token according to all the established rules for the king in playing the game. Yet if this is our belief about what is essential and what is accidental to the king in chess, then we must offer some sound basis for going against the letter of the law in the rules of chess that specify this preliminary ceremonial role for the king, without the equivalent of which the game cannot begin. Wittgenstein turns next to this problem:

> 567. But, after all, the game is supposed to be defined by the rules! So, if a rule of the game prescribes that the kings are to be used for drawing lots before a game of chess, then that is an essential part of the game. What objection might one make to this? That one does not see the point of this prescription. Perhaps as one wouldn't see the point either of a rule by which each piece had to be turned round three times before one moved it. If we found this rule in a board-game we should be surprised and should speculate about the purpose of the rule. ("Was this prescription meant to prevent one from moving without due consideration?")

568. If I understand the character of the game aright—I
might say—then this isn't an essential part of it.
((Meaning is a physiognomy.))

If a particular rule is to be essential to a game, its point or
purpose must be clear in the context of other game activities
defined by the other predominant rules of the game. We have a
good sense of the purpose of chess from the rules that define the
endgame and the moves of all the pieces on the board. When we
consider an additional rule that appears to define an extracur-
ricular role for the king, such as being used to draw lots to decide
which player is to begin the game by making the first move, we do
not see the choice of the king in particular as contributing anything special to the game's purpose. We imagine other pieces or
other things and methods of decision that would equally serve
the purpose of getting the game started by identifying which of
two players plays white. If we take away the king's ability to
move on the diagonal or for ecclesiastical reasons to capture a
bishop, or if we add to its repertoire the ability to move two
squares in any direction when it is in check by a knight, then we
have changed the game to something other than chess, and the
new 'king' to something other than the chess king. We have by
comparison no similar reaction to allowing the queen or a rook or
knight to serve the purpose of deciding by lot which player is to
begin. Insisting that only the king can be used in this way as a
preliminary to play, Wittgenstein says, insofar as we otherwise
understand the game's purpose, lacks point. It would be like requiring a player to twist each piece around when moving it on the
board, which has no evident purpose intrinsic to the game.

The practical constraints on concept choice are fixed by the
point or purpose of life activities. The examination of language
games to explain meaning by essential rules from the standpoint
of their praxeological foundations in a form of life can only be
understood by reference to the point or purpose for which a language game is played. We thus require a way of distinguishing
between the essential and inessential rules of a language game,
and in so doing we uncover its philosophical grammar.

The point or purpose of a game can only be understood if it
belongs to our form of life. We must know something about chess
and what constitutes normal play in the game in order to know
that drawing lots to decide who plays first by holding the king
rather than another piece or something else or by some other fair
method is an inessential ceremonial rather than an essential rule
of chess. Using the king in particular or going first by rightly choos-

ing the hand in which the king is concealed is a detachable part of chess, even though it must somehow be decided who is to play first. (Other conventions are possible and some are often followed; choosing hands is the standard practice for amateurs, while in official play among chess masters the one with the highest tournament ranking always plays white and always plays first.)

Something similar is true of language games. We must share in at least some of the relevant form of life in order to determine the point and purpose of the game, in order to distinguish its essential from its inessential rules. This is comparable to but obviously rather different than the *Tractatus* distinction between sign and symbol, between the sign as something inessential to the logic of language and the transcendent symbol as essential. Now, in the later period, Wittgenstein scorns the transcendental, and requires that what is essential to language belongs to empirical reality, that both are to be distinguished by reference to the point and purpose of particular language games. For this, we must be able to do something, we must be masters of a technique whereby we can participate in the activities that constitute the relevant form of life by which the point and purpose of a particular language game is determined.

The task of identifying the essential rules of a language game is difficult. There is a difference between understanding the point and purpose of chess and understanding the point and purpose of language use in the United Nations debate about the future of world trade. It is related to the problem of distinguishing between acting from or acting in way that involves a rule as opposed merely to acting in accord with a rule. In the same way that the movement of a finger in space can be interpreted as pointing to just about anything, so a physical or symbolic move in a game including a language game can be understood as following an unlimited number of differently interpreted rules. Wittgenstein illustrates the problem in the extrapolation of a series of numbers in arithmetic, where the series and any continuation of the series can be interpreted as issuing from many distinct rules, or from any specially interpreted rule. The underdetermination of meaning by a practice that may occur merely in accord with a language game rule concerns Wittgenstein already in the *Blue Book,* where he says:

> We must distinguish between what one might call "a process being *in accordance with a rule*", and, "a process involving a rule" . . .

Take an example. Some one teaches me to square cardinal numbers; he writes down the row

$$1 \qquad 2 \qquad 3 \qquad 4,$$

and asks me to square them. (I will, in this case again, replace any processes happening 'in the mind' by processes of calculation on the paper.) Suppose, underneath the first row of numbers, I then write:

$$1 \qquad 4 \qquad 9 \qquad 16.$$

What I wrote is in accordance with the general rule of squaring; but it obviously is also in accordance with any number of other rules; and amongst these it is not more in accordance with one than with another. In the sense in which before we talked about a rule being involved in a process, *no* rule was involved in this. Supposing that in order to get to my results I calculated 1×1, 2×2, 3×3, 4×4 (that is, in this case I wrote down the calculations); these would again be in accordance with any number of rules. Supposing, on the other hand, in order to get to my results I had written down what you may call "the rule of squaring", say algebraically. In this case this rule was involved in a sense in which no other rule was. (13)

In the *Philosophical Investigations,* we are led by a series of steps to the underdetermination of meaning in language games by rules considered only in themselves. This follows previous discussion of the underdetermination of ostension by body movements considered only in themselves. The first question is whether rules can be so carefully defined or observed in practice as to fix the meaning of a linguistic term, an individual word such as a name or sentence, without any possibility of doubt. If we were in possession of such a rule, we would know with absolute certainty what any language user in the respective language game means by the use of the term as a token in the game:

84. I said that the application of a word is not everywhere bounded by rules. But what does a game look like that is everywhere bounded by rules? whose rules never let a doubt creep in, but stop up all the cracks where it might?—Can't we imagine a rule determining the application of a rule, and a doubt which *it* removes—and so on?

But that is not to say that we are in doubt because it is possible for us to *imagine* a doubt. I can easily imagine someone always doubting before he opened a front door whether an abyss did not yawn behind it, and making sure about it before he went through the door (and he might on some occasion prove to be right)—but that does not make me doubt in the same case.

The question of whether or not a rule admits the possibility of doubt is different from the doubt that occurs in trying to understand an explanation. Wittgenstein shakes our faith in the determination of meaning by rules by describing a sequence of language games in which the rules of simple arithmetical language games are taught, and the success of teaching or training in using the rule is tested by a performance criterion. Different mutually incompatible rules are then offered as equally plausible in explaining game playing practices in the teaching, learning, and proof of having learned the rules, where what would ordinarily be described as blatant failure to follow an obvious rule is characterized under special interpretation instead as an instance of following the rule precisely as intended and understood.

There is always a plurality of different ways to understand the instructions or directions given by a rule. Wittgenstein regards such rules as convenient reminders for those who already have sufficient mastery of their application contextually to interact with them in a particular way. To see a sign along a path pointing with an arrow or stylized finger in one direction where the path forks would usually be understood as identifying the route by name or giving its destination. If you want to go to Spring Mill, continue to walk in this direction. That is how virtually anyone in almost any human culture would understand the meaning of the sign as a practical rule for guiding a journey from place to place. But does the sign by itself determine its own standard application in this way? The sign just stands there, and we must interpret it, which in principle we can do in any number of different ways with any number of different results:

> 85. A rule stands there like a sign-post.—Does the sign-post leave no doubt open about the way I have to go? Does it shew which direction I am to take when I have passed it; whether along the road or the footpath or cross-country? But where is it said which way I am to follow it; whether in the direction of its finger or (e.g.) in the opposite one?—And if there were, not a single sign-post, but a chain of adjacent ones or of chalk marks on the ground—is there only *one* way of interpreting them?—So I can say, the sign-post does after all leave no room for doubt. Or rather: it sometimes leaves room for doubt and sometimes not. And now this is no longer a philosophical proposition but an empirical one.

The pure behavioral act of extending a finger in space is no better and no worse a determinant of exact meaning than the sign along the path. We must know what to do with such an object or event in order to derive or attribute its meaning. The body motion or physical facts of the sign by themselves do not contain the instructions about how they are to be understood. If they do contain further instructions, the instructions by themselves do not contain further complete univocal instructions about how they are to be followed in following the first sign or set of instructions, and so on.[1]

Through any number of iterations of attempts to specify precisely how a rule is to be followed by articulating further rules, the problem of giving a final determination of meaning is pushed back but never definitely settled. By virtue of sharing a common form of life, a point is usually quickly reached after which further explanation of the application of a rule by a regression of rules becomes as unnecessary as it is unprofitable. Then, Wittgenstein says, we simply act. It is the way we act and the fact that we act in the way we do, the activity of life and the practices in which we are involved in our form of life, that determine the meanings of terms in language games and game playing tokens like chess pieces. We engage in language games in which we explain meanings by ostension and by explicit rules. But body movement by itself is not pointing, pointing by itself is not naming or explaining the meaning of a name, and a language game rule by itself does not fix its own interpretation or application in naming, teaching, or explaining the meaning even of technically and explicitly rule-governed words or sentences as symbolic tokens or playing pieces in a language game.

Wittgenstein demonstrates the problem graphically by means of alternative methods of coordinating the information in a written table used as a language game implement according to a definite set of rules. We see clearly how different interpretations of what may present itself as a single language game rule results in entirely different applications with entirely different results as the language game is played. The rule by itself admits of so many different interpretations that we can only try to stop some of the leaks, the doubts that may crop up about its exact determination of meaning, by giving yet another rule or set of rules explaining how the first rule is to be followed. This rule or set of rules will be in no more privileged position to decide these matters, and so their exact interpretation and application must be determined by the introduction of yet another rule or set of rules, in turn variously interpretable and applicable, *ad indefinitum*. From this, Wittgenstein concludes that rules alone and by themselves like body motions alone and by themselves do not resolve the problem of meaning or fix meaning precisely and without possibility of doubt in any definite way. We return to the builders:

> 86. Imagine a language-game like (2) played with the help of a table. The signs given to B by A are now written ones. B has a table; in the first column are the signs used in the game, in the second pictures of building stones. A shews B such a written sign; B looks it up in the table, looks at the picture opposite, and so on. So the table is a rule which he follows in executing orders.—One learns to look the picture up in the table by receiving a training, and part of this training consists perhaps in the pupil's learning to pass with his finger horizontally from left to right; and so, as it were, to draw a series of horizontal lines on the table.
>
> Suppose different ways of reading a table were now introduced; one time, as above, according to the schema:

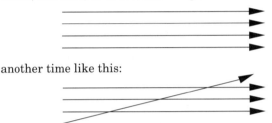

> another time like this:

> or in some other way.—Such a schema is supplied with the table as the rule for its use.
>
> Can we not now imagine further rules to explain *this* one? And, on the other hand, was that first table incomplete without the schema of arrows? And are other tables incomplete without their schemata?

Are we to learn the principles of philosophical semantics only from fruit merchants and construction workers? The answer is yes, because it is in such real life and fictionalized language game scenarios that language is put to practical use at its regular day job and not on philosophical holiday. What we discover in the refinement of language game (2), where A communicates to B his need for building blocks in a certain order by writing down a table, is that A and B must share in the expectation that the lists of items are to be correlated horizontally in parallel alignment, and not by any of several possible criss-crossing patterns. For that matter, it must be assumed that A and B understand that the list is not to be burned and the order of stones chosen by watching which way the sparks and ashes fly when tossed into a passing breeze. We know well enough that this is not how the table is to be used. But why? What forbids such interpretations and applications of the rules? How do rules work, and what if anything can they accomplish by themselves? What are the implications of the proper functioning of rules in understanding the role of rules and rule-following in language use and language game play?

Wittgenstein approaches these questions by shifting to examples of rule-following in extrapolating sequences of numbers according to arithmetical rules. These are also genuine language games, as we know from Wittgenstein's list of the multiplicity of kinds of language games in §23. Wittgenstein shows repeatedly that with a little perverse ingenuity any activity can be interpreted as following any rule, if we consider only the rule itself, standing there like a signpost awaiting our decision about how to use it:

> 185. Let us return to our example (143). Now—judged by the usual criteria—the pupil has mastered the series of natural numbers. Next we teach him to write down other series of cardinal numbers and get him to the point of writing down the series of the form
>
> o, n, 2n, 3n, etc.
>
> at an order of the form "+n"; so at the order "+1" he writes down the series of natural numbers.—Let us suppose we have done exercises and given him tests up to 1000.
>
> Now we get the pupil to continue a series (say +2) beyond 1000—and he writes 1000, 1004, 1008, 1012.
>
> We say to him: "Look what you've done!"—He doesn't understand. We say: "You were meant to add *two:* look how you began the series!"—He answers: "Yes, isn't it right? I thought that was how I was *meant* to do it."—Or suppose he pointed to the series and said: "But I went on in the same way."—It would now be no use to say: "But can't you see . . . . . ?"—and repeat the old examples and explanations.—In such a case we might say, perhaps: It comes natural to this person to understand our order with our explanations as *we* should understand the order: "Add 2 up to 1000, 4 up to 2000, 6 up to 3000 and so on."
>
> Such a case would present similarities with one in which a person naturally reacted to the gesture of pointing with the hand by looking in the direction of the line from finger-tip to wrist, not from wrist to finger-tip.

The context is one of teaching or training someone to master a technique. A rule is explained, and its application begins. The student after a certain point is required to continue the series of numbers by following the rule in what is supposed to be understood as the same way. Yet, no matter what the student does thereafter, regardless of the numbers adduced as continuing the series, any choice of numbers whatsoever can be justified as following an appropriately slanted interpretation of the rule. Wittgenstein does not imagine nonstandard rule-following as deliberate violations of the rule by those pretending to observe it, but as the result of a sincere interpretation that comes naturally to the student but quite unexpectedly to the teacher.[2]

If I am given the series 2, 4, 6, 8, 10, . . . , I might conclude that the numbers in sequence have been generated by any of many different algebraic rules. A simple rule that gives the series is x+2. But the same series is produced, for example, by $2(x+2)/2$, $(x+4) - 2$, $(x - 5) + 7$, $2y$ for $y = <1,2,3, . . . >$, and countlessly many others. When I think I understand and am able correctly to continue the series, it is natural to ask *which,* if any, of all these rules is actually being followed? If I continue the series 2, 4, 6, 8, 10, . . . , by next writing down 11, 19, 256, 7, 7, 7, . . . , in fact, by adding any numbers whatsoever to the series, then this too by appropriate interpretation and adjustment can be understood as in perfect conformity to any of the above rules, or, indeed, to any chosen rule whatsoever. We can, even under the 'right' interpretation, regard the series 2, 4, 6, 8, 10, . . . , as produced by the rule x^2, x^2+1, etc., for example, by giving a special spin to the meanings of these terms or to the rules themselves at different stages of their application. The rule by itself considered only on its own stands there like a signpost, like dead syntax, and we must give life to it by deciding how it is to be interpreted and applied in use.

The analogy with the underdetermination of the meaning of names or other individual words by body movement in pure behavioral ostension is explicit in Wittgenstein's reference to finger pointing in the explanation of a term. The motion of the hand, the signpost along the path, the rule 'add 2' for an arithmetical language game, are all helpless in and of themselves to fix meaning. We must rightly know or correctly decide how to apply them, and this is a matter in which the rules by themselves cannot definitively instruct us, and to clarify which by supplementing the rules with rules for following rules begins an infinite regress:

> 198. "But how can a rule shew me what I have to do at *this* point? Whatever I do is, on some interpretation, in accord with the rule."—That is not what we ought to say, but rather: any interpretation still hangs in the air along with what it interprets, and cannot give it any support. Interpretations by themselves do not determine meaning.
>
> "Then can whatever I do be brought into accord with the rule?"—Let me ask this: what has the expression of a rule—say a sign-post—got to do with my actions? What sort of connexion

is there here?—Well, perhaps this one: I have been trained
to react to this sign in a particular way, and now I do so react
to it.

But that is only to give a causal connexion; to tell how it
has come about that we now go by the sign-post; not what this
going-by-the-sign really consists in. On the contrary; I have
further indicated that a person goes by a sign-post only in so
far as there exists a regular use of sign-posts, a custom.

There is an element of the elementary school teacher that
still clings to Wittgenstein's examples of rule-following. Wittgenstein may be drawing on his experiences teaching young students
the rudiments of arithmetic, geometry, and algebra, in which he
must often have found himself beginning a series, attempting to
explain the general rule he was following in the elements he had
already produced, and then encouraging students to continue the
series according to the same rule as a criterion of determining
whether or not they had understood his instructions—and
of whether or not he had succeeding in explaining his meaning.
When a student can correctly continue the series long enough to
be relatively sure that the answers are not merely a result of
guesswork, extrapolating and interpolating values in the required
way, then the teacher has positive evidence that the meaning of
terms in a particular language game has been adequately communicated, expressed and understood, and that the student has become master of the relevant language game technique.[3]

The practice of rule teaching and following as a form of life
must now be critically investigated. Wittgenstein asks, given the
ways in which we actually develop, use, and communicate rules,
whether it is thinkable to follow a rule as an activity for one person only, or only once in life. The rhetorical tone implies that
Wittgenstein rejects such possibilities, and offers the problems as
contributions to the grammar of what it means to obey a rule:

> 199. Is what we call "obeying a rule" something that it would
> be possible for only *one* man to do, and to do only *once* in his
> life?—This is of course a note on the grammar of the expres-
> sion "to obey a rule".
>
> It is not possible that there should have been only one oc-
> casion on which someone obeyed a rule. It is not possible that
> there should have been only one occasion on which a report
> was made, an order given or understood; and so on.—To obey
> a rule, to make a report, to give an order, to play a game of
> chess, are *customs* (uses, institutions).
>
> To understand a sentence means to understand a language.
> To understand a language means to be master of a technique.

The picture Wittgenstein's discussion of rule-following brings
to mind, especially in continuing an arithmetical series, is one in

which, trying to explain the determination of meaning by rules alone, we are sent from one set of instructions to the next, each of which we find equally puzzling and in need of further explication. The process never comes to an end, and meaning is never fixed in any language game, so long as we suppose that rules alone and by themselves can settle the problem of the meaning of a term. We must look outside the regress of rules to the practices and activities presupposed as part of a shared form of life. The application of rules is determined only in the context of what people do and how people live in cooperation with the development of language. If the sequence of rules needed to follow other rules needed to explain meaning never comes to an end, then the sequence cannot explain the meaning of language. The explanation of meaning works well enough in makeshift everyday rapid-fire semantic interactions; while explanation, along with the rules by which we seek to explain explanation, eventually has an end:

> 201. This was our paradox: no course of action could be determined by a rule, because every course of action can be made out to accord with the rule. The answer was: if everything can be made out to accord with the rule, then it can also be made out to conflict with it. And so there would be neither accord nor conflict here.
>
> It can be seen that there is a misunderstanding here from the mere fact that in the course of our argument we give one interpretation after another; as if each one contented us at least for a moment, until we thought of yet another standing behind it. What this shews is that there is a way of grasping a rule which is *not an interpretation,* but which is exhibited in what we call "obeying the rule" and "going against it" in actual cases.
>
> Hence there is an inclination to say: every action according to the rule is an interpretation. But we ought to restrict the term "interpretation" to the substitution of one expression of the rule for another.

The regress of rules for understanding rules is unnecessary. Wittgenstein asks whether the table of instructions that builder A shows helper B would be complete without the schema of arrows showing the proper alignment of entries in each of the facing columns. Of course, the table is complete and perfectly understandable as it is. In all but the most unusual circumstances, the table would be interpreted in the usual way by going directly across from left to right without criss-crossing or using the table as an implement in any sort of prophecy ritual.

The point is rather that these facts about what we assume to be the correct use of the table are not attributable to the table alone, nor generally to rules considered only in themselves. They acquire meaning only as expressions of a particular form of life, in which natural activities have naturally determined that certain practices are to be followed in the use of rules. Why do we not conclude that a pointed finger indicates an object in the direction of fingertip to knuckle rather than knuckle to fingertip? Why, when we see an arrow-shaped sign along the path, do we not conclude that the sign indicates the way we are to proceed from arrow tip to shaft rather than shaft to tip? Why do we not suppose that we must begin to dig a tunnel at the base of the sign or go straight up in the air to get to where we are trying to go?

Such conventions could be part of our form of life. For a variety of reasons, with as complex a natural history as the course of human life, they are simply not. This is not what we do; these imaginary alternative applications of rules have not evolved as part of our linguistic and extralinguistic culture, and there is nothing more to say. The arrow in a sign is understood rightly and without further ado as pointing in the way it does because arrows have a certain function in our way of life. They have acquired this implicit value by being thrown or shot from bows in hunting, aimed and propelled toward a target in what we consequently think of as a forward-pointing direction. The same is true for other generally more complicated background practices that in some ways uphold and in others blend almost indistinguishably into linguistic activity. The purposes by which essential rules are distinguished from inessential rules in language games are deeply interrelated with these human practices in our complicated forms of life.

If as children or foreigners we are not yet sufficiently familiar with these activities to function effectively in the relevant practices, if we make what those training us in the use of a rule regard as a mistake in passing along this part of a form of life in which we are to participate, then we are soon behaviorally corrected, provided we share at least enough sublinguistic practice in common to grasp the difference between approval and disapproval in the responses of others who are already masters of the technique. Here is also the clue to the problem of identifying and individuating the open-ended family resemblance concept of a form of life. We can say that a form of life is at least partially shared by any persons capable of at least partially understanding each other's meaning. Wittgenstein argues that meaning is impossible without this common pragmatic background and stage-setting:

> 211. How can he *know* how he is to continue a pattern by himself—whatever instruction you give him?—Well, how do I know?—If that means "Have I reasons?" the answer is: my reasons will soon give out. And then I shall act, without reasons.

He returns to the same point several passages later:

> 217. "How am I able to obey a rule?"—if this is not a question about causes, then it is about the justification for my following the rule in the way I do.
>
> If I have exhausted the justifications I have reached bedrock, and my spade is turned. Then I am inclined to say: "This is simply what I do."
>
> (Remember that we sometimes demand definitions for the sake not of their content, but of their form. Our requirement is an architectural one; the definition a kind of ornamental coping that supports nothing.)

When we are properly trained to follow a rule, we simply act in accord with it. To stop and question how the rule is to be interpreted and followed, to begin to examine all the limitless possibilities for other conventions that might be embodied in or intended by the rule, is only a sign that we have not yet assimilated the rule as a procedure to be followed in practice, that we are not yet at home in the particular conventions presupposed by and embodied in the rule. Wittgenstein accordingly says that to follow a rule is to follow it blindly, without hesitation or doubt, and without the paralyzing skepticism that occurs only in philosophy in its abstraction of concept terms from their real practical rule-following contexts:

> 219. "All the steps are really already taken" means: I no longer have any choice. The rule, once stamped with a particular meaning, traces the lines along which it is to be followed through the whole of space.—But if something of this sort really were the case, how would it help?
>
> No; my description only made sense if it was to be understood symbolically.—I should have said: *This is how it strikes me.*
>
> When I obey a rule, I do not choose.
>
> I obey the rule *blindly.*

A rule is also regular. Rule-following requires the same response under the same conditions. Wittgenstein takes these implications as a further comment on the grammar of the word 'rule' and the words 'same' and 'agreement'. What is not regularly followed, or what is supposed to be followed differently on different occasions without special instruction is simply not a rule:

> 223. One does not feel that one has always got to wait upon the nod (the whisper) of the rule. On the contrary, we are not on tenterhooks about what it will tell us next, but it always tells us the same, and we do what it tells us.
>
> One might say to the person one was training: "Look, I always do the same thing: I . . . . . ."

224. The word "agreement" and the word "rule" are *related* to one another, they are cousins. If I teach anyone the use of the one word, he learns the use of the other with it.

225. The use of the word "rule" and the use of the word "same" are interwoven. (As are the use of "proposition" and the use of "true".)

The discussion at this point is clearly related to Wittgenstein's prior questions about whether it is possible for one person only to follow a rule, or for anyone to do so only once in a lifetime. When we try to think of rules abstractly, as though disengaged from the densely interwoven cultural practices and practical activities of which they are so intimately a part and by which they must be explained and applied, then we may become wrongly convinced that the interpretation of a rule is up for grabs on every occasion in which rule-following occurs. This, Wittgenstein maintains, is not the case for anything we can correctly call a rule. To delay and deliberate over what a rule requires is not to follow the rule, nor can we follow a rule by first deciding how we are to follow it. If we must ask whether a putative rule applies in the same way now as on any other occasion, then what we are considering does not deserve to be called a rule. The fact that a rule applies to a different content in its application on distinct separate occasions does not make the rule itself different:

226. Suppose someone gets the series of numbers 1, 3, 5, 7, ... by working out the series $2x + 1$[1]. And now he asks himself: "But am I always doing the same thing, or something different every time?"

If from one day to the next you promise: "To-morrow I will come and see you"—are you saying the same thing every day, or every day something different?

227. Would it make sense to say "If he did something *different* every day we should not say he was obeying a rule"? That makes *no* sense.

228. "We see a series in just *one* way!"—All right, but what is that way? Clearly we see it algebraically, and as a segment of an expansion. Or is there more in it than that?—"But the way we see it surely gives us everything!"—But that is not an observation about the segment of the series; or about anything that we notice in it; it gives expression to the fact that we look to the rule for instruction and *do something*, without appealing to anything else for guidance.

The essential rules of a language game are its rules of philosophical grammar. By following these rules blindly language users accomplish the purposes for which language tools have entered into language, and at the same time are assured of avoiding philosophical problems. There can be no philosophical problems associated with correct rule-following in language games, and apparent philosophical problems are dissolved by recognizing the rules of philosophical grammar connected with the terms that enter into their formulation only when they are removed from their natural habitats where they have a particular purpose to fulfill. To explicate the rules of philosophical grammar requires what Wittgenstein calls a perspicuous representation of the terms and ordinary language game tokens that give rise to philosophical paradoxes when language goes on holiday. Wittgenstein writes:

> 116. When philosophers use a word—"knowledge", "being", "object", "I", "proposition", "name"—and try to grasp the *essence* of the thing, one must always ask oneself: is the word ever actually used in this way in the language-game which is its original home?—
>
> What *we* do is to bring words back from their metaphysical to their everyday use.

The philosophical grammar of color predications finally provides the solution in Wittgenstein's later philosophy that had defeated the logical atomism and picture theory of the *Tractatus*. Wittgenstein does not return to the color incompatibility problem in *Philosophical Investigations,* but he discusses the problem at length in some of the other posthumously published manuscripts, such as those that became the *Philosophical Grammar* and *Philosophical Remarks*. Already in the *Blue Book,* Wittgenstein describes color incompatibility as prohibited by a 'grammatical rule'. A rule of philosophical grammar for space-time-color descriptions forbids simultaneous color predications occupying the same location in space. The restriction reflects a logical impossibility, but not in the narrow sense of syntactical contradiction.

The rules of philosophical grammar that define and must be followed in playing the color predication language game do not permit the conjunction, R P T & B P T. Any language game allowing its construction would have no practical application, and could only arise as intellectual mischief in the improper conduct of philosophy. We discover the grammatical rules of color predication in the practical activity of describing facts undertaken with a definite purpose. The essential rules of such a language game preclude incompatible color predication conjunctions as failing to contribute to the point or purpose of color fact description. That is why color incompatibility is both like the necessity of tautology in some ways and unlike it in others. The essential rules of philosophical grammar for color predication language games codify the fact that color incompatibility statements have no use and serve no point or purpose in practice. The long road Wittgenstein travels from the color incompatibility problem in the *Tractatus* and "Some Remarks on Logical Form" leads at last to the rules of philosophical grammar in color predication language games. The necessity of color incompatibility is accounted for without exerting pressure on what were supposed to have been the watertight distinctions between sense, nonsense, and the senseless established by the general form of proposition.[5]

Wittgenstein concludes that rule-following cannot be done privately. He has already argued that it is nonsense to suppose that a rule could be followed by only one person in the history of the world or on one and only one occasion. Now he claims that rules cannot be followed privately, on the grounds that were it possible, then there could be no basis for distinguishing between actual rule-following and merely believing that one is following a rule. This conclusion has the greatest consequences for a topic Wittgenstein first raises in §36, concerning the explanation of naming and the meaning of names by internal psychological ostension or private mental pointing. It is the 'spirit' to which he says we naturally resort when the 'body' or pure behavioral ostension account of meaning fails. Wittgenstein's discussion of rule-following closes with these important remarks, by which he prepares us for more extended reflections on the impossibility of private naming, in what is perhaps the most famous and difficult part of the *Philosophical Investigations,* the private language argument:

> 202. And hence also 'obeying a rule' is a practice. And to *think* one is obeying a rule is not to obey a rule. Hence it is not possible to obey a rule 'privately': otherwise thinking one was obeying a rule would be the same thing as obeying it.[6]

❚ NOTES

1. Wittgenstein 1968a §§156–78. An insightful if controversial analysis is offered by Kripke 1982, 45–49.

2. Rule-following is also discussed at Wittgenstein 1967a §§293–96, 299–310, 320–21, 331, 440–41; 1983, 36–37, 156, 160, 192, 229, 238, 335, 341, 345, 347–48, 360–61, 404–5, 409, 413–22, 429.

3. See Monk on Wittgenstein's corporal pedagogy, 201–2: "[Karl] Gruber was a gifted boy who responded well to Wittgenstein's methods. Like many of Wittgenstein's pupils, he initially found algebra difficult. 'I could not grasp', he recalled later, 'how one could calculate using letters of the alphabet.' However, after receiving from Wittgenstein a box on the ears, he began to knuckle down: 'Soon I was the best at algebra in the class.'"

4. Wittgenstein 1958, 56. Wittgenstein in *Tractatus* 3.325 similarly speaks of: "A symbolism . . . which obeys the rules of *logical* grammar—of logical syntax."

5. See Ferré 1961.

6. See also Ackermann, 129–32; Ayer, 61–73; Baker and Hacker 1985, 25–228; Cook 1994, 286–315; Fogelin 1987, 159–81; Garver 1994, 42–60; 201–8; 223–32; Hacker 1989, 247–55; Hallett 1977, 239–305; Hanfling, 146–51; Hardwick 1971; Holtzman and Leich 1981; Kenny 1973, 161–78; Malcolm 1986, 154–81; Schulte 1992, 115–28.

The Private Language Argument

The private language argument is strewn about a series of remarks in Wittgenstein's *Philosophical Investigations*. Wittgenstein
denies advancing any philosophical theses, yet appears to argue for
the substantive philosophical conclusion that a private sensation
language is impossible.[1] There is disagreement about what Wittgenstein means by a private language, and about whether Wittgenstein offers an argument concerning the impossibility of private
language, and if so about the exact structure and overall significance of the private language argument in Wittgenstein's later
philosophy.[2]

What is more universally accepted is that Wittgenstein's rejection of private language depends on the requirement that the
naming of objects satisfy 'criteria of correctness', a condition he
claims cannot be met in the case of private sensations. Wittgenstein's concept of criteria of correctness implements what he takes
to be an essential rule of naming language games. The philosophical grammar of naming entails that to name means always to designate the same thing by the same term. We can see this by
contrasting names with definite descriptions. The word 'Ringo',
insofar as it functions as a proper name, must refer to the same
individual on every occasion of its use. The definite description,
'The winner and new champion . . .', on the other hand, in each
application presumably refers to a different individual. If two or
more things are named 'Ringo', then, except where specific reference to an individual is contextually understood, 'Ringo' does not
function as a proper name. Wittgenstein shows that what might
be called the 'Same thing, same name' rule, arguably the main
part of the philosophical grammar of naming or naming language
games, implies that there can be no private language in which

private objects are named, and therefore no language in which objects are privately named.[3]

The private language argument in Wittgenstein's *Philosophical Investigations* is one of the most celebrated parts of the book. More ink has been spilled trying to understand, refute, and defend it than any other single topic in Wittgenstein's later philosophy. What is important about the argument for our purposes is that it brings us back round to the problem of naming, with a refutation of the idea that naming might take place by internal psychological ostension or private mental pointing. The most fundamental question the private language argument addresses is that with which Wittgenstein's investigations begins, the problem of how names name. Wittgenstein considers a family of naming language games, from which he concludes that we cannot privately name, and that there can be no private language of privately named private mental objects. The philosophical grammar of naming precludes private language as impossible, because there are no criteria of correctness for verifying even in principle whether the same private mental name is being used to refer to the same object, let alone the same private mental object, in a private-sensation-naming language game. This makes it impossible privately to observe the 'Same thing, same name' naming rule.

The private language argument eliminates the possibility of naming by private psychological ostension or private mental pointing. This, along with Wittgenstein's earlier rejection of pure body movement or behavioral ostension, does away with the spiritual as well as purely bodily explanations of naming and of the meaning of names, mentioned in §36. The argument thereby clears the way for Wittgenstein's instrumentalist theory of language, and of naming as understandable only in connection with the essential rules of naming language games, determined by its point or purpose in a form of life. The three categories of philosophical semantic principles Wittgenstein considers in the later philosophy are body, spirit, and action. The body alone, as Wittgenstein's criticism of the underdetermination of reference in Augustine's ostensive account is supposed to show, cannot explain naming. Spirit as an internal psychological ostension or private mental pointing is refuted by the private language argument. By eliminating body and spirit as explanations of naming, Wittgenstein's argument leaves action as the only alternative. Action is not merely body movement, but purposive behavior. Language as an activity is part of a larger form of life that gives particular speech acts their point or purpose, without which the essential rules of their philosophical grammars cannot be discerned. The

276 I CHAPTER TWELVE

actions that many different kinds of linguistic tools permit us to perform in language game play are interconnected in Wittgenstein's later instrumentalist account of language with the extralinguistic actions that constitute a form of life as the extrasemantic praxeological foundations of semantics.[4]

Wittgenstein's private language argument eliminates the possibility of spirit as a philosophical explanation of meaning. The impossibility of a private language in which private mental objects are privately named defeats the theory of naming by internal psychological ostension or private mental pointing. To explain the private language argument and its role in refuting the spiritual account of naming, we must first try to clarify how Wittgenstein understands the philosophical grammar of naming language games. Wittgenstein asks:

> 244. How do words *refer* to sensations?—There doesn't seem to be any problem here; don't we talk about sensations every day, and give them names? But how is the connexion between the name and the thing named set up? This question is the same as: how does a human being learn the meaning of the names of sensations? —of the word "pain" for example . . .

As a thought experiment, we are to imagine a diarist using a private sensation language to record recurring pains. The diarist annotates sensations in a symbolism that cannot be translated or decoded into a public language, but that only the diarist as first-person experiencer can understand.[5] Wittgenstein argues that, despite appearances, the conceptual requirements for naming sensations presupposed by a private sensation language are unsatisfiable. From this he concludes, contrary to the thought experiment's assumption, that there cannot be a private sensations diary written in a private sensation language. He appears at first to dispute the privacy of sensation even prior to launching the private language argument:

> 246. In what sense are my sensations *private?*—Well, only I can know whether I am really in pain; another person can only surmise it.—In one way this is wrong, and in another nonsense. If we are using the word "to know" as it is normally used (and how else are we to use it?), then other people very often know when I am in pain.—Yes, but all the same not with the certainty with which I know it myself!—It can't be said of me at all (except perhaps as a joke) that I *know* I am in pain. What is it supposed to mean—except perhaps that I *am* in pain?
> Other people cannot be said to learn of my sensations *only* from my behaviour,—for *I* cannot be said to learn of them. I *have* them.

> The truth is: it makes sense to say about other people that
> they doubt whether I am in pain; but not to say it about myself.

Yet Wittgenstein on examination does not question the existence or the privacy of sensations. His point is rather that the philosophical grammar of the epistemic evaluation terms 'know' and
'doubt' are involved in a kind of implicational modal polarity, by
which if it makes no sense to say that something can be doubted,
then similarly it makes no sense to say that it can be known.[6]
When Wittgenstein appears to deny the privacy of sensation
in §246, he is only denying that sensations are private in the
sense that only the person experiencing the sensation can know
or know with certainty that the sensation is occurring or know or
know with certainty the particular content or quality of the sensation. This is unintelligible because of the knowing-doubting
polarity. It is an essential philosophical grammatical rule for the
language game of describing sensations that if it makes no sense
to say that I doubt whether or not I am in pain, then it makes no
sense to say that I know I am in pain. By virtue of the fact that
others from a third-person perspective can doubt whether I am in
pain, it follows by the same reasoning involving the same rule
that they rather than I can know that I am in pain. The argument
seems to entail only the impossibility of having defeasible first-
person knowledge of private sensations, since it is certainty by
definition rather than defeasible knowledge that logically excludes the possibility of doubt. The knowing-doubting polarity
rule in that case need not contradict the possibility of knowledge
of first-person mental states, if, as some philosophers after Descartes believe, introspection yields absolutely certain incorrigible
knowledge of mental occurrence and content.[7]
The argument at best does not contradict the privacy of sensation, but only the epistemology of privileged knowledge of private sensation. Wittgenstein seems to regard it as a tautology or
analytic truth that sensations are private. He makes a crucial
point about the philosophical grammar in what he takes to be the
essential rules for proper language game use of the terms 'private' and 'sensation', according to which sensations are necessarily private:

> 248. The proposition "Sensations are private" is comparable to:
> "One plays patience [the card game of solitaire] by oneself".

The question is whether there can be a language game in
which particular private sensations are named in a private sensation language. A private language is a language that can be
understood only by the person who privately names a privately

experienced sensation. Privacy is supposed to hold not merely by virtue of the name user's keeping the name's designation or manner of designation a secret from other language users, but in the sense that no one other than the individual who tries to privately name private sensations can possibly understand the meanings of private sensation names. If such a thing is even possible, it implies the private language designation of a private sensation by a private language private sensation name in a private sensation language game:

> 256. Now, what about the language which describes my inner experiences and which only I myself can understand? *How* do I use words to stand for my sensations?—As we ordinarily do? Then are my words for sensations tied up with my natural expressions of sensation? In that case my language is not a 'private' one. Someone else might understand it as well as I.—But suppose I didn't have any natural expression for the sensation, but only had the sensation? And now I simply *associate* names with sensations and use these names in descriptions.—

The idea that naming can occur merely by one-one association of name and object recalls the *Tractatus* oversimplification of the semantics of naming. Wittgenstein's private language argument finally obliterates all hope of avoiding the problem of naming by transcendental reasoning. After criticizing the Augustinian ostension or 'body' type of theory, Wittgenstein in the private language argument turns his attention to the 'spirit' component of the body-spirit dichotomy of §36. The private language argument cuts off the only remaining possibility of rescuing a theory of naming with a much-revised *Tractatus*-type logic, logical atomist metaphysics, and picture theory semantics. The *'geistiges'* ('spiritual') approach to the theory of naming is refuted by Wittgenstein's criticisms of the concept of a private language. If there can be no private language, then there can be no private spiritual naming. If sensation is private, it would appear that an otherwise linguistically competent sensation subject could name particular sensations simply by associating with them a special term or symbol. This would constitute a private naming of private sensations that no one other than the private name user could possibly understand. We might think of it as occurring concretely in thought or expressed by use of language signs or abstractly in the transcendent order of symbols. The reason no one else could understand the private sensation language is that if sensation is private, then no one other than the private name user can possibly have the same experiences by which a name is privately associated with a privately experienced sensation. Wittgenstein undermines all of these assumptions in a single stroke when he disproves the possibility of a private sensation language.

Wittgenstein first raises the pragmatic question of the point or purpose of the private naming of private sensations. He inquires counterfactually about what the world and our language would have to be like if there were no external indications of private sensations by which they could be publicly named and described. He concludes that in that case there could be no public language of private sensation, no words whatsoever in any human language game for pains or pleasures. Wittgenstein considers the objection that it might nevertheless occur to an unusually gifted person to make up a word by analogy with public language terms in order privately to designate a particular private sensation. No such word with a privately intended meaning could possibly be understood by any other language user. What then of the point or purpose of privately naming private sensations? If there is none, as Wittgenstein finally concludes, then there is no private sensation language game for privately naming private sensations in any imaginable form of life:

> 257. "What would it be like if human beings shewed no outward signs of pain (did not groan, grimace, etc.)? Then it would be impossible to teach a child the use of the word 'tooth-ache'."—Well, let's assume the child is a genius and itself invents a name for the sensation!—But then, of course, he couldn't make himself understood when he used the word.—So does he understand the name, without being able to explain its meaning to anyone?—But what does it mean to say that he has 'named his pain'?—How has he done this naming of pain?! And whatever he did, what was its purpose?—When one says "He gave a name to his sensation" one forgets that a great deal of stage-setting in the language is presupposed if the mere act of naming is to make sense. And when we speak of someone's having given a name to pain, what is presupposed is the existence of the grammar of the word "pain"; it shews the post where the new word is stationed.

The naive expectation is that naming a particular private mental occurrence is easy to accomplish. A private sensation occurs, it is intimately known only in the immediate private experience of the individual psychological subject. The subject then decides to designate it by a private sensation name 'S', which no one else by virtue of the privacy of the experience and of its being privately named can possibly understand.

Wittgenstein continues his criticism of the possibility of private naming by considering a fictional language game in which a plausible purpose is attributed to ostensible acts of privately naming private sensations. Wittgenstein imagines himself privately experiencing a pain of which he wants to keep a record by writing in a diary of private sensations, using a private sensation name always to designate the same particular private pain sensation whenever it recurs:

> 258. Let us imagine the following case. I want to keep a diary about the recurrence of a certain sensation. To this end I associate it with the sign "S" and write this sign in a calendar for every day on which I have the sensation.—I will remark first of all that a definition of the sign cannot be formulated.—But still I can give myself a kind of ostensive definition.—How? Can I point to the sensation? Not in the ordinary sense. But I speak, or write the sign down, and at the same time I concentrate my attention on the sensation—and so, as it were, point to it inwardly. —But what is this ceremony for? for that is all it seems to be! A definition surely serves to establish the meaning of a sign.—Well, that is done precisely by the concentrating of my attention; for in this way I impress on myself the connexion between the sign and the sensation.—But "I impress it on myself" can only mean: this process brings it about that I remember the connexion *right* in the future. But in the present case I have no criterion of correctness. One would like to say: whatever is going to seem right to me is right. And that only means that here we can't talk about 'right'.

Again, the naming of the private sensation is supposed to take place merely by 'associating' a sign with a particular privately recurring sensation. Such a sign cannot be defined, as Wittgenstein remarks. If it were, then it would be possible for another language user to understand the definition, contrary to the assumption that the sign is used privately to name a particular private pain sensation in such a way that no one else can possibly understand its privately determined meaning.

Wittgenstein argues that while the supposedly private language sign 'S' cannot be defined in the ordinary sense as naming a particular private sensation, it might yet be privately defined. Even if it is an essential rule of the philosophical grammar of naming in ordinary naming language games that the meaning of names be definable or at least in some way explicable, the private sensation naming language game might have different rules. We might think, unless or until we prove otherwise, that private sensation names are privately defined, not externally by behavioral ostension, but internally or 'spiritually' by a private psychological ostension or private mental pointing. The private name user defines the private sensation name by concentrating his attention on how the sensation feels at the same that he writes down the private sensation name in the private sensations diary. The focusing of introspection is supposed to impress on the memory precisely what the sensation is like, so that the next time it is encountered the name user is able to recognize it and use the same name in referring to precisely the same pain. Wittgenstein rejects this suggestion in his remarks on private language, and with it the possibility of privately naming private sensations in a private sensation naming language game.

Concentrating attention on the experience while trying to give it a name accomplishes nothing. Wittgenstein dismisses the attempt to associate a sensation with a name as a mere ceremony that serves no useful purpose in any language game. An internal psychological ostension or private mental pointing is supposed to enable the private name user to remember correctly the same particular pain when it recurs, so as to be able to use the same name to designate precisely the same pain on later occasions. This requirement is so firmly a part of the philosophical grammar of naming and so essential a rule of naming language games that we do not speak of naming something unless we suppose that the same name can be used to designate the same object whenever it is used. The concept of a rule that is followed only once is meaningless, as Wittgenstein argues in §§199-202. If the private sensation diarist privately names a private sensation by writing sign 'S' in the diary, then it must be possible to use the same private name repeatedly for the same private object. The private sensation name user must therefore be able correctly to identify the same particular private sensation if and when it recurs in subsequent pain episodes. But the requirement that the very same sensation be correctly remembered for future applications can never be satisfied. There can be no criteria of correctness by which actual recurrences of the same object are confirmed as distinct from what the subject may merely believe or have the psychologically convincing impression is the same previously experienced private sensation:

> 259. Are the rules of the private language *impressions* of rules?—The balance on which impressions are weighed is not the *impression* of a balance.
>
> 260. "Well, I *believe* that this is sensation S again."—Perhaps you *believe* that you believe it!
>
> Then did the man who made the entry in the calendar make a note of *nothing whatsoever?*—Don't consider it a matter of course that a person is making a note of something when he makes a mark—say in a calendar. For a note has a function, and this "S" so far has none.

(One can talk to oneself.—If a person speaks when no one
else is present, does that mean he is speaking to himself?)

The objection returns to Wittgenstein's remark in §202, that
merely "to *think* one is obeying a rule is not to obey a rule," from
which he concludes, "Hence, it is not possible to obey a rule 'privately': otherwise thinking one was obeying a rule would be the
same thing as obeying it."

Criteria of correctness are reliable practical procedures by
which any name user can determine in principle when the same
numerically identical object is correctly reidentified and referred
to by the same name on different occasions. There must be criteria of correctness to distinguish situations in which a putative
name user actually follows the naming language game rule always to use the same name for the same thing, from those in
which a person merely thinks or believes himself to be following
the rule. If this condition is not satisfied, then putative name users are not really naming, but only going through the motions of
naming. The requirement that there be criteria of correctness is
an essential rule of naming language games as Wittgenstein understands the philosophical grammar of 'name' and 'naming' for
anything that might be named.

Wittgenstein concludes that there can be criteria of correctness only in naming public particulars, such as a subject's body
or the Eiffel Tower. For these, there is always a way of deciding
whether the same name is used on different occasions to refer to
precisely the same object. Wittgenstein assumes that in such
cases we can distinguish actually following the rule from merely
believing that we are following it by checking up in various ways
on the object's public spatiotemporal continuity. In trying to
name particular private sensations, by contrast, there are no criteria of correctness. There is no test, independent of my belief
that I am following the rule always to use the same name for the
same pain, by which I can determine whether I am actually following the rule, or merely believe that I am doing so.[8]

An internal private psychological ostension or private mental pointing is supposed to impress on memory precisely what the
particular private sensation is like, so that a private name user
can use the same name to refer to precisely the same particular
private sensation if and when it recurs. There can in that case be
no practical distinction between actually following and merely
believing that one is following the rule. It is the belief itself that
stands in need of a criterion of correctness, the belief that the
same sensation has recurred. But in deciding whether or not it is
precisely the same sensation that has recurred, the private name

user can only appeal to the vividness of the belief as testimony to the identity of its content with that of a previously experienced sensation. The belief that the 'Same thing, same name' naming language game rule is actually being followed would have to justify itself, with no possibility of being overruled as mistaken by any independent check:

> 261. What reason have we for calling "S" the sign for a *sensation?* For "sensation" is a word of our common language, not of one intelligible to me alone. So the use of this word stands in need of a justification which everybody understands. — And it would not help either to say that it need not be a *sensation;* that when he writes "S", he has *something* — and that is all that can be said. "Has" and "something" also belong to our common language. — So in the end when one is doing philosophy one gets to the point where one would like just to emit an inarticulate sound. — But such a sound is an expression only as it occurs in a particular language-game, which should now be described.

If I am a private sensation diarist, then I have no reliable way to confirm that I have correctly reidentified the very same recurring sensation, or merely a similar but strictly different sensation. In the latter situation, I will not have followed the 'Same pain, same name' sensation particulars naming rule. I will merely believe that I am following it, because I merely believe that the same sensation has recurred. As a putative private name user, I can only rely on belief in the form of impression and memory. But if this is my only resource, then I am limited to the closed circle of my beliefs in whatever identity test I may try to apply. If mere belief cannot be verified or disproved by something beyond or outside itself, then in Wittgenstein's sense there are no criteria of correctness for naming private sensations. If criteria of correctness are required for naming particular private sensations, but are strictly unavailable, then private sensations cannot be named, and in that sense there cannot be a private sensation language.[9]

The private naming of a private sensation is supposed to be incommunicable. The description of the private sensation diarist's putative private sensation sign 'S' as naming a sensation may already be going too far, since 'sensation' is a public language expression. Nor does the problem disappear if we try to speak instead of the private sensation name user as referring more generally to an 'experience', 'psychological occurrence', or even to say that the name user 'has something' when the name is used. Any such words or phrases are part of our ordinary language by which private psychological sensations are publicly named and described, and therefore seem equally beyond the limits of a private sensation language. Wittgenstein concludes that out of desperation we are tempted at this stage in doing philosophy simply to utter an inarticulate sound. Only such an outcry will have no prior established role in a public language game, and might therefore be used to try to say what must be strictly publicly unsayable about the privately experienced properties of private mental objects. We are better off grunting 'Aarghh . . .', as an expression of primal frustration at the inability to say anything substantive about the meaning of a putative private sensation name, than lapsing into the domain of public language by saying what may appear at first to be so semantically harmless and ontically neutral as that a private name user is experiencing something or that a private sensation name user uses a private sensation name when the name user has or experiences 'something'. Yet to limit ourselves to inarticulate grunts is not likely to advance our understanding of the concepts of naming and private sensation in philosophical psychology and semantics.

What is important is that in §261 Wittgenstein distinguishes names for 'a' putatively particular private sensation from public language terms for generic experiences like 'sensation', together with such publicly understood auxiliary expressions as 'has' and 'something'. Sign 'S', on the contrary, cannot have any public meaning. But this conclusion of the private language argument holds only if 'S' is supposed to designate a particular recurrent private sensation, an individual mental object, and not a generic sensation type or kind like 'pain', 'sharp pain', or 'sensation'. If 'S' names a sensation type or kind, then it must "belong to our common language," where it functions as a public sensation predicate, rather than as a private sensation name. This is what leads Wittgenstein half-seriously to consider the idea of replacing such terms with an inarticulate sound, a dummy variable with no prior public language connotations. Yet even this inarticulate primal squawk, he admits, could only advance philosophical discussion if its pragmatic surroundings or stage-setting in a particular language game were first described, whereby a public meaning is attached.[10]

Wittgenstein reinforces the need for and unavailability of criteria of correctness in the attempt to name private sensations in the private sensation diary language game by comparing the limitations of private naming with public language games. There must be a way of distinguishing in practice between correctly re-identifying the same private sensation and merely believing that one has done so. The limitations of relying on belief as the only possible criterion for the correctness of the same or another belief is caricatured in some of Wittgenstein's most memorable analogies. He argues:

> 265. Let us imagine a table (something like a dictionary) that exists only in our imagination. A dictionary can be used to justify the translation of a word X by a word Y. But are we also to call it a justification if such a table is to be looked up only in the imagination?—"Well, yes; then it is a subjective justification."—But justification consists in appealing to something independent.—"But surely I can appeal from one memory to another. For example, I don't know if I have remembered the time of departure of a train right and to check it I call to mind how a page of the time-table looked. Isn't it the same here?"—No; for this process has got to produce a memory which is actually *correct*. If the mental image of the time-table could not itself be *tested* for correctness, how could it confirm the correctness of the first memory? (As if someone were to buy several copies of the morning paper to assure himself that what it said was true.)
>
> Looking up a table in the imagination is no more looking up a table than the image of the result of an imagined experiment is the result of an experiment.

Wittgenstein's private language argument has direct implications only for the impossibility of naming particular private sensations. The private language argument leaves the question open whether there can be a language game involving generic public sensation predicates for publicly describing private sensation kinds or types. If higher manometer readings happen to correlate with the diary keeper's use of sign 'S', then the sign can be used as evidence of increasing blood pressure in the absence of the manometer:

> 270. Let us now imagine a use for the entry of the sign "S" in my diary. I discover that whenever I have a particular sensation a manometer shews that my blood-pressure rises. So I shall be able to say that my blood-pressure is rising without using any apparatus. This is a useful result. And now it seems quite indifferent whether I have recognized the sensation *right* or not. Let us suppose I regularly identify it wrong, it does not matter in the least. And that alone shews that the hypothesis that I make a mistake is mere show. (We as it were turned a knob which looked as if it could be used to turn on some part of the machine; but it was a mere ornament, not connected with the mechanism at all.)
>
> And what is our reason for calling "S" the name of a sensation here? Perhaps the kind of way this sign is employed in this language-game.—And why a "particular sensation," that is, the same one very time? Well, aren't we supposing that we write "S" every time?

The idea is to invent a pragmatic context for a private sensations diary. It might be useful, Wittgenstein states, to keep track of the recurrence of a private sensation if the sensation were correlated with manometer measurements. This would make it possible to determine blood pressure increase without the manometer. Wittgenstein then denies that the usefulness of the sign requires that the sensation be correctly identified. This is puzzling at first, because, if the particular private sensation is not correctly identified, then the correlation that is supposed to justify the private sensation sign as evidence of increasing blood pressure without the manometer seems to lack foundation.

By the manometer argument in §§270-271, Wittgenstein eliminates the possibility of a pragmatic or instrumentalist defense of the possibility of a private sensation language. He holds that the apparent use of sign 'S' as the name of a particular sensation is misleading. Relying on the occurrence of sensation signs in the diary is just as effective in determining blood pressure, even if it is not exactly the same particular recurring sensation identified on separate occasions, but other, so to speak, S-like sensations, provided only that they coincide with blood pressure fluctuations measurable (perhaps counterfactually) by the manometer. That is, Wittgenstein regards sign 'S', which is supposed (for purposes of reductio ad absurdum) to name a particular private sensation, as functioning in the manometer example not as a private sensation name but as a public sensation predicate. What sign 'S' actually does in place of the manometer does not prove that 'S' is a name, because its service is equally explained as a generic type or kind term for the members of a class of sensations, indistinguishably collected by a single predicate term by virtue of their common dispositional correlation with public manometer readings.

This is what Wittgenstein means when he writes in §270: "And now it seems quite indifferent whether I have recognized the sensation right or not. Let us suppose I regularly identify it wrong, it does not matter in the least." He claims that it makes no practical difference in our use of sign 'S' as a substitute for manometer readings whether or not we have correctly reidentified recurrences of the same numerically identical particular private sensation. The utility of using 'S' in the diary as a linguistic blood pressure gauge is equally served, not by supposing that 'S' names a particular recurring private sensation, but that it functions as a publicly definable predicate for a class of numerically distinct sensations, the occurrence of any one of which is as good as any other in indicating blood pressure increase in the absence of the manometer. If the practical payoff for naming sensations obtains equally on the assumption that similar kinds of sensations rather than numerically identical particulars are designated by 'S', then there is no pragmatic justification for supposing that 'S' names a particular as opposed to a type or kind of similar sensation. It is pointless from a pragmatic or instrumentalist point of view in that case to try assigning names to pains and other sensations as particulars, because the pragmatic use of the sign as a substitute manometer does not require 'S' to be a name.

To interpret 'S' as the name of a particular sensation as opposed to a predicate subsuming individually indistinguishable private sensations with a common public manifestation makes no practical difference in using the sensation diary as a paper and pencil blood pressure gauge. The naming of particular private sensations has, after all, no pragmatically justifiable use, and as such constitutes what Wittgenstein likes to call a useless gesture or idle ceremony. "(We as it were turned a knob which looked as if it could be used to turn on some part of the machine; but it was a mere ornament, not connected with the mechanism at all.)" (§270)

The pragmatic rationale for keeping a 'private' sensations diary at most justifies a public sensation predicate for a class of similar sensations in principle with publicly observable manifestations, not a private sensation name or sign for a particular private sensation in a private sensation language. Wittgenstein concludes the manometer example on the same note, with another reference to the literal pragmatic uselessness of pretending by the application of a term privately to name a private mental object when the term actually functions as a public psychological predicate:

> 271. "Imagine a person whose memory could not retain *what* the word 'pain' meant—so that he constantly called different things by that name—but nevertheless used the word in a way fitting in with the usual symptoms and presuppositions of pain"—in short he uses it as we all do. Here I should like to say: a wheel that can be turned though nothing else moves with it, is not part of the mechanism.

It follows that insofar as sign 'S' has a pragmatic role in a language game, it functions as a term for a kind of sensation, rather than as the name of a particular sensation, where the diarist "constantly call[s] different things by that name." Then the pragmatic justification for sign 'S' does not legitimize its use as the name of a particular private sensation, but at most as a generic public sensation kind or type.

What fails to move the machinery, the ornament that is not really connected with the mechanism, is the assumption that a mistake is made in designating the same particular. It is as though, had it turned out that a different sensation strictly non-identical to the first was designated by 'S', then this would somehow affect the use of the sign in predicting blood pressure increase. But the machine is unaffected. The hypothesis that the sensation as a particular private object is regularly wrongly identified in substituting the private sensations diary for the manometer does nothing whatsoever to alter its effect, even if numerically distinct but sufficiently S-like sensations correlated with public manometer readings were all 'mistakenly' designated by 'S' as a private language name for the same recurring particular private pain.

It is only in this way that it can be a matter of (pragmatic) indifference whether the sensation is regularly wrongly identified as a particular private sensation ostensibly named 'S'. Although the sensations by hypothesis are different, they are correlated with an increase in blood pressure as indicated by the manometer while it is still in place. By analogy, this is what it would be like if the person described in §271 could not remember what the generic sensation term 'pain' meant, and constantly referred to different things by the word, yet it made no difference in ordinary pragmatic contexts because the person "used the word in a way fitting in with the usual symptoms and presuppositions of pain." This is at most an analogy for Wittgenstein, either because the generic word 'pain' as a public sensation type or kind term has acceptable criteria of correctness by which rule-following in principle can be distinguished from merely thinking that one is rule-following, or because the philosophical grammar for the language game of describing sensations by predicates as opposed to naming particulars does not require criteria of correctness.

The diary sign 'S' fails to name a recurrent particular sensation without making any difference to its usefulness in tracking blood pressure increase. Although the diarist does not realize it, 'S' functions by referring to numerically different things of a similar type. The first part of §271 is placed in quotations, indicating that it may be the response of Wittgenstein's imaginary interlocutor to the rhetorical question posed at the end of §270. Wittgenstein had asked what reason there could be in the manometer case for calling 'S' the *name* of a particular private sensation. Here he demands: "And why a 'particular sensation,' that is, the same one every time? Well, aren't we supposing that we write 'S' every time?" The use of the same sign is not enough to guarantee that naming has taken place or that a "particular sensation" is designated. From a pragmatic or instrumentalist standpoint, the most that can be inferred is the existence of a generic kind or type of sensation that regularly occurs in conjunction with an increase in blood pressure, but not necessarily with a particular recurring private sensation ("the same one every time"). The manometer example shows that sensation terms function as public predicates for generic sensation types or kinds even when we think we are using them as private sensation names referring to particular private sensations.

A polarity principle now comes into play. If there is no pragmatic difference between mistakenly identifying the same private sensation as a particular recurring object, then it makes no sense in the manometer case to say that sensation S is wrongly reidentified. The philosophical grammar of reidentification implies a correct-mistaken polarity similar to the knowing-doubting polarity, whereby if S cannot be wrongly reidentified, then it also cannot be rightly or correctly reidentified. Thus, there is no pragmatic justification for correct tokenings of diary sign 'S' as the name of a particular private sensation.[11]

The argument implicit in Wittgenstein's discussion of the manometer problem can be reconstructed in this way:

1. Suppose (for purposes of indirect proof) that in a number of situations I experience a recurring particular private sensation S and record it in my diary.

2. Suppose that on the occasions described in (1) a manometer reading indicates an increase in my blood pressure.

3. Then I can do away with the manometer, and determine an increase in blood pressure by the recurrence of S as recorded in the diary.

4. But for this purpose it does not matter whether S regularly is correctly or incorrectly identified *as a recurring particular* (provided that *some* (so-to-speak *S-like*) experience occurs on each such occasion; it is sufficient for the experience of any number of individually indistinguishable private sensations to coincide with an increase in blood pressure counterfactually measured by the manometer; they will thereby belong to the extension of the public sensation predicate 'S' by virtue of sharing the same relevant publicly distinguishable properties).

5.   Therefore, I cannot be mistaken in (mis-) identifying S as a particular private sensation (the 'hypothesis' in (4) that I am mistaken is "mere show").

6.   By the correct-mistaken modal polarity principle implied by the philosophical grammar of 'reidentify', it follows that if I cannot be mistaken, then I cannot also even in principle be correct in identifying S as a particular private sensation, contrary to the assumption in (1).

The logic of Wittgenstein's private language argument establishes the philosophical grammar of naming particulars. The essential rules of any naming language game require criteria of correctness. There is a right way for each of the many instruments of language to do its job. Wittgenstein believes that criteria of correctness are available for publicly naming any public object, but not for privately naming any private mental object. The private language argument can thus be understood as a reductio ad absurdum of the assumption that there can be a private sensation language. A private language in Wittgenstein's sense implies that private sensation particulars can be named. Particulars can be named only if there are criteria of correctness for their reidentification. There are criteria of correctness for all and only publicly nameable public entities, and not for private mental objects. As a result, private sensation particulars cannot be named and there can be no private sensation language.[12]

The effect of Wittgenstein's private language argument is to refute the explanation of naming as an internal psychological ostension or private mental pointing. The 'spiritual' approach to naming is ruled out by the consideration that sensation particulars cannot be privately named if the philosophical grammar of naming requires criteria of correctness, and if criteria of correctness are necessarily unavailable in the case of private sensations. But how does the private language argument show this? What is the connection between the private language argument and the failure of internal psychological ostension or private mental pointing as an inadequate account of naming? Wittgenstein's discussion leaves us dangling precisely here, and we can proceed only by trying to connect the dots in the incomplete argument he has sketched.

The best way to fill in the blanks is by interpreting pain as a particular example of a private experience from which Wittgenstein draws a more general moral about the impossibility of naming by private mental pointing or internal psychological ostension. The private language argument precludes naming by internal psychological ostension or private mental pointing because it (supposedly) shows that private experiences like mentally pointing to an object cannot constitute namings. It does this (supposedly) by showing that we cannot follow the generalized 'Same thing, same name' naming rule. And it does this (supposedly, on the present account) by showing that we cannot satisfy the requirement of knowing as opposed to merely believing on distinct occasions that we are using the same name or naming the same object by means of the same name, if naming is itself an unnameable private psychological occurrence of private psychological ostension or private mental pointing.

The analysis completes Wittgenstein's argument against naming as an internal psychological ostension or private mental pointing by maintaining that private sensations are not sufficiently identifiable to constitute names or namings in applying the 'Same pain, same name' rule. The problem is not just that pains will not hold still, so that we cannot be sure when have the same pain to which we can then apply the same name. Rather, the fact is that private mental pointings or private psychological ostensions construed as namings will not hold still, so that we cannot be sure when we have the same name to apply to pains and other private sensations, or to any other object, public or private. Thus, the hypothesis offered to complete this part of Wittgenstein's criticism focuses on the second of two components (sameness of pain and sameness of name) of the 'Same pain, same name' equation in explaining Wittgenstein's objections to internal psychological ostension or private mental pointing as an inadequate theory of naming.

Far from concluding that thought is not private, the proposed interpretation of Wittgenstein's private language argument presupposes the privacy of sensation. If sensation is not private, then there is no failure of naming private sensations by private mental pointing or private psychological ostension, nor can strictly unre-identifiable private mental pointings or internal psychological ostensions fail as satisfactory namings. Wittgenstein's private language argument offers no support to reductivism in the cognitive sciences as against phenomenology. Wittgenstein's interest in the private language argument is linguistic and semantic rather than ontological; it is about language and the limitations of language, which is always his central concern, rather than the nature of mind.[13]

The language game of naming particulars in Wittgenstein's account of the rules of its philosophical grammar requires criteria of correctness for reidentifying and attributing the same name to the same entity on different occasions, without which there is no point and indeed no utility, and hence, on the instrumentalist 'meaning is use' doctrine of the later philosophy, no pragmatic semantic justification, for concluding that the same particular is named. The peculiar nature of private sensation implies there can be no criteria of correctness for distinguishing instances when the rule always to use the same name for the same particular is actually followed in the case of private sensation particulars, as opposed to a subject's merely believing that the naming rule has been observed. This again is because whatever 'mental' or 'internal' evidence might be offered to confirm or disconfirm the correct following of the rule will belong to the self-enclosed circle of the subject's thoughts, and as such is dependent on rather than providing an independent check on the subject's belief that the rule is correctly followed. It is like comparing multiple copies of the same newspaper to determine if a story printed in it is true.[14]

When Wittgenstein criticizes the idea of a private language, he means to reject the possibility that there could be a language game in which private sensations are designated as particulars, as individual recurring reidentifiable things. This is different from and not meant to contradict the possibility that there are general terms for private sensations, which, in predicating generic types or kinds of sensations, are public rather than private. This divides Wittgenstein's relatively permissive thinking about sensation from his more stringent thinking about sensation language. That sensation is private is a redundancy or analytic truth. Particular sensations cannot be named, because private occurrences necessarily lack criteria of correctness. Sensation is private (which is to say only that sensation is sensation), but there can exist no genuine language game in which private sensations are designated as particulars.[15]

Wittgenstein in §49 and elsewhere explains naming as a preparation for description. Although he targets this thesis in his sustained critique of logical atomism and the picture theory of meaning, he also seems to see an element of truth in its way of organizing the tasks of language use. He finds it natural to turn from the impossibility of a private language of privately named private sensations to a parallel treatment of the impossibility of privately describing private sensations in a private sensation language. This appears in his famous example of the beetle in the box. Wittgenstein acknowledges a potential ambiguity even in language games describing ordinary physical objects.

290. What I do is not, of course, to identify my sensation by criteria: but to repeat an expression. But this is not the *end* of the language-game: it is the beginning.

But isn't the beginning the sensation—which I describe?— Perhaps this word "describe" tricks us here. I say "I describe my state of mind" and "I describe my room". You need to call to mind the differences between the language-games.

Wittgenstein begins by drawing on the conclusions of the previous discussion of private language. The impossibility of privately naming private sensations also has implications for privately describing them. We use a similar turn of phrase in describing physical objects, like the contents of a room, and the mental contents of thought, as though these too could be contained in a private Cartesian receptacle. Wittgenstein recommends that we look critically at this assimilation of expressions to see if they do not disguise quite different philosophical grammars.

291. What we call *"descriptions"* are instruments for particular uses. Think of a machine-drawing, a cross-section, an elevation with measurements, which an engineer has before him. Thinking of a description as a word-picture of the facts has something misleading about it: one tends to think only of such pictures as hang on our walls: which seem simply to portray how a thing looks, what it is like. (These pictures are as it were idle.)

292. Don't always think that you read off what you say from the facts; that you portray these in words according to rules. For even so you would have to apply the rule in the particular case without guidance.

We have a tendency to regard the description of mental states by a false analogy. Wittgenstein reminds us of the ordinary meaning of 'description' as an instrument for practical purposes. We describe the workings of a machine by giving a blueprint that may show the relation of its parts in cross-section, or a topographic map that describes a particular geography with conventions for elevation measurements, a physical entity that encodes information. Wittgenstein resists this analogy as inadequate for phenomenology, because he finds descriptions in the ordinary sense to be static, lifeless, and 'idle', something to be framed and hung on a wall, by contrast with the living dynamic contents of thought and language.

The point of §292 seems to be to break the grip of the analogy between ordinary description and what might otherwise be thought to occur in attempts to describe the private contents of mental states. Wittgenstein observes that we should not take it for granted that we proceed in the same way in the two kinds of 'description'. It is too simplistic to suppose that we can transcribe the facts directly into language according to definite rules. He reminds us that in any case the rules do not guarantee their own correct application. For description language games in particular we lack guidance for correctly applying the essential rules of their philosophical grammar. This remark floats in the air until Wittgenstein offers a more concrete illustration in the following paragraph. He claims that we can have no rule for the public description of private mental states. He draws an analogy between the attempt to give a private phenomenological description of the contents of a state of consciousness with the contents of a box, which he refers to as its 'beetle'. He stipulates that each box owner is to have privileged epistemic access to look into the box and try to describe its beetle:

> 293. If I say of myself that it is only from my own case that I know what the word "pain" means—must I not say the same of other people too? And how can I generalize the *one* case so irresponsibly?
>
> Now someone tells me that *he* knows what pain is only from his own case!—Suppose everyone had a box with something in it: we call it a "beetle". No one can look into anyone else's box, and everyone says he knows what a beetle is only by looking at *his* beetle.—Here it would be quite possible for everyone to have something different in his box. One might even imagine such a thing constantly changing.—But suppose the word "beetle" had a use in these people's language?—If so it would not be used as the name of a thing. The thing in the box has no place in the language-game at all; not even as a *something:* for the box might even be empty.—No, one can 'divide through' by the thing in the box; it cancels out, whatever it is.
>
> That is to say, if we construe the grammar of the expression of sensation on the model of 'object and designation' the object drops out of consideration as irrelevant.

When I speak of what my box contains, I use the code word 'beetle'. I try to describe what my beetle is like in terms of the properties it has. Of course, no one else knows exactly what I mean by speaking of my beetle. I predicate properties to something in my description, which Wittgenstein imagines remains unknown to outsiders except by my characterization of its attributes. The word 'beetle' does not function as the name of a thing in this language game. Wittgenstein says that we can "divide through" by the beetle, and that it "cancels out whatever it is." The beetle as a distinguishable nameable entity drops out of consideration as irrelevant in preference to the description of a generic type or kind of object by a general predication of properties. Wittgenstein concludes that naming and describing private mental phenomena cannot be understood by the ordinary essential naming language game rules for "object and designation," which is to say, object and name. But if naming is a preparation for description, how can I privately describe what I cannot privately name?

> 294. If you say he sees a private picture before him, which he is describing, you have still made an assumption about what he has before him. And that means that you can describe it or do describe it more closely. If you admit that you haven't any notion what kind of thing it might be that he has before him—then what leads you into saying, in spite of that, that he has something before him? Isn't it as if I were to say of someone: "He *has* something. But I don't know whether it is money, or debts, or an empty till."

Two participants play Wittgenstein's beetle description game: 'he' and 'you'. He has a private picture in front of him, displayed to introspection in a private phenomenological theater, which he examines and then tries to describe. If he succeeds to any extent, then you, any other person, can describe it too, and hence you or any third person can characterize it more closely in descriptions of several possible levels of contentual detail. If he fails to describe the private picture in his phenomenology, then the second horn of Wittgenstein's dilemma entails that there may be nothing private to be described.

Wittgenstein does not make his position totally clear. He presupposes multiple minds as a prerequisite for the possibility of rule-following, which suggests that he would probably prefer the first part of the dilemma to the effect that private psychological experiences can only be publicly described. If there are irreducibly private properties of psychological experience, they will be just as privately indescribable as they are publicly inaccessible. If the intentionality or 'aboutness' of thought, or the *qualia* or lived-through experiential content of what it feels like to have a certain mental state, are privately knowable only to the first-person psychological subject, then the subject cannot describe them publicly or privately. Private sensations like the beetle in the box must therefore vanish from consideration altogether as neither publicly nor privately nameable or describable. This leaves generic description of kinds or types of psychological experience in a public sensation language, whatever can be publicly said about the publicly inaccessible beetle in the box, as the only language game in town.[16]

Wittgenstein claims that there is no epistemic privilege in private experience. As in *Tractatus* 5.634, Wittgenstein in *Philosophical Investigations* now concludes on quite different grounds that the uniqueness of the psychological subject's first-person access to experience cannot provide the basis for a foundationalist epistemology of a priori truths. Wittgenstein repeats the conclusion of §248 that to say that sensations are private is to make a grammatical point comparable to the statement that solitaire is a card game played by one person alone, and that to do so is to illustrate the point with language use samples:

> 295. "I know . . . only from my *own* case"—what kind of proposition is this meant to be at all? An experiential one? No.—A grammatical one?
>
> Suppose everyone does say about himself that he knows what pain is only from his own pain.—Not that people really say that, or are even prepared to say it. But *if* everyone said it—it might be a kind of exclamation. And even if it gives no information, still it is a picture, and why should we not want to call up such a picture? Imagine an allegorical painting take the place of those words.
>
> When we look into ourselves as we do philosophy, we often get to see just such a picture. A full-blown pictorial representation of our grammar. Not facts; but as it were illustrated turns of speech.

The beetle in the box refutes a common philosophical confusion. First-person psychological experience is sometimes touted as providing infallible foundations of knowledge. To suppose that all subjects individually have privileged first-person access to the contents of their thoughts depends on mistaken views about the philosophical grammar of phenomenological description, limited by the essential rules that more generally govern description language games. Privileged phenomenological description moreover entails a superficial methodological solipsism. In *Tractatus* 5.62, Wittgenstein argues that solipsism is nonsensical, while admitting that what solipsism tries to convey about the transcendence of the metaphysical subject "is quite correct." Now in *Philosophical Investigations* he builds into his account of meaningful language use a pragmatic requirement that presupposes the coexistence of other minds socially engaged in a common form of life:[17]

> 307. "Are you not really a behaviourist in disguise? Aren't you at bottom really saying that everything except human behaviour is a fiction?"—If I do speak of a fiction, then it is of a *grammatical* fiction.

Wittgenstein accordingly asks whether by rejecting private language he embraces behaviorism. If there is no private language, then it appears that phenomenology, epistemic foundationalism, and other philosophical programs are groundless. What remains is the hard cognitive sciences, behaviorism, materialism as the philosophical ideology of neurophysiology, and what today is called functionalism or computationalism as the philosophical ideology of the information and computer sciences. Wittgenstein addresses himself explicitly only to behaviorism, as the predominant form of reductivist philosophical psychology in his day. Once again he clarifies his position by distancing himself from any substantive philosophical thesis, and explaining his investigations as an attempt to describe the philosophical grammar of public sensation language.[18]

I N O T E S

1. Wittgenstein 1968a §109.

2. See Thompson 1964, 20. Binkley 1973, 172: "The discussion of private language is . . . contrapuntal, and not the development of a theory which claims that private language is impossible." And 173: "If [Wittgenstein] does not want to put forward theses, he avoids negative as well as positive claims: his task is ultimately neither to affirm nor deny philosophic claims or theories. If p is a philosophical thesis, so is $-p$, and Wittgenstein will have nothing to do with the assertion of either one." Hintikka 1969, 423–25; Smerud 1970, 14–15.

3. Albritton 1959, 845–57. Not all interpretations associate Wittgenstein's criteria of correctness specifically with the naming of particulars. See, for example, Kenny 1978, 11: "To use Wittgenstein's technical term, the physical expression of a mental process is a *criterion* for that process: that is to say, it is part of the concept of a mental process of a particular kind (a sensation such as pain, for instance, or an emotion such as grief) that it should have a characteristic manifestation." Yet by comparison with criteria for names there are no criteria of correctness for many ordinary public language predicates. There is no practical criteriological method of deciding whether a painting deserves the predicate 'beautiful', or a fetus the predicate 'person', etc., though there is at least some reason to think that there may be criteria of correctness for the public naming of public particulars. It seems uncharitable to suppose that Wittgenstein is committed to such an implausible version of the criteria of correctness as applies to generic (and public) sensation predicates like 'pain' or 'grief', as opposed to names for particular sensations. See Wellman 1962. Wellman's notion of Wittgenstein's demand for criteria of correctness to reidentify sensations in their *infima species* comes closest to accurately interpreting Wittgenstein's demand for criteria of correctness in reidentifying recurring sensation particulars.

4. Wittgenstein 1968a §§62, 564–67.

5. For the sake of conformity with the text, and not through any gender bias of my own, I follow Wittgenstein's practice of using masculine pronouns exclusively in referring to the private sensations diarist.

6. Hacker 1989, 276–306; Garver 1994, 159–76.

7. The same polarity does not seem to govern all epistemic-psychological predications according to Wittgenstein. See his 1967a §395: "A man can pretend to be unconscious; but *conscious?*"

8. See Hacker 1989, 307–35; Garver 1994, 177–96; Suter, 137–53.

9. Wittgenstein seems at least implicitly committed to the idea that public and private phenomena are distinguishable on the basis of the availability of criteria of correctness for public, but not for private, phenomena. If even one public phenomenon were to lack such criteria, it would not only be unnameable, breaking down the distinction between the public and putative private naming of public and private sensation particulars. More importantly, the discrepancy would undermine the argument that private sensations are unnameable, since there is otherwise no intuitive justification for supposing that any public particular is unnameable. The distinction between public and private might then be understood in terms of the availability or unavailability of criteria of correctness. It is by virtue of a particular's admitting of the practical determination of its genidentity or persistence or recurrence through change in real time by means of reliable external extramental checks that the public is distinguished from the private. It also follows in this extension of Wittgenstein's terminology that private states or occurrences are at least a subset of if not coextensive with the mental or psychological.

10. The problem is illustrated in a fascinating brochure by Melzack, Paris, and Rogers 1987, 2: "The pain that *you* experience is unique. It can't be compared to another person's, and only you can know how much pain you have and when you have it." There follows a list of seventy-seven terms for distinct types of pains, including Flickering, Quivering, Pulsing, Throbbing, Beating, Pounding, Jumping, Flashing, Shooting, Pricking, Boring, Drilling, Stabbing, Sharp, Cutting, Lacerating, etc., and a pain intensity scale. The pain descriptions are taken from the McGill Pain Questionnaire compiled by Melzack in 1970.

11. I shall not discuss other interesting accounts of Wittgenstein's manometer argument. But consider Kenny 1973, 194–95: "Why does Wittgenstein say no mistake is possible? Cannot I say 'S' and then find my blood pressure is *not* rising? Yes, but that is not what Wittgenstein is rejecting: he is talking about a would-be intermediate step between having the sensation and judging 'Now my blood pressure is rising', a step which would consist in recognizing the sensation as a sensation of a particular kind, and remembering that a sensation of that kind indicated a rise in blood-pressure. Misidentification here would not matter, provided that I both misidentified the kind of sensation *and* misremembered what kind of sensation indicated the blood-pressure rise. It is this, according to Wittgenstein, which shows that the hypothesis of a mistake is a mere show. Suppose that I say 'S' and the blood-pressure does not rise: what reasons have I to say that I have misidentified the sensation rather than misremembered which kind of sensation goes with the rise? None at all, unless 'identifying the sensation' means 'identifying it as the blood-pressure-rising sensation'; but if it does then there is no room for the intermediate step, and 'S' is not the name of a private object but a word in a public language." This interpretation seems faulty because it assumes from the outset that sign 'S' in the manometer example, in Kenny's words, is supposed to designate a "kind of sensation", whereas Wittgenstein explicitly requires that it designate a "particular sensation." Nor for that matter does Wittgenstein in the example ever mention the quite different problem of misremembering which kind of sensation is correlated with blood pressure increase. See Müller 1978.

12. Many commentators have interpreted the structure of Wittgenstein's private language argument as a reductio. See Jones, ed. 1971, part 5, "The Private Language Argument as a *Reductio ad Absurdum*," pp. 132–82. Jacquette 1994a.

13. See, for example, Armstrong 1968, 54–55: "Gilbert Ryle's book *The Concept of Mind* seems to be a defence of Analytical Behaviourism. I think the same is true of Wittgenstein's *Philosophical Investigations,* although this interpretation is hotly denied by many disciples. The problem of interpreting Wittgenstein's book may perhaps be reduced to the problem of interpreting a single sentence: '580. An "inner process" stands in need of outward criteria.' When Wittgenstein speaks of 'outward criteria' he means bodily behaviour. . . . But there is one difficulty in interpreting Wittgenstein and Ryle as Behaviourists. Both writers deny that they hold this doctrine! I think, however, that the only reason that these philosophers denied that they were Behaviourists was that they took Behaviourism to be the doctrine that there are no such things as minds. Since they did not want to deny the existence of minds, but simply wanted to give an account of the mind in terms of behaviour, they denied that they were Behaviourists." I interpret Wittgenstein's remark in §580 differently than Armstrong, in a way that allows me to take Wittgenstein at his word in §307 when he distances himself from thetic commitment to behaviorism. When Wittgenstein claims that "inner processes stand in need of outward criteria," I take him to be acknowledging rather than disputing the existence of inner processes, while in context I understand him to assert that inner processes need outward criteria in order to be *named*—the only connection in which Wittgenstein speaks of criteria in the *Investigations*—rather than in order to be *described* or *explained.*

14. Wittgenstein 1968a §§258, 265. Wittgenstein's view that "meaning is use" (together with the qualifications he attaches) is discussed in §§30, 43, 120, 138, 197, 247, 454, 532, 556–57, 561. See Hallett 1967.

15. See Werhane 1989. Wittgenstein seems to regard sensation types as publicly designatable if they must have something external in common by virtue of which they can be grouped together under a generic sensation category term. This means that satisfaction of exact identity conditions is not necessary, so that different persons in principle could experience the same more loosely associated generic sensations, such as pain, stabbing pain, wincing pain, and so on (see note 9 above).

16. Wittgenstein 1968b, 271–74. An expanded version appears in Wittgenstein 1993, 202–88. Rhees's notes on Wittgenstein's 1936 lectures on "The Language of Sense Data and Private Experience" appear in Wittgenstein 1988, 290–369 (see xii for complete documentation of original sources).

17. See Kripke, esp. 114–45. Kripke's interpretation of Wittgenstein's private language argument has been widely discussed. I shall not try to recapitulate the main points of Kripke's analysis, but remark only that Kripke does not accept, and claims that Wittgenstein would not endorse, outright skepticism about the meaningfulness of language. But if Kripke's community of language users solution to Humean skepticism about the meaning of language is unsatisfactory, then his account of Wittgenstein's private language argument makes meaning impossible. The problem, as with body movement in pure behavioral ostension, is that absolutely any reaction of the language community can be regarded by the Humean skeptic as expressing approval or disapproval of any use under any assertibility conditions of any term (say, the continuation of the series 2, 4, 6, . . . by 19), just as any number placed after 6 in the series can be regarded by the Humean skeptic as satisfying the appropriate assertibility conditions for correctly continuing the series. The Humean skeptic disappears from Kripke's book by the time Kripke offers his own community of language users solution to what he takes to be Wittgenstein's Humean skeptical challenge to the meaningfulness of language. Other criticisms of Kripke's interpretation are found in McGinn, and Baker and Hacker 1984b.

18. See also Bloor 1983; Budd 1989; Cook 1994, 316–42; Fogelin 1987, 166–85; Garver 1994, 205–15; Gram 1971; Hacker 1989, 245–75; Hallett 1977, 306–85; Hanfling, 112–15; Hintikka and Hintikka 1986; Jacquette 1994b; 1998; Kenny 1973, 178–202; Oldenquist 1971; Paskow 1974; Pears 1987, 2, 328–422; Price 1973; Reeder 1979; Rhees 1954; Saunders and Henze 1967; Schulte 1992, 129–54; Schulte 1993, 37–74; Wisdom 1972.

| **An Ancient City of Languages**

The most provocative insights in Wittgenstein's early and later thought are those concerning the nature of philosophy itself. What is philosophy? Is there anything for philosophy to do? Is there a proper method of philosophy, and if so, what is it? The *Tractatus* tried to answer these questions, but the *Tractatus* metaphysics, semantics, and logic are thoroughly demolished in the *Philosophical Investigations*.

What is the proper practice of philosophy when there is no longer an antiphilosophical justification for dismissing philosophical discourse as a babble of logically meaningless pseudopropositions? The *Philosophical Investigations* rethinks this important metaphilosophical question just as it reinterprets the meaning of language in terms of language tools, language games, family resemblance concepts, and forms of life. We might expect that Wittgenstein in the later period would regard philosophy as just another language game intertwined in the form of life of philosophers, with essential rules of metaphilosophical grammar determined by the point or purpose of philosophy, whatever he now takes this to be. But Wittgenstein excludes philosophy as an exception to the account of meaning in language. The practice of (anti-) philosophy is still not an ordinary use of language, a mode of expression in which genuine philosophical problems can be stated or within which they can be solved. There are no philosophical theses, and the proper practice of (anti-) philosophy is the clarification of meaning in language by which apparent philosophical problems disappear.

The *Tractatus* and *Philosophical Investigations* agree in their meta-anti-philosophy. The persistence of Wittgenstein's basic attitude toward philosophy represents the most important line of continuity from the early philosophy through the transition period to the later philosophy. It defines Wittgenstein's (anti-) philosophy, meta-anti-philosophy, and anti-meta-philosophy as a coherent ideal concept about the nature and proper practice of philosophy that makes a unique contribution to philosophy's evolving self-image, its history and future direction.

Wittgenstein struggled through all three major phases of his philosophical development with the intellectual and emotional demands of philosophy. He is almost desperately eager to set philosophy aside and put it in its place, to finally be free of its questions. The *Tractatus* tries to do so by using philosophy against itself, like a ladder to be tossed back when Wittgenstein thinks he can discharge its apparent problems as nonsensical pseudo-problems. With the rejection of logical atomism and the picture theory of meaning in the transition period, Wittgenstein finds new ways to neutralize the problems of philosophy.

Returning to philosophy at Cambridge in 1930, Wittgenstein began converting his early antiphilosophy into a kind of therapy. Instead of quieting philosophical problems by reducing them to nonsense, in the later period he seeks relief by describing language games and their essential rules of philosophical grammar. Now he holds that philosophical difficulties arise pathologically only through the urge to remove words from their natural settings in language games where they have a definite purpose. If we understand this, and come to see how philosophical puzzles occur in psychology, mathematics, and everyday knowledge claims and denials, then we may be in a position to resist the temptation to commit the same kinds of mistakes and be free at last from the semantic bewitchment of our intelligences by means of language. The therapy requires the painstaking uncovering of philosophical grammars for every troublesome concept by describing its natural function in a form of life from which it cannot be extracted without philosophical confusion. Wittgenstein remarks in *Philosophical Investigations:*

> 109. We must do away with all *explanation,* and description alone must take its place. And this description gets its light, that is to say its purpose, from the philosophical problems. These are, of course, not empirical problems; they are solved, rather, by looking into the workings of our language, and that in such a way as to make us recognize those workings: *in despite of* an urge to misunderstand them. The problems are solved, not by giving new information, but by arranging what we have always known. Philosophy is a battle against the bewitchment of our intelligence by means of language.

There are philosophical problems, but no philosophical solutions comparable to those offered in the natural sciences. When we comprehend how language works, as Wittgenstein concludes in the *Tractatus,* we see that what may impress us as real philosophical problems are only based on linguistic confusions. These are not grammatical errors in the ordinary sense, but mistaken concepts and inferences drawn from misunderstandings of the philosophical grammar of language games.

Philosophical problems arise, Wittgenstein says in §38, only when language goes on holiday. This occurs when words and sentences are removed from the natural nonphilosophical work they are meant to do in practical human transactions. Philosophical solutions do not involve new discoveries in a special field of knowledge, but require instead a rearrangement of the facts of language use in language games, from which philosophy uncovers their philosophical grammar. The correct characterization of philosophical grammar proves thought and language capable in principle of being entirely free of all philosophical confusions, puzzles, problems, or paradoxes.

As in the *Tractatus,* so now in *Philosophical Investigations,* Wittgenstein believes that philosophical problems simply disappear when we properly understand the semantic workings of language. The difference between Wittgenstein's early and later philosophy is partly one of emphasis in describing the dissolution of philosophical problems by arriving at a correct understanding of language. This shift in Wittgenstein's later (anti-) philosophy from the early results from his later rethinking of philosophical semantics and philosophical psychology.

Wittgenstein agrees in both his early and later (anti-) philosophy on dissolving philosophical problems by a proper understanding of the meaning of the language in which philosophical problems are supposed to be expressed. The following passage from *Philosophical Investigations* might just as easily have been written by Wittgenstein at the time of and in the spirit of the *Tractatus:*

> 119. The results of philosophy are the uncovering of one or another piece of plain nonsense and of bumps that the understanding has got by running its head up against the limits of language. These bumps make us see the value of the discovery.

Wittgenstein's reflections about the nature and practice of philosophy belong to the category of what is usually called the philosophy of philosophy or metaphilosophy. Wittgenstein resists this terminology, just as in the *Tractatus* he rejects the stratification of

different types of things and different types of syntax into the ordered hierarchy of Russell's theory of types.[1] Wittgenstein pre-
fers a leveled plane of philosophical categories, with every
concept logically on a par with every other. Wittgenstein argues
that there is no justification for treating the philosophy of philosophy as any sort of higher-ordered metaphilosophy. In the
early period, Wittgenstein denounces metaphilosophy as logically meaningless because no sample of discourse considered as a
picture-fact among other facts in the world could possibly picture
itself. In *Philosophical Investigations,* he offers a similar syntactical analogy from the standpoint of the later philosophy's inquiry into the philosophical grammars of language games:

> 121. One might think: if philosophy speaks of the use of the
> word "philosophy" there must be a second-order philosophy.
> But it is not so: it is, rather, like the case of orthography,
> which deals with the word "orthography" among others
> without then being second-order.

The proper practice of philosophy requires what Wittgenstein
calls the "perspicuous representation" of language use. This involves the articulation of philosophical grammar as the essential
rules of particular language games from an accurate description
of nonphilosophical linguistic practice. Ordinary language is so
complicated and its philosophical grammar so difficult to discern
that there is no choice but to proceed step by step through a series
of progressively complicated language games. These invented scenarios will nevertheless describe real features of language use in
their pragmatic contexts that reveal their extrasemantic praxeological foundations embedded in a form of life:

> 122. A main source of our failure to understand is that we do
> not *command a clear view* of the use of our words. — Our
> grammar is lacking in this sort of perspicuity. A perspicuous
> representation produces just that understanding which con-
> sists in 'seeing connexions'. Hence the importance of finding
> and inventing *intermediate cases.*
>   The concept of a perspicuous representation is of funda-
> mental significance for us. It earmarks the form of account we
> give, the way we look at things. (Is this a 'Weltanschauung'?)

The alienation of philosophy from other types of language use
is emphasized by Wittgenstein in an ongoing series of remarks
about the nature of philosophy. What passes for a philosophical
problem Wittgenstein first reduces to conceptual confusion or uncertainty of direction in a language game. The confusion can
manifest itself as an unfamiliarity with the purpose of a particular set of language tools resulting from their unknowing misappli-

cation in tasks for which they are not naturally suited or intended.

When philosophy is properly practiced it produces a perspicuous representation of language use in which apparent philosophical problems disappear, but does nothing to change language, and imposes no refinements of its own. Modifying, correcting, or improving language is a task only for philosophy in its more traditional role as queen of the sciences or managerial efficiency expert. Wittgenstein does not think of philosophy as cleaning house by throwing out the confusions and ambiguities of ordinary language and imposing a preferred set of philosophically acceptable concepts in an ideal language.[2] The philosopher should instead work toward the perspicuous representation of actual linguistic practice in selected language games, from which to discern the essential rules of philosophical grammar, leaving ordinary language in its practical applications entirely untouched:

> 123. A philosophical problem has the form: "I don't know my way about".

> 124. Philosophy may in no way interfere with the actual use of language; it can in the end only describe it.
> For it cannot give it any foundation either.
> It leaves everything as it is.
> It also leaves mathematics as it is, and no mathematical discovery can advance it. A "leading problem of mathematical logic" is for us a problem of mathematics like any other.

Why is ordinary language innocent, while philosophical discourse is corrupt? Wittgenstein believes that ordinary language has a legitimate job to do, with a definite point and purpose rooted in a form of life and bound up with the practical activities by which language maintains its self-justifying place in our cultural lives. The use of language in formulating and trying to solve philosophical problems is abstracted from this living cultural context. The application to mathematics cannot be ignored, because of the importance attaching to mathematical logic as a field of traditional philosophical problems, and in the use of logic and mathematics in attempts to clarify and resolve these and related philosophical problems in the philosophy of Frege, Russell, and the analytic tradition generally. Here Wittgenstein explains the nature of contradiction and paradox in logic, mathematics, and philosophy:

> 125. It is the business of philosophy, not to resolve a contradiction by means of a mathematical or logico-mathematical discovery, but to make it possible for us to get a clear view of the state of mathematics that troubles us: the state of affairs

before the contradiction is resolved. (And this does not mean that one is sidestepping a difficulty.)

The fundamental fact here is that we lay down rules, a technique, for a game, and that then when we follow the rules, things do not turn out as we had assumed. That we are therefore as it were entangled in our own rules.

This entanglement in our rules is what we want to understand (i.e. get a clear view of).

It throws light on our concept of *meaning* something. For in those cases things turn out otherwise than we had meant, foreseen. That is just what we say when, for example, a contradiction appears: "I didn't mean it like that."

The civil status of a contradiction, or its status in civil life: there is the philosophical problem.

Wittgenstein has more to say about the meaning of contradiction in *Remarks on the Foundations of Mathematics*. Interestingly, in this passage he attributes the occurrence of contradiction to faulty rules. If we are bothered by the contradiction, then we are simply mistaken to accept the inconsistent rules. Deny the rules, and the contradiction disappears; whereupon we may find other rules for what we need to do.

But are we always free to deny inconsistent rules? Are there always consistent rules available for whatever we may need to do that do not also entangle us in unwanted ways? What if I find it unacceptable to have a contradiction anywhere in my thought or expression of thought? What if I can never escape contradiction, but at best exchange one type of contradiction for another? Wittgenstein does not consider the possibility that we might have contradiction-entangling rules absolutely forced on us by inherent inconsistencies in our thought about the world, or by deep contradictions in the essential rules of philosophical grammar in ordinary nonphilosophical language games. Yet it should be an open question for an empirical realist like the later Wittgenstein whether in the end a correct description of the world, thought, or language can avoid inconsistency.

Wittgenstein blocks the pernicious effects of contradiction in two ways: (1) He presupposes that the world and language are ultimately logically consistent. This unexamined assumption runs through Wittgenstein's early, transitional, and later philosophy, as an implicit article of faith in the fundamental logical consistency of world, thought, and language. (2) He explains and tries to justify a sense in which we can confine and thereby live with certain kinds of contradictions, by adopting a tolerant attitude toward them after coming to understand their potential language game functions.

If contradictions exist, they are either our avoidable fault, or they have always existed in thought and language, where they have obviously not derailed ordinary language use in practice, nor hindered its development as a vital part of our culture. All language as the semantic realist acknowledges is language use in practice. What we call contradictions, if they are not merely the result of our own slovenly conceptual housekeeping, do not prevent language from working, but at most show that we may be playing a different language game than we thought. If we are bothered by these contradictions, we should at least muster the ingenuity to work out a system of essential rules for the language games we think we need and are able in practice to play. The pragmatic fact that a language game works leads Wittgenstein back to the assumption of ultimate logical consistency in the world, thought, and language. If, on the other hand, unavoidable contradictions exist, they must have existed alongside the development of all our practically effective language, where they have been harmless enough. We may lose interest in the question of contradiction altogether when we fully embrace a pragmatic instrumentalist philosophical semantics. What could contradiction possibly matter to the everyday facts of human life and culture? This is what Wittgenstein in §125 means by "The civil status of a contradiction, or its status in civil life", of which he remarks with rare emphasis, "there is the philosophical problem." Wittgenstein seems to be saying that the one and only or most important philosophical problem is the pragmatic functioning of contradictory language games, or that it is the only or most important business of philosophy to avoid and untangle logical inconsistencies in the perspicuous representation of actual language use as a way of investigating its philosophical grammar.

Wittgenstein denies that philosophy discovers substantive theses. It proceeds on the contrary by rearranging what is given to experience in a perspicuous representation. In the later period, Wittgenstein denounces transcendentalism as pretending to inquire into an unknowable realm beyond human interests. He limits proper philosophical methodology to describing language use by means of what is unhidden before us:

> 126. Philosophy simply puts everything before us, and neither explains nor deduces anything. —Since everything lies open to view there is nothing to explain. For what is hidden, for example, is of no interest to us.
> One might also give the name "philosophy" to what is possible *before* all new discoveries and inventions.

127. The work of the philosopher consists in assembling reminders for a particular purpose.

128. If one tried to advance *theses* in philosophy, it would never be possible to debate them, because everyone would agree to them.

Philosophy must leave everything as it is. The method of doing philosophy in Wittgenstein's later period is one in which philosophy as therapy offers peace of mind by eliminating philosophical problems through the perspicuous representation of relevant language games as a way of disclosing their philosophical grammar. When this is rightly done there is no basis for philosophical concern about traditional philosophical problems. When the therapy is successful, all apparent philosophical problems disappear, unable to withstand the cleansing light of clarity:[3]

133. It is not our aim to refine or complete the system of rules for the use of our words in unheard-of ways.

For the clarity that we are aiming at is indeed *complete* clarity. But this simply means that the philosophical problems should *completely* disappear.

The real discovery is the one that makes me capable of stopping doing philosophy when I want to.—The one that gives philosophy peace, so that it is no longer tormented by questions which bring *itself* in question.—Instead, we now demonstrate a method, by examples; and the series of examples can be broken off.—Problems are solved (difficulties eliminated), not a *single* problem.

There is not *a* philosophical method, though there are indeed methods, like different therapies.

As a second entomological emblem, to complement the beetle in the box, Wittgenstein offers this striking image of the purpose of philosophy. The goal of philosophy, as Wittgenstein thinks of it consistently throughout the three phases of his philosophical transition, is to set the thinker free from philosophical concern:

309. What is your aim in philosophy?—To shew the fly the way out of the fly-bottle.

It is as therapy that philosophy is rightly practiced to avoid the intellectual ills engendered by traditional philosophy in its misunderstandings of language. For Wittgenstein in the later as in the early period there is only one correct theory of language and one correct practice of philosophy, that go together to free us from philosophical problems.

We must then ask whether the fly is shown the way out of the fly bottle by avoiding or learning to live with contradictions, or by a little of both. It would appear, depending on how seriously we take the metaphor, that if the fly actually finds its way out of the bottle, then contradiction is avoided. The fly does not settle down to a contented existence inside the bottle to be somehow reconciled with its limitations; rather it escapes. The fly and fly bottle are images of Wittgenstein's faith that there is always a way out of philosophical problems if we only retrace the false steps that got us into trouble in the first place. If we share his confidence that there are no real philosophical paradoxes, then we can rise above pedestrian obsessions about the detection and avoidance of contradiction. In *Remarks on the Foundations of Mathematics,* Wittgenstein writes:

> 55. It is one thing to use a mathematical technique consisting in the avoidance of contradiction, and another to philosophize against contradiction in mathematics.
>
> 56. Contradiction. Why just this *one* bogy? That is surely very suspicious.
>
> Why should not a calculation made for a practical purpose, with a contradictory result, tell me "Do as you please, I, the calculation do not decide the matter"?
>
> The contradiction might be conceived as a hint from the gods that I am to act and *not* consider. (RFM)

Wittgenstein considers a number of possible functions or roles for contradiction in ordinary language games, including one in which a practical activity is linked to the occurrence of contradiction as a sign from the gods. The same inventive application of language games to accommodate contradictions in practical ways and with pragmatic justification is then turned to the problem of contradiction in mathematics:

> 57. "Why should contradiction be disallowed in mathematics?" Well, why is it not allowed in our simple language-games? (There is certainly a connexion here.) Is this then a fundamental law governing all thinkable language-games?
>
> Let us suppose that a contradiction in an order, e.g. produces astonishment and indecision—and now we say: that is just the purpose of contradiction in this language-game. (RFM)

Now Wittgenstein considers the role of contradiction in a traditional problem of philosophical logic, the so-called Liar paradox. When someone says 'I always lie', the assertion is true only if it is false. If the liar's sentence is true, it is false, because it is true in that case that whatever the liar says is false. Wittgenstein considers a number of potential reactions to the puzzle. Perhaps we are using basic terms differently than the liar; perhaps the liar means to convey something different than what we naturally take to be the literal meaning of the liar sentence; perhaps the liar does not intend to make an assertion:

> 58. Someone comes to people and says: "I always lie". They answer: "Well, in that case we can trust you!"—But could *he* mean what he said? Is there not a feeling of being incapable of saying something really true; let it be what it may?—
>
> "I always lie!"—Well, and what about *that?*—"It was a lie too!"—But in that case you don't always lie!—"No, it's all lies!"
>
> Perhaps we should say of this man that he doesn't mean the same thing as we do by "true" and by "lying". He means perhaps something like: What he says flickers; or nothing really comes from his heart.
>
> It might also be said: his "I always lie" was not really an *assertion*. It was rather an exclamation . . . (RFM)

The Liar paradox as a paradigm of conceptual self-non-application is the basis also underlying Russell's paradox about the set of all sets that are not members of themselves. Wittgenstein asks why the Russell paradox should automatically be conceived as a symptom of a philosophical mistake, and why it could not just as reasonably be understood as the Janus-headed two-faced mascot of logic, or even the source of the unparadoxical propositions of logic from which it is distinguished without threatening their logical integrity:

> 59. Why should Russell's contradiction not be conceived as something supra-propositional, something that towers above the propositions and looks in both directions like a Janus head? N.B. the proposition $F(F)$—in which $F(\xi) = \sim\xi(\xi)$—contains no variables and so might hold as something supra-logical, as something unassailable, whose negation itself in turn only *asserts* it. Might one not even begin logic with this contradiction? And as it were descend from it to propositions.
>
> The proposition that contradicts itself would stand like a monument (with a Janus head) over the propositions of logic.
>
> 60. The pernicious thing is not: to produce a contradiction in the region in which neither the consistent nor the contradictory proposition has any kind of work to accomplish; no, what *is* pernicious is: not to know how one reached the place where contradiction no longer does any harm. (RFM)

A cadre of commentators has called attention to Wittgenstein's disclaimers of giving substantive theses or doctrinal propositions in philosophy, of philosophy as theorizing or metaphilosophy. But while Wittgenstein denounces such talk, he does not always observe these official scruples in his own practice, in the language he allows himself to use in explaining his ideas. Even in the *Tractatus,* where nonsense is so fluently spoken, Wittgenstein, possibly in connection with his early thinking about solipsism, makes his own heuristic use of language a privileged exception, *eine Ausnahme,* to the limitations of meaningful discourse prescribed by the general form of proposition.

Throughout the *Philosophical Investigations,* Wittgenstein similarly offers arguments, defends and rejects substantive principles, makes definite contributions to what almost any other philosopher would call metaphilosophy, and explains as well as describes many things about the nature and workings of thought, language, and the world, just as he quite meaningfully does, despite equally vehement denial, in the early philosophy. Kant in the *Critique of Judgment* had defined the concept of genius as someone who defines for others but is exempt from and stands outside the rules of art.[4] Kant's idea may have reached Wittgenstein through Schopenhauer, a full third of whose writings is devoted to aesthetics and dominated by the topic of the concept of aesthetic and philosophical genius. Schopenhauer discusses Kant's definition, and adds his own different but in some ways also generally Kantian treatment of the concept of genius.[5] Does Wittgenstein try in all his writings to fulfill the promise of the Kantian-Schopenhauerian genius by making himself an exception to his own rules of philosophical semantics?

I have preferred up to this point to let Wittgenstein speak for himself, rather than observing his official avoidance of philosophical explanation and substantive philosophical theses. But it is crucial now in understanding Wittgenstein's later philosophy to recall that philosophy is supposed to be a purely descriptive enterprise. Precisely as Wittgenstein offers an album of scenery sketches in the *Philosophical Investigations,* philosophy is to consist of pragmatically contexted descriptions of actual language use as we might collect them standing out on a street corner with a tape recorder and microphone. The perspicuous representation of language use in turn provides the data for discovering the essential rules of particular language games in philosophical grammar. In the process of giving such descriptions, philosophy as therapy relieves us of concerns about traditional philosophical problems. We can relax about the words that give us trouble in philosophy when we see them functioning normally and unproblematically as part of the forms of life in and for which they were introduced. Philosophy fails its mission in the later as in the early philosophy for Wittgenstein when it does not recognize its task of eliminating philosophical concerns as real answerable problems. Philosophy must try to put everything in the right place so that what had tormented us as philosophical puzzles no longer arise in our thinking, and in so doing shows the fly the way out of the fly bottle (after which we need not care about the bottle—or the fly!).

Wittgenstein proposes a semantic pluralism in the later philosophy. Yet he continues to believe that there is only one right way of doing philosophy. The right way of doing philosophy is to leave everything as it is, to offer no explanations, but to give pure descriptions in which what is empirically open to inspection in linguistic and extralinguistic practice is correctly arranged in therapeutic ways that eliminate the unnatural malaise of philosophical problems.[6]

> 435. If it is asked: "How do sentences manage to represent?—the answer might be: "Don't you know? You certainly see it, when you use them. For nothing is concealed."
>
> How do sentences do it?—Don't you know? For nothing is hidden.
>
> But given this answer: "But you know how sentences do it, for nothing is concealed" one would like to retort "Yes, but it all goes by so quick, and I should like to see it as it were laid open to view."

The later parts of *Philosophical Investigations* illustrate Wittgenstein's method in application to the problem of naming. Wittgenstein asks in effect, in endlessly different ways, 'What makes my thought about him a thought about *him?*' The discussion is generally about the intentionality of names and pronouns in thought and language, within the scope of such propositional attitudes as belief, doubt, hope, and fear. The *Tractatus* analysis of propositional attitude in 5.54–5.5422 leaves only the logical picturing of fact by fact, from which subject and attitude are eliminated as transcending the world. The *Philosophical Investigations* renounces transcendentalism, but allows families of language games involving propositional attitudes to be considered at face value in philosophical semantics. Wittgenstein accordingly finds it necessary to describe the philosophical grammar of intentional discourse. With the new concepts of language games, language tools, forms of life, and family resemblance relations at his disposal, Wittgenstein develops a pragmatic account of naming by describing the language games in which a thinker or speaker intends an object, usually a person. The exercise makes possible the perspicuous representation of language use to uncover the philosophical grammar of naming, in the course of which philosophical anxieties about the concept of meaning disappear.

The question Wittgenstein now resumes is the central problem of the *Philosophical Investigations*. What is the meaning of a word and how do names name? Wittgenstein asks in effect how a name intends an object, how the intentional relation that links a particular name to a particular object functions in language games involving the description of psychological states and propositional attitudes. What person, for example, do we mean when:

> 577. We say "I am expecting him", when we believe that he will come, though his coming does not *occupy our thoughts.* (Here "I am expecting him" would mean "I should be surprised if he didn't come" and that will not be called the description of a state of mind.) But we also say "I am expecting him" when it is supposed to mean I am eagerly awaiting him. We could imagine a language in which different verbs were consistently used in these cases. And similarly more than one verb where we speak of 'believing', 'hoping' and so on. Perhaps the concepts of such a language would be more suitable for understanding psychology than the concepts of our language.

Wittgenstein distinguishes two different things that might be meant by the ordinary language expression, 'I am expecting him'. These involve different meanings of the term 'expecting', which might mean merely 'I would be surprised if he did not come' and 'I am eagerly awaiting him'. These are by no means the same. The first is, roughly speaking, reportorial of an epistemic stance. The second is more emotionally charged, indicating an attitude toward the intended state of affairs that goes beyond dispassionate judgment of the likelihood of its occurrence. Wittgenstein observes the accident of language by which these two meanings are conveyed by the same natural language expression, and recommends their disambiguation as a contribution to understanding their philosophical grammar. Yet the real question for Wittgenstein about the semantics of 'I am expecting him' and the sentences into which its meaning can be disambiguated is who (or what) 'him' (he) is. The problem applies to all such thoughts and sentences:

> 584. Now suppose I sit in my room and hope that N.N. will come and bring me some money, and suppose one minute of this state could be isolated, cut out of its context; would what happened in it then not be hope?—Think, for example, of the words which you perhaps utter in this space of time. They are no longer part of this language. And in different surroundings the institution of money doesn't exist either . . .

> 585. When someone says "I hope he'll come"—is this a *report* about his state of mind, or a *manifestation* of his hope?—I can, for example, say it to myself. And surely I am not giving myself a report. It may be a sigh; but it need not. If I tell someone "I can't keep my mind on my work today; I keep on

thinking of his coming"—*this* will be called a description of my state of mind.

Wittgenstein considers examples of many different kinds of ordinary language use to distinguish semantic from psychological components. What we really need to know about such constructions is not the psychology of propositional attitudes, but the arrow of intentionality that is common to them all, that in naming and related psychological and phenomenological description language games somehow point to or intend different things (though never private sensations or mental beetles in a box). Wittgenstein first reorients us to the methodological limitations within which inquiry must be conducted:

> 654. Our mistake is to look for an explanation where we ought to look at what happens as a 'proto-phenomenon'. That is, where we ought to have said: *this language game is played.*
>
> 655. The question is not one of explaining a language-game by means of our experiences, but of noting a language-game.

He concludes that occurrent mental processes or states are logically irrelevant to the intentionality of a name or other referring term (personal pronoun like 'him', etc.). There are several ways in which this appears in the description of propositional attitude language games. Naming and reference unlike mental states or processes among other differences do not occur over definite intervals of time.[7]

> 661. I remember having meant *him.* Am I remembering a process or state?—When did it begin, what was its course; etc.?
>
> 662. In an only slightly different situation, instead of silently beckoning, he would have said to someone "Tell N. to come to me." One can now say that the words "I wanted N. to come to me" describe the state of my mind at that time; and again one may *not* say so.

Whatever mental accompaniments happen to be correlated with intending can always be thought away. We can imagine another psychological process occurring instead in its place, so that there seems to be no necessary connection between the intentionality or aboutness of thought and the experienced content of any particular occurrent psychological state. Thought experiments like the ones Wittgenstein considers in §33, in which we are asked on cue to intend different things by use of the same name, now a color, now a shape, should also convince of this. When I intend the color as opposed to the shape I experience no particular characteristic or distinguishing psychological occurrence, and certainly none different than when I intend the shape as opposed to the color. If I did, there would be no obvious reason why on another occasion I might not intend the same object by the same term to the accompaniment of a qualitatively different phenomenological experience, a flashing red mental light instead of steady amber, a pleasure instead of a pain, a sound instead of a picture. If I happened always to have the same experience in a mental state or process occurring simultaneously with my intending a particular object in a propositional attitude, there is no reason to assume that intending the same object could not coincide with a qualitatively quite different type of experience. The contents of mental accompaniments to intendings by themselves do not determine the particular objects a thought intends, and as such provide no adequate answer to Wittgenstein's *Hauptfrage,* 'What makes my thought about him a thought about *him?*'

> 663. If I say "I meant *him*" very likely a picture comes to my mind, perhaps of how I looked at him, etc.; but the picture is only like an illustration to a story. From it alone it would mostly be impossible to conclude anything at all; only when one knows the story does one know the significance of the picture.

This is a move Wittgenstein is no longer tempted to make. We could only consider resemblance a requirement for representation if we accepted the logical atomist picture theory, according to which resemblances are supposed to obtain in the depths of logical analysis. As a matter of empirical correlation, any imaginable combination of associations is possible. I might use a mental image of the Taj Majal to represent the Eiffel Tower, or I might use a language or even a logical notation that refers but in no way pictures what it names or represents:

> 683. I draw a head. You ask "Whom is that supposed to represent?"—I: "It's supposed to be N."—You: "But it doesn't look like him; if anything, it's rather like M."—When I said it represented N.—was I establishing a connexion or reporting one? And what connexion did exist?

Wittgenstein repeats the same question in different ways, getting the feel of its use and looking for clues in what we find it reasonable to say about our thought, language, psychological states, and the outside world, turning the most elementary propositional attitude expressions around to see them from different angles as they occur in a particular family of language games:[8]

> 687. Instead of "I meant him" one can, of course, sometimes say "I thought of him"; sometimes even "Yes, we were speaking of him." Ask yourself what 'speaking of him' consists in.

689. "I am thinking of N." "I am speaking of N."

How do I speak *of* him? I say, for instance, "I must go and see N today"—But surely that is not enough! After all, when I say "N" I might mean various people of this name.—"Then there must surely be a further, different connexion between my talk and N, for otherwise I should *still* not have meant HIM."

Certainly such a connexion exists. Only not as you imagine it: namely by means of a mental *mechanism.*

(One compares "meaning him" with "aiming at him".)

Here Wittgenstein refuses to reduce the intentionality of reference to the content of a mental state or process. An adequate description of the relevant language games requires that the use of a name or other referring term be directed toward a specific object. I could use the name 'N' to mean anything whatsoever. If I merely say 'I must go and see him [N] today', I still have not yet said exactly who this is or exactly which person I mean. There must be more to intentionality than this, Wittgenstein reasons, or else my thought about him would not yet be a thought specifically about *him:*

691. When I make myself a sketch of N's face from memory, I can surely be said to *mean* him by my drawing. But which of the processes taking place while I draw (or before or afterwards) could I call meaning him?

For one would naturally like to say: when he meant him, he aimed at him. But how is anyone doing that, when he calls someone else's face to mind?

I mean, how does he call HIM to mind?

How does he call him?

The question has no answer for Wittgenstein except to say that intending is simply something we do. Referring is among the primitive activities that makes other language games possible. We do not do anything else in order to intend an object by using its name; we merely intend one thing rather than another as a basic action. Yet it would be misleading to characterize intending as a basic *mental* action, because it has no essentially associated accompanying mental state or process.

Wittgenstein pursues the question in part 2 of *Philosophical Investigations,* originally intended to replace or be collated with unidentified parts of the later sections of part 1. The problem of intentionality remains unanswered except to reassert that a particular object is meant by a particular use of a name or referring term. We are not to expect an explanation in any case, but at most a description of how the language game is played:

What makes my image of him into an image of *him?*

Not its looking like him.

The same question applies to the expression "I see him now vividly before me" as to the image. What makes this utterance into an utterance about *him?*—Nothing in it or simultaneous with it ('behind it'). If you want to know whom he meant, ask him.

(But it is also possible for a face to come before my mind, and even for me to be able to draw it, without my knowing whose it is or where I have seen it.) (2, 177).

In using language to explain our intentions, we mesh further with the extralinguistic praxeological background that grounds all language, and that includes what we do in those thought and speech acts in which we refer to a particular object. If someone asks us what we mean, which person we believe, doubt, fear, hope, or expect will come, we can only try to indicate in various ways the person we intend. To explain to another the meaning of a word, such as the referent of a name, we play a special language game. We must take advantage of a shared background of practical activities that constitutes a common form of life. Otherwise there is no possibility of conveying our intentions, no matter what we say or how we gesture, point, or flap our arms. Intending a particular object is something we simply do. This makes Wittgenstein's later philosophy thoroughly pragmatic in its interpretation of the most basic semantic instruments by which we name.

When he has (dis-) solved the problem of naming, Wittgenstein's constructive task remaining from his criticism of the *Tractatus* is complete. The relation between language and philosophy is thereby reconceived. Whereas in the early (anti-) philosophy, Wittgenstein wields logical atomism, the picture theory of meaning, and general form of proposition to reduce all philosophical discourse to the nonsense of meaningless pseudoconcepts and pseudopropositions, in the later period he describes language use in its workaday practical context as a way of understanding the philosophical grammar of language games in which philosophical problems no longer arise. Wittgenstein's later attitude toward the meaning of language and its implications for philosophy is symbolized by his metaphor of language as an ancient city. The city has a center and suburbs, old quarters and modern developments. Language games are complexly interrelated in similar ways, sometimes built upon or overlapping with one another, with older unused parts and newer more frequented locales. We can imagine naming as a primitive foundation of the city, belonging to the trenches of its first settlements. The intending of objects precedes other linguistic activities as a preparation for description in more specialized language games by which the city is built. Language as a whole has a dynamic ongoing natural history to be uncovered by a kind of philosophical archaeology in much the same way as the foundations of an ancient city might be unearthed:

> 18. Do not be troubled by the fact that languages (2) and (8) consist only of orders. If you want to say that this shews them to be incomplete, ask yourself whether our language is complete;—whether it was so before the symbolism of chemistry and the notation of the infinitesimal calculus were incorporated in it; for these are, so to speak, suburbs of our language. (And how many houses or streets does it take before a town begins to be a town?) Our language can be seen as an ancient city: a maze of little streets and squares, of old and new houses, and of houses with additions from various periods; and this surrounded by a multitude of new boroughs with straight regular streets and uniform houses.

The cityscape, as Robert John Ackermann explains in *Wittgenstein's City*, contains a number of ethnic districts. They include clear factual assertion, as in the *Tractatus*, mathematics, color, sensation, pain, knowledge, emotion, gesture, expectation, and dreams. The items are different in category; many but not all are psychological states, including color construed as a secondary quality. Cities are complex things, and Wittgenstein cautions us not to judge similarity of kind or category by superficial appearance, as when we seek the essential characteristics of sundry tools in a toolbox, or control handles in a locomotive cabin. The subjects of each distinct language game might all be precincts of the same city despite their dissimilarities, each occupying different quarters in areas outlying the arrondissements of color, pain, and certainty.[9] Hence the problem of the specifically civic status of contradictions. The mixed categories of neighborhoods in Wittgenstein's city are an important feature of his later semantic pluralism. Yet if Ackermann is right, philosophy itself is no part of Wittgenstein's city; not the acropolis, not even a tiny slum.[10]

Wittgenstein describes philosophical problems as originating from the complex interrelations among languages games in similar terms as a matter of being in unfamiliar surroundings. It is a matter of the difference Wittgenstein frequently urges, between seeing and seeing-as:

> 203. Language is a labyrinth of paths. You approach from *one* side and know your way about; you approach the same place from another side and no longer know your way about.

A philosophical problem is eliminated by arriving at the point in the descriptive characterization of the philosophical

319 I An Ancient City of Languages

grammar of language games in which philosophically problematic words and sentences originate are seen as familiar, in which
we come at last to know our way about, in the way we might learn
to get around in a city where we have lived, in which we can recognize the necessary landmarks.[11]

Wittgenstein in the early and later periods uses the word
'philosophy' in two different ways. Philosophy is both torment and
therapy for the torment it induces. There is traditional philosophy
as most others practice it, that spawns a havoc of urban ghettos and
requires philosophy as Wittgenstein thinks it should be practiced
to undo the damage of bad philosophy and contribute to linguistic
municipal renewal.[12] Philosophy, even though it uses language in
the examination of language, cannot be just another language
game, because in the process of describing the philosophical
grammar of language it must not change or add to what is described, but leave everything precisely as found. If there is a distinction between a selection of discourse to be described and the
discourse in which it is described, then Wittgenstein's *Tractatus*
4.111–112 separation of philosophy as something above or below
but not a par with empirical science appears committed to a
methological hierarchy, between language and metalanguage,
theory and metatheory, philosophy and metaphilosophy. The
problem of whether philosophy resides somewhere within or outside the gates of Wittgenstein's city is the later reflection of his
lifelong (anti-) philosophical ambivalence toward the aims and
methods of philosophy.[13]

I NOTES

1. See chapter 6, notes 3 and 4.
2. Wittgenstein 1975 §3: "How strange if logic were concerned
with an 'ideal' language, and not with *ours!*"
3. Rhees 1984, 219, n. 7: "Years later Wittgenstein said to me:
'You know I said I can stop doing philosophy when I like. That is a lie! I
can't.'"
4. Kant 1952, 168–69, 180–82.
5. Schopenhauer, 1, esp. 186–208. See Weiner 1992; Lange 1989.
6. Wittgenstein 1967a §382: "In philosophizing we may not *terminate* a disease of thought. It must run its natural course, and *slow* cure
is all important. (That is why mathematicians are such bad philosophers.)" Compare Wittgenstein's (anti-) meta-anti-philosophy in 1968a
with his essay "Philosophy" (§§ 86-93 of the *Big Typescript*), in Wittgenstein 1988, 161–99 (xii gives complete documentation of the editing and
translation). See Hallett 1977, 192–232; Peterman 1992.
7. Wittgenstein does not deny that mental images sometimes ac-
company naming or other word use. See his 1968a §6: "This ostensive
teaching of words can be said to establish an association between the
word and the thing. But what does this mean? Well, it may mean various

things; but one very likely thinks first of all that a picture of the object comes before the mind when one hears the word. But now, if this does happen—is it the purpose of the word?—Yes, it *may* be the purpose.—I can imagine such a use of words (of series of sounds). (Uttering a word is like striking a note on the keyboard of the imagination.)"

8. Epigrams of the same sort occur in Wittgenstein 1967a §§7, 9, 12–14, 18–19, 24–26, 31–32, 64–65.

9. A rough idea of Wittgenstein's division of the subject matter of one conception of a more complete philosophical grammar is given in his 1974a, 31–35.

10. Ackermann, 15: "What is the crude, large-scale map of Wittgenstein's City? First of all, no section of the City represents logic, grammar, or philosophy. Philosophy is the process of surveying the City, constructing its map, using the fixed spaces of logic and grammar as the reference points for the survey. Logic and grammar, as well as the philosophical assertions marking their horizons, appear everywhere on City boundaries." See Ackermann, 34–35, 147–48, 174–80. Wittgenstein 1967a §455: "(The philosopher is not a citizen of any community of ideas. That is what makes him into a philosopher.)"

11. Drury in Rhees 1984, 81: "In the *Philosophical Investigations* [Wittgenstein] compares his method to that of teaching someone his way about a strange city, numerous journeys have to be made in which the same place is constantly approached by different routes. Only when many journeys have been made can the learner say 'now I can find my way about' [P (§§) 18, 123, 203; cf. p. vii]."

12. Ackermann, 208–9: "Kenny . . . quotes Wittgenstein to the effect that the philosopher is not a citizen of any human community and also quotes him as saying that people must do philosophy *individually*, deciding for themselves how to deal with their own pressing conceptual puzzlements. . . . We are all tempted, at times, into bad philosophy, and we need to overcome our own temptations. The philosopher, however, lives *in* the human community, inside the City. Accurate citation reveals that Wittgenstein held that the philosopher is not a citizen of any particular community of ideas, that is, is not the apologist for any particular interests or ideologies. The philosopher is free to root out nonsense anywhere." See Kenny 1984, 38–60.

13. See also Ackermann, 204–25; Baker and Hacker 1980, 1, 457–559; Fann 1969, 82–96; Findlay 1984; Hacker 1989, 146–78; Hacker 1996, 228–73; Hallett 1977, 553–609; Hunter 1985; Jacquette 1990b; Koethe 1996; Suter, 3–24.

CONCLUSION | **Wittgenstein's Philosophical Legacy**

> In a certain sense one cannot take too much
> care in handling philosophical mistakes, they
> contain so much truth.
> —Wittgenstein, *Zettel* §460

Wittgenstein stands at the crossroads of two major trends in contemporary philosophy. Although his place in both traditions has frequently been oversimplified, Wittgenstein's early philosophy remains among the most enduring paradigms of logical-philosophical analysis, and, with due qualifications, of the logical and methodological program of logical positivism. Wittgenstein's later lectures and posthumous writings at the same time continue to inspire a second Wittgensteinian philosophical revolution in ordinary language philosophy.

Wittgenstein's thought is more complex than either of these descriptions suggests. The logical positivists of the Vienna Circle who took the *Tractatus* as a guidebook were disappointed to find that Wittgenstein, despite agreements on certain matters of logical form and literal significance, had little sympathy for positivism as a philosophical movement. Many philosophers today profess greater affinity with and loyalty to Wittgenstein's early formalistic approach to logic and philosophy than with his later emphasis on the practical cultural contexts of language games in forms of life. Yet many modern-day proponents of Wittgenstein's early philosophy do not accept his semantic transcendentalism, of which they are either unaware or which they find ideologically embarrassing. Thus, there is a philosophical predisposition for some commentators to interpret the *Tractatus* as a purely extensionalist theory of sentence meaning, without acknowledging its underlying Kantian-Schopenhauerian transcendental idealism, nor seriously integrating the text's religious and ethical-aesthetic dimensions with its logic, metaphysics, and semantics.

In Wittgenstein's early philosophy, meaning is abstract; in the later philosophy, it has a very human pulse. Many philosophers

| 321

who by contrast believe themselves to be philosophically more sympathetic to the later Wittgenstein, who identify themselves as Wittgensteinian in their own work, often misunderstand, misapply, or simply ignore some of Wittgenstein's most important methods and conclusions in the later philosophy of language. There are various movements in recent analytic philosophy that claim to follow the later Wittgenstein, but that do not make use of anything like Wittgenstein's framework for investigating the philosophical grammar of language games in forms of life. Wittgenstein's later discovery of the praxeological foundations of language admittedly takes much of its data from ordinary ways of speaking, and assumes as does the early philosophy that everyday language is somehow logically correct. But the concept of a Wittgensteinian philosophy of language is sometimes implausibly made to cover virtually any philosophy of ordinary language in the most general sense. Wittgenstein's later philosophy has a specific content and a characteristic way of selecting and handling examples that cannot be reduced to and is not adequately practiced by any and every attempt to shake off philosophical problems by refining definitions of terms from their occurrence in ordinary language.

In the later period, Wittgenstein rejects his early logical atomism and picture theory semantics. He seems thereby to leave behind any trace of positivism along with the rest of the *Tractatus* wreckage. Yet Wittgenstein in the *Philosophical Investigations* insists that there can be no private mental naming or private mental describing of private mental objects, precisely because there can be no publicly verifiable criteria of correctness for naming private mental objects. The later philosophy in its antitranscendentalism no longer supports a transcendental solipsism of the metaphysical subject or philosophical I. But Wittgenstein's obsession with solipsism and the impossibility of a private language in the later philosophy appear to be different expressions of much the same philosophical yearning for nothingness. The self vanishes into thin air in Wittgenstein's early philosophy if there is no logically possible language in which anything intelligible can be said about the transcendent metaphysical subject or philosophical I, or about the subjective propositional attitude states of the psychological ego, self, or soul. The person equally disappears in the later philosophy when Wittgenstein concludes that there can be no private mental naming or private mental describing of private mental occurrences. By excluding all discourse about irreducible subjectivity from any possible language game, Wittgenstein again but in quite a different way reduces everything about the human condition to the world of facts in what he refers to in the early philosophy as "superficial psychology."

I have tried to explain the evolution of Wittgenstein's thought as a transition from transcendental idealism to empirical realism. The remarkable turn in Wittgenstein's later philosophy was necessitated by the color incompatibility problem. It posed a challenge for the early logic and semantics that could not be satisfactorily addressed except by giving a logical analysis of the facts of experiential phenomena. At this point, Wittgenstein has already crossed over from transcendentalism to the recognition that nothing is hidden, and he is prepared to admit the irreducible diversity of language as a real human activity in a dynamic cultural context. The conviction that persists through Wittgenstein's thought from the early to the later philosophy is that there is only one correct way of doing philosophy, and that the only correct nontraditional method of philosophy requires philosophers to arrive at an adequate understanding of the conditions of meaning in language whereby all philosophical problems disappear.

The early philosophy's commitment to a single correct way of doing philosophy is explicit in *Tractatus* 6.53, where Wittgenstein speaks of "The right method of philosophy," which he also describes as "the only strictly correct method." The later philosophy substitutes a different but equally parochial conception of the proper therapeutic conduct of philosophy. Wittgenstein's explanation of how language works and how meaning in language is supposed to preclude philosophical problems is dramatically transformed in the transition from the early to the later philosophy. Wittgenstein's thought remains faithful throughout to his early vision of the proper conduct of philosophy as the activity of clarifying the presuppositions of meaning by which we can satisfy ourselves that there are no real philosophical problems.

Philosophical problems do not arise in Wittgenstein's early philosophy because they are excluded as logically meaningless nonsensical pseudopropositions. In the later philosophy, philosophical problems occur only when language goes on holiday, when the improper practice of philosophy misappropriates ordinary language expressions in violation of the essential rules of philosophical grammar. Philosophy is not a language game and is not a part of any form of life; philosophy is pragmatically unjustifiable except as a clarification of meaning to undo the conceptual damage of philosophy. In Wittgenstein's later (anti-) philosophy, the correct practice of philosophy is a therapeutic activity in which apparent philosophical disorders are diagnosed and cured. Philosophical problems evanesce in Wittgenstein's later philosophy when philosophical anxieties are alleviated through the clarification of otherwise philosophically problematic concepts as they are determined in a pragmatically grounded natural language game. We reassure ourselves in this way that no genuine philosophical problems ever existed in the first place.

There are parallel similarities and differences in Wittgenstein's application of his philosophy of language to his early and later philosophy of mathematics and philosophical psychology. After Wittgenstein discards the *Tractatus* logic, he can no longer reduce the methods of mathematics to logic. He is unable to interpret mathematical equations as disguised tautologies about numerical relations involving iterated truth-functional logical operations. Nor can Wittgenstein in the later period eliminate psychological subjects and their propositional attitudes in the transcendental solipsism of the metaphysical subject or philosophical I. Mathematics in Wittgenstein's later thought is a family of language games with a complex dynamically evolving structure. Alternative mathematical language games are played according to different formal rules designed by mathematicians for different pragmatic purposes, in which even contradictions can be tolerated as answering imaginable needs. Wittgenstein's later philosophy has no concept of the transcendent metaphysical subject. Yet Wittgenstein rejects private psychological occurrences as having no pragmatic consequences by which they could be privately named or privately described, and hence no legitimate part to play in any possible language game.

As in the early philosophy, but now for quite different reasons, the metaphysics of individual subjectivity is affirmed rather than denied, but interpreted-away as philosophically irrelevant. Wittgenstein's later reflections on what makes a thought about something a thought about just that thing implies that intentionality as in the early philosophy is a primitive relation. In an important series of remarks following the private language argument, Wittgenstein describes reference as something thinkers and language users simply do as an irreducible psychological or linguistic activity. Thinking about or referring in language to an object is an action that combines an irreducibly intentional purpose with an accompanying mental ('spiritual') event or a physical ('body') movement. Wittgenstein's early and later philosophy agree in principle though for quite different reasons that the privacy and subjectivity of thought offers no meaningful basis for a superficial psychological solipsism or Cartesian foundational epistemology. Wittgenstein's early philosophy reduces ethics and aesthetics indistinguishably to one transcendental nonsense. But the later philosophy has no logical-semantic basis for collapsing or excluding ethics and aesthetics from the world of facts. Wittgenstein is obligated instead to examine the point and purpose of natural language expressions of epistemic, religious, ethical, and aesthetic value in order to understand their unique pragmatic contributions to particular language games.

Why does Wittgenstein believe that clarity of meaning has power over philosophical problems? It is noteworthy that some traditional philosophical problems do seem to fade away even in conventional philosophical analysis by clarifying the language in which they are wrongly or misleadingly expressed. Wittgenstein was undoubtedly impressed with the most famous classical applications of logical analysis in Frege and Whitehead and Russell, from which he then generalizes the idea to try to make all philosophical problems disappear like magic in a puff of smoke. The elimination of philosophical problems as nonsensical pseudopropositions in the early philosophy may be capable of bestowing the sort of wisdom Wittgenstein believes can only retire in silence about what cannot be said. In Wittgenstein's later (anti-) philosophy, relief from the torments of philosophical paradox is more laboriously gained by a difficult demanding therapy of philosophical grammatical investigation.

Again, Schopenhauer's concept of the aesthetic genius and ascetic saint is vital to understanding Wittgenstein's early and later (anti-) philosophy. Wittgenstein tries in different ways to follow both paths of genius and sainthood to the silencing of individual will that Schopenhauer regards as the most profound achievement and salvation of the soul. Yet even if we accept an ideal of philosophical quietude as a worthy goal—and Wittgenstein does not try to persuade us that we should—it still does not follow that we can reasonably expect to eliminate all philosophical problems. Why should Wittgenstein suppose that there are no deep philosophical problems, but that apparent paradoxes arise only through abuses of language or failure to understand the logic or philosophical grammar of ordinary language? Why should we agree with Wittgenstein that it is possible even in principle to lay philosophical doubts to rest? Why assume that the only philosophical problems are those of the fly in the fly bottle?

The only answer Wittgenstein can give is that philosophy correctly understood and properly practiced cannot possibly contain problems of its own because it is the lens through which all other problems are considered. Philosophy as Wittgenstein thinks of it in the later period cannot contain genuine problems if its proper practice advances no theses but is merely the activity of clarifying meaning. Describing special language games to see how language works in miniature models is part of the antiphilosophical remedy by which philosophical problems are eliminated. But the effectiveness of Wittgenstein's later antiphilosophy depends on the extent to which the explanation of meaning itself can be known to be free of philosophical paradox, so that the analysis or pure description of the conditions of meaning with no beam in its own eye can see clearly enough to remove the mote from traditional philosophy's.

What might then be said by way of critical assessment of Wittgenstein's lifelong philosophical project? The early philosophy has much of value, especially in its rigorous application of a minimalist conception of logic and a logically correct symbolism to the (pseudo-) problems of philosophy. Logical atomism, the picture theory of meaning, and general form of proposition are nevertheless seriously flawed, as Wittgenstein later concludes. The color incompatibility problem and lack of attention to the requirements of naming are the final undoing of Wittgenstein's early philosophy. Wittgenstein was driven by his melancholy genius to see compromise and error even in his best work. But it is surely no accident that his later turn from logical atomism and the picture theory of meaning toward the philosophical grammar of language games in forms of life dates almost immediately from the time of disowning his 1929 essay, "Some Remarks on Logical Form."

Wittgenstein's later thought resists easy summary because he self-consciously abstains from sharply defined concepts and explanatory philosophical theses, and substitutes painstaking elaborate descriptions. We do not have the benefit of Wittgenstein's probing self-criticism of the later philosophy as we do in the case of his early thought. But the insights of Wittgenstein's later philosophical grammar are an equally valuable legacy. The most severe criticism of Wittgenstein's early or later thought can do nothing to detract from the wealth of concepts, methods, and colorful images he has made a permanent part of philosophy. That Wittgenstein left so many previously unimagined questions to take philosophy in new directions is the true measure of his philosophical achievement.

▌Works by Wittgenstein

1913.   "Review of Peter Coffey, *The Science of Logic.*" *Cambridge Review* 34:351.

1922.   *Tractatus Logico-Philosophicus.* C. K. Ogden, ed. London: Routledge & Kegan Paul.

1929.   "Some Remarks on Logical Form." *Aristotelian Society Supplementary Volume 9, Knowledge, Experience and Realism,* 162–71.

1933.   Letter to the Editor. *Mind* 42:415–16.

1958.   *The Blue and Brown Books.* New York: Harper & Row.

1967a. *Zettel.* G. E. M. Anscombe and G. H. von Wright, eds. Anscombe, trans. Oxford: Basil Blackwell.

1967b. *Letters from Ludwig Wittgenstein with a Memoir by Paul Englemann.* Brian McGuinness, ed. Oxford: Basil Blackwell.

1968a. *Philosophical Investigations.* 3d ed. Anscombe, trans. New York: Macmillan.

1968b. "Wittgenstein's Notes for Lectures on 'Private Experience' and 'Sense Data'." Rush Rhees, ed. *Philosophical Review* 77:275–320.

1969a. *Notebooks 1914–1916.* Von Wright and Anscombe, eds. Anscombe, trans. Oxford: Basil Blackwell. [Includes "Notes on Logic" and "Notes Dictated to G. E. Moore in Norway."]

1969b. *On Certainty.* Anscombe and von Wright, eds. Oxford: Basil Blackwell.

1971.   *Prototractatus: An Early Version of Tractatus Logico-Philsophicus.* McGuinness, T. Nybert, and von Wright, eds. David Pears and McGuinness, trans. Ithaca, N.Y.: Cornell University Press.

1973.   *Letters to C. K. Ogden with Comments on the English Translation of the Tractatus Logico-Philosophicus.* Von Wright, ed. Oxford, London: Basil Blackwell/Routledge & Kegan Paul.

1974a. *Philosophical Grammar.* Rhees, ed. Anthony Kenny, trans. Oxford: Basil Blackwell.

1974b. *Letters to Russell, Keynes and Moore.* Von Wright and McGuinness, eds. Oxford: Basil Blackwell.

1975. *Philosophical Remarks*. Rhees, ed. Raymond Hargreaves and Roger White, trans. Chicago, Ill.: University of Chicago Press.
1977a. *Wörterbuch für Volksschulen*. Werner Leinfellner, Elisabeth Leinfellner, and Adolf Hübner, eds. Vienna: Hölder-Pichler-Tempsky.
1977b. *Remarks on Color*. Anscombe, ed. Linda L. McAlister and Margarete Schättle, trans. Oxford: Basil Blackwell.
1980. *Culture and Value*. 2d ed. Von Wright, ed., in collaboration with Heikki Nyman. Peter Winch, trans. Oxford: Basil Blackwell.
1983. *Remarks on the Foundations of Mathematics*. Rev. ed. Von Wright, Rhees, and Anscombe, eds. Anscombe, trans. Cambridge, Mass.: MIT Press.
1989. *Wittgenstein's Lectures on Philosophical Psychology 1946–47: Notes by P. T. Geach, K. J. Shah, and A. C. Jackson*. Geach, ed. Chicago, Ill.: University of Chicago Press.
1993. *Philosophical Occasions: 1912–1951*. James Klagge and Alfred Nordmann, eds. Indianapolis, Ind.: Hackett.

I Selected Secondary Literature

Ackermann, Robert John. 1988. *Wittgenstein's City*. Amherst: University of Massachusetts Press.
Albritton, Rogers. 1959. "On Wittgenstein's Use of the Term 'Criterion'." *The Journal of Philosophy* 56:845–57.
Allaire, Edwin B. 1958. "*Tractatus* 6.3751." *Analysis* 19:100–105.
Ambrose, Alice, and Morris Lazerowitz, eds. 1972. *Ludwig Wittgenstein: Philosophy of Language*. London: George Allen and Unwin.
Anscombe, G. E. M. 1971. *An Introduction to Wittgenstein's Tractatus*. Philadelphia: University of Pennsylvania Press.
Aristotle. 1930. *The Complete Works of Aristotle*. W. D. Ross, ed. Oxford: Clarendon Press.
Armstrong, D. M. 1968. *A Materialist Theory of the Mind*. London: Routledge & Kegan Paul.
Auerbach, David. R. 1985. "Intensionality and the Gödel Theorems." *Philosophical Studies* 68:337–51.
Austin, James. 1980. "Wittgenstein's Solutions to the Color Exclusion Problem." *Philosophy and Phenomenological Research* 41:142–49.
Ayer, A. J. 1985. *Wittgenstein*. Chicago, Ill.: University of Chicago Press.
Baker, G. P., and P. M. S. Hacker. 1980. *An Analytical Commentary on the Philosophical Investigations,* vol. 1, *Wittgenstein: Understanding and Meaning*. Oxford: Basil Blackwell.
———. 1984a. *Frege: Logical Excavations*. Oxford: Oxford University Press.
———. 1984b. *Scepticism, Rules and Language*. Oxford: Basil Blackwell.
———. 1985. *An Analytical Commentary on the Philosophical Investigations,* vol. 2, *Wittgenstein: Rules, Grammar and Necessity*. Oxford: Basil Blackwell.
Baker, Gordon. 1988. *Wittgenstein, Frege and the Vienna Circle*. Oxford: Basil Blackwell.
Baker, Lynne Rudder. 1984. "On the Very Idea of a Form of Life." *Inquiry* 27:277–89.

Bambrough, Renford. 1960–61. "Universals and Family Resemblances." *Proceedings of the Aristotelian Society* 61:207–22.

Barrett, Cyril, Margaret Paton, and Harry Blocker. 1967. "Wittgenstein and Problems of Objectivity in Aesthetics: A Symposium." *The British Journal of Aesthetics* 7:158–74.

Barrett, Cyril. 1991. *Wittgenstein on Ethics and Religious Belief.* Oxford: Basil Blackwell.

Binkley, Timothy. 1973. *Wittgenstein's Language.* The Hague: Martinus Nijhoff.

Black, Max. 1964. *A Companion to Wittgenstein's 'Tractatus'.* Ithaca, N.Y.: Cornell University Press.

———. 1978. "*Lebensform* and *Sprachspiel* in Wittgenstein's Later Work." In *Wittgenstein and His Impact on Contemporary Thought, Proceedings of the Second International Wittgenstein Symposium,* edited by Leinfellner et al., 325–31. Vienna: Hölder-Pichler-Tempsky.

Bloor, David. 1983. *Wittgenstein: A Social Theory of Knowledge.* London: Macmillan.

Bolzano, Bernard. 1972. *Theory of Science: Attempt at a Detailed and in the Main Novel Exposition of Logic with Constant Attention to Earlier Authors.* Rolf George, ed. and trans. Berkeley and Los Angeles: University of California Press.

Bradley, Raymond. 1992. *The Nature of All Being: A Study of Wittgenstein's Modal Atomism.* Oxford: Oxford University Press.

Brentano, Franz. 1969. *The Origin of Our Knowledge of Right and Wrong.* Oskar Kraus, ed. London: Routledge & Kegan Paul.

———. 1973. *The Foundation and Construction of Ethics.* Franziska Mayer-Hillebrand, ed. Elizabeth Schneewind, trans. London: Routledge & Kegan Paul.

Budd, Malcolm. 1989. *Wittgenstein's Philosophy of Psychology.* London: Routledge.

Campbell, Keith. 1965. "Family Resemblance Predicates." *American Philosophical Quarterly* 2:238–44.

Cantor, Georg. 1952. *Contributions to the Founding of the Theory of Transfinite Numbers.* P. E. B. Jourdain, trans. New York: Dover.

———. 1966. *Grundlagen einer allgemeinen Mannigfaltigkeitslehre, ein mathematisch-philosophischer Versuch in der Lehre des Unendlichen.* Leipzig: Teubner (1883), first published in *Jahresbericht der deutschen Mathematiker-Vereinigung* I (1890–91), 75-78; rpt. Cantor, *Gesammelte Abhandlungen mathematischen und philosophischen Inhalts, mit erlauternden Anmerkungen sowie mit Ergangzungen aus dem Briefwechsel Cantor-Dedekind.* Ernst Zermelo, ed. Hildesheim: Georg Olms.

Caruthers, Peter. 1989. *Tractarian Semantics: Finding Sense in Wittgenstein's Tractatus.* Oxford: Basil Blackwell.

———. 1990. *The Metaphysics of the Tractatus.* Cambridge: Cambridge University Press.

Cavell, Stanley. 1962. "The Availability of Wittgenstein's Later Philosophy." *The Philosophical Review* 71:67–68.

Chisholm, Roderick M. 1986. *Brentano and Intrinsic Value.* Cambridge: Cambridge University Press.

Cook, John W. 1972. "Solipsism and Language." In *Ludwig Wittgenstein: Philosophy of Language,* edited by Ambrose and Lazerowitz, 37–72. London: George Allen and Unwin Ltd.

———— 1994. *Wittgenstein's Metaphysics*. Cambridge: Cambridge University Press.

Copi, Irving M., and Robert W. Beard, eds. 1966. *Essays on Wittgenstein's Tractatus*. London: Routledge & Kegan Paul.

Dallago, Carl. 1912. *Otto Weininger und sein Werk*. Innsbruck: Brenner Verlag.

Descartes, René. 1984. *Meditations on First Philosophy*, in *The Philosophical Writings of Descartes*. John Cottingham, Robert Stoothoff, and Dugald Murdoch, trans. 3 vols. Cambridge: Cambridge University Press.

Dummett, Michael. 1981. *The Interpretation of Frege's Philosophy*. Cambridge, Mass.: Harvard University Press.

Edwards, Cliff. 1989. *Van Gogh and God: A Creative Spiritual Quest*. Chicago, Ill.: Loyola University Press.

Engel, S. Morris. 1969. "Schopenhauer's Impact upon Wittgenstein." *Journal of the History of Philosophy* 7:285–302.

————. 1970. "Wittgenstein and Kant." *Philosophy and Phenomenological Research* 30:483–513.

Engelmann, Paul. 1967. *Dem Andenken an Karl Kraus*. Vienna: Otto Kerry.

Fann, K. T. 1969. *Wittgenstein's Conception of Philosophy*. Berkeley and Los Angeles: University of California Press.

————. 1978. *Ludwig Wittgenstein: The Man and His Philosophy*. Atlantic Highlands, N.J.: Humanities Press.

Ferré, Frederick P. 1961. "Colour Incompatibility and Language Games." *Mind* 70:90–94.

Field, Frank. 1967. *The Last Days of Mankind: Karl Kraus*. New York: St. Martin's.

Finch, Henry LeRoy. 1971. *Wittgenstein — The Early Philosophy: An Exposition of the "Tractatus"*. Atlantic Highlands, N.J.: Humanities Press.

Findlay, J. N. 1973. "My Encounters with Wittgenstein." *The Philosophical Forum* 4:167–85.

————. 1984. *Wittgenstein: A Critique*. London: Routledge & Kegan Paul.

Fogelin, Robert J. 1976. *Wittgenstein*. London: Routledge & Kegan Paul.

————. 1982. "Wittgenstein's Operator *N*." *Analysis* 42:124–27.

————. 1987. *Wittgenstein*. 2d ed. London: Routledge & Kegan Paul.

Frege, Gottlob. 1950. *The Foundations of Arithmetic*. J. L. Austin, trans. Oxford: Basil Blackwell.

————. 1970. "On Sense and Reference." In *Translations from the Philosophical Writings of Gottlob Frege*, edited by Geach and Black, 56–78. Oxford: Basil Blackwell.

————. 1977a. "Thoughts." Trans. Geach and R. H. Stoothoff. In Frege, *Logical Investigations*, 1–30. Oxford: Basil Blackwell.

————. 1977b. *Logical Investigations*. Geach and Stoothoff, trans. Oxford: Basil Blackwell.

Garver, Newton. 1984. "Die Lebensform in Wittgenstein's *Philosophischen Untersuchungen*." *Grazer Philosophische Studien* 21:33–54.

————. 1994. *This Complicated Form of Life: Essays on Wittgenstein*. LaSalle, Ill.: Open Court.

Geach, P. T., and Max Black, eds. 1970. *Translations from the Philosophical Writings of Gottlob Frege*. Oxford: Basil Blackwell.

331 I WORKS CITED

Geach, P. T. 1981. "Wittgenstein's Operator *N.*" *Analysis* 41:168–71.
———. 1982. "More on Wittgenstein's Operator *N.*" *Analysis* 42:127–28.
Gier, Nicholas F. 1981. *Wittgenstein and Phenomenology: A Comparative Study of the Later Wittgenstein, Husserl, Heidegger, and Merleau-Ponty.* Albany: State University of New York Press.
Goddard, Leonard, and Brenda Judge. 1982. *The Metaphysics of Wittgenstein's Tractatus.* Melbourne: *Australasian Journal of Philosophy* Monograph.
Gödel, Kurt. 1931. "Über formal unentscheidbare Sätze der Principia mathematica und verwandter Systeme I." *Monatshefte für Mathematik und Physik* 38:173–98.
Goodman, Russell B. 1994. "What Wittgenstein Learned from William James." *History of Philosophy Quarterly* 11:339–54.
Gram, Moltke S. 1971. "Privacy and Language." In *Essays on Wittgenstein,* edited by Klemke, 298–327. Urbana: University of Illinois Press.
Gravagnuolo, Benedetto. 1982. *Adolf Loos: Theory and Works.* C. H. Evans, trans. New York: Rizzoli Press.
Griffin, James. 1964. *Wittgenstein's Logical Atomism.* Seattle: University of Washington Press.
Griffin, Nicholas. 1974. "Wittgenstein, Universals and Family Resemblances." *Canadian Journal of Philosophy* 3:635–51.
Griffiths, A. Phillips. 1974. "Wittgenstein, Schopenhauer, and Ethics." In *Understanding Wittgenstein,* edited by Vesey, 96–116. Royal Institute of Philosophy Lectures, 7, 1972–1973. London: The Macmillan Press Ltd.
Hacker, P. M. S. 1972. *Insight and Illusion: Themes in the Philosophy of Wittgenstein.* Oxford: Oxford University Press.
———. 1989. *Insight and Illusion: Themes in the Philosophy of Wittgenstein.* Rev. ed. Oxford: Oxford University Press.
———. 1996. *Wittgenstein's Place in Twentieth Century Philosophy.* Oxford: Basil Blackwell.
Hackstaff, L. H. 1966. "A Note on Wittgenstein's Truth-Function Generating Operation in *Tractatus* 6." *Mind* 75:255–56.
Haller, Rudolf. 1988. *Questions on Wittgenstein.* Lincoln: University of Nebraska Press.
Hallett, Garth. 1967. *Wittgenstein's Definition of Meaning as Use.* New York: Fordham University Press.
———. 1977. *A Companion to Wittgenstein's Philosophical Investigations.* Ithaca, N.Y.: Cornell University Press.
Hamburg, Carl. 1953. "Whereof One Cannot Speak." *Journal of Philosophy* 50:662–64.
Hanfling, Oswald. 1989. *Wittgenstein's Later Philosophy.* Albany: State University of New York Press.
Hardwick, Charles S. 1971. *Language Learning in Wittgenstein's Later Philosophy.* The Hague: Mouton.
Herbert, Zbigniew. 1991. *Still Life with a Bridle: Essays and Apocryphas.* John Carpenter and Bogdana Carpenter, trans. Hopewell, N.J.: Ecco Press.
Hervey, Helen. 1961. "The Problem of the Model Language Game in Wittgenstein's Later Philosophy." *Philosophy* 36:333–51.
Hilmy, S. Stephen. 1987. *The Later Wittgenstein: The Emergence of a New Philosophical Method.* Oxford: Basil Blackwell.

Hintikka, Jaakko. 1958. "On Wittgenstein's 'Solipsism'." *Mind* 67:88–91.
———. 1969. "Wittgenstein on Private Language: Some Sources of Misunderstanding." *Mind* 78:423–25.
———. 1981. "Wittgenstein's Semantical Kantianism." In *Ethics: Foundations, Problems, and Applications, Proceedings of the Fifth International Wittgenstein Symposium,* edited by Morscher and Stranzinger, 375–90. Vienna: Hölder-Pichler-Tempsky.
Hintikka, Merrill B., and Jaakko Hintikka. 1986. *Investigating Wittgenstein.* Oxford: Basil Blackwell.
Hodges, Michael. 1973. "Wittgenstein on Universals." *Philosophical Studies* 24:22–30.
Holtzman, Steven H., and Christopher M. Leich. 1981. *Wittgenstein: To Follow a Rule.* London: Routledge & Kegan Paul.
Huby, Pamela M. 1969. "Is 'Tractatus' 5.542 More Obscure in English Than It Is in German?" *Philosophy* 44:243.
Hume, David. 1978 [1739–40]. *A Treatise of Human Nature* . 2d ed. L. A. Selby-Bigge, ed. P. H. Nidditch, rev. Oxford: Clarendon Press.
Hunter, J. F. M. 1968. "Forms of Life in Wittgenstein's *Philosophical Investigations.*" *American Philosophical Quarterly* 5:233–43.
———. 1985. *Understanding Wittgenstein: Studies of Philosophical Investigations.* Edinburgh: University of Edinburgh Press.
———. 1990. *Wittgenstein on Words as Instruments: Lessons in Philosophical Psychology.* Edinburgh: University of Edinburgh Press.
Huntington, Edward V. 1917. *The Continuum and Other Types of Serial Order, with an Introduction to Cantor's Transfinite Numbers.* 2d ed. New York: Dover.
Iggers, Wilma Abeles. 1967. *Karl Kraus: A Viennese Critic of the Twentieth Century.* The Hague: Martinus Nijhoff.
Jacquette, Dale. 1990a. "Wittgenstein and the Color Incompatibility Problem." *History of Philosophy Quarterly* 7:353–65.
———. 1990b. "Metaphilosophy in Wittgenstein's City." in *Ludwig Wittgenstein: A Symposium on the Centennial of His Birth,* edited by Tegharian, Serafini, and Cook, 31–42. Rpt. in *International Studies in Philosophy* 25 (1993): 27–35.
———, trans. 1991. Mojzesz Presburger, "On the Completeness of a Certain System of Arithmetic of Whole Numbers in Which Addition Occurs as the Only Operation." *History and Philosophy of Logic* 12:225–33. [With commentary.]
———. 1992–93. "Wittgenstein's Critique of Propositional Attitude and Russell's Theory of Judgment." *Brentano Studien* 4:193–220.
———. 1994a. "Wittgenstein on Private Language and Private Mental Objects." *Wittgenstein Studien* 1, Article 12. [Computer disk format textname: 12-1-94.TXT) (89K) (c. 29).]
———. 1994b. "Wittgenstein's Private Language Argument and Reductivism in the Cognitive Sciences." In *Philosophy and the Cognitive Sciences: Proceedings of the Sixteenth International Wittgenstein Symposium,* edited by Roberto Casati, Barry Smith, and Graham White, 89–99. Vienna: Hölder-Pichler-Tempsky.
———, ed. 1996a. *Schopenhauer, Philosophy, and the Arts.* Cambridge: Cambridge University Press.
———. 1996b. "Haller on Wittgenstein and Kant." In *Austrian Philosophy Past and Present: Essays in Honor of Rudolf Haller,* edited

by Keith Lehrer and Johannes Christian Marek. Boston Studies in the Philosophy of Science. Dordrecht: Kluwer Academic Publishing.

———. 1996c. Review of Andrés Rivadulla, "Wahrscheinlichkeitsaussagen, statistische Inferenz und Hypothesenwahrscheinlichkeit in L. Wittgensteins Schriften der Übergangsperiode." *Mathematical Reviews* 95i, 1995, 5080.

———. 1997a. "Wittgenstein on the Transcendence of Ethics." *Australasian Journal of Philosophy* 75:304–24.

———. 1997b. Review of P. M. S. Hacker, *Wittgenstein's Place in Twentieth Century Philosophy: History and Philosophy of Logic* 18:109–14.

———. 1998. "Wittgenstein's Manometer and the Private Language Argument." *History of Philosophy Quarterly* (forthcoming).

Janik, Allan, and Stephen Toulmin. 1973. *Wittgenstein's Vienna.* New York: Simon and Schuster.

Janik, Allan. 1966. "Schopenhauer and the Early Wittgenstein." *Philosophical Studies* 15:76–95.

———, ed. 1985. *Essays on Wittgenstein and Weininger.* Atlantic Highlands, N.J.: Humanities Press.

Joachim, H. H. 1951. *Aristotle: The Nicomachean Ethics.* Oxford: Clarendon Press.

Johnston, Paul. 1989. *Wittgenstein and Moral Philosophy.* London: Routledge.

Johnston, William M. 1972. *The Austrian Mind: An Intellectual and Social History 1848–1938.* Berkeley and Los Angeles: University of California Press.

Jones, O. R., ed. 1971. *The Private Language Argument.* London: Macmillan.

Kant, Immanuel. 1952. [1790] *Critique of Judgement.* James Creed Meredith, trans. Oxford: Clarendon Press.

———. 1959. [1785] *Foundations of the Metaphysics of Morals.* Lewis White Beck, trans. New York: Macmillan.

———. 1965. [1787] *Critique of Pure Reason.* Norman Kemp Smith, trans. New York: St. Martin's.

———. 1977. [1783] *Prolegomena to Any Future Metaphysics That Will Be Able to Come Forward as Science.* Paul Carus, trans. James W. Ellington, rev. Indianapolis, Ind.: Hackett.

Kapfinger, Otto. 1984. *Haus Wittgenstein: Eine Dokumentation.* Cultural Department of the People's Republic of Bulgaria.

Kelly, John C. 1995. "Wittgenstein, the Self, and Ethics." *Review of Metaphysics* 48:567–90.

Kenny, Anthony. 1973. *Wittgenstein.* Cambridge, Mass.: Harvard University Press.

———. 1978. *Freewill and Responsibility: Four Lectures.* London: Routledge & Kegan Paul.

———. 1984. *The Legacy of Wittgenstein.* Oxford: Basil Blackwell.

Khatchadourian, Haig. 1957–58. "Common Names and Family Resemblances." *Philosophy and Phenomenological Research* 18:341–58.

Klemke, E. D., ed. 1971. *Essays on Wittgenstein.* Urbana: University of Illinois Press.

Koethe, John. 1996. *The Continuity of Wittgenstein's Thought.* Ithaca: Cornell University Press.

Kraft, Werner. 1961. "Ludwig Wittgenstein und Karl Kraus." *Die neue deutsche Rundschau* 72:812–44.

Kripke, Saul A. 1982. *Wittgenstein on Rules and Private Language.* Cambridge, Mass.: Harvard University Press.

Kubinszky, Mihaly. 1970. *Adolf Loos.* Berlin: Henschelverlag.

Lange, Ernst Michael. 1989. *Wittgenstein und Schopenhauer: Logisch-philosophische Abhandlung und Kritik des Solipsismus.* Cuxhaven: Junghans-Verlag.

Leblanc, Hugues. 1972. "Wittgenstein and the Truth-Functionality Thesis." *American Philosophical Quarterly* 9:271–74.

Leinfellner, Elisabeth, Werner Leinfellner, Hal Berghel, and Adolf Hübner, eds. 1978. *Wittgenstein and His Impact on Contemporary Thought, Proceedings of the Second International Wittgenstein Symposium.* Vienna: Hölder-Pichler-Tempsky.

Leitner, Bernard. 1970. "Wittgenstein's Architecture." *Art Forum,* 59–61.

———. 1973. *The Architecture of Ludwig Wittgenstein: A Documentation.* Halifax: Nova Scotia College of Art and Design.

Loos, Adolf. 1962. *Sämtliche Schriften.* Vienna: Verlag Herald.

Malcolm, Norman. 1958. *Ludwig Wittgenstein: A Memoir, with a Biographical Sketch by Georg Henrik von Wright.* Oxford: Oxford University Press.

———. 1963. *Knowledge and Certainty: Essays and Lectures.* Englewood Cliffs, N.J.: Prentice Hall.

———. 1986. *Wittgenstein: Nothing Is Hidden.* Oxford: Basil Blackwell.

———. 1994. *Wittgenstein: A Religious Point of View?* Peter Winch, ed. Ithaca, N.Y.: Cornell University Press.

Manser, A. R. 1967. "Games and Family Resemblances." *Philosophy* 42:210–24.

———. 1970. "Some Remarks on Tractatus 5.542." *Southwestern Journal of Philosophy* 1:113–20.

Margolis, Joseph. 1980. *Art and Philosophy.* Atlantic Highlands, N.J.: Humanities Press.

———. 1984. *Culture and Cultural Entities: Toward a New Unity of Science.* Dordrecht: D. Reidel.

———. 1986. "Constraints on the Metaphysics of Culture." *Review of Metaphysics* 39:653–73.

Maslow, Alexander. 1961. *A Study in Wittgenstein's Tractatus.* Berkeley and Los Angeles: University of California Press.

McGinn, Colin. 1984. *Wittgenstein on Meaning: An Interpretation and Evaluation.* Oxford: Basil Blackwell.

McGuinness, Brian. 1966. "The Mysticism of the *Tractatus.*" *Philosophical Review* 75:305–28.

———. 1988. *Wittgenstein: A Life. Young Ludwig 1889–1921.* Berkeley and Los Angeles: University of California Press.

Melzack, Ronald, Paul M. Paris, and Ada G. Rogers. 1987. "How to Talk to Your Doctor about Acute Pain." Wilmington, Del.: DuPont Pharmaceuticals. [Pamphlet.]

Miller, Hugh, III. 1995. "Tractarian Semantics for Predicate Logic." *History and Philosophy of Logic* 16:197–215.

Monk, Ray. 1991. *Ludwig Wittgenstein: The Duty of Genius.* New York: Penguin Books.

Moore, G. E. 1903. *Principia Ethica.* Cambridge: Cambridge University Press.

———. 1954–55. "Wittgenstein's Lectures in 1930–33." *Mind* 63–64: 289–316; 1–27.

Morrison, James C. 1968. *Meaning and Truth in Wittgenstein's Tractatus.* The Hague: Mouton.

Morscher, Edgar, and R. Stranzinger, eds. 1981. *Ethics: Foundations, Problems, and Applications, Proceedings of the Fifth International Wittgenstein Symposium.* Vienna: Hölder-Pichler-Tempsky.

Müller, Anselm W. 1978. "No Need for Criteria?" In *Wittgenstein and His Impact on Contemporary Thought, Proceedings of the Second International Wittgenstein Symposium,* edited by Leinfellner et al., 306–9. Vienna: Hölder-Pichler-Tempsky.

Munz, Ludwig, and Gustav Kunstler. 1966. *Adolf Loos: Pioneer of Modern Architecture.* New York: Praeger.

Musil, Robert. 1953–60. *The Man without Qualities.* Eithne Wilkins and Ernst Kaiser, trans. 3 vols. London: Secker and Warburg.

———. 1964. *Young Törless.* Wilkins and Kaiser, trans. New York: New American Library.

Nagel, Thomas. 1971. "Brain Bisection and the Unity of Consciousness." *Synthese* 22:396–413.

Nedo, Michael, and Michele Ranchetti. 1983. *Wittgenstein: Sein Leben in Bildern und Texten.* Frankfurt: Suhrkamp.

Nicod, Jean. 1917. "A Reduction in the Number of the Primitive Propositions of Logic." *Proceedings of the Cambridge Philosophical Society* 19:32–41.

O'Shoughnessy, Edna. 1953. "The Picture Theory of Meaning." *Mind* 62:181–201.

Oldenquist, Andrew. 1971. "Wittgenstein on Phenomenalism, Skepticism, and Criteria." In *Essays on Wittgenstein,* edited by Klemke, 394–422. Urbana: University of Illinois Press.

Parfit, Derek. 1984. *Reasons and Persons.* Oxford: Oxford University Press.

Paskow, Alan. 1974. "A Phenomenological View of the Beetle in the Box." *New Scholasticism* 48:277–304.

Pears, David. 1971. *Wittgenstein.* Glasgow: William Collins Sons & Co.

———. 1977. "The Relation between Wittgenstein's Picture Theory of Propositions and Russell's Theories of Judgement." *Philosophical Review* 86:189–95.

———. 1987. *The False Prison: A Study of the Development of Wittgenstein's Philosophy.* 2 vols. Oxford: Oxford University Press.

Peterman, James F. 1990. *Philosophy as Therapy: An Interpretation and Defense of Wittgenstein's Later Philosophical Project.* Albany: State University of New York Press.

Peterson, Donald. 1990. *Wittgenstein's Early Philosophy: Three Sides of the Mirror.* New York: Harvester Wheatsheaf.

Pitcher, George, ed. 1966. *Wittgenstein: The Philosophical Investigations.* New York: Doubleday.

Plato. 1937. *The Dialogues of Plato.* Benjamin Jewett, trans. and ed. 2 vols. New York: Random House.

Pole, David. 1958. *The Later Philosophy of Wittgenstein.* London: University of London, The Athlone Press.

Pompa, Leon. 1967. "Family Resemblance." *Philosophical Quarterly* 2:63–69.

Presburger, Mojzesz. 1930. "Über die Vollständigkeit eines gewissen Systems der Arithmetik ganzer Zahlen, in welchem die Addition als einzige Operation hervortritt." *Sprawozdanie z I Kongresu Matematyków Krajów Slowianskich* (Warszawa), 92–101, 395. [Trans. Jacquette 1991.]

Price, Jeffrey Thomas. 1973. *Language and Being in Wittgenstein's Philosophical Investigations*. The Hague: Mouton.

Priest, Graham. 1995. *Beyond the Limits of Thought*. Cambridge: Cambridge University Press.

Quine, W. V. O. 1960. *Word and Object*. Cambridge, Mass.: MIT Press.

Ramsey, Frank P. 1923. "Review of 'Tractatus'." *Mind* 32:465–78. Rpt., *Essays on Wittgenstein's Tractatus*, edited by Copi and Beard, 9–23. London: Routledge & Kegan Paul.

Rankin, K. W. 1967. "The Role of Imagination, Rule-Operations, and Atmosphere in Wittgenstein's Language-Games." *Inquiry* 10:279–91.

Redpath, Theodore. 1990. *Ludwig Wittgenstein: A Student's Memoir*. London: Duckworth.

Reeder, Harry P. 1979. "Language and the Phenomenological Reduction: A Reply to a Wittgensteinian Objection." *Man and World* 12:35–46.

Rhees, Rush. 1954. "Can There Be a Private Language?" *Proceedings of the Aristotelian Society Supplement* 28:77–94.

———. 1960. "Wittgenstein's Builders." *Proceedings of the Aristotelian Society* 60 (1959): 171–86.

———, ed. 1984. *Recollections of Wittgenstein*. Rev. ed. Oxford: Oxford University Press.

Riemann, Bernard. 1990. *Gesammelte mathematische Werke, wissenschaftlicher Nachlaß und Nachträge*. Heinrich Weber and Richard Dedekind, eds. Berlin: Springer-Verlag.

Rosenberg, Jay F. 1968. "Intentionality and Self in the Tractatus." *Noûs* 2:341–58.

Rundle, Bede. 1990. *Wittgenstein and Contemporary Philosophy of Language*. Oxford: Basil Blackwell.

Russell, Bertrand. 1897. *An Essay on the Foundations of Geometry*. Cambridge: Cambridge University Press.

———. 1919. *Introduction to Mathematical Philosophy*. London: George Allen and Unwin.

———. 1929. *My Philosophical Development*. New York: Simon and Schuster.

———. 1938 [1903]. *The Principles of Mathematics*. 2d ed. New York: W. W. Norton.

———. 1975. *The Autobiography of Bertrand Russell 1914–1944*. 3 vols. London: George Allen & Unwin.

———. 1985. *The Philosophy of Logical Atomism* (Lectures 1917–1918). Ed. Pears. LaSalle, Ill.: Open Court.

Sachs, Oliver. 1995. *An Anthropologist on Mars: Seven Paradoxical Tales*. New York: Vintage Books.

Saunders, John Turk, and Donald F. Henze. 1967. *The Private Language Argument: A Philosophical Dialogue*. New York: Random House.

Schopenhauer, Arthur. 1969. [1859] *The World as Will and Representation*. E. F. J. Payne, trans. 2 vols. New York: Dover.

Schulte, Joachim. 1992. *Wittgenstein: An Introduction.* William H. Brenner and John F. Holley, trans. Albany: State University of New York Press.

———. 1993. *Experience and Expression: Wittgenstein's Philosophy of Psychology.* Oxford: Clarendon Press.

Schwyzer, Hubert. 1986. "Thought and Reality: The Metaphysics of Kant and Wittgenstein." In *Wittgenstein: Critical Assessments,* edited by Shanker, 2:150–62. London: Croom Helm.

Sellars, Wilfrid. 1954. "Some Reflections on Language Games." *Philosophy of Science* 21:204–8.

Shanker, Stuart, ed. 1986. *Wittgenstein: Critical Assessments.* 4 vols. London: Croom Helm.

Sheffer, Henry Maurice. 1913. "A Set of Five Independent Postulates for Boolean Algebras, with Application to Logical Constants." Transactions of the American Mathematical Society 14:481–88.

Shields, Philip R. 1993. *Logic and Sin in the Writings of Ludwig Wittgenstein.* Chicago, Ill.: University of Chicago Press.

Smart, Harold. 1957. "Language-Games." *Philosophical Quarterly* 7:224–35.

Smerud, Warren B. 1970. *Can There Be a Private Language? An Examination of Some Principal Arguments.* The Hague: Janua Linguarum, Series Minor.

Soames, Scott. 1983. "Generality, Truth Functions, and Expressive Capacity in the *Tractatus.*" *Philosophical Review* 92:573–89.

Sraffa, Piero. 1960. *The Production of Commodities by Means of Commodities.* Cambridge: Cambridge University Press.

Stenius, Erik. 1960. *Wittgenstein's Tractatus: A Critical Exposition of Its Main Lines of Thought.* Ithaca, N.Y.: Cornell University Press.

Stern, David. 1991. "The 'Middle Wittgenstein': From Logical Atomism to Practical Holism." *Synthese* 87:203–26.

———. 1995. *Wittgenstein on Mind and Language.* Oxford: Oxford University Press.

Sternfeld, Robert. 1966. *Frege's Logical Theory.* Carbondale: Southern Illinois University Press.

Stewart, Dugald. 1818. *Philosophical Essays.* Edinburgh: Archibald Constable & Co.

Strawson, P. F. 1954. "Review of Wittgenstein's *Philosophical Investigations.*" *Mind* 63:70–99.

———. 1959. *Individuals: An Essay in Descriptive Metaphysics.* London: Methuen.

Suter, Ronald. 1989. *Interpreting Wittgenstein: A Cloud of Philosophy, a Drop of Grammar.* Philadelphia, Pa.: Temple University Press.

Tanner, Michael. 1966. "Wittgenstein and Aesthetics." *Oxford Review* 3:14–24.

Tegharian, Souren, Anthony Serafini, and Edward M. Cook, eds. 1990. *Ludwig Wittgenstein: A Symposium on the Centennial of His Birth.* Wakefield: Longwood Academic.

Thompson, Judith Jarvis. 1964. "Private Languages." *American Philosophical Quarterly* 1:20–31.

Tilghman, Benjamin R. 1991. *Wittgenstein, Ethics and Aesthetics: The View from Eternity.* Basingstoke: Macmillan.

Vesey, Godfrey, ed. 1974. *Understanding Wittgenstein.* Royal Institute of Philosophy Lectures, 7, 1972–1973. London: Macmillan.

Von Wright, G. H. 1942. "Georg Lichtenberg als Philosoph." *Theoria* 8:201–17.

———. 1978. "Wittgenstein in Relation to His Times." In *Wittgenstein and His Impact on Contemporary Thought, Proceedings of the Second International Wittgenstein Symposium,* edited by Leinfellner et al., 73–78. Vienna: Hölder-Pichler-Tempsky.

———. 1982. *Wittgenstein.* Minneapolis: University of Minnesota Press.

Waismann, Friedrich. 1979. *Wittgenstein and the Vienna Circle: Conversations Recorded by Friedrich Waismann.* McGuinness, ed. Schulte and McGuinness, trans. Oxford: Basil Blackwell.

Walker, Jeremy. 1968. "Wittgenstein's Earlier Ethics." *American Philosophical Quarterly* 5:219–32.

Weiner, David Avraham. 1992. *Genius and Talent: Schopenhauer's Influence on Wittgenstein's Early Philosophy.* Rutherford, N.J.: Fairleigh Dickinson University Press.

Weininger, Otto. 1903. *Geschlecht und Charakter.* Vienna-Leipzig: Braumüller.

———. 1906. *Sex and Character.* New York: G. Putnam's Sons. [Anon. trans. of Weininger 1903.]

———. 1918. *Die letzten Dinge.* Vienna-Leipzig: Braumüller.

Wellman, Carl. 1962. "Wittgenstein's Conception of a Criterion." *Philosophical Review* 71:433–47.

Wennerberg, Hjalmar. 1967. "The Concept of Family Resemblance in Wittgenstein's Later Philosophy." *Theoria* 33:107–32.

Werhane, Patricia H. 1989. "Must We 'Always Get Rid of the Idea of the Private Object'?" *Southern Journal of Philosophy* 27:299–317.

White, R. M. 1974. "Can Whether One Proposition Makes Sense Depend on the Truth of Another? (*Tractatus* 2.0211–2)." In *Understanding Wittgenstein,* edited by Vesey, 14–29. London: Macmillan.

Whitehead, A. N., and Bertrand Russell. 1925–27 [1910]. *Principia Mathematica.* 2d ed. 3 vols. Cambridge: Cambridge University Press.

Whittaker, J. H. 1978. "Language Games and Forms of Life Unconfused." *Philosophical Investigations* 1:44–45.

Wijdeveld, Paul. 1994. *Ludwig Wittgenstein, Architect.* Cambridge, Mass.: MIT Press.

Wisan, R. H. 1956. "A Note on Silence." *Journal of Philosophy* 53:448–50.

Wisdom, John. 1972. "Wittgenstein on 'Private Language'." In *Ludwig Wittgenstein: Philosophy of Language,* edited by Ambrose and Lazerowitz, 26–36. London: George Allen and Unwin.

Worthington, B. A. 1988. *Selfconsciousness and Selfreference: An Interpretation of Wittgenstein's Tractatus.* Brookfield: Avebury.

Wünsche, Konrad. 1985. *Der Volksschullehrer Ludwig Wittgenstein.* Frankfurt: Suhrkamp.

INDEX

I Index of Names

∎ Index of Subjects

Manometer (blood-pressure
gauge), 285–89, 298
Mastery of a technique, 238, 261,
264; training in a technique,
261, 263–64, 268–69
Materialism, 175, 297; material object, 17–18, 175; material complex, 29. *See also* Physical object
Mathematical multiplicity
(*mathematische Mannigfaltigkeit*), 40–41, 52–54, 57, 101–2,
139, 154–55, 157, 159, 162,
164–65, 170–71, 176, 178–79,
183–84, 191, 212, 215, 236–37,
241, 244, 251, 264. *See also*
Logical multiplicity
Mathematics, xii, 3–4, 7, 9–11, 122,
148, 160–61, 163, 178, 189, 236,
238, 244, 254, 302, 305–6, 309,
318, 324; mathematical analysis, 58; mathematical form, 73,
121–22, 125; mathematical language, 324; mathematical
language games, 324; mathematical operation, 61; mathematical
logic, 3, 5, 305
Meaning, xi–xii, 10–12, 17–19,
24–25, 27–28, 33, 35–37, 39–
41, 46–51, 54–60, 63–64, 76,
78, 82–85, 90–95, 97–98, 101,
103–4, 106–7, 116, 121, 128–
32, 134–35, 137–38, 140–49,
153, 161–65, 172, 174–75, 181–
82, 185–88, 191, 195–202, 205–
10, 212–22, 224–27, 229–30,
232–35, 237, 239–41, 243, 245–
48, 254, 256, 258–63, 265–69,
272, 275–76, 279–80, 284, 292–
93, 299–303, 306, 309, 312–13,
316–17, 321, 323, 325–26;
meaninglessness, xi–xii, 62,
66–67, 72–73, 79, 83, 93, 95–
96, 102, 104, 107, 111, 124,
128–30, 133–35, 138–39, 142,
144–49, 164, 186–87, 226, 281,
301, 304, 317, 323; meaning of
life, 138, 142, 145, 147
Memory, 14, 230, 238, 281–83,
285, 287, 316
Mental, 9, 59, 96–97, 106, 188,
201, 205, 220–22, 272, 275–77,
279–82, 284–85, 287, 290–95,

297–98, 314–16, 319, 322, 324;
mental state, 96–97, 295, 315–
16. *See also* Mind; Psychology;
Spirit
Metalanguage, 90, 140, 319;
metalinguistic, 73, 108;
metatheory, 319
Metamathematics, 128
Metaphilosophy, 128, 130, 301,
303–4, 310–11, 319;
metaaesthetic, 130; metaethics,
114, 116, 128–30, 133; anti-
meta-philosophy, 302; meta-
anti-philosophy, 301–2, 319;
metaphilosophical grammar,
301
Metaphysics, metaphysical, xix, 4,
17, 19, 22 24–26, 28, 33, 73, 79,
92–93, 98, 101–2, 104–7, 109–
12, 118–22, 124–26, 128–30,
132–35, 142, 144–45, 147–48,
161, 174–75, 195, 228, 271, 296,
301, 312, 321–22, 324; metaphysical subject, 79, 92–93, 98,
101–2, 104–7, 109–12, 118–22,
124–25, 132, 134, 147–48, 296,
322, 324; metaphysical ego, 4
Mind, 46–47, 92, 103–4, 106, 108,
134, 214, 221–23, 231, 260,
285, 291, 293, 295–96, 299,
313–17, 320. *See also* Mental;
Psychology; Spirit
Mirror, 53, 78; mirroring, 25, 35,
57, 169, 213, 215; mirroring relations, 169; 'the great mirror',
78, 199
Modality, 277, 290
Model, 28, 41, 48, 58, 93, 142,
187, 217, 230, 235, 294; model
of reality, 41
Monism, 84
Morality, xi, 4–6, 9, 99, 110–17,
119–20, 123–28, 131–33, 147–
48, 290; moral agents, 117, 128;
moral law, 131; moral pluralism, 117; moral-aesthetic
value, 124, 126. *See also* Ethics
Multiplication, 88, 91
Music, 50–51; musical notation,
score, 50; musical, 48–51
Mysticism (*das Mystische*), 4–5,
111, 144–45